Shortlisted for:

- The British Academy's Global Cultural Understanding
- The Hindu
- The Kamalac ʙook Prize
- The Sahitya Aka uraskar Prize

A *Hindustan Times* 'India @ 70' book

'Aanchal Malhotra is a new star of Indian non-fiction.' — William Dalrymple

'This is a book of startling originality, weaving stories of intimate connections with objects and harrowing histories of displacement into beautifully cadenced prose. It is a book to treasure.' — Edmund de Waal, author of *The Hare With Amber Eyes*

'This is a quietly powerful book; poignant, delicate and reflective. It is an alternative telling of the history of the Partition as a meditation on identity, belonging, and home.' — *Brown Girl Magazine*

'A well-researched and richly readable book.' — Ramachandra Guha, author of *India After Gandhi*

'A wonderful idea stylishly executed.' — Andrew Whitehead, former BBC India correspondent

'Aanchal Malhotra evokes one of the world's great tragedies in moving, beautiful prose, woven through everyday objects treasured as relics of a shattered age.' — Shashi Tharoor, Indian MP and author of *Inglorious Empire*

'This is a truly original way to approach the history of Partition. Malhotra's writing is evocative and, through the finely observed details of everyday life, brings depth and empathy to understanding this event.' — Yasmin Khan, author of *The Great Partition*

'Artfully weaves travel, memory and materials—all without guile— reminding us why India is one of the world's greatest storytelling cultures.' — Gurcharan Das, author of *India Unbound*

'One of the most compelling books I have read in a long time. It is a searing account of the power of memory to shape and reshape worlds … This is oral history at its best.' — *Family and Community History Journal*

REMNANTS OF PARTITION

AANCHAL MALHOTRA

Remnants of Partition

21 Objects from a Continent Divided

HURST & COMPANY, LONDON

First published in hardback in the United Kingdom in 2019 by
C. Hurst & Co. (Publishers) Ltd.,
41 Great Russell Street, London, WC1B 3PL
© Aanchal Malhotra, 2021

This paperback edition first published in 2021 by
C. Hurst & Co (Publishers) Ltd.,
83 Torbay Road, London, NW6 7DT

Foreword © Kavita Puri, 2021

A Cataloguing-in-Publication data record for this book
is available from the British Library.

ISBN: 9781787386037

The map on pp. viii–ix is reproduced with the kind permission of
HarperCollins Publishers India. All photographs are the author's own,
© Aanchal Malhotra.

This book is printed using paper from registered sustainable
and managed sources.

www.hurstpublishers.com

For her, who taught me the importance of one's soil
And for him, who tried so hard to forget it

CONTENTS

FOREWORD TO THE PAPERBACK EDITION

Kavita Puri

Memory is never just that, never finished or 'done.' Edmund de Waal, the author and potter, made this observation in an interview with *The Times,* in reference to the Jewish experience of the Holocaust. But he could just as well have been talking about the recollections of the Partition generation and their descendants. 'As second or third generation [Jewish],' de Waal explained,

> you [grow up] aware of the silences [around the past], you're completely aware of what you're not being told, of those protected spaces of anxiety. What do you do with that? You can either just move on or you can go into them. And the moment you go into them, you have to go through to the end. You are in freefall.[1]

We, in the second and third generation since Partition, knowing elderly family members who lived through that traumatic period, must make the same choice. Do we dare to delve deeper, or do we not, respectful of the silence or accepting without question the grains of history scattered before us? And if we do dig deeper to excavate that difficult past, what should we then do with that knowledge, with that load? But if we do not ask, how much of our own stories are we missing?

These are not light questions. But Aanchal Malhotra chose to ask them, and not just of her family. Asking, listening and documenting have consumed almost a decade of her life. What began as a fine art project as part of her MFA in Canada evolved into a vital piece of oral history and literature.

Partition memory takes many forms—the official, the political, the personal, the generational. But Aanchal has considered Partition through a different and largely unexplored lens: material memory. An object—whether carried at the time, later retrieved or even discarded—be it a *gaz*, a sword or a shawl, can retain memory and 'act as a prompt to its recollection.'

Material memory, Aanchal acknowledges, 'works in mysterious ways. It hides in the folds of clothes, [in] old records, boxes of inherited jewellery, the yellowing pages of books, furniture and handkerchiefs. Memory merges into our surroundings, seeps into our years, and remains quiet, accumulating the past like layers of dust, only to manifest itself in the most unlikely scenarios generations later.'

Objects, like memories, are handed down; some keep their secrets, others reveal them. The meaning of the object shifts constantly in different times and contexts. Each generation develops their own relationship with it, and it gathers another layer of dust.

Interviewing the Partition generation in Britain, I saw the power, as well as the sanctity, of such objects—how an ordinary physical possession is elevated and transformed in the telling of the story. I've seen how a brick taken from a place you once lived, and carried across a border, acquires the status of an ancestral home. A stone taken from the earth of one country decades before, when touched in the twenty-first century in another, can—in an instant—transport the interviewee over seventy years back in time. A single roof tile can be fought over by subsequent generations, as the only physical evidence that their family once lived in Pakistan. As an interviewer, I often felt that if I too touched the object, I could connect with that history, as if it were a physical bridge to a distant time.

The twenty-one objects documented by Aanchal in this book tell their own story of flight, retrieval, loss and promise. In one memorable story, the object—a sword—saves one life and brings another into the world, cutting an umbilical cord during a dramatic escape. Objects also reveal memories through their owners, in what the interviewee chooses to remember so many years on, and in the complex emotions the items stir up—whether trauma, joy, wistfulness or longing. There can be gaps too, when remembrance becomes too heavy, and the words stop. This is a work that is deeply personal to each of the twenty-one interviewees, the keepers of the objects. But the telling and recording of their stories is also a strand in an intricate tapestry of collective Partition memory.

Aanchal's commentary demonstrates the relationship between her and her interviewee. In the same room as the object and its keeper, she absorbs the weight of their words, hears their pauses, sees their expressions, feels their silences—that, too, is a part of their story all these years on. Azra Haq tells Aanchal that she doesn't want to remember what she witnessed on her arrival in Lahore: 'If you don't mind, I'd rather not talk about what I saw. I'm sorry, I cannot repeat those things. I cannot bring them to life again. I don't want to remember them.'

Aanchal is listening. She writes, 'I held my breath, not wanting to disturb that silence, not wanting to utter even a single word. I needed to know what she saw … but I didn't know how to ask … or what to ask.'

There is something delicate in this relationship. Aanchal is aware of the privilege of listening to these stories (all this time she is holding the catalyst of the memories—a pearl earring, bequeathed to Azra by a Maharajah); she knows the toll it takes to speak, and is mindful that a single question could go too far, and the interviewee could close up. In the back of the interviewer's mind is always the knowledge that dredging up difficult memories could be harmful so many years later. You cannot push too hard. Instinctively the interviewer must know that there are times for silence. These dynamics are all playing out in the room, often in the presence of the object in question.

Memory is by no means free of flaws. But the recollection of stories, no matter how imperfect, is an important part of the history of Partition. Memories are malleable, but *how* they are remembered and spoken about matters, as Urvashi Butalia notes in her seminal work *The Other Side of Silence: Voices from the Partition of India*. The objects will live on, but the sun is setting on the living memory of Partition. The number of survivors is ever dwindling. Soon, all we will have left are the stories they have passed down.

Re-reading *Remnants of Partition,* I thought about the power of objects, and, in particular, the power of my grandmother's jewellery, carried from Lahore to what would become India— some pieces of which I still possess. All I know about the gold filigree earrings and bracelet is that she chose to take these objects on that one-way journey. I was never old enough to ask her about their story: when she was given them, why she took them, the secrets they held. I now wear them in Britain, the country which was once her colonial ruler and which drew that calamitous line across the map of the subcontinent, forcing her to flee to India more than seventy years ago. I am now their keeper. They are the only physical objects I own which connect me to Lahore. But sadly my grandmother's memories have been permanently lost to time.

So why does recording these memories matter today?

If you listen closely to the stories that Aanchal records, if you search the layers of memory, of course there is violence and horror, but there are other things too, which confound current political narratives. Nazmuddin Khan asks Aanchal, 'Weren't *Musalmaans* also born here [in India]? Isn't this our country too?' Khan goes on to say, 'India is my country, regardless of my religion.' Reading this today, in the early 2020s, there is an added poignancy given the state of politics on the Indian subcontinent. These testimonies matter because they recall a time before borders, before *them and us*—a time when what united you was not only religion but food, traditions, culture, land. As Aanchal notes, the object's story is also about 'soil and rain, fields and clouds … love and relationships … children and the sound of their crying; it was about landscape and language, music, art, literature and poetry.' It is about profound connections that transcend man-made frontiers. As long as these memories are recorded, they exist, and show the complexity of that time of Undivided India, where Hindus, Sikhs and Muslims could live side by side.

Edmund de Waal spoke of the choice we must make as members of the second and third generations. Aanchal made hers. She walked towards these stories; she carried on to the very end. And now she is in freefall. She is a young author with an old soul. Her work never stops. I remember being in a rickshaw with her in Jaipur as she spoke to the Sikh driver, who happened to tell her a Partition story about his family. I watched as she quickly became the interviewer, and, with his permission, began to record their conversation. It is a life's work now to document the experiences of the Partition generation and their descendants. It has become a part of her, as vital as walking and breathing.

I first read *Remnants of Partition* just after completing the initial draft of my own book on survivors in Britain. Reading Aanchal's work felt like being reunited with a long-lost sister. So many similar themes came up throughout the chapters: familiar feelings about the responsibility of careful recording, as well as about the heaviness these stories leave behind. But above all, what came up was the importance of remembering.

London, April 2021

PREFACE

THE INDIAN EDITION OF this book, called *Remnants of a Separation*, was first published in 2017 to mark the seventieth anniversary of Indian Independence and the Partition of the subcontinent two days later into India and Pakistan. In the months following the book's release, I revisited all the men and women I had written about, on both sides of the border. I took along my personal copy, asking them to sign their respective chapters. They would often look over the pages carefully, smiling, recalling a memory associated with the text, sometimes even reading passages out. Over time, this master copy transformed into a codex with inscriptions in many languages and voices—much like the book itself.

'Thanks for recording these old experiences—long forgotten by our people and often deliberately ignored,' Lt Gen. S.N. Sharma wrote, signing off with his nickname, Tindi. 'What a wonderful way you have told my story,' Azra Haq noted in slightly trembling letters. 'What I appreciated the most,' Mian Faiz Rabbani wrote, 'was the impartiality in narrating each story.' Narjis Khatun simply signed and dated the page with the help of her daughter, Lisa. And then her granddaughter, Bano, wrote below: 'Grateful for this story and our friendship that formed along the way.' Savitri Mirchandani's chapter also bore a third-generation inscription: 'With love from an indebted granddaughter, Maya.'

Sitara Faiyaz Ali's chapter, partly about the home her father built in Dalhousie several years before the Partition, was inscribed both by Ali and by the family that bought the house some years after Partition: 'The two brothers who lived there,' signed Ambassador Gurdip Bedi and Col. Harinder Bedi. The Bedis, who had moved into the house as compensation for the home they themselves left behind in Pakistan, had serendipitously contacted me on reading the chapter and invited me to come up to Dalhousie. This is how I was able to take the colour photograph of the house that opens Chapter 18 of this new, UK version of the book. At the end of my visit, the Bedi brothers also invited Sitara Faiyaz Ali and her family to come and spend time in 'their' house, restoring to my interviewee the house she thought she'd never see again, and which I had thought consigned to history.[1]

The only chapters that remained unsigned were the ones whose protagonists had since passed—the ones on my paternal grandfather, Balraj Bahri; the eminent Punjabi poet, Prabhjot Kaur; the proudly Hindustani Englishman, John Grigor Taylor; and the gentle, childlike Sunil Chandra Sanyal, who passed away suddenly in 2018 and whose daughter Sangita, unable to bear the blankness of his page, wrote in his place, 'This book used to be my dad's favourite possession.'

***

For many writers, the publication of a book—especially one that has involved years of research—marks the culmination of that particular project, a release from their mind into the world. But that has not happened to me yet, nor do I think it ever will, for the research is still continuing. This is not with the active intention of writing another book on the subject, but simply because the work cannot stop. *Remnants* seems only to have opened the doors to a larger, more cavernous excavation of migratory memory and its living consequences, particularly with regards to the second and third generations of families who lived through the Partition.

Despite the sheer volume of information on the Partition available to us today, we are still only just learning how to speak both thoroughly and sensitively about the event, how to encompass its many facets and countless individual accounts. Traditional means of narration have failed to do justice to the depth of historical trauma, and yet it is so necessary to continually express it in words and discuss it, thereby gradually eradicating this notion of the unspeakable. The trauma experienced by many during the Partition has been submerged for long years. Perceptions that there was never a 'need' to speak about it, which several of the people I spoke to expressed, may also have led to an unnaturally detached and unemotional narration of that time.

Dr Dori Laub, a professor of psychiatry at Yale and co-founder of the Fortunoff Video Archive for Holocaust Testimonies, writes that 'the horror of the historical experience is maintained in the testimony only as an elusive memory that feels as if it no longer resembles any reality'.[2] In other words, fathoming and untangling memory demands a form of retreat from reality. And so I have realized that, in these interviews with the generation that lived through Partition, I, the interviewer, become the point of retreat, as it were—a person who does not carry the burden of the experience, but participates in reliving the events, within a larger history reaching to the present day.

I have wondered many times how reliving moments of trauma affects those recalling the story, but the interviewer and interviewee together go beyond the scope of the recollection itself, striving not to be engulfed, but to attempt to untangle. The unwillingness of many to talk about their experience of Partition over decades betrays some kind of hope that suppression might remove all traces of it. Yet, no one truly finds peace in silence, even when it is their choice to remain silent.[3] The great difficulty of crossing the bridge and giving voice to the experiences of 1947 does eventually result in some form of lightness, because even a crisis that is no longer active will persist latently, and remains a possible source of lingering trauma.[4] We need to talk about what happened, as things have not yet settled. There is still so much we do not know and Partition is not yet an event of the past, for its consequences are still very much alive today. Its heaviness continues to weigh down—sometimes only subconsciously—both those who lived through it personally as well as those who have inherited fragmented stories and memories of it.

***

It might seem strange to some that I have written a book about mere objects carried across the border, when I could very well have written about the enormity of memory and experience that survives. And I must admit that at times, during my interviews, I did feel uncomfortable and perhaps even petty to be continually asking about things people brought, when clearly they had witnessed so much horror along the path to safety. But still, I would persist.

What did you bring? How much did you bring? How did you bring it? What did you leave behind? Why these things? Things. Things. Things. I have learnt to say 'things' in so many different languages that it alarms me. But I will say this: that continuing to remember clearly is very difficult. And so my entry point into the memory of that time remains the material object, the personal possession. It is still my main gateway to 1947 and the life before it—fabrics and documents and soil and stones and touch and smell and caress.

But there are many ways to go back, I have discovered. In particular, since the publication of the original Indian edition of *Remnants*, people have sought me out and offered me their own versions of the paths that lead them 'home'. There are many kinds of objects—present or not—that help people to return. Holding on to a Karachi Club membership card issued to her father before the Partition, Pushpa Bhatia told me, 'I'll cut out my right arm if they don't let me in with it now. I'm sure they will!' She said this jokingly, but I realize that, living as the family does now in Mumbai, this membership card had become a portal to the Karachi they had unwillingly left behind.

Born in Chittagong and having migrated to West Bengal, the memory of Kalyani Ray Chowdhury was lined with green hill tracts. 'I tried to sow the plants I knew growing up; I wanted to feel at home. I thought that maybe if I grew the same plants in Calcutta, it might feel like my own private Chittagong—an escape into the past. But nothing grew here, as even trees bear allegiance to their soil, you see. Just like people,' she told me wisely. 'It is difficult to uproot them and place them where they don't belong. Sometimes, life is full of sorrow.'

Balbir Singh Bir, born in Sillanwali, close to Sargodha, drew a map of his city from memory in my notebook. It was detailed beyond imagination for a place he had fled seventy years ago, complete with where the neem trees grew, where the grain market was, and where the boys of the government school set up by the British celebrated the victory of the Allied Forces in World War II. When I asked him if he wished to go back, he smiled softly. 'It is my heart's desire to find a way home, but now I have no strength—neither in my heart nor in my body. But memory—that is the saving grace. And so I close my eyes and I make the journey back. Every single day I plunge into the heart of my memory.'

I have also met those who have been lucky enough actually to go back and find their homes still standing, occupied by new residents. Krishan Mohan Sharan, who once lived on Lodge Road in the Walled City of Lahore, narrated an amusing tale of what happened when he visited his hometown. Before migrating, he recalled, his older brother had buried some valuables at their home, in the hope that they would return. When they did return many decades later, a lovely Muslim family was living in the home and, surprisingly, still using all the objects that the Sharan family had left behind. When he asked, Sharan was told that no valuables had been excavated. When he came back a day or two later, though, he was welcomed by the sight of the whole floor having been dug up in order to find these aged treasures!

***

In February 2018, I was grateful to be invited by the Karachi Literature Festival to speak about this book and the research involved in writing it. This time, I decided to cross the border on foot. So many of my interviewees had stressed how both sides looked identical, how they couldn't even tell where one country ended and the other began, and I wanted to know for myself how that felt. Of course, seventy years ago, the border and its accompanying regulations were nowhere near as overwhelming and inflexible as they are today, as many of the characters in this book point out. But even today, at the Attari–Wagah border, there is just a single white line painted across six inches that separate India from Pakistan. Ironically, it is over these six inches that the passport, visa and luggage procedures are conducted. So much so that I didn't quite realize when I had simply walked over. Just as my documents were being checked, my foot unknowingly crossed the white line, and, much to my disappointment, rather than savouring the moment of stepping into 'the other side', I would look over my shoulder, alarmed that India had already been left behind.

The reception of this project has helped me recognize—much to my surprise—how curious the youth of both countries are about each other. This realization came not only from the messages I received or the questions I was asked before going to Pakistan, or on arrival, but also through the lament with which people narrated the stories of their ancestors, wishing they could visit 'where they were from'. It is through these conversations that I have understood that it is in fact possible to slowly and gradually obscure this border. There might never come a day when the Radcliffe Line no longer separates India and Pakistan, but through gentle, continuous and engaging conversations, one day this boundary might not feel so definite. The 'other' might not feel like the other any more.

On the same trip, Nazeer Adhami *sahab* (Chapter 10) welcomed me back into his home in Lahore. Our first meeting had just been him, his wife Najma-ji, and me. But this time three generations of the family were present. '*Ab aise hi toh Hindustan aur Pakistan milte hain,*' Najma-ji said to the room at large, 'this is the only way our two countries can meet.' Holding my hand, she told her grandchildren, 'We have now woven her into the web of our life.' And I remember nodding, agreeing, feeling completely at ease. Adhami *sahab* said, 'She has come to Pakistan to find her own, like we used to go to India to find our own.' He said this with a smile on his face, but I knew the sadness that ran beneath the surface. Having migrated in 1953 from Aligarh to Karachi, leaving his whole family in India, he had travelled back many years later to visit the living in their homes and the dead in their graves. Burial, after all, binds you to a place.

Khizar-ji, who had taken me around the city during my first visit when writing the Indian book, was my companion this time around as well. As always, he sat behind the wheel of the car, generously doling out the wisdom of his years. 'In the old days,' he began, 'people used to care for one another. But now they only think of themselves. The relationships between people have diminished, between communities too, and especially between our two countries.' He manoeuvred the car through traffic and then continued. '*Talluq. Urdu ka lafz hai "talluq"*, in English you call it "relation", *aur Punjabi vich ennu kehnde ne "jor … jor-jamma"*,' he laughed, reminding me how important it is to keep all these relationships I have built in his city alive and intact. And I sat wordless in the back, listening and reflecting, as always, on the poignancy of his words.

***

Many years ago, when my paternal grandfather turned seventy-five, my father presented him with a book. A document on his life—from birth to setting up a career as a bookseller; from Malakwal to Delhi; from what became Pakistan to what became Independent India. Listening to hours and hours of interview tapes of the generation before his, my father painstakingly traced our family history.

No matter how many years have passed, I still go back to this book from time to time, especially now that my grandfather is no more. It keeps him alive in some way. In it, his stories seem like stories of the present; as if he's narrating them, as if he's still here. In his poignant book about his family, *The Farthest Field*, Raghu Karnad writes that people have two deaths: the first at the end of their lives, and the second at the end of the memory of their lives, when all who remember them are gone. Then a person quits the world completely.[5] Today I think I finally understand what he means when he says this.

In my book, I have archived the lives of many people whom I didn't know before. People who have now, over the course of so many years, become intimately connected with me. In return, I have become intimately connected with them and everyone in their lives: their wives, husbands, sons and daughters, grandchildren and even the household help. The heaviness of the lives of others that I felt while working on this book was deposited within its seams. I know now that, just like my father and the book about his father, my book too is about so many people's fathers and mothers and sisters and brothers and grandparents. It remains a way to keep these people alive, immortalized in ink on paper.

Professor Partha Mitter, whose wife I wrote about in Chapter 12, sent me an email to say that the family read excerpts about her from my book on her death anniversary. Imogen Taylor, whose father is the protagonist of Chapter 7, wrote to say that she read a section from the book at his memorial service, that the soil I had once brought from India to England for him was sprinkled in the garden he loved so much. To my staggering amazement, messages of this sort continue to pour in even from people I hadn't interviewed—photos and recordings of grandchildren reading parts of the book to their grandparents, people looking for their birthplaces on maps, dreaming in languages they once spoke as children on 'the other side', and, with eyes closed, crossing over every single day.

I used to feel almost uncomfortable holding on to these intimate moments of the lives of people I interviewed, but I know now that it is the only way not to forget—for me, for the families, and for future generations. It fills my heart with joy to know that this book is able to keep people alive even after they are gone. To encase their memory, to remember.

INTRODUCTION

THE PAST SURFACES FREQUENTLY and unexpectedly these days.

It is March 2016. I return home from work to find my paternal grandmother, my *dadi*, hunched over the bed, sifting through a pile of coins. A plastic sheet has been spread over the mattress, and her elusive collection, unseen by me but talked about frequently by my father, has been spilled out onto the sheet. For as long as I can remember, this coin collection has lived discreetly inside a blue velvet pouch. Rupees, paise, annas, takas, dhelas—a veritable hoard amassed by my grandmother over the years. Mementos of monetary change in the subcontinent, some passed down from her mother and some her own. Today, they are strewn across the sheet, and my grandmother's long fingers pick at them erratically.

But this is not an unusual sight in our house, especially of late. My grandfather died a few weeks ago and the plastic sheet has been ceremoniously spread many, many times since. As drawers and cupboards are gradually emptied, belongings are laid out— some his, some theirs—to be classified for keeping or discarding. Coupled with this sorting are memories, which inevitably tumble out alongside.

I stand at the door and watch my grandmother. Her eyebrows are knit together. Though I'm not surprised to find her this way, I am curious since this is the first time I've actually seen the collection.

'What are you doing?' I ask, visibly startling her.

1

'I was sorting through some things and I found this pouch. It has my old coins. *Purane zamane ke.*' She is speaking to me but her eyes have already returned to the pile. I come in and sit down on the wicker chair next to her bed.

She is singling out the larger silver coins and laying them in a line, chronologically. She picks one up and holds it to the light. Then she wipes it clean and places it in the middle of my outstretched palm. It is heavier than I expect, minted in solid silver, dulling at the edges but still brilliant. 'ONE RUPEE INDIA 1920'. The amount is written in English and Urdu and is surrounded by a floral wreath. I flip it over to find an image of the King, embossed in all his regal glory. 'George V King Emperor', it reads proudly.

'*Humne kya kya din nahi dekhe,*' she says distantly.

As I study the coin, I think about what she means when she says this. *What have I not seen in my time.* My grandmother was born in the North-West Frontier Province (NWFP, now Pakistan's Khyber Pakhtunkhwa province) to an affluent family of landowners in 1932. Her father, the youngest of four brothers, passed away when she was a child, and her mother became a widow at the age of only twenty-five. They were cheated out of their share of the family property, leaving them in dire circumstances. In 1947, at the onset of the Partition, my great-grandmother and her five children fled across the border and arrived in Delhi.

'In those days, one rupee was worth a lot of money.' My grandmother is sitting next to me, yet her voice seems to be emanating from elsewhere. 'I remember this incident from when I was six or seven years old. We needed money for something important and my mother had none. It had to be something important or I wouldn't have done it, I wouldn't have asked. It was always me when money was involved. I was always the one sent out.'

She pauses and runs her flattened palm over the sea of one-rupee coins.

INTRODUCTION

'I can still see the scene play out before me. The ancestral house was large and each of my father's brothers had his separate quarter. I walked across the house to the room of my cousin—my eldest uncle's daughter-in-law, who was much older than me. She had had nothing to do with the division of family property and seemed kind enough. So there I was, knocking on the door innocently, hoping that she would understand our plight. She opened the door and asked me what I wanted. "Five rupees," I had said to her. "Just five rupees, *didi*. We don't have anything, and this will last us the whole month."'

Suddenly, she stops and looks at me, her moist eyes boring into mine, and I realize that my grandmother has extracted perhaps the single most heartbreaking memory from her past. Now she separates from the pile she's made five of the one-rupee coins and stacks them on top of one another. Five rupees.

'That was what I asked for,' she gestures to them. 'And she said no. She didn't help us. No one in that house did.' A small river trickles down her cheek and lands in a pool at the neck of her kameez. 'What I have not seen in my time,' she repeats slowly.

Her palm tightens around the five silver coins, claiming them. She brings her fist up to her chest and holds it against her heart, as though owning the currency now brings her delayed consolation.

As she weeps, coins still clutched tight, I sit with a void in my heart for a memory that is not mine. I am just a listener, a passive contributor to the vulnerable act of unfolding a painful past. Yet, at the same time, it is my grandmother's very vulnerability and the intimate nature of this experience that provokes within me a sense of guilt. And I think to myself: am I an intruder?

The Beginning

Although this incident became crucial to my understanding of material memory and left a deep impression on me, it was not my first experience with the concept, nor did it mark the beginning of this project. For that, we must go back a few more years to 2013, when I was in Delhi on a research sabbatical from my Master of Fine Arts at Concordia University, Montreal. It was October, and I was on my way with Mayank Austen Soofi—a writer, also known as the Delhi Walla—to my maternal grandparents' home in north Delhi, for a story he was writing on old houses in the city (Chapter 1).

That day, the conversations between my family and the Delhi Walla mostly revolved around the construction of the house, Vij Bhawan, and its neighbourhoods of Roop Nagar and Kamla Nagar. But somewhere in the middle of their discussion, a few objects of old were brought out from the recesses of closets and shelves. According to my grandfather's eldest brother, the patriarch of the Vij family, 'If times of old must be discussed, they must be discussed in their entirety,' and the family's possessions were as much a part of history as the house itself.

Each item placed before us was visibly aged and possessed a unique history, but there were two whose histories ran parallel with that of the family itself. A medium-sized metallic vessel—a *ghara*—and a yardstick—a *gaz*. These had travelled from Lahore to Amritsar and then to Delhi just before the Partition. The *ghara*, belonging to my grandfather's mother, and the *gaz*, belonging to his father, were by far the oldest surviving items in that house, older than him. And when they were picked up, grazed, studied, remembered and situated in anecdotes from a time gone by, they proved to be the most effortless yet effective stimulus for extracting memory.

This was the first time that the importance of material memory truly dawned on me—the ability of an object or a possession to retain memory and act as a prompt to its recollection. But more curious than this unexpected revelation was the context in which it had arrived. Despite the fact that I was born and raised in Delhi—a city thick with Punjabi migrants who had flocked here from across the border after the Partition—and although I was a descendant of migrants on both sides of my family, this desire to study the Great Divide had never been as strong in me as in that brief encounter with the *ghara* and the *gaz*.

The Other Side

I have grown up listening to my grandparents' stories about 'the other side' of the border. But, as a child, this other side didn't quite register as Pakistan, or not-India, but rather as some mythic land devoid of geographic borders, ethnicity and nationality. In fact, through their stories, I imagined it as a land with mango orchards, joint families, village settlements, endless lengths of ancestral fields extending into the horizon, and quaint local bazaars teeming with excitement on festive days. As a result, the history of my grandparents' early lives in what later became Pakistan essentially came across as a very idyllic, somewhat rural, version of happiness. Many a time, I'd imagine what my life would have been like had I too been born and raised on 'the other side', for, in these seemingly superficial tales of the past, the words 'religion', 'faith' and 'Partition' were never mentioned.

My paternal grandfather, my *dada*, hailed from Malakwal, a small town in the Mandi Bahauddin district of Punjab about 250 km from Lahore, and my *dadi* from Muryali, Dera Ismail Khan, in NWFP. Both my maternal grandparents, my *nana* and *nani*, came from Lahore. The syncretic feeling that each of their families harboured for land and community was drastically altered by the events of the Independence and Partition of India in 1947. And, what's more, the journeys of migration that they and many other families were forced to undertake covered their existence in a shroud of painful silence that only magnified as the years went by.

'An unholy rush' was how the award-winning Punjabi poet Prabhjot Kaur (Chapter 13) described this massive exercise in human misery.[1] Having been displaced in the communal riots herself, she penned heartbreaking, soulful verses recounting an event that is considered one of the largest mass migrations of people in world history, leaving up to 1 million dead and forcing approximately 14 million to flee in both directions across a newly created border.[2]

* * *

So how did it happen, I wonder to myself, as the third generation of a family affected by the Partition. How was it that the division of a land was so easily conceptualized? Was it really possible to carve out a new country from within India, consolidating most of the Muslims living across the expanse of the subcontinent into one nation? How could Indians—Hindus, Muslims and Sikhs, but Indians all the same—be suddenly drawn apart for their differences, despite being children of the same soil?

At the historic Lahore Conference of the Muslim League in March 1940, the future Pakistani governor-general Muhammad Ali Jinnah listed the inherent 'differences' between the two peoples as the basis of the demand for the country of Pakistan:

> We are a nation with our distinctive culture and civilization, language and literature, names and nomenclature, sense of values and proportions, legal laws and moral codes, customs and calendar, history and traditions, aptitude and ambitions. In short, we have our own distinct outlook on life and of life. By all canons of international law, we are a nation.[3]

Taking me back to his teen years in pre-Partition Lahore, Pran Nevile—former diplomat, art historian, and author of several books including *Lahore: A Sentimental Journey*—recalled for me the amity and brotherhood he had witnessed between the people of various communities. 'When Hindus, Muslims and Sikhs broke sugarcane, or ate *aloo-puri*, they did so in the same fashion. When they went to buy wares at Anarkali bazaar, they did so together. This was—is—our shared Punjabi culture and it had little to do with religion.'[4] In stark contrast, my grandmother Bhag Malhotra (Chapter 5) recalled walking to school in NWFP in the early months of 1947 and being called a *kafir*, a disbeliever, all the way, despite having lived there her whole life. Amir Ahmed, a resident of Nawabganj, Delhi, was eleven years old at the time of Partition, and his family had decided not to migrate. 'Partition,' he claims, based on the sights of Delhi at that time, 'had brought out the ugliest, most vehement side of humanity, showed us what the word insanity truly meant.'

How, I wondered, did families who had lived for generations on the same soil suddenly find themselves on the 'wrong' side of the border? How, having celebrated both Diwali and Eid, eaten sugarcane and *aloo-puri* with people of all religions, did they suddenly become 'the other'? Were our land, our languages, our food, our habits, really as dissimilar as some had declared them to be?[5]

During my time in Pakistan researching this book, Lahore embedded itself into the same place in my heart otherwise occupied by my hometown of Delhi. There was no sense of homesickness or unfamiliarity. On the contrary, its streets seemed to be alive with the same history as the streets of Delhi; its monuments boasted of the same civilizations; and its government buildings and old bazaars structurally felt the same. And what had I been expecting, really, if not just that? I didn't stand out as someone from across the border, apart from the fact that I spoke more Hindi than Urdu. But in terms of physicality, I was folded seamlessly into the public landscape by the skin tone, angular jawline and pronounced chin I had inherited from my great-grandmother from the Frontier; I became like every other woman walking the streets of urban Lahore.

Through the stories I had heard and the interviews I had conducted previously in various parts of India, with people who had migrated from this Garden City, I was certain that somewhere amidst my research, I had slipped through the cracks of time, existing alternatively in the Lahore of an Undivided India. That I could belong to it and it could belong to me became more and more apparent with every layer the city allowed me to peel off. Strange as it may be to think this way, it had felt like an appropriate homecoming to a place I had never been before.

My own experience makes me question the concreteness of citizenships, both inherited and adopted. My conversations with those who migrated across the border make me wonder about their psyche in the days of the Partition. Apart from a physical displacement, there would have been a traumatic mental displacement, a sudden uprootedness, an unlearning and relearning of identity. 1947 would have created an involuntary distance between where one was born before the Partition and where one moved to after it, stretching out people's identity over the expanse of this distance. As a result, somewhere in between the original city of their birth and the adopted city of residence lay their essence—strangely malleable.

Noor Qadir, a young architect from Lahore, described how both sets of his grandparents, having migrated from Jullundur (now Jalandhar), still long for their land and life as it was before 1947. Even the *rishta*, the betrothal, between the children of the two families was agreed simply due to their common origins on the other side of the border. 'Jullundur was his weakness,' he wrote in an email about his maternal grandfather. 'Everything was forgiven if you were from there. My *nana* would even send his car to Jullundur Autos in his adopted city of Multan.' But most poignantly of all, his *nana*, Pirzada Abd-e-Saeed Pakistani—who had believed so fervently in the creation of Pakistan that he had added the suffix to his name—ceremoniously renounced it after the Partition. Unable to comprehend that his beloved hometown wouldn't be part of the new country, he became Pirzada Abd-e-Saeed Jullunduri, carrying his identity with him across the border.

This newly carved boundary would act as a physical manifestation of the Divide in the two new national identities, adopted and defended with fervour. A definitive event in the histories of many families, it was used as a tool to archive, dividing lives into two phases: pre and post.

* * *

Though the Divide will always hold utmost importance in the minds of people directly affected by it, what I have hoped to do through this work is to provide an alternative lens to view it with. Seven decades have passed since 1947, and still there continues to be new and original scholarship emerging from various disciplines, contributing to a more comprehensive understanding of it. This book certainly draws from that traditional paper trail, but also breaks away from it.

Remnants uses methods of oral history to commemorate those affected by the Great Divide. This has proved to be a remarkable resource, distilling an enormous event down to something that is graspable: the experience of the individual. However, to speak of the human dimension is not to say that it exists in isolation from the political or social context. What is important, and what I have attempted to do in each chapter, is to weave together a cohesive narrative of personal experiences vis-à-vis the past as well as the present. Memorialization is an active and continual process, a conversation. The evolution of personal histories from the time of Partition allows us to further unravel and better understand its legacy.

An Empire Falls: Disbelief and Denial

The immediate years following World War II were fraught with great uncertainty about whether India would remain a part of the Empire. But Britain's condition in the aftermath of the War, coupled with the environment of extreme communal unrest in the subcontinent, made it quite clear that Independence was in the foreseeable future. On 3 June 1947, citizens of the subcontinent learned that it would be partitioned.[6] The Indian Independence Act, formulated by Prime Minister Clement Attlee and Viceroy of India Lord Louis Mountbatten (in agreement with various representatives of the subcontinent community), declared that India would be free from British rule on 15 August 1947, partitioned into the dominions of India, which was to be a secular nation despite its Hindu majority, and Pakistan, intended to be a homeland for Muslims.

On 5 July, in his daily prayer meeting, Mahatma Gandhi proclaimed in response to this decision that 'the very creation of two nations is poison. The Congress [Party] and the Muslim League have accepted this but a vice does not become a virtue merely because it is accepted by all.'[7]

* * *

The demand for Pakistan had indeed been accepted, albeit theoretically, but what did this Partition really mean? Even the Muslim League's propaganda failed to define concretely the geographic nature of the new country.[8] So who would draw the border and where would it lie? What provinces would become a part of Pakistan? Were people expected to move across this border, or would they be allowed to remain where they were, despite their religious beliefs?

Savitri Mirchandani (Chapter 17), hailing from a Sindhi family for whom the concepts of Hindu or Muslim meant little, remained in Karachi until late 1947. In Delhi, Begum Ikramullah's husband assured her that the capital city they currently inhabited would certainly be a part of the new country. 'The frontiers of Pakistan had not yet been defined, and it never entered our heads that Delhi would not be within it.'[9] As a result, the creation of Pakistan became an imaginary nationalistic dream, as well as a cold territorial reality.[10]

Simultaneously, what also existed within the population was an enormous sense of disbelief that the country would actually be divided. Even within the close community of those who served in the British Indian government, this was a legitimate doubt. Author Gurcharan Das has told me about a *guchchha* with fifty-one rustic keys belonging to his maternal grandmother, Shib Dai Verma, married to the lawyer Wazir Chand Verma. She was so convinced that they would return to their home in Lyallpur, now in Pakistan, that before leaving for Ludhiana she locked every single cupboard and every single room, including the kitchen, making sure the house was secure and safe. Fifty-one locks for fifty-one keys. In fact, she even made arrangements with a local woman to make sure the house would be cleaned before they returned, overlooking the fact there was no way to actually enter the rooms, due to all the locks! '*Ke saade aan de pehle, safai toh ho jaani chahiye*,' Das imitated his grandmother's voice in Punjabi, stressing the conviction with which she believed that they would return home.

Sumohini Bhagat, daughter of the late Justice (Dr) Bakshi Tek Chand, has attempted to describe to me the family's lack of preparation for the Divide. 'The truth was,' she said, sitting in what her family now calls 'The Lahore Room' of their Lutyens' Delhi home, 'despite the fact that my father was one of the advisors to the Punjab Boundary Commission, he didn't actually believe that Partition would happen. In that, there is something to be said about unwavering belief. We refused to believe that such a vivisection would—could—ever occur. I think about it now and am still astonished. Just weeks before independence, I remember my father constantly writing letters, being engaged in meetings, long phone calls and closed-door conversations with Lord Mountbatten, Pandit Nehru and all the others, and yet we left in haste, completely unprepared and unwilling.' The family had migrated from Lahore to Dalhousie in the hope that it was just temporary. 'We should have realized it sooner, at least my father should have, that there was no coming back. Not in September when the riots died down, not in October when the subcontinent still lay in shock, not even in November as he had hoped and promised us. Lahore was now lost forever.'[11]

The Anatomy of the Radcliffe Line

British barrister Sir Cyril Radcliffe was the architect of the new border. Owing to the evident Muslim majority, areas of the north-east and north-west would naturally be carved out for the new country, resulting in West and East Pakistan (the latter becoming Bangladesh in 1971), with India sandwiched in between. The contentious border would concern, for the most part, the provinces of Punjab in the east and Bengal in the west, where there was the most intermingling of religious groups.[12] To aid the actual creation of the border, two Boundary Commissions were announced on 30 June, a week before Radcliffe's arrival in India.

Then, a few days later, on 4 July, Christopher Beaumont, a district officer in the Punjab, mentioned the name Radcliffe for the first time in his nearly unreadable scrawl. His correspondence confirms that a new post had been created for the mapmaker of Independent India and Pakistan, and that Beaumont had been appointed secretary, Rao V.D. Ayer assistant secretary.[13] Finally, on 8 July, Radcliffe made his first appearance on Indian soil, seemingly equipped with everything but time.

The Crown had sent Radcliffe, a man who had never set foot in India before, to partition it, believing that his very lack of knowledge of the subcontinent would result in a neutral division of the territory.[14] And though he tried to maintain this belief till the end of his assignment, the politics of Indian Independence eventually infiltrated his final decision of the Awards.

On 12 July, he travelled with Beaumont to the north-eastern province of Bengal to survey the land and its people. On the plane back from Calcutta to Delhi, looking down at the vast terrain soon to come under the sharp knife of the Award, Beaumont writes, 'Sir Cyril had two very adequate days in Calcutta staying in the Government House and we made some progress in the difficult task of partitioning Bengal.'[15]

In the crevasses of the India Office Archives at the British Library, a thick khaki green file holds within it the earliest drafts of Radcliffe's proposed border. Over the course of his five weeks in India, this murderous boundary would shift one way then the other as effortlessly as the tides of the oceans he had crossed to be there. Depending on perspective, bias and convenience, it would falter to favours and concede to the needs of the elite over the needs of the many, much against the mapmaker's better judgement. Moreover, Radcliffe, as a person, would forever be changed in his own eyes after his time in India. The task that had been entrusted to him was an impossible one, with no single outcome being acceptable to all parties involved. On 28 July, Beaumont wrote the following words, making it quite clear:

> The actual job is difficult. Neither the Punjab nor Bengal were ever intended to be partitioned, and it will not be possible to do it otherwise than by leaving nearly everyone with a grievance, more or less legitimate. The position of the Sikh in Punjab will be particularly hard. Altogether, a thankless task.[16]

In June 1947, the *Times of India* published an article where Viceroy Mountbatten was asked the essential question: whether he foresaw a mass transfer of population. 'Personally, I don't see it,' he responded. 'There are many physical and practical difficulties involved. Some measures of transfer will come about in a natural way … perhaps governments will transfer populations.'[17] This answer, coming just months before the Partition and lacking any sort of definition, in some sense did prefigure the nature of the Divde, unfolding as it did very suddenly, amid chaos and uncertainty.

* * *

The dangers of being stranded on the 'wrong' side of a line—a fate no one could know for certain they would avoid or encounter, as the border had not yet been announced—led many families to migrate prematurely by the end of 1946 or the beginning of 1947, though the wrath of relocation and sheer magnitude of the exodus would emerge only later.

Seventy-six-year-old Harmeet Singh Baweja has shared with me his memories of fleeing with his family from Mintgumri or Montgomery (now Sahiwal) to Amritsar in June 1947. He was seven years old at the time and had helped in carefully rolling up all the family's valuables into a large carpet and burying it in the floor of their *haveli* (townhouse) at Akhtali Chakk. Under a cloak of heavy rainfall, they left with only the most basic belongings, hopeful and confident of coming back as soon as the riots subsided.

Professor D.P. Sengupta, now at the National Institute of Advanced Studies, Bangalore, was barely eleven years old at the time. He remembers the journey from Barisal, East Bengal, to Calcutta. '*Udbastu*,' he tells me in Bengali. '"Without *bastu*", without home, a refugee, a displaced person. I remember, as the train arrived at Calcutta station, in the distance one could see people living in pipes. Those large cement pipes served as homes to men, women and children, all in rags. These were the *udbastu*, people living in the shadows of an imminent Partition.'

Swarna Kapur, travelling from Jhelum to Delhi in September 1947, recalls the warnings given to her family at the start of their long journey. 'We brought nothing, absolutely nothing, for fear of being looted along the way. The only possession my father-in-law dared to bring was a receipt stating that his shipment of Hitkari cycles [which would later expand to the more popular Hitkari crockery and timepieces] would now be delivered to Bombay instead of Karachi. Every time the train stopped at a station, we would all hold our breath, making sure not a single sound drifted out of the closed windows. We were hungry and our throats parched. From inside the train we heard voices travelling up and down the platform, saying, "Hindu *paani*," and, from the other side, "Muslim *paani*." Apart from land and population, even the water had now been divided.'

Renowned Pakistani playwright and actor Naeem Tahir recalls the extent to which one remained loyal to the land of one's birth, refusing to migrate. 'The population of Bhoptiyan village in district Lahore consisted of a Sikh majority and Muslim minority, a gurudwara at one end of the village and a mosque at the other. During the days of the riots, the village saw its entire Sikh population converting to Islam to be able to continue to live on a land that was as much as theirs as their Muslim brothers'.'

INTRODUCTION

* * *

Strangely Raj-less and seemingly out of place, there also existed a sliver of the British elite in the midst of millions of Indians and soon-to-be Pakistanis. The impending news of Independence had left these British families serving the Empire in India to 'return' and seek a life in their ironically foreign motherland. After the official announcement of the Partition, the governor of Assam, Sir Andrew Gourlay Clow, wrote with a heavy heart to Mountbatten, 'Leaving India is a big wrench, particularly as I shall, in my own country, be rather a stranger in a strange land.'[18]

Harold Neville Blair had been given command of the Black Watch in India in early 1947. His daughter, Juliet Cheetham, has told me that she remembers he could barely contain his excitement. Not because he had any geographic connection to India, but simply because two generations prior to him had served there, and so, for him, it was the continuation of a legacy. His father, Alexander Neville Blair, who was also a part of the Black Watch, had left for India in January 1917, but unfortunately died in the Colaba War Hospital in Bombay two months later and was never to be seen again by his family.

'When we arrived in India in 1947, my father's task was quite different from what had been the role of British officers up until then,' she explained to me. 'He was responsible for the safety of the remaining British citizens in this historic period of Independence and Partition. He had hoped to travel across India to see the landscapes and sights which would have been familiar to his family, but that was not to be, since travel at this time was largely forbidden. On train trips we did make, he made sure that my sister and I looked out the window as we passed through towns and the countryside where our ancestors had lived and worked, and sometimes died. Perhaps the most emotional moment of our time there was when we visited the Sewri Cemetery in Bombay, where my grandfather was buried in 1917. It was the first time my father had met his father in over thirty years, and because of that connection to the land he was buried in, there was a sense of belonging for us as well. That we could be some part of India and it could be some part of us was never as certain as it had been in that moment.'

In a letter written on 26 September 1947, Mrs Freda Evelyn Olivier, wife of an English civil servant, describes how the family had to flee with other refugees from Ludhiana to Lahore, in shared convoys of twenty-eight trucks, despite their foreign pedigree. She describes being on the 'wrong side of Amritsar', fearing having to spend the night at a refugee camp. 'On the roads, of course, were bullock carts laden sky-high, refugees walking, riding, driving cattle or goat. It is quite impossible to even begin to describe the scene for you to imagine it.'[19]

And, in thinking about British lives in the Raj bound by their duty to the Empire, it is difficult to discount the predicament of our mapmaker. On 14 August, Pakistan and on 15 August, India celebrated their Independence, two days before the borders were even published. Radcliffe, upon seeing the bloodshed his actions had caused, so repulsed by the horrifying consequences of his particular imperial duty, refused to accept his fee, left for England, destroyed all his maps and papers pertaining to the Divide and made sure, in his long illustrious career as a judge, never again to speak of what had happened in India.[20] And yet the border bears his name; that is the paradox of his legacy.

What continues to fascinate me, though, is the anatomy of the Radcliffe Line. It is by no means an isolated or invisible boundary, but one that is firmly and physically present. The line might as well have been drawn in blood and littered with the possessions of those who crossed it—a piece of cloth here, utensils scattered there, jewellery, riches and money strewn across the sand. What follows in the chapters of this book is an exploration of these contested objects—artefacts that were carried across or, at times, discarded and mourned, at the conjoined birth of these two countries—and of the memories infused within them.

INTRODUCTION

* * *

Why does this matter? The Partition of India in 1947 is a complex event even today, one that cannot be attributed to a single cause or community. We cannot say with certainty that it was the Hindus, Muslims, Sikhs or even the British who were responsible, for ultimately everyone suffered, in one way or another. Even more elusive is the question that comes to me when I weigh the violence, plunder, loot, murder, rape, rehabilitation, strength, unity and nationalism: was it worth it? And there is an even larger question behind it: could there have been a version of history where we remained an Undivided India? Could I have been born in a city that is now 'on the other side'?

For as long as these questions live with us, on the subcontinent and beyond, the Partition is a living event. Similarly, the exploration of memory is not something that is or can be finite.[21] It is impossible to think that there will come a day when, due to the reservoir of research built up, we can cease recording memories of the Partition. The more you search, the more there is that opens up.[22] If I considered the Partition an archaeological site, and the many experiences of those who witnessed it as layers of sediment, then the deeper I excavated, the more I found, in innumerable variants. And, as I have discovered both while researching *Remnants* and since its Indian publication, there is a hunger for these layers of lost heritage and family history among the younger generations.

Leena Naqvi, a Pakistani designer living in Sweden, has described to me how it was only after she married an Indian that her grandparents finally opened up about the life they had left behind in India. 'The whole time while I was growing up,' she wrote to me, 'there was no denying their Indian roots, but there was never an instance where I heard anyone mention the word [India].' And though she still had family on the other side, her mother only met her Indian cousins for the first time when Naqvi was to travel there on a school trip. As she arrived in a land seemingly foreign yet familiar to her—India—she found at the heart of her family's unity a curious source: food. 'I reconnected with the Indian side of my family [during that first trip] and was force-fed everything they could get their hands on. *Katthal sabzi* that my grandmother had liked, *motichoor laddus* and all kinds of sweets!' After years of being strangers, the two branches of the family were finally reunited, and her grandmother, having rekindled her love for her lost land, became the window onto the roots Naqvi had so wished to explore growing up.

In Lahore, Fateeha Saleem told me of a comical incident during the very first meeting with the part of her family that had remained across the border in Khopoli, a city at the base of the Sahyadri mountains in Maharashtra. 'I had never seen my aunt, my *phupho*, before, only heard about her. The first time we went to visit India, I was ten years old and didn't know what to expect. How would the people be, what would they look like? Would our *phupho* be like us, or…?' She let her voice trail off, revealing her childhood concerns. 'I had never seen an Indian before, you see. The only thing I had seen was the currency, the banknotes, and on every single one was drawn the Ashoka pillar, with its four lions standing back to back. Four heads. So when we met for the first time, I looked at my *phupho*'s face and then looked to her side and back, and in a very confused tone asked, "But where are the rest of your heads?" I was only a child, I had never seen an Indian before; how could I have known any better? Nobody in our family had told us that we were the same people; nobody had talked about what life used to be like before we separated.'

'Ask me quickly before I forget' was what my own grandmother said to me when I finally convinced her to part with the story of her migration, my own history which I did not know (Chapter 5). I don't really know what her reason was for keeping the past locked away, but I'd like to imagine it was because she had never really been asked before. As she began to open up, rather cautiously at first, and later as confidently as a seasoned storyteller, what was apparent in her was a sense of relief at having finally poured the past out of herself and into me. In doing so, I became the collector of her memories. A transference of memory was occurring as she wrung out every small, muffled detail. And once it had begun, it was difficult to interrupt or stop.

The act of forgetting the Partition, either inevitably or purposefully, seems to play as much of a part as the eventual remembering itself. People often recall the Great Divide as the darker side of Independence, the price we paid for it. Hence, remembering it continues to be a difficult and sensitive act. For the most part, those who witnessed it have either consigned parts of their memory to old age, or have sheathed them in utter silence. As my interviewees' migratory experiences began to unravel, I realized it was not just loss that they were concealing, but a number of feelings—sadness, shame, pain, anxiety, horror—that had risen within them as they had fled their homes. These feelings have never truly been unravelled, and the silence surrounding them has itself been concealed.

So there is both a need to remember the Partition, and a reluctance, a failure, or a lack of impetus to remember among those who experienced it in 1947. How to unlock these memories, before they fall into the abyss of forgetting?

* * *

As I saw for myself with my grandmother's coin collection, and my great-grandparents' *gaz* and *ghara*, personal belongings can serve, in some cases unknowingly, as the repository for memories. Orhan Pamuk writes in *The Museum of Innocence*, 'We can bear the pain only by possessing something that belongs to that instant.'[23] Preserving an object of a particularly painful time can be somewhat therapeutic if it is allowed to envelop that memory of suffering. This means that such objects also serve as the catalyst for memory, a trigger for remembering and a portal into the past.

This should be obvious if we think about how we interact with objects in our daily lives. We surround ourselves with things and put parts of ourselves in them: clothes, old records, boxes of inherited jewellery, the yellowing pages of books, furniture and handkerchiefs. Memory merges into our surroundings, seeps into our years, and remains quiet, accumulating the past like layers of dust, only to manifest itself in the most unlikely scenarios generations later. In *Contested Objects*, Dominiek Dendooven examines the importance of war souvenirs and other objects that remain from World War I, stating:

> We all know how unreliable memory can be, how transient reminiscences are, and how inaccessible the past will always remain. Experiences can never be duplicated or revived … by those who took no part in the struggle. Herein lies the beauty and power of conflict-related objects, some of which withstand the ravages of time in a way that memories do not.[24]

In other words, there is an immediacy to physical remnants of the past that faded memories may not be able to bring to the same history. Events that occurred during the Partition, unthinkable acts of violence and communal disruption, need to be understood in the context in which they occurred, not rationalized by immersing them in the present. While our memory dilutes over time, an object remains unaltered.

And when we confront a traumatic event of great and often permanent rupture like the Partition, there is a particular power in the personal possessions that were abandoned, lost or brought over the border at that time: they tell a story of belonging through belongings.[25] We can unpack rich and sensitive ideas of identity and attachment through them, especially if the places they involve are now inaccessible due to a national border. Families living with a sense of lost identity or displacement can draw history from these heirlooms.

INTRODUCTION

I witnessed this power of objects for myself when speaking to my family. Five coins awoke in my grandmother a memory that had caused her great pain, creating an incision in the comfortable life she now led in Delhi and inserting into it the extreme penury of her childhood in NWFP. And though I was simply a listener, it left in my heart a sadness that didn't really belong to me. Somehow I was able to feel an emotion created by an incident I did not witness. It had transferred to me, and I had made it mine.

In the Pursuit of Objects

Once an idea takes root in one's mind, it is difficult to retract it. Such was the case with my family *gaz* and *ghara*—I thought of little else. As I contemplated the notion of home and what it might have felt like to flee from it hastily, I pictured an arduous journey to a future you couldn't foresee. I tried to imagine emptying out your whole home, an entire life, every single belonging, and hoping to take it with you. Alternatively, I tried to imagine leaving every single thing behind. And in doing so, I thought of all that refugees brought with them, the objects that became their companions on the way to a new citizenship—from things as banal as household items to those of precious value. These belongings have become reservoirs of memory and experience, their physical mass outweighed by the emotional load they have borne over the years: the weight of the past.

At the same time, considering my great-uncle's relationship with his parents' belongings, I realized that the Partition wasn't just about those who crossed the border, but also about those who remained behind. It affected even those who never moved and never had to, sometimes consuming their lives as they remained amidst the chaos. They too had seen the riots, the violence, the disorder, but from a different perspective. Their belongings, too, had a place in the history of the Partition, a colossal historical event that persists into the present.

The more I immersed myself in my research, the more my intentions for the project began to coalesce. This was not just about objects from another time, but a collated experience of their physicality, both for their original owners and for us looking back on the Partition today. I wanted to know what it felt like to hold in one's hands a tangible part of one's history. How do you approach it? Has it been a prized possession or something too mundane to be considered of value? Will it be allowed the luxury of touch and feel and smell, the sensual caress of fingers and living skin, or is it to remain elusive and out of reach, behind a glass display or safely stored at the back of a closet? Moreover, what does this object convey to its owner? Is its importance immediately recognized, does it demand an audience, is the story of its serendipitous survival known and celebrated, or abandoned and forgotten? Could it be used as a guide for recollection, a key to the past? It became my aim to record the minutiae of interacting with such history-heavy objects: the change in one's facial features, the lilting of a voice narrating its history.

* * *

'*Kuch nahi laaye the*. We brought nothing. We came with nothing,' was easily the first response I got from whoever I asked about their belongings from 1947. But then things would eventually crawl out of the backs of closets, suitcases and trunks, sheathed in dust and infused with dormant memories. In the autumn of 2013, I began my quest for objects and, predictably enough, it began at home. My great-grandmother had brought with her a piece of jewellery, a *maang-tikka*, given to her by her mother-in-law for her wedding; she would later pass it on to her daughter, my *dadi*, for hers. She had carried it across with the hope of selling it, coming into some money, and using that to pay for the education of her children. My *dadi* herself had brought, almost accidentally, a small foldable knife. My *dada*'s family, having fled their home in Malakwal and having to stay in a makeshift refugee camp in the local cotton factory, were not able to bring much. His mother's main concern had been food but, because they couldn't flee with perishable items, she made sure to carry their utensils, so that at least if rations were given in the camp they would have a means to cook them. So what accompanied their flight were *peetal* plates, spoons, tumblers and pots, all with my great-grandfather's initials on them, given to him as part of his wife's trousseau.

Soon, my research expanded beyond the peripheries of my own family to include complete strangers. As a young researcher, then twenty-three years old, I struggled with how to begin. How would I learn of refugees who had crossed the border? How would I search for these objects? I would like to say that I had a structured model in mind but, really, the project grew as sporadically and organically as the initial idea. It is not difficult to locate Partition refugees or their descendants, especially in Delhi, but as I found out within the first few months, finding objects was a laborious task. My family and word of mouth became my main means of forage, and gradually I began to visit people who shared with me their belongings and memories from across the border. My aunt, during her daily walks in Delhi's Defence Colony, would fearlessly approach older men and women from the neighbourhood, armed with questions about their potential memorabilia. My parents, who run Bahrisons Booksellers in the capital, would do the same when they learned of a customer's connection to the Partition in any way.

After half a year, I had collected what I felt were enough stories of objects to pen a cohesive dissertation and curate a gallery show. But, very soon, I realized that the project was actually nowhere close to being done. I could not talk about the objects that had migrated to India without also discussing the objects that had migrated to what became Pakistan. And so, a few months later, I travelled to Lahore to continue my research. I located and recorded stories of the most unexpected objects, unearthed incredible memories of a syncretic India and cultivated in my heart an unshakeable love for Delhi's twin city across the border.

Part of this also had to do with Khizar-ji, who drove me
around Lahore. In fact, his first '*As-salaam-alaikum*, Aanchal-ji!'
of the morning became such a ritual that, in the weeks following
my departure from the Garden City, his cheerful voice
continued to linger in my head. At first, Khizar-ji could not
understand what a young girl from India was doing there all
alone, why we were driving across the city from morning to
night meeting grandmothers and grandfathers. But, after a long
conversation over lunch one day, when I explained to him
exactly what I was trying to do, we became quite the team.
When I visited someone's home to conduct an interview,
Khizar-ji, in all his inquisitive Punjabi glory, would speak to the
household help, extracting anecdotes that I would never have
had the chance to hear otherwise. We would later compare
notes in the car and, between his information and mine, try to
weave together a colourful tapestry of migration. If he was in a
generous mood, Khizar-ji would divulge bits of old Punjabi
layman's wisdom and I would dutifully listen, both amazed and
appreciative. 'All five fingers of the hand are not equal,' he told
me as I sulked after a particularly unfruitful interview one
evening in Lahore. Some fingers are long and some short. Some
interviews are good and some are not. '*Koi masla nahi hai*, it's no
problem. Tomorrow's will be better!' he assured me, smiling
through his bushy moustache.

* * *

Human memory is fragile. It is the form in which we store our
experiences.[26] However, it is important to understand that our
memory is not a recording device.[27] It cannot be assumed that
whatever we experience will be stored as an exact and precise
trace of that moment, especially when time gradually begins to
wear it down. If you imagine an experience as the construction
of a memory, then its recollection years later is its reconstruction.
As the years pass, memory, inherently malleable, accumulates

holes that can be filled with new experiences—imagined, fabricated or, sometimes, seamlessly integrated together where connections didn't previously exist.

During our conversation in his London home, John Grigor Taylor (Chapter 7) experienced a fascinating tangling of memories. Over the years, he has begun, subconsciously, to bind seamlessly together details from his years of service in the British Indian Army and his father's, both of whom coincidentally served in the Rajputana Rifles regiment. Throughout our conversation, he often used his father's experience in World War I and his in World War II interchangeably. Between my grandmother Bhag Malhotra and her younger sister Dharam Bali (Chapter 5), there is an ongoing animated discussion about how things really unfolded during the days of their migration from NWFP to Delhi. Did they take the train from Dera Ismail Khan, or did they take a boat over the river Sindh? Did they stop to pick up their sister from Lahore, or did she come later? Did they actually see the corpses lined up at the railway station, or merely hear of them?

These are examples of how emerging narratives of a time long gone sometimes become fabricated, amalgamated and almost fictitious. And though this leads us to question the notion of 'true' memory, it's still the case that recorded oral recollections and histories, especially of a traumatic time, often become the primary means for us to understand and collate collective memory.

My interviewees weren't always convinced of this at first. My requests to see someone's belongings from the time of the Partition were usually met initially with confused looks and raised eyebrows. The inherent misfortune of everyday objects belonging to ordinary people, unlike those preserved in museums and private collections, is that they are often underappreciated. But what I noticed during my interviews was that, from the moment I infused importance into an otherwise mundane personal possession, the emotions and memories hidden within it came to the surface and, all of a sudden, the thing became precious. If in the course of our conversation I happened to wrap a shawl around my own shoulders rather than its owner's, or put a ring on my finger instead of theirs, I would witness in them a surge of sudden, fervent possessiveness. As I asked about objects, their significance to their owner emerged.

'This belongs to my mother,' they would suddenly claim, rather than it simply being an old shawl from before the Partition. 'This is the lock and key we used to lock our house,' they would beam, placing the rust-encrusted object on the table before us. And thus it would gradually dawn on the possessor that the singular object surviving from his or her home, village or childhood could be a vessel for memory. Mine, my mother's, my father's, our family's—the transition, in most cases, from indifference to proprietorship was unexpected, yet understandable. It was as though the object had found a new life.

With this revival—the recovery of memories of the Partition preserved within these belongings—the Divide itself also came back to life. When people described to me vivid scenes of massacres and rivers of red from before my birth, I was able to taste in my mouth the metallic tinge of blood. By collecting the memories of those who witnessed the Partition, I have collected also their prejudices, biases, fears, hesitations, nightmares, dreams, longings and, of course, their belongings. I have transformed from a person who makes things—an artist—to a person who collects things.

I have collected stories about everything from plain kitchen bowls to parrots and crocodile skins. I have encountered objects carried over the border during Partition that now bind together several generations of a family living in different parts of the world, or childhood friends separated by the Divide. I have also discovered objects carried across the border years after the Partition, by people who made the journey back to their homelands to retrieve items of great value or emotional significance. I have even learnt of objects that were brought across in a spirit of goodwill and continued fellowship between pre- and post-Partition inhabitants of a house (Chapter 8). Other possessions have been rediscovered, decades later, through sheer serendipity, even on the other side of the world.[28]

Particularly remarkable to me are those objects whose stories and memories have been unearthed and preserved not by their original owners, but by their offspring—second- and third-generation inheritors of Partition's lingering trauma; children and grandchildren sat in on and participated in many of the interviews described in these chapters, both asking and answering questions. The photo on the cover of this book is of the vibrantly dyed *naale*, silk threads handwoven into a thick drawstring with which a pyjama or salwar is held in place, which Jasminder Gulati's mother Gurdeep Kaur carried to New Delhi from Multan in West Punjab. When I interviewed her about the *naale*, Jasminder's mother began humming an old Punjabi folk song about such ladies' accessories.

At the outset, I had not accounted for such an expansive topography of storytelling. In fact, and quite naively so, I believed that a story of the object would remain just that. However, dozens of interviews later, what has emerged is a way of life in an inclusive and interwoven Undivided India. The longer I sat with those who had lived through the exodus, the more convinced I became that a story from the days of the Partition was about so much more than the Partition itself. It was a story about soil and rain, fields and clouds, families and their traditions and customs; it was about love and relationships, children and the sound of their crying; it was about landscape and language, music, art, literature and poetry.

* * *

How did an item cross the border, what were the experiences of its bearer and, moreover, what is the relevance of the object today? *Remnants of Partition* attempts to answer these questions: to try to understand memories of this great migration in a visceral way. Personal possessions are an invaluable means of unearthing social and material culture and, through the chapters that follow, I attempt to unravel the often quieter, more hidden aspects of an Undivided India.

This book is a collection of conversations with individuals who witnessed and experienced unforgettable moments in the subcontinent's history and who have themselves become manifestations of that history—living libraries, as it were. They divulge personal histories that can, given the nature of their content, also be perceived when put together as a kind of collective history. The experience of one can speak of the experiences of many. As a child, I remember that almost every story my parents or grandparents told me was born out of mundane conversation. Words of wisdom and advice, ideas and opinions, and teachings from their own childhood would embroider the landscape of our everyday interactions.

The language of these childhood stories was a mixture of Hindi, Urdu and English, with generous dollops of Punjabi. The same went for the stories that unfold in this book, and I have tried to preserve where possible the flavour of these languages and the way Indians and Pakistanis mix them together, without obstructing the reader's understanding. I have also kept the names of places as their residents used them, an amalgamation of ancient and modern: Dilli and Dehli for Delhi, for instance, or Jullundur as the British name for Jalandhar. It is in this informal style, where history, memory and life meet at the heart of oral storytelling, that this book has been written.

In my family, 'Partition' was a word unspoken for years, a feeling unexplored, a wound untouched. Partition. I listen to my lips release it into the world and ponder its lingering aftertaste: the very weight of the word, how I enunciate its every syllable with clarity and care in a way that has been subconsciously instilled in me. How I use it with an almost extreme fragility, considering at all times its innate heaviness in the context of the Indian subcontinent—what it means to be Indian, to be Pakistani and, later, to be Bangladeshi. The entire concept of a cultural identity has been enveloped within a single event, a single six-inch white line, a single word: Partition. This book is a modest attempt to unravel that word, if such a thing is even possible.

1

A *GAZ* FOR MY FATHER AND
A *GHARA* FOR MY MOTHER

THE HEIRLOOMS OF Y.P. VIJ

IT WAS AN EARLY Sunday morning and the by-lanes of Delhi University's sprawling North Campus were devoid of their usual commotion. Riding through a maze of intricate lanes and small stores, a cycle-rickshaw delivered me to my destination on a quiet suburban street in the neighbourhood of Roop Nagar: Vij Bhawan, an aged and frayed two-storey house with an old silver gate.

As far as I could remember, I had always thought this house to be old. Not just because of how it looked—simply existing, enduring time and weather, the off-white exterior yellowing with the passing of years—but also because of what it contained. Living within those ancient walls were generations of my mother's side of the family. For me, it had stood as an age-old symbol of the firm bonds of ancestry and lineage, and inside its archaic structure I'd always found comfort. But standing before Vij Bhawan that day, I realized I was experiencing it differently from how I had growing up. I had ceased to be someone who knew the house intimately, someone who had spent weekends and vacations there as a child, and had become an observer of the house, looking up at it with the objective eye of an archivist. This had to do with my friend, the blogger and columnist Mayank Austen Soofi, popularly known as the Delhi Walla.[1] A few weeks ago, he had told me that he wanted to do a short story on Delhi's old houses. He knew that my mother's family lived in one such house in the northern part of the city and asked me if I could take him there so he could speak to its residents. A simple enough request, so I agreed. On a pleasant October afternoon I took him to meet my grandfather,

Vishwa Nath Vij, and his eldest brother, my great-uncle, Yash Pal Vij, both of whom I called *nana*, maternal grandfather. They sat together for a long time in the first-floor living room, sipping sweet lemonade, talking about how Roop Nagar had been part of the rehabilitation plan for refugees arriving in Delhi from Pakistan at the time of Independence in 1947.[2] They talked about how the house had been designed by T.R. Mahendru, the architect behind famous Delhi buildings like Hans Raj College and Sir Gangaram Hospital, and built in 1955. They talked about how, though sections of the house had been renovated over the years, parts of its original structure still remained.

The room that we were seated in, with large windows and a floor of white marble, had been renovated only recently. I remember the original tiles being jade-green and maroon squares, with white marble chips embedded in them. The original doors were made of dark *sheesham*, Indian rosewood, with brass latches and rectangular wooden doorstops. On the wall there used to be mounted a glass cabinet, overstocked with family photographs and curios. All this had changed now.

The three men talked about the residents of the house—how, though my great-grandfather was no longer alive, his desire for the family to live together was still respected. How the seventeen rooms and five kitchens were inhabited by sixteen family members of three generations. They spoke extensively of the past, the Partition of British India, the modernization of Delhi and its many neighbourhoods, and the importance of a joint family structure.

After a while, my great-uncle slowly rose and left the room. My eyes followed his tall, wiry frame as he walked out and closed the door behind him. He returned minutes later with an array of objects and carefully placed them on the glass top of the rectangular coffee table in the middle of the room.

The conversation came to a halt as we examined them, I being more eager than anyone else to touch and experience each item: a cursory graze to begin with and then a more confident, prolonged caress, patient and intentionally lingering. I allowed my fingers to dip lazily into the curves, and my nails to get caught in the cracks of each surface. Taking a deep breath, I selected what was closest to me and inhaled its scent. It was an old lock of unusual shape, the kind one finds on the shelves of an antiquities museum. It smelt predictably musky, metallic, tangy. Satisfied, I put it back down next to its key, equally old and quaint with a small, thick stem and a larger hand-carved bow in the shape of a flower. The pair were encrusted entirely with age and rust. I wondered what door this had belonged to, what the key would have unlocked. Beside it sat a long foldable bookend made of dark wood and hand-carved with a filigree pattern of leaves and flowers, the ends standing up in the shapes of smoothly carved elephants. There were also some old photographs, dusty and yellowed with age, and a few dog-eared books. I took particular note of the dust gathered in the corners of books and in the creases of photographs, for these were the real treasures, evidence of age and markers of the passing of time.[3]

Placed on the glassy surface of the table, the lustreless objects looked particularly antique and interesting, carrying within them a suffocated sense of the past. I also noticed that two items had been kept away from the rest of the pile of objects brought into the room: a round-bottomed vessel and a long, thin metal stick. Both brothers looked at these somewhat differently from the rest.

'What are all these things?' I asked.

My great-uncle straightened his lean frame, focused his large beady eyes on me, and in his typically slow and lilting tone said, 'This is an old house full of old things. We are talking about the past, so it is only fitting that I show you some of the objects that have lived here for decades. But these...' he said, gesturing to the pair kept to one side, '... these are older than the rest and far more special. They belonged to our parents, who brought them from Lahore before the Partition.'

Then, as he began to stroke the surfaces of the two objects from his past, something changed in him. A slow and almost unnoticeable change, born purely of memory, dictated the way in which his hands carefully and gently moved across them. And when he spoke about them, his whole demeanour transformed. He became child-like, his face lit up and his voice excited, unlike his usual quiet self. It seemed as though he was physically there in front of us, but at the same time he was not. Within those objects he had found a pathway into the past and had wandered along it all the way back to Lahore, exploring and rediscovering.

'My mother used to churn *lassi* in this *ghara* for us when we were young,' he said of the metal vessel that sat in his hands. It was medium-sized, round at the bottom with a graceful neck, and made up of a combination of alloys. It was rusting in places, and metallic hues of dark and light merged on its surface. Engraved on it was a pattern of foliage and line work typical of the Indian subcontinent. It was not particularly heavy but it weighed down his hands. As he drummed his fingers over its smooth exterior, it created a hollow metallic sound.

My great-uncle described how his mother would pour yoghurt and water into the vessel and churn them with a long wooden churner called a *phirni*. She would hold it in her hands and move it forward and back, gracefully, with skill, creating clockwise and anti-clockwise ripples in the liquid. Out of the corner of my eye, I saw my grandfather smiling at the words.

'It is from Lahore,' his brother said. 'She brought it with her when she got married. In those days, bringing utensils to your husband's home at the time of the wedding was common for new brides, part of their trousseau, even. This *ghara* is made of German silver, if I remember correctly. She used it throughout her life, and now we use it just like her—to make *lassi*.' He smiled and laid it back down.

I had tasted Vij Bhawan's *lassi* many times but hadn't had the slightest inkling of the history of the container in which it was made. The sheer thought made me smile—an object of such banality laid claim to a historic past, travelling through generations and still in use today.

'And what about this?' the curious Delhi Walla asked, holding up the metallic stick.

'This is a yardstick, a *gaz*,' my great-uncle answered. 'Nowadays we use the metre to measure fabric, but earlier it would be measured by the *gaz*, the yard. This also came from there. My grandfather used to own a clothing store in Lahore. When my father worked there, this is the yardstick he used.'

He stretched out his long arms, holding the stick in between. It was completely ordinary at first glance—not even straight, slightly bent in places—but on closer inspection I saw there were markings at set distances that indicated specific measurements: ½ *gaz*, ¼ *gaz* and so on. The stick was smooth and cold to the touch, made of a dark metal, maybe iron or lead. Its dense chestnut colour stood out against his wrinkled sandy-brown arms. He held it up with ease. It was light, as you might expect, since it would have had to be manoeuvred through layers and layers of fabric fairly quickly.

'Did they bring these with them at the time of the Partition?' I asked.

'We were already in Delhi at the time,' my great-uncle replied. 'But yes, when our parents moved from Lahore to Amritsar, they did bring the *ghara* and *gaz* with them. During the Partition, we lived in the old city, and I remember just how thankful we felt not to have to cross over the border during those days. My parents often spoke about what would have happened if they had continued to live in Lahore.'

The afternoon light streamed in. Seated on a low sofa, he stretched out his arms, placing both hands on his knees, and continued. 'We were safe, but from what we saw on the streets and in train stations, people came with nothing, pouring into Delhi every day. For weeks they continued to arrive from various places across the new border. The sheer mass of people was unbelievable, and it seemed as though overnight the population of Delhi had nearly doubled![4]

'If you were a refugee crossing the border, there were many, many difficulties at every step of the way. So who knows what people brought with them when they came here, *beta*. I suppose they took what they could, but most of the time even those objects didn't survive the journey. They staggered in, with their clothes barely covering their bodies, their families barely alive, looking for any means to survive.' He shook his head slowly from side to side.

We hung onto his every word, and I thought immediately back to the photographs I had seen and the books I had read about the Partition. Flashing before my eyes were black-and-white images of refugees crossing the border into cities, setting up tents and makeshift kitchens to cook meagre meals. Until then they had just been images—of an event far removed from me, in both time and perspective. But as my great-uncle spoke about the Great Divide as something my living family had seen, witnessed, survived, it made my skin crawl. This monumental exodus that I had viewed purely academically became a living, breathing entity that had affected the people I knew.

'These things,' he said, gesturing to the vessel and the yardstick, bringing me back to the first floor of Vij Bhawan, 'these things belonged to my parents and they are from pre-Partition.'

* * *

That was the very first time I realized the power of an object to retain memory, years before I saw my grandmother's coin collection. On touching the items that belonged to his parents, my great-uncle had drifted back into his past and arrived at a time where he could see those objects being used by them in everyday life. What I had just witnessed was the physicality—texture, scent—of an object serving as a catalyst to preserve and invoke the memory of a person, a time, an event that was regarded as the most catastrophic in the contemporary history of the Indian subcontinent.

Partition, he had said to me, had divided India. He had then gone on to apply it as a unit of division within himself. He had divided his own life into pre- and post-Partition. The objects belonged to pre-Partition times, an Undivided India; his memories lived in post-Partition, in a subcontinent divided.

Until then, I had not thought much about the Partition. Having grown up in India, I couldn't divorce myself from it, but I also don't remember ever laying any special emphasis on it despite its traces being present in my own family history. It sat effortlessly at the very back of my mind, like one of those things one is supposed to remember but that never quite surfaces. But with the visit to my grandfather's home, and having seen for myself how such memory can be drawn to the surface through personal belongings, I found myself completely drawn to the Partition.

That afternoon, after we had spoken about the past, about the house and its residents, the Delhi Walla and I left Roop Nagar. He filed his story on the old houses of the city and October passed fairly quietly. But the objects and the memories attached to them wouldn't leave my mind. For weeks I thought of nothing else. I knew that each of my grandparents was originally from what became Pakistan, but I had always glossed over this fact with detachment. I had never probed any of them for details, never even wondered how they, or we, got to where we were today. And they in turn had never spoken about it either. As a result, what dwelled in my mind now were only questions.

I thought back to my *nana*'s descriptions of the capital in the early days of Independence and couldn't help but wonder about all those people who had been displaced on either side of the newly created border. How would they have vacated their homes, left their towns, villages and cities? How would they have figured out where to go? What modes of transport would they have used, if any? Did they travel with the hope and expectation of a better future, or did they travel by force and in fear of death? All these questions ran through my mind, coupled with an innate curiosity for the stories of my own family members. I didn't know what I was feeling exactly, but in those first few weeks after I visited Vij Bhawan, it consumed me completely.

* * *

Weeks later, I found myself on the doorstep of the house once again, this time alone. I sat with my great-uncle and his wife in the oldest part of the house—it reminded me of the original roots of the Vij family, for in this wing the past was clearly discernible. Despite all the modern construction around it, it had remained untouched: the simple wooden door with its vintage metal latch, the archaic electric switchboard, the peeling walls moist from the recent monsoon, the stone floors with old-fashioned tiles, and the round bathroom mirror encased in a square wooden frame. But the most endearing part of this section was the large open *aangan*, a courtyard with stone flooring at the back of the house where we sat that afternoon. Returning to the house after many weeks made me acutely aware of one thing: that though everything was exactly how it had always been, it seemed suddenly new to me. Every dust-covered alcove seemed more intriguing than ever. Even the *aangan* seemed to hold within it the weight of an old, undiscovered secret.

As we sat under Delhi's crisp winter sun, the couple spoke to me about a time that once was. He spoke first, his wife listening intently. He laid emphasis on certain things, speaking mostly in English but pronouncing words the Punjabi way—*roits* instead of riots, *maiyer* instead of measure. At first I smiled, but very soon I realized that these were the details that needed to be archived; these were the gems, the gifts, the lingering nuances. And so, I extracted them from his speech and noted them down them as extraordinary quirks and oddities of a dying generation, for these were what built his essence, his character.

'I was born in 1930 in Lahore, which is now in Pakistan,' he said. 'Though my parents had already moved to Amritsar by then, they had both grown up in Lahore, and when I was born, my grandparents were still living there. So, my mother went back to her parents' house for the delivery, as was the custom, and I was born in Lahore. My father's family left Lahore for Amritsar when he was a teenager. When he was twenty years old, he moved to Nairobi for a few years. I think there was a very large Indian population there at the time, so he moved there in search of employment. But during his stay there he noticed the community was full of drunkards and smokers. Since he neither drank nor smoked, the people made him feel uncomfortable and he moved back to India. On his return he began a jewellery business with three partners.'

Pad-ner, he said.

'How come he didn't join his father's clothing business? That's what your family used to do in Lahore, right?' I gestured to the yardstick in the corner.

'I don't know. He just chose to work with his friends. Together they began a store called Bratha-ji di Hatti Jewellers in 1942. The first store opened in Amritsar, then here in Chandni Chowk, and one in Bombay—three in total. A year later, we moved to Delhi and so my father ran the one in Chandni Chowk, where the neighbouring shop owners spared no chance to tell us that our store wouldn't survive. They didn't like the competition; they were all anti-Punjabi, you see. I remember them saying to us, "*Tumhe toh phook maar ke bhaga denge.*"'

He laughed jovially and held out his palm in front of his mouth and blew at it, demonstrating what the shopkeepers had said—that they would blow their business away in no time.

'What do you mean they didn't like Punjabis? What were the other shopkeepers around you?' I asked.

'They were Hindu, from Delhi. They spoke Hindustani.[5] We were from Amritsar in Punjab. We spoke Punjabi. They were averse to anyone who was not from here, anyone who posed a threat to their business. This behaviour prevailed for *years* before the Partition too. At that time, there were not so many Punjabis in Delhi. It was like when you make *roti*, you add a pinch of salt to the dough. When my father began the store, the Punjabis living and working in Delhi were like that pinch of salt in dough.'

'But that all changed when the Partition happened…' I began.

'Oh, yes! The entire demography of the city changed considerably after the Partition.[6] Millions of Punjabi refugees came into the city, and the shop owners disliked them the most. Punjabis are enterprising people, you see. They flooded into the country with nothing: no job, no future, no money. But everyone has got to eat and feed their families in some way. So they did whatever they could to survive. They took the monopoly of trade away from the original shopkeepers, they were competition and, most of the times, they even sold their goods at a lower price—at cost price—never making a profit but earning just enough to keep their families alive. They would sell items on the streets, in trains, on bicycles, however they could. They were relentlessly hardworking, a quality that Punjabis have managed to retain even today.'

His wife, a petite woman with grey hair tied in a neat bun, spoke. 'My uncle's family came to Delhi from Pakistan during the days of the Partition,' she said. 'Because of the commotion, they ended up boarding a train to Delhi instead of Amritsar, where they had chosen to live. And so they had to stay here in very cheap accommodation for a week before they could find a way to get to Amritsar. One day, my uncle, a young boy at the time, went out to get food for everyone. When he got to the stall, extending his money, he placed his order. The shopkeeper told him lunch was over, that there was no more food. "What do you mean there is no more food?" he said. "I am paying for it." The shopkeeper gave him a nasty look and said, "Go away! You don't belong here. You've run away from your country and now…"

'He didn't even have a chance to finish his sentence since my uncle grabbed his collar and pulled him into the street. "We don't belong here?" he asked in a fit of rage. "What do you mean run away? We eat anything we can get because we need to survive. We even eat your rotten grains and spoilt food because we need to live—we have nothing. Nothing. And rather than helping us, you are telling us to go back where we came from? Go back to the riots, the violence?

'"You don't give us food; in fact, you increase the prices to make a profit when we buy anything. Do we complain? No, because we are dependent on you for survival right now. We are just like any other customer … we make money where and how we can, and buy your goods just like any other customer and still you curse us?" In that moment, my uncle was livid. He let go of the man's collar and left him in the middle of the street.'

She sighed.

'It really was like that,' my great-uncle added. 'Refugee or no refugee, Delhi wasn't always kind to those who weren't from here.'

* * *

'But your father's business—it survived?' I asked.

'Oh yes! Regardless of what the other shopkeepers said, our business grew! We fast became north India's leading jewellers. We had a very clever strategy that made us number one,' my great-uncle chuckled to himself. 'The partners got two Muslim painters to advertise the store on every possible wall surface they could find, beginning in Delhi and slowly making their way south up to Bombay and west to Peshawar. Remember, this was before the Partition and the country was still one, so it was relatively easy to travel around. We paid these painters two rupees per day, plus for all their meals.'

'How much was two rupees in 1943?' I asked, wondering what one could buy with that sum now.

'Oho! In those days, two rupees were plenty! Probably the equivalent of about 200 rupees now! You would get a *tolah* of gold, which is about 11.6 grams, for 20 rupees. Today, that would probably be worth over 40,000 rupees! Anyway, we would pay these men to paint on any surface they saw—houses, offices, sometimes even cremation grounds. "Bratha-ji di Hatti Jewellers—Amritsar. Delhi. Bombay." This worked. It made us very popular all over India. I would also sit in the shop in Chandni Chowk every day after school.

'We used to have the most beautiful designs as we would get them made from various cities—some from Jaipur, some from Madras, some from Bombay. They would always be new and different from the designs of the local jewellers in Delhi. Any time someone tried to copy our designs, we would just stop selling them altogether and get new ones. But one thing was for sure, the price would always be fixed! Just like the Bata shoe company—fixed prices always, all over India, with no exceptions!'

'So where did you live when you moved to Delhi from Amritsar?' I asked.

'Mori Gate, on Nicholson Road. Close to Kashmere Gate. We lived there until this house was built in 1955.'

'What kind of neighbourhood was it then? Was it affected during the Partition?' I asked. Mori Gate stands erect even today, an ever-prominent part of the old city.

'It was a predominantly Muslim neighbourhood, with the exception of a few families. Actually, before the Partition, nearly half the population of the old city was Muslim! During the riots, everyone—Hindus, Muslims, Sikhs—everyone was scared. Even at the onset of August, the *maahaul*, the atmosphere, was not okay. We heard stories about trains coming in and going out of Old Delhi railway station laden with dead bodies and injured passengers. We were instructed to stay inside our houses.

'I remember, there were announcements made on the radio one or two days *after* Independence, informing people of the exact location of the new border—what remained in India and what became Pakistan. Violence broke out all over Old Delhi and continued well into the weeks after the Partition, up till September.[7] Our Muslim neighbours asked us to help them and of course we agreed because they were all innocent people, just like us. We assured them that we would protect them, but eventually they moved across the border anyway. Maybe they thought it would lead to a more secure future. I am told that many waited for days in special refugee camps set up for Muslims in Purana Qila and Jama Masjid as they were deemed safer than other parts of the city. From there they were eventually put on trains to Pakistan.[8] After that, every day we saw new inhabitants occupy the abandoned homes of our various neighbours.

'I remember there was a middle-aged Sikh man who had come to visit his daughter in Mori Gate and, amidst the riots, he decided to go back to his home in Punjab. Everyone told him not to go, that it was too dangerous, that there would be no trains, but he was adamant. He packed his bags, walked out about 200 *gaz* from the lane and asked a rickshaw driver to take him to the railway station. The driver, who happened to be Muslim, stuck a knife into his passenger's chest. Though middle-aged, the Sikh man was significantly stronger and managed to throw the young driver off the rickshaw and ride it back into the lane till he reached his daughter's house. Just as he made it to the door, we saw him fall off the rickshaw into a lifeless pile, blood oozing out of his open gash onto the ground.'

A pause.

'In the months leading up to Partition, whenever my father made a visit to Amritsar, he would come back weighed down by stories of horrific communal violence. Hindus, Muslims and Sikhs engaged in a bloody communal war. Slogans of "*Le kar rahenge Pakistan!* We will take Pakistan!" would resound in the air as a demand for the new country. But for most people, even the thought of such a division was absurdity. In fact, even after the Divide happened, the people expected to stay where they were— continue to live in India or Pakistan, whichever side of the border they were on, regardless of their religion. No one anticipated the extent of what happened in 1947; no one was prepared for such an exodus or the violence that followed. No one ever imagined the magnitude of the communal hatred and conflict that eventually seized both nations.'

I nodded, and then in my naivety asked, 'Nana, what do you think the world would have been like if there hadn't been a Partition?'

In the last few weeks I had thought of this question many times over, worded it in many different ways, never quite able to come up with a definitive answer. I kept thinking about 'the other side' beyond the border. What would life have been like if it didn't exist, if the land had remained unified? I suppose there was no concrete answer to these questions; it was all relative and speculative. But I was curious to know what he would say, whether he'd ever even thought about it or not.

'I don't know, *beta*—who knows?' he replied. 'All I can say is that what happened, happened. But the truth is that many such inconceivable things happen in our lives, and after a while even their memory fades and eventually becomes dormant, we just forget. Then years later we recollect them in conversations like this one, with a sense of disconnect, as though these were not the lives we had lived but incredible snippets of fiction that had sprung out of mere imagination.'

Leaning against the wooden chair, he continued, 'How do these moments of magnanimity become reduced to sheer anecdotes with the passing of time? *Yeh samajh nahi ata*, this I fail to understand. I think about the Partition now, and as I'm talking to you about it I'm amazed at the smoothness and ease with which I am describing the madness I witnessed in my youth. As though I'm recounting a dream so immeasurably far away, so far removed from reality, so impossible to have actually occurred...' His voice trailed off, his head still slowly swaying from side to side. 'And though our family was not displaced per se, the consequences of the Partition live in our memories till today. That is what makes me feel bad. But, like I said, what is done is done. No matter what, there is nothing we can do now that will take us back to the time of Undivided India. And Delhi ... Delhi has truly evolved; it has changed so much since we moved here in 1943. Life is moving at a rapid pace; technology has changed the world completely. Taking all this in stride, Delhi is progressing, moving forward.'

'Do you think we are moving forward too fast? That in that rapidity we are forgetting our culture, our history?'

'*We* are not forgetting! The children are!' he laughed.

I studied his kind face as he smiled widely.

'The truth is, one cannot prevent change. The world has always been changing and it will continue to do so. What I say is that it can change as much as it wants to, Delhi can progress and evolve and transform, and it will. But some things will always remain the same. Our family. We lived together then—in Lahore, in Amritsar, through the Partition in Delhi—and we live together even today. I consider myself lucky that that has not changed till now.'

He sat back in his chair, crossed his right leg over his left and sighed in satisfaction. His face still bore a smile, his hands curled atop one another in his lap. His wife beamed as she sat across from him, nodding in agreement.

I looked around the verandah. Surrounding me were antique walls and tradition. Every time I thought of this house, I was invariably struck by the sheer expanse of history that lived there. From the oldest member of the family to the youngest, I tried to imagine the accumulation of collective memory. From a pre-Partition Lahore to a twenty-first-century Delhi, how much memory had coursed through the veins of that grand building and how much was still to unfold?

* * *

My great-uncle, now the patriarch of the Vij family, was indeed a lucky man, sitting before me with his wife, in the resplendent glory of Delhi's winter sun and memories of a lifetime. His family still lived together under one grand roof. The notion was so simple and sincere that its existence seemed almost impossible in today's day and age. The changes in the world usually and inevitably affected familial relations too.

But here, the holiness of those relations still existed, and this brought the family patriarch peace and solace. His mother's *ghara* and his father's *gaz* weren't the only things that had survived over the years. It was also the seemingly antiquated principle of a joint family structure, of which Vij Bhawan had become an embodiment, and which it had somehow managed to keep alive all these years.

Four brothers—the eldest a chartered accountant, the second a general manager in Dabur who had worked in Canada for over twenty years, the third also a chartered accountant, and the youngest a radio broadcaster in Toronto who had passed away in 1991—none of whom had taken over the family business of Bratha-ji di Hatti Jewellers since their father had wanted them to educate themselves—had chosen to live together as one with their wives, children and grandchildren in a large house in Roop Nagar.

As the sun began to set and we retreated into the dark rooms, the *gaz* and *ghara* in hand, I thought of my *nana*'s words: 'We lived together then—in Lahore, in Amritsar, through the Partition in Delhi—and we live together even today.' This was the legacy of Vij Bhawan, I decided; this was what had withstood the time and dark events. This was what had remained, despite the separation.

2

BETWEEN THIS SIDE AND THAT

THE SWORD OF AJIT KAUR KAPOOR

SHE HELD IN HER hands a small sepia-toned photograph of herself and her husband, gently, like a souvenir. Careful to touch only the edges, she placed it on the table. 'Listening to the stories, speaking about that time and actually witnessing the atrocities of Partition are very different things,' she said, eyes downcast. 'You can write this story, but we have seen everything with our own eyes. When I try to remember that time, my life feels as though it's slipping away, I want to die. Remembering that long, long walk to India makes me feel ... almost lifeless now.'

Finally, Ajit Kaur Kapoor looked straight into my eyes, and it was not anger that I saw in hers, but, rather, a quiet and aged fear.

'Why should I remember it?'

I set my notebook down and looked around the room, where her daughter-in-law, Sukhmeet, and grandson, Gurshane, were sitting across from us. 'For them, you should remember for your family, and...' I gestured to myself, having travelled from Delhi to Chandigarh just to hear her story, '... and for my generation, and those who come after, those who will have no way of listening to a first-hand account. It is important for them to know what happened.'

Nervously, her eyes met those of her *samdhan*'s, her son's mother-in-law, who sat on the other side of the sofa, nodding knowingly. And so the story unfolded.

* * *

'The city we are from was called Mirpur,' she said, raising her forefinger in the air and placing it as if at the top of an imaginary map. 'It was in the very north of Hindustan, on the western edge of Jammu and Kashmir state, and our Maharaja was named Hari Singh. My father, Sardar Singh Soni, was the secretary of the local gurudwara. Secretary *sahib*, he was called. The population was not large, but it was diverse—Musalmaan, Sikh, Hindu[1]— people were happy and healthy. Each had different neighbourhoods. For instance, the Sikhs lived in a [lane] called Purana Qila and the Mahajans, a well-known trader community, lived in a place called Mahajan ka Mohalla, or Buna Mohalla. I remember having friends from all communities. The legend we heard growing up was that the city of Mirpur was founded nearly 600 years ago by two saints—Hazrat Ali Mira Shah Ghazi and Gosain Budh Puri. "Mir" was taken from the former's name and "Pur" from the latter's, together making "Mirpur", a symbol of interfaith unity.[2] The language we spoke there was a sweet form of Punjabi called Pothwari.'

'Who lived with you?' I asked.

'Our father, mother, four brothers and a sister.' She then giggled and said, 'Our 100-year-old grandfather lived with us too, I think his name might have been Jassa Singh—a sweet-looking man with Pahari features, whose eyesight was so good that he never had to wear spectacles.'

I smiled. 'Do you still remember what Mirpur looked like?'

'It is difficult to forget … even if one wants to. Mirpur was surrounded by mountains; it was beautiful but simple. We had no electricity, even radios were battery-powered. For light, we used only kerosene lanterns. And until the day we left, all our drinking water still came from deep-water wells. In the evenings, we would play games like marbles and skipping rope. Mirpur had masjids and holy shrines, temples and gurudwaras. At the eastern end was Hazrat Ghazi's tomb, and at the western end Gosain Puri's temple.[3] The city had a rich syncretic culture. None of that remains now; the city has gone, and so have its people. The entire old city is submerged.' Her hands made a sinking gesture.

'What do you mean, submerged?' I asked.

'Old Mirpur is under the water of the Mangla dam constructed over it many years after Partition,' she smiled sadly. 'When the water level decreases in the winter months, the city shows itself. You can see houses, roads and even graveyards.[4] But we will never get to see it again, the city is caught between this side and that.'

'Would you *want* to see it again, don't you miss it?'

'In the years immediately after '47, I used to want to, but not any more. It's become a tale of old times. There is nothing for us there, and I dread to even think back to that time, dread even talking about it now.'

I uncapped my pen and put it to paper.

* * *

'I was married at the age of sixteen, while still in grade 9 in the local government school. For grade 10, I enrolled into a high school affiliated with Punjab University, whose central office at the time was in Lahore. But because my husband worked in the bus service at Chaklala airfield in Rawalpindi, we lived there and would return to Mirpur only for exams. It was a full day's journey, where one would travel by boat, train and bus.

'See, I remember clearly that in 1947, my husband dropped me to Mirpur in June, both for exams as well as because I was pregnant with our first child. We had heard that Punjab was no longer safe, mass murder was happening. In fact, the population of Mirpur swelled considerably because refugees from the Punjab began migrating there. They were confident that nothing would happen to them there because it was part of an independent princely state.'[5]

'What happened in Mirpur when Partition was announced?' I asked, wondering what went on when the division of the country was declared in August 1947; Maharaja Hari Singh of Jammu and Kashmir signed the Instrument of Accession to India only in October of that year.[6]

'Mirpur was quiet. At the time of Independence, the princely states were given a choice to join either India or Pakistan, but the Maharaja chose neither immediately.[7] On 14 August, the Pakistani green flag went up on Muslim shops, homes and mosques. The next day, Sikhs and Hindus waved the Indian tricolour. But though things were civil between the communities, tension had begun to build between those who were pro-India and those who were pro-Pakistan.

'We heard of terrible communal violence in other parts of Jammu and Kashmir.[8] In Jammu district, many villages were destroyed and their populations, which once had a Muslim majority, brutally massacred.[9] But still Mirpur was quiet, apart from some isolated incidents of violence. Everyone is not alike, are they? Sometimes someone would throw stones at a person, or abuse them. But every Muslim, every Hindu and every Sikh is not the same, so we didn't pay much attention to these incidents. But, all the while, more and more Hindu and Sikh refugees poured into the city and used it as a stopover on the way to East Punjab [assigned to India].[10] They would come on foot, in buses, on carts, and sometimes even escorted by armed personnel. Eventually, a curfew was put in place, only the afternoons remaining free to roam outside.

'We had no idea at the time about the events that were unfolding outside of our periphery, outside of Mirpur. It was only later we learnt that the Pakistani army and militants had attacked several cities that bordered Pakistan. And we were right next to it all. So, eventually, some troops of the Jammu and Kashmir army took up posts in our area.'

'Had you made arrangements to migrate elsewhere by then?'

'We didn't think we would have to leave,' she said flatly. 'Even after the army came in, even after they began handing out rifles to all the able-bodied men in every household, even after the men began keeping watch, we didn't think we would actually have to leave.'

I looked at her, but she didn't meet my eye; she just continued to stare ahead. The tale she narrated that afternoon was unlike any I had heard before, its fabric spun with a level of violence and terror that I was absolutely unprepared for. It was harrowing to the extent that, at times, it seemed almost unreal, impossible for one family to have endured so much tragedy and to continue living with the burden of those memories. As I listened, I expected Ajit Kaur's tone to gradually change, to become infused with anger, horror or even despair, but it hardly wavered. The soft, supple Mirpuri Punjabi merely relayed what had happened, minute by minute, in a detached voice. 'I still remember it clearly. It was November and we had been sitting in our garden all afternoon. Gurupurab was just a few days away,' she said, placing her hands over her knees, creating soft folds in her baby-pink salwar kameez. 'It was a day like any other, and then suddenly, out of nowhere, gunfire rained from the sky—airplanes flying over Mirpur, shooting bullets everywhere.'

'Bullets?' I asked, confused.

'*Ji haan*, bullets. They began firing and the whole village was suddenly caught in a frenzy.'

'*Who* began shooting?' I persisted.

'It could have been Pakistan's military, Pathans, rioters, mercenaries![11] It could have been anyone. But they were shooting at everything, anything and anyone they could see. We never even had a chance to go back inside our house to take anything. Everything was left as it was. People left whatever they were doing, wherever they were and began taking cover from the downpour of bullets. Houses were set on fire, causing chaos all over. Screams and cries engulfed the city—they echo in my ears even today and I cannot forget them.

'My husband had been keeping watch at his post with the other men and I had no idea how to find him. This was an organized attack. Thousands of Hindus and Sikhs were killed, and those who weren't made their way to the courts. I don't know who told us to go there, but it had a basement and people decided it would be safest to hide there until the firing stopped. Amidst the mayhem, I was separated from my family, and those who were not as quick to escape were either killed or captured and abducted.[12] So many women were taken, so many were abused and raped. Horrified by the infernos blazing around them, some people even took their own lives.[13] My own father was shot and died right outside our house. My father-in-law was killed, my sisters-in-law were all killed, so many Sikh men and women were killed, even their children massacred. My mother, sister and two brothers were taken prisoner.'

'What did you think was happening when the firing began?' I asked, still shocked.

'There was no time to think about anything! I had no idea what was happening, or who was doing it. Everyone was just being herded into the basement of the courts, and so I followed. I had nothing with me, no possessions, no money, no clothes. I was wearing a light cotton suit with no shawl—we had been sitting outside in the sun, after all. But everyone was in the same situation.

'This was just the beginning, for when I reached the basement we realized that apart from the few soldiers who had accompanied us for our safety, the rest of the army that had been manning the city had fled. But the bullets were still being fired, and so we waited. No one dared leave the basement, and no one went back to their homes. The rest of my family had already been separated, but thankfully my husband found me in the basement. Janak Singh, that was his name. When he found me, he was carrying only two things—the gun that the army had given him, and this sword.' She motioned to the long piece of rusted metal placed before us.

It sat idly on the table, seeming rather out of context. The curtains of the living room had been drawn, and the yellow light from the ceiling created dark shadows on the sword's surface.

'This sword is from Mirpur?' I asked, picking it up. Though I tried to be gentle, it was heavier than I expected, and I awkwardly cradled it in my arms, quite unlike the weapon it was meant to be. Longer than a regular sword, it was slim and frail. It was likely forged out of a combination of different metals, but due to oxidation and weathering, it was difficult to figure out its make. In parts, the metal had been so laden with moisture that its layers had either flaked off or sat in pockets of air bubbles. Rust and black patches covered its surface, and the bottom of the sword had broken off. A single line, the fuller, ran across the length of the blade, darker and denser in colour. But the real beauty was the grip—it had been hand-carved in dark wood and bore a crosshatch pattern. Its metallic cross-guard had been welded in a way that it rounded on one side and dipped into a graceful curve on the other. Given its condition, I was amazed that it had survived the years.

'*Nahi*, it's from Rawalpindi,' she said. 'My husband received it when he was working at the airfield there and brought it to Mirpur when he came, about ten or twelve days before we finally left. Look closely, you will see markings on it.'

Her grandson Gurshane brought out a magnifying glass and offered it to me. 'Look right underneath the cross-guard,' he said, pointing out the place.

Barely two or three inches below, where the blade began, one could see an engraving, like a code or a serial number. 'R B B… S.' I peered closely and, unable to make out all the letters, moved on to the next line. 'R. PINDI… R. Pindi? Rawalpindi?' My eyes grew wide.

Gurshane nodded. 'Rawalpindi.'

Under that was a small white gash, where the sword was slightly bent. The family told me that the point had broken during a particularly bad monsoon when they lived in Lucknow. Water had seeped into the scabbard, and when the sword was retrieved from it, the tip had been so badly affected by rainwater that it broke off, leaving a jagged edge at the end.

As I was studying its surface, Ajit Kaur placed a hand on it and said, 'This and the gun were the two things we had on us that day. I don't remember how long we stayed in the basement, whether it was hours or days, but I remember still being able to hear the firing outside. I was scared, I didn't know if we would get out of there alive or not. More people had gathered underground with us, some had run to the army cantonment, and some had hidden in a gurudwara. But so many others had been killed. Houses had been set ablaze, stores and shops burned to the ground. The city was destroyed. Mirpur had fallen, it was gone.'[14]

And as she said those last words, her eyes returned again to meet those of her son's mother-in-law, Satwant Kaur.

* * *

'When the last of the soldiers left the basement, we followed them out, ran through the city and straight into the jungles. Not one person went back home, we all simply followed the uniformed men. We didn't have any possessions. I think my husband only had three rupees and nine annas in his pocket, but there was no time to go home, and who knew whether our home still stood or not, so we just continued running. Ahead there was nothing but jungle, so people just ran whichever way they could. There were thorny shrubs, bushes and trees all around us. No one knew where they were going, and because the firing continued every now and then, people just ran in whatever direction they thought was safe. Some of the army men were on their *khachar*, the mules they used in the mountains, and suddenly, scared by the gunfire, one of the mules trotting close to me jumped, threw off his soldier and hurled me across to the other side...'

She extended her right arm forward, showing us how far she had been flung.

'And then it just ran off. But I was pregnant, and the violent movement made me unwell. In the fall, my dupatta, my slippers, everything had been thrown in different places. As we continued walking behind the caravan of people, the firing continued from the sky as well. So, from time to time, we lay on the ground and moved as and when we could. My husband had been trained at the Chaklala airfield, so he knew a little bit about such drills. We would lie flat and move with our elbows and knees. My movements were, of course, constrained, but he made me continue. We were not thinking straight about anything except getting to safety. We just kept walking, following, the whole day and night.'

'But where did you think you were going?'

'India. But no one really knew the way…' She shrugged and then turned to Satwant Kaur, saying, 'Did you know where we were going, do you remember?'

Satwant Kaur shook her head. 'Our house was right in front of theirs,' she explained to me. So we knew one another even before our children got married. In 1947, I was barely four or five years old, so whatever I remember is what my elders have told me. I was the youngest sister, and my brother, who was younger than me, was barely eight or nine months old at the time. When the rioters entered our city, just like she said,' she pointed to Ajit Kaur, 'they began shooting everyone and everything. We ran in different directions trying to avoid the firing. They killed my mother, and were about to kill my father as well. But he gestured to my eldest sister, Inderjit—a beautiful eighteen-year-old, who was already engaged—and said that, before him, the rioters must kill her. He said he would rather she died in front of his eyes than have her honour besmirched in worse ways later. Inderjit was holding our brother at the time and the bullet hit her thigh, where she still has a very deep gash—as a child, I could fit my hand in there—and then the bullet grazed our brother's lower stomach and left. But they both were bleeding badly. In the chaos that followed, my sister got separated from us. And the baby, our baby brother Billa, well, my grandmother placed him on top of my parents' corpses.'

She picked up a pillow from beside her and showed us how the child had been placed. 'Like this, they lay him on his stomach. He was badly wounded, and who knew how long he would last? We had no choice, we just left him there, and followed the caravan through the jungle and to a refugee camp. But little did we know that the fates of my sister and brother would not end there, for neither had died with that one bullet. My sister was picked up and taken to a Muslim man's house; she was eventually rescued and sent to a camp of other young women who had been abducted from Mirpur. She was returned to us after two years in a population exchange between India and Pakistan...'

Her eyes became moist and she wiped her tears away. 'The family said that her honour had been tarnished. They didn't think about what she had gone through, to be away for all that time, under what circumstances. And my brother—you won't believe this—he too was picked up by a Muslim man, who had three wives at home, but none had borne him children, and so he raised my brother ... as a Pakistani. I think they named him Ashiq. But my brother's life was fraught with difficulty and many hurdles. It's a long, long story, but he managed to find his way back to us after twenty-eight years.'[15]

Tears collected in her eyes. Placing both hands over her face, she said, 'Eventually, we were all reunited, but at what cost? That November in Mirpur fractured so many families and left so many others dead. Don't you remember,' she asked Ajit Kaur, 'how many children were just abandoned on the walk?'

'What do you mean?' I asked, horrified.

'Lots of people abandoned their children in the jungle. So many small children could not walk and so they walked ahead and left them behind. So many families even buried their children in the forest itself,' Ajit Kaur said.

'Newborn children, or those who had died?'

'*Nahi*, children who were two or three years old. They dug holes in the ground—graves, really—and buried them there, right there and then.'

Goosebumps shot up my arms and my body immediately turned cold.

'*Zinda?*' I asked, in a voice I hardly recognized.

'*Zinda*. Alive,' she responded unflinchingly.

'Why did no one stop them?' I clenched my jaws.

Finally, she peeled her eyes away from the blank wall ahead and looked at me. Her vacant gaze revealed far more distance than I could ever have imagined. Even the voice telling this story seemed only to be reporting it—somehow not belonging to the person who had endured these circumstances but, rather, someone for whom this memory had simply become a shadow of actual events, no longer resembling the depth of traumatic reality.[16]

'What could we do?' she shrugged. 'Each and every person wanted to reach safety. Nothing else mattered. Some people even placed large stones on the children so that they wouldn't be able to go any further.[17] Would they take care of themselves or their families or their children or just try and escape the firing? It was only when we reached the refugee camp in Jammu that people began talking about all the unthinkable acts they had committed along the way. They wept for the children they had buried or killed. We saw all of this on the way to India. Those nights were perhaps the worst I have ever experienced in my life.'

'Mummy, *Malkeet didi kede hoe si?*' her daughter-in-law asked about the child born to the couple along the way.

'I have only told you about one day. Many women even gave birth along the way … and so did I. Malkeet, my daughter, was born on the third and last day of our walk.'

'By the second day, some people were abducted from the caravan itself, some were killed and some succumbed to starvation and thirst. There was no food or water. When I felt really faint, I began licking the mud on the ground, and finally felt a bit of wetness on my lips. But apart from that, the path that we had taken through the forest had no lakes and no wells, no sources of water at all.[18]

'Night had set in, it was *puranmashi*, full moon, and Guru Nanak-ji's birthday, and in the moonlight we continued our journey on foot. Then we saw a small hill in the distance and, with great difficultly, people began to climb. When we had almost reached the top, a voice came from below: "*Wahan Pakistan hai, uss paar Pakistan hai!*" They were warning us that Pakistan lay on the other side of that hill and we needed to come down immediately. It was 4 a.m. and the moon shone bright. In its light, many women who had ascended ended up giving birth on the top of that very hill, and later were unable to climb down. There were women I knew as well and I was trying to help them down, but I, myself, was in no state to climb down, and told my husband that. He swiftly caught hold of my arm and dragged me down for fear of someone from the other side abducting me. I slid down that hill. The sides of my body were badly scraped by the rocky surface of the hill and the thorny bushes that grew on it. There was blood everywhere, and on top of that I neither had my dupatta to wipe it off nor any shoes. The holiest night brought forth our worst and most unthinkable horrors. But we had no choice, we continued on, and the firing from the sky also continued every now and then.'

Ajit Kaur then picked up the sword herself. Holding its grip, she said, 'We used this on the third night. This sword saved my life.' But even though her words were suffused with the past, her touch didn't speak the same language. She ran a forefinger over the dulled blade in a cool and restrained way, and put it back down.

'I told my husband again and again to leave me and go ahead. I just could not walk any more. I had had no food and no water and, in my pregnant condition, I knew I was only slowing him down. So I insisted—I cannot walk any further, you should just go ahead. But he just held my arm and made sure I continued walking, until the third day when I just couldn't walk any more. In the evening, my labour pains began, and I simply slumped down next to a tree in the forest. My husband began running around frantically, asking people to help, and finally a woman agreed. She assisted me through the birth and then asked for something sharp to cut the umbilical cord.

'She told us to find anything sharp, a knife or even a sharp stone. My husband offered her this sword,' she said. 'She took it and swiftly cut the cord and placed the baby on the ground. My husband rushed to my side immediately to make sure that I was still breathing and alive. Both my baby and my body had cuts and bruises from the thorny ground of the forest. There was blood everywhere. I was losing consciousness and didn't think I could continue walking, so I insisted that my husband go ahead and I would continue when I could with the baby. Without even thinking, he threw the baby aside and picked me up to my feet.

She paused and looked at me. 'Can you imagine the circumstances we were in, for him to do that? Imagine how desperate he must have been. He didn't even think twice, just put the child to the side and made sure I could continue. I had no energy to even protest; the only thing he kept repeating was that we had to get out alive.

'He just couldn't take care of both of us just then, keep us both alive, and so we left our daughter behind. Then, slowly leaning on him, I began walking. We must have gone just five or seven paces when we heard the cries of our newborn. Imagine, you nurture a child inside your body for nine months, how could you just… Anyway, he was torn, but he couldn't leave her. So he told me to wait, swiftly undid his turban, picked up the baby and swaddled her in it. He held us both, as well as the gun and the sword.'

She paused, breathed in heavily and again looked at the sword. 'He really loved this sword. He would have been very happy to see it out today, to see someone writing about it. I have always wondered about the sheer strength he showed on that journey to India. He just refused to let me go, refused to allow me to stop. He was the only reason I continued for as long as I did.'

'Do you think he loved the sword because of what it had been through with you—what it represented?' I asked, now looking more closely at the eroded spine, weathered and worn.

'*Nahi, nahi*,' she laughed. 'He loved it not because of this journey, but because it was from the other side. He made sure to carry it. He loved his home and his land dearly. We weren't able to get anything else…' Her voice trailed off for a few seconds before she returned to her story.

* * *

'So, at 2 a.m, some hours after our daughter was born, we finally reached a large military base manned by the Indian Army in a village called Sarya, now in the Nowshera district.[19] There was really no provision for any food or water there, but people rested for a while. We had to return the rifle to the army, but the sword was ours, so it remained. The old, the sick, the wounded and those who needed immediate medical attention were sent in trucks to Jammu,[20] and the rest were told to continue on foot. It would take them seven more days. But I was barely paying attention to my surroundings, because I had had no rest at all after the childbirth. Thankfully the three of us were sent on the truck. A kind officer took pity on my condition and gave us whatever he could find—some pieces of dried coconut and a box of powdered milk for our child.

'On the way to Jammu came Nowshera town, where my husband's brother worked, so he told the truck driver to let us off there. But fate plays cruel jokes on us all, for when we reached their house, we found it locked. Every second house in the neighbourhood had a lock on it. Later we were told that much of the non-Muslim population had left the city and gone to Jammu for fear of being attacked like in other areas of the state. So, with nowhere to go and no one else we knew, my husband and I sat on the side of the road with our newborn daughter.

'Then a young man in a car came up to us. He saw that I was unwell, that our daughter was an infant and that we were clearly stranded, and he offered to drive us to Jammu. He took off his socks, shoes and overcoat and gave these to me; I had been shivering. Finally, we arrived at a refugee camp in Jammu, but it was full! So many people had arrived from the state and also from parts of West Punjab [allocated to Pakistan] that all the camps were overflowing. Somehow I got admitted to the local hospital, and because there was no space for my husband to wait with me, he took our daughter and waited under a tree outside. He sold a ring for 20 rupees and, with that money, bought milk and some food. I only came to consciousness after the doctors had operated on me. I had lost so much blood and there were so many wounds that…'

She didn't complete her sentence but took a short breath instead and looked at me, almost confused. 'Are you not tired of listening to this story by now? It's so disturbing and old … and forgotten now.'

I glanced through the six pages of notes I had taken while she was narrating. 'Just because a certain truth is old doesn't make it any less true. No matter how long or disturbing the story, I'm listening,' I assured her.

She nodded slowly but for a while said nothing, and I wondered if, rather than my listening, it was her own telling that had overwhelmed her. After all, the story had been set aside to languish in silence for decades. She played nervously with her hands in her lap, her eyes ignoring the sword sitting before us, and her soft forehead now bore lines it hadn't had when I'd first entered the room. The narrative had caused her pain, this much was clear, but my heart went out to her bravery. This was, without a doubt, a story of remarkable courage and survival. I wanted to tell her that her recollections were important, they mattered, they would make a difference, but then I remembered what she had said about just listening to a story versus living it. No narration could undo the past, and no story would bring back those who had died at the hands of others, all at the cost of freedom.

* * *

'Uh … your family, what happened to the rest of your family?' I asked her.

'Well, after Jammu, my husband and I travelled to Punjab to a place called Doraha Mandi, where his cousin lived. My two younger brothers had somehow found their way there as well, but we had no news from the rest of the family. My father had been killed already, but my mother, sister and two brothers had been taken as prisoners to the Alibeg Camp. We didn't see them until six months later.' After a moment, she asked me softly, 'Have you heard anything about that camp? The circumstances, the living situations … do you know about it?'

I shook my head.

'Hmm … I also only came to know later, when I was reunited with the family. I could barely recognize them. There was barely any flesh on their bones. They had been kept like animals. Thousands of Hindus and Sikhs were marched out of Mirpur and its surrounding areas, and kept as prisoners in the camp, which was an old gurudwara in Alibeg, just a few kilometres away from the Pakistan border.[21] Dozens of people had been stuffed into the rooms, where they were expected to live, sleep, defecate and spend their days. They were given no food.[22] My family later told me that they used to boil leaves and eat those. Apple leaves. For six months.'

I stared at her.

'In the beginning, many people committed suicide on seeing the conditions of the camp. Many were executed, many were taken advantage of, and many just suffered, day after day. My younger sister was a nice-looking girl, and so my mother feared that the troops from the other side would take her.[23] She tried three times to drown my sister in the river. Three times. But each time, my sister refused to die. "I will not die here," she insisted. And so, my mother started to crush up coal and darken her beautiful face. One of my younger brothers, Charan Singh, had a *joora*, a topknot on his head. In the camp, one of the men just chopped all his hair off. They made him Hindu! This happened to so many Sikhs inside that prison camp.'

'H-how did they get out of the camp?' I asked, my voice barely a whisper.

'The government retrieved them with the help of the Red Cross. A team of foreigners came in 1948, took photos, helped the refugees imprisoned there, provided food and aid, wrote reports and documents, and brought them to India to the Kurukshetra camp.'[24]

'How did you find them?'

'Well, from Doraha Mandi we came to Amritsar. But we didn't know anyone there and had no means of employment to earn money, so we decided to go to Patna Sahib. There is a big gurudwara there, built to commemorate the birthplace of Guru Gobind Singh-ji. We thought that we would go there and at least, if not work, be able to feed ourselves in the *langar* and also have a safe place to sleep. So we took the train from Amritsar to Patna. But somewhere near Lucknow, the train stopped and my uncle's daughter also fell violently ill. We had barely had anything to eat, so the child died of starvation in the train compartment itself. We didn't know what to do or where even to dispose of her body. Lucknow was a new city for us. Someone on the platform told us that people dispose of bodies in the Gomti river, and so we made our way there.'

As she remembered the details of their journey, I couldn't help but wonder about the nature of death in the days of the Partition. It seemed to be such an overwhelming consequence of the Divide that people's voices turned almost callous when speaking of the loss of a loved one. Perhaps that was just one way to overcome the loss, I comforted myself. *Dispose*, she had said. Dispose of the body. I swallowed hard and continued to take notes.

'When we came back to the station, the whole day had passed. The child had died, arrangements had to be made, and that took up time. As a result, we missed our train to Patna and now our group stood on the platform, deciding our next steps, when a man came to us and told us about the Talkatora refugee camp at Charbagh. He was the camp commandant. Night was setting in, it was starting to get quite cold; it was the month of December now. He offered us food and a place to stay, so we agreed. I stayed close to my two brothers and we were put in the same tent. Every single person got bedding and food—one *pau* dal and one *pau* flour—and for the first time in many days we slept a good night's sleep. Over the next few weeks, we realized that the Talkatora camp housed many people who had migrated from various towns and villages that were now across the border. There was even an employment exchange in the camp for those who had finished high school, and so they helped us find work. Sometimes, foreigners would come visit the camp and bring us gifts or treats, rice and biscuits.

'One day, we heard an announcement on the radio—it was some time in the spring of 1948—that some residents of Mirpur, who had been taken as prisoners to Alibeg Camp, had been brought to Kurukshetra. So I travelled from Lucknow to Kurukshetra, where a very large camp had been set up, with thousands and thousands of tents.[25] I found them there, and when I saw them I barely recognized them. They were just bones— skeletons. And shall I tell you the worst thing?'

I nodded gravely.

She scrunched up her nose. 'They hadn't changed their clothes or bathed in six months. Their bodies and hair were full of infections and lice. They would simply shake their heads and lice would fall around them like rain. My youngest brother had become so frail that he had to be hospitalized, and it was only after he was discharged that we took them back to Lucknow with us. From then on we lived in Lucknow city, and now we are in Chandigarh.'

She heaved a deep sigh, and for a few minutes the whole room was quiet. Everyone's thoughts perhaps lingered on Mirpur and Alibeg, and the horrific acts that humans are capable of committing against one another.

* * *

I asked her again, as I had at the beginning of our conversation, 'Do you miss your life in Mirpur, as it had once been?'

'After seeing so much bloodlust and death, after losing my father, my father-in-law, and so much of my family to the

Partition, I don't think I want to see Mirpur again. To this day, I cannot explain why Partition happened. We had all been living together—Hindus, Muslims, Sikhs, Christians. I still don't understand it. Partition ruined us, turned us into…' she paused, '… beggars. It sucked the life out of us, reduced us to penury.' Her eyes fell on the sword again. 'Every time I cleaned the house, I used to tell my husband to get rid of this sword. Throw it out. But he insisted that we keep it. And now after his death, it has passed down to my son and further down to Gurshane,' she said, gesturing to her grandson.

'Do you feel angry when you look at it?' I asked, unsure of the words I had chosen.

She scoffed, '*Gussa nahi*, but why should I remember that time? What is the need to remember your land, your home? It didn't help us, it didn't protect us. And yet, till his last day, he kept this sword close, saying: "It's from Pakistan, it's from home…"' Her voice trailed off into the mechanic whirring of the ceiling fan.

Suspecting that the interview had come to an end, I began closing my notebook and putting away my recorder.

'So, you have heard our story,' Satwant Kaur now said.

I nodded.

'But you have *only* heard the story; we have lived the days she described.'

'Even listening can cause you pain…' I offered.

'Yes, to some people, but not to all. Everyone's heart is not the same.'

My eyes met hers and she continued unflinchingly. 'Now, think about all those people who have been through such a traumatic event. Think about what continues to remain in our minds, continues to haunt us till this day. Then think about how much it must have pained those of us who went through it.'

3

GIFT FROM A MAHARAJA

THE PEARLS OF AZRA HAQ

IN THE SULTRY SEPTEMBER heat of Lahore, I was welcomed into a single-storey home in the neighbourhood of Gulberg just as the electricity went out. 'Load-shedding,' the young girl who answered the door called it. She showed me into the living room and returned after a few minutes, escorting the woman I had come to see, Azra Haq. The air, which had just moments ago been dark and stagnant, suddenly felt lighter. An aura of pinkness surrounded her, perhaps emanating from the rose-coloured shalwar kameez she was wearing, perhaps from the light rouge that coloured her cheeks or the soft crimson tinge of her lips. As the curtains were drawn open, natural light flooded into the small room, illuminating her left side, and I saw her more clearly: a delicate oval face, brown eyes, a sharp hooked nose and silver hair pulled into a ponytail. The woman, now likely in her nineties, looked every bit as elegant as I had been told.

'Oh my dear, sit down, sit down,' she said. 'I'm sorry there is no electricity, so common these days in Lahore. But help yourself to a *pankhi*.' She pointed to a hand fan placed on the table—multi-coloured with a golden rim. In her lap sat a small black pouch, which she safeguarded with both hands. The girl who had welcomed me brought a tray with glasses of cool almond sherbet, then glided out the door.

'Ah, now we can talk,' the woman said in a crisp accent, more English than anything else. Her eyes studied my face for a few minutes. 'Delhi … you have come from Delhi? I went there once. We accompanied the Pakistan Army polo team on their visit to

India in 1955. We saw all the sights, went shopping in Connaught Place, and the people, oh, they were so hospitable. Hardly any difference between the Lahoris and the Delhiites, the same Punjabi warmth.'

'Were you born in India?' I asked her.

Her grasp tightened around the black velvet pouch in her lap and, ever so gracefully, with her posture erect and neck long, she smiled. 'Oh yes. I was born in 1925 in Ludhiana. Lu-dhee-yaana. But because of my father's transfers through the excise and taxation department of the government, I spent most of my life in Jullundur, where we had an ancestral *haveli*.' She pronounced the name of the city in the British way, sharpening the otherwise rounded word with a distinct colonial twang. 'It was a good life, we had a good life. I was educated in convent schools until the age of sixteen, learning foreign languages like French, Latin and English, of course. Though we spoke Urdu at home, in formal education it came to us belatedly, and only for refinement. My parents, Mian Ata-ul-Haq and Zohra Jabeen, were very broadminded people and the privileges I had were the same as any British girl would have had.'

I raised my eyebrow at the intentional distinction.

'Yes, well, it's true,' she continued, 'because we were educated in British schools, and all our neighbours were British as well. The family had...' she paused, as if contemplating the right words to position her pedigree, 'the family had stature in society. There was a certain reputation one was expected to uphold. Upon finishing our convent education, my parents hired a governess for my sister and me: a Scottish woman, Mrs Bellamy, tall, grey-haired with rimless glasses. She taught us many things that could perhaps be considered part of a finishing course: table manners, grooming and posture, delivery and enunciation of speech, how to behave in public gatherings, always with grace and elegance, always like a lady. She would often tell us stories from Scotland, would discuss the history of Europe, and I remember insisting that I wanted to learn Indian history as well. She stayed with us for five years, spoke no Urdu, though she managed around the house and neighbourhood.'

As I watched Azra Haq conduct herself, I became convinced that some attributes, if sown deep enough, end up being second nature, habitual and inherent. Her every gesture was choreographed and graceful, as if life around her played out in slow motion. Her demeanour, demure yet confident, felt like it had the ability to captivate even the most resistant audience. My gaze then fell on her lap, where her long, slim fingers were still fidgeting with the black velvet pouch.

'What is inside?' I asked.

'Inside lies my childhood from across the border.' Soft laughter rang through the room like a melody. Her eyes danced, beckoning me to come closer, as if what she was going to extract from the pouch was a great and valuable secret. Eyes wide with interest, I sat down cross-legged at her feet. She untied the string and opened the pouch. And as she turned it upside down in her lap, what fell out were a long necklace and a pair of earrings made of exquisitely rare Basra pearls. She held the necklace up to the light coming in through the window, each pearl iridescent in the sunshine, the chain that held them together glimmering like a golden rope. Then she offered it to me and, holding my left palm out gingerly, I accepted it. With my right hand, I scooped it up and brought the string closer to me, inspecting it.

'Let me tell you a story.'

There was something in her voice that evoked the uncomplicated calm I associated with childhood. It reminded me of my grandmother's voice as she told us stories when we were young. Azra Haq's was one that wove history and memory together into magic. I leaned my back against the coffee table in the centre of the room, eager to explore her India. And as she began narrating, what I felt unfurl before me was a tapestry of royalty and resplendence, a story embroidered with gold and infused with the perfume of the past.

* * *

'My father's elder brother, Mian Ehsan-ul-Haq, who would later also be my father-in-law, was the chief judge for the princely state of Bikaner under Maharaja Ganga Singh, who was a visionary and a reformist. He represented India on the Imperial War Cabinet and at the Paris Peace Conference just after World War I, and was also the first ruler in India to establish a Chief Court, presided over by Mian Ehsan-ul-Haq. Since my uncle was the legal advisor, they were quite close and moved in the same social circles of Indian royalty, aristocracy and British officials. The year was 1943, it was summer and I was visiting Bikaner with my uncle and aunt. It was rare for families to join the employees when at work, but I had vacations. The maharani was throwing a grand shindig, a tea party in the palace, and we all were invited. "Azra," I had told the maharaja when he asked me my name as we were introduced. "Azaria? Asia?" He couldn't understand or remember the name but was completely smitten by it.' She giggled.

I noticed that she pronounced her own name with the same bubbly pinkness that floated in the air around her. I asked her what it meant.

'Oh, I really don't know. But my father did. He told me once that it meant a young girl, to which I replied, "How ridiculous, Abba-ji, you know I won't be young forever!" But that man, bless him, he said to me, "Keep your heart young, Azra, just keep your heart young." And I have, I still have. After all these years, I feel that my father was right, for I have kept my heart youthful!'

'So the maharaja couldn't remember your name?'

'He could not, and listen to this. We were close to the end of the summer vacations. I had to go back to Jullundur. But before that my aunt and uncle asked me what I wanted as a parting present. Now remember I was just about eighteen and had this very English mentality, so I said that I'd like some pearls. In those days, we used to wear all kinds of keyrings and other silver junk on our hands and fingers, but pearls, now those were refined. Those were a mark of elegance and class.

'So, as it turned out, my uncle was speaking to the maharaja one day and just happened to mention to him that his niece had asked for pearls. And so, the next morning, a very big sort of bag arrived from the maharaja's residence, carried by two bearers. Naturally, we were all very curious and excited, and my cousins and I—four young girls—we all got permission to be present when the bag was opened. My aunt picked up the bag and toppled it over on the bed, and out fell volumes and volumes of pearls. There were earrings and necklaces and rings and stray pearls in various sizes. Beautiful whites and pinks and dull golds, it was like a sea of pearls had cascaded on the bed.

'Accompanying the bag was a letter, which read: "Pearls for your daughters Para, Razia and Zarina, and for your niece Aziria." You see, he was trying so hard to remember the name that I became Aziria. But I did not mind, the gesture was so sweet and surprising. I remember writing him a letter, this charming Maharaja of Bikaner, to thank him.'

My mouth, half open with both awe and shock, curled into a smile. 'So what did you take, what could you take from the pile?' I asked in anticipation.

The pearls that I had held against the light were brought out once again. They were admired and caressed and given their rightful place in history. 'Well, I was a little shy, so I only picked up a pair of earrings. These ones, in fact, here in this bag. But my aunt, she selected two more necklaces from the pile, one *saat lada*, a seven-strand, and one *paanch lada*, a five-strand, and presented them to me.' She showed me with her hands how deep the necklaces sat when she wore them.

'Unfortunately, those two are in a safe at the bank and I couldn't find the key. But this one single string and the matching earrings I keep at home. This set of jewellery is what I brought with me when we left during the Partition. That's why I hold it so close, that's why it's so valuable to me. It survived migration. When we were leaving, it was so difficult to decide what to take and how to take it. You just picked up what you could afford to, and this was small enough to slip into the folds of clothes. It has survived and, with it, so many memories of the maharaja and the decadent parties and luxurious lifestyle…'

Her tone was soaked in lament as she turned her face towards the window. I thought about what it must have felt like to leave all that behind, a life of stature and comfort. As I studied the contours of her face, it became clear that it would have felt like a deep plummet. When I asked whether I could help her put the pearls back into the bag, she politely declined. 'I think I will wear them for a while. You have brought them out from the past and I think they deserve a little air, don't they? They *are* rather lovely.'

Smiling to herself, she put the necklace on, wrapping it around her neck twice, the matte pearls striking against her light skin. She adjusted it several times until she was satisfied with how they sat against the folds of her pink georgette dupatta, and then she looked up, beaming.

'There is an important part of my life that I must tell you about before it escapes me completely. Forgive me, I hope I won't confuse you but I must go back a little in time. Memory is like that … hardly ever chronological when you want it to be.

'In 1940 or 1941, just after I had finished my convent education, I remember reading an advertisement in the newspaper. I think it was in the *Dawn*, which used to be published out of Delhi at the time. "Join the WACI and see the world. Work at home and abroad with the forces." The WACI,' she repeated slowly, 'Women's Auxiliary Corps (India), was essentially formed with the aim of giving women of British and Indian nationalities duties with the British Army during World War II.[1] Really, it was made for the British ladies who had come to India or the Anglo-Indians, to include them in the war efforts and provide them with a means of livelihood. Recruitment began in 1940 and the unit itself was officially formed in 1942.

'I read this ad in the newspaper and my mind was made up. I wanted to join the forces. For days I worked on my Abba-ji, trying to persuade him in any way I could. "I'll never let you down, I'll never embarrass you. I want to make something of my life, please, Abba-ji. I want to join the army."'

'Did you know of other women your age and upbringing who were keen on joining?'

'Oh no, not at all. All the girls I knew were keener on getting married at that age, looking for suitors, starting families. And it was my father's worry as well that I would end up alone, that no one would marry me. But that was of little concern to me. I wanted to have my own life, make something of myself before I could even consider spending a life with anyone else. Joining the army was a matter of pride. I was adamant … and he eventually gave in!' she chuckled.

'So I was with the WACI from 1942 to 1947 and was trained in mostly administrative skills and intelligence work. This was the only time women were allowed to join the army in a non-medical capacity. As with our counterparts in the United States and Europe, we were not allowed to serve in combat roles but worked behind the frontlines as typists, switchboard operators, drivers, and we were posted anywhere the Indian Army went.[2] As it happened, I was one of the few Indian girls in the headquarters. Most of the others were, as I said, British or Anglo-Indian, or Anglo-Burmese or Indian Christian. I was made to follow the work of General [William] Slim's campaign in Burma quite intently.[3] Another time, I worked directly under the area commander, a Major General Farrwell, doing shorthand typing of documents and driving him around wherever he needed to go. The army provided housing in the cantonment and there were different messes for the various officers of different ranks. As part of the force you were required to do so many tests regularly, and when you passed them you'd be up for promotion. I think I retired as a captain with a salary of about Rs 600 per month, which was very good in those days.'

'Was it worth it, then, persuading your father to allow you to join?' I asked.

'Oh, yes. I felt like I belonged to the army. I loved it very much and was quite sorry to leave. It was such a disciplined and clean life. To be honest, there are many things to be told about the past when one really sits down to remember. It's true that sometimes I forget the smaller details—the names, the ranks, the dates—but at other times this part of my life is clearer than anything else. Clearer than today, clearer than even now. And it was so different from the sheltered life I had led up until then that it gave me a sense of purpose, of mission. Later, after Independence, I even joined the Pakistan Women's National Guard.'

After a short pause, her voice just as calm and leisurely as before, she said, 'I'm not complaining at all, I hope you understand. My parents provided us with the best possible upbringing, but the army, it was like nothing else I'd ever experienced before.

'In Jullundur we had this grand, lavish *haveli* [townhouse] with a lush garden where my parents would host parties. There were women in beautiful gowns and hats, British women who had come to India. They had all even learnt a little Urdu in order to blend with the landscape. Oh and puppets, we would have puppet shows … and *qawwali* nights where, once a month, famous *qawwals* would be invited to perform [Sufi devotional music]. *Durrees*, large carpets, would be laid out and the whole *mohullah*—neighbours and workers alike—would be invited to watch and we would sit with them on the ground. In front of our *haveli*, my grandfather had built about forty houses—with longer rooms at the back, smaller rooms at the front, a *chulha* to cook on, a washbasin and bathroom—and these were given to forty families, mostly agricultural workers, free of charge. Good man, he had a very big heart.'

'And what was the city of Jalandhar like when you were growing up?'

'It was … well, we lived…' For a moment, her face turned blank, hesitant and unsure of what to say next and then, shaking her head, she spoke. 'I'm sorry, I don't remember the city. I don't remember it at all. I only remember the small market around our house ... there was Jeevaram, the fruit and vegetable-*walla*, selling everything from apples to potatoes, then there was Jagannath, who made the most wonderfully sweet *mithai* and *halwa puri*. I would often go there with my *amma*, the nanny, who was from Meerut. When I was young, all these people were like friends or family. I would spend time with them and all the servants who worked in the house. There were about twenty in total. I still remember there were two women, one with a large *paraat* of *atta*, a large metal dish full of dough, and another woman with a *tawa*, a coal oven, this big'—she opened her arms wide— 'and they would make rotis for all the servants twice a day, once in the morning and once late in the evening, as my parents would insist on feeding everyone. There were Motiya and Jagan, who insisted on calling me Ujjo *bibi*. Now Azra became Ujjo!'

She pronounced these traditional Hindu names, which to me sounded strange and foreign coming from her polished Urdu tongue, in a voice that held the naivety and magic of childhood. I sat with my palm rested against my chin and listened as she continued.

'Then one day there was a wonderful addition to our family. Remember, there is strangeness in this world beyond our comprehension: events, incidents, things and people that live within the cracks of plausibility. This was one such thing. One morning, in the second week of November 1943, a sudden noise woke me up. The guards were bickering outside. I looked at the clock on the wall: 6.30 a.m., still too early to rise. I looked beside me. Amma-ji was still asleep. It was a strange, grey sort of laden sky, an unhappy-looking morning. Back then, November brought with it the winter chill and so I put on my chadar to go out and see what the commotion was about, careful not to wake Amma up. But, still half asleep, she held my wrist tight.

'"Not alone, *bibi*," she said, "never alone."

'Slowly, she too rose and covered her head with her own chadar. I was already waiting by the door and, barely awake, she followed me. When we got to the garden, we saw a small, wizened old man being pushed around by the guards. His skin was dark and he was wearing that … I've seen men in India wearing them … oh yes, a *dhoti*. He was wearing a *dhoti*, with a sacred thread draped across his torso, and he had a bald patch right in the middle of his head.

'"*Kahan se aaye ho?*" Amma asked him, but he was silent. "Where have you come from?" she tried again but got no answer.

'The guards had been manning both the front and back of the house and had not seen him jump over either gate. After discussing it amongst themselves, they offered us a strange and extraordinary explanation. The man had come from above, they deduced, looking up to the heavens. Fallen from the sky, smack into our compound in the heart of Jullundur. He had fallen from the sky.'

'Did he not say anything?' I asked, curious.

'He hardly ever spoke, but eventually we learnt that his name was Mohanlal. He stayed in our house till the Partition.'

'A complete stranger?'

'Well, my parents had a very big heart. They decided that he had come to our house for a reason—that, in some way, God had sent him. He had come from above. He would always just sit around the garden under the plum trees watching the sky, and so my father had this little room built for him there.'

With her hands she sketched a room in the air, not very large, rectangular and raised about two feet above the ground, with a door on the side. 'Inside the room was a bed with a warm *razai*, a blanket my mother brought him from the house. The most beautiful thing about that small room in the garden was that its roof was made of glass. As it was being constructed, Mohanlal looked up at the sky and said to my father, "Baba, up there, put glass up there." And so the roof became an invitation to the heavens, where he could lay down in peace and get lost in the firmament. After all, he had come from above. I remember, even in the storms and terrible rains, Mohanlal refused to leave the periphery of that room. Every morning before sunrise, he would look up at the sky and talk, well, yell, as if he were speaking to someone up there. Gibberish mostly, repeating words and phrases. He would go on for hours at the top of his voice. And he had strange names for us all. My mother was "*maiya*" and I was "*amma*". Imagine, he called me Amma!' she laughed. 'Abba-ji wanted Mohanlal to come to Lahore with us, but one day he just disappeared.'

'Without a trace?'

'Exactly. When the Partition was announced, my parents decided to take all the servants across the border with them. But one day he disappeared, along with the things he had brought with him when he first came, and nothing else. My mother had made him jackets for the winter, brought new and clean cloth for his *dhotis*, given him utensils to eat with so he felt part of the household. But he didn't take any of it. He just vanished … without a trace.' She smiled. 'Dear old Mohanlal.'

'How did you come to learn of the Partition?'

'Partition. Well, I was in the army, so naturally I heard of it there. The family was very well connected and we would continually get news, if not from friends then from newspapers and radio broadcasts. But did anyone anticipate it? It's difficult to say. There was certainly talk about it.

'Once, in 1944, Mr Jinnah came to Jullundur and I attended the meeting, though not in uniform. The room was silent, there was pin-drop silence as he spoke. I sat on the floor next to this woman, straight out of a village, who was listening to him with such care and interest. Her eyes were fixed on him as he spoke in flawless English, such an orator he was! So I leaned over and asked her in Punjabi if she understood at all what he was saying. And without so much as batting an eyelash, she responded that she understood everything perfectly: "I know every word he is saying. Long live Jinnah *sahab*!" I didn't know whether she really understood or was just transfixed by this charismatic person who knew well how to manipulate the crowd, but there you had it. Even the women had begun to be mobilized and seduced by the idea of the promised land of Pakistan. He talked of our rights, our different culture and, would you believe it, in the days that followed, when I had come home from work, I would join the women on the streets as they chanted nationalist slogans: "*Humein Pakistan chahiye*, we want our Pakistan! *Humare dil mein Quran hai*, we hold the Quran in our hearts. *Pakistan zindabad*, long live Pakistan!" I remember saying these things.'

'Yes, but did you actually believe them? Despite the status of your family, all the English eccentricities, did you truly believe in home rule?'

'My dear, many things changed after the army, after the war. Even in the upper crust of Indian society, we began to see the drawbacks of the Raj. We were still friends with the officials, but it was clear that the British government had slowly taken everything from us. We, the jewel in their crown, no longer sparkled. And so, as 1947 approached, yes, we too believed in Pakistan.'

Was it so strong, the strength of nationalism, I wondered, that it could diminish even the most English of Indians? Was it easy to shed a lifestyle like a snakeskin? Had it been simple to forego the garden parties, the gowns and hats, the puppet shows, the language, the customs and mannerisms? Was there such power in speech and elocution and in the mere idea of freedom? I thought of the beautiful young woman, impeccably groomed, trained in the army, now protesting for independence with slogans of '*Leke rahenge Pakistan*, we will take our Pakistan!'

* * *

'I had got engaged to Mehboob-ul-Haq in May 1945,' she continued, her memories swimming against the chronology of time. 'He was my first cousin. And though everyone was quite keen on the match, and this kind of marriage within families was quite normal, I was unsure. Not because of him—mostly because I wasn't ready. However, when I met him, I saw he was a good man. He was also in the army, with the Lancers, had been educated at Doon School in Dehra Dun, very refined, very cultured. So I agreed. We had a big party in Jullundur to celebrate the union. Bobby, everyone called him Bobby!

'Then, in the summer of 1947, I fell very ill with typhoid and the sweltering heat wasn't doing me any good. Bobby and my marriage had been set for later that summer, and so to make sure I'd be well by then, my uncle and aunt—who were soon to be my in-laws—took me to Dalhousie, where our family had built summer homes. The cool was indeed refreshing, I was getting better with every passing week. But closer to August, we got a message from friends of the family, chemists, who had heard of riots across the Punjab. Hindus, Muslims and Sikhs causing agitation and killings. Independence was certain, Partition its by-product, but this kind of communal madness was unexpected. So my uncle asked them about the situation in Jullundur. This was around mid-August now, just a few days before Independence. He found out that my parents, who had remained behind to prepare for my wedding, were making provisions to leave the city.

'Sir Francis Mudie, who was appointed by Jinnah *sahab* as the first Governor of West Punjab in 1947 and was one of the few Europeans to remain in the subcontinent after the departure of the English, was an avid supporter of the creation of Pakistan.[4] A great sympathizer, if you will, of the Muslim cause. Because he was a close acquaintance of my uncle, he was kind enough to help us leave Dalhousie and travel across the new border in army-manned trucks.

'In the summer house, my uncle had kept his grand collection of carpets from around the world, and these were systematically rolled and carefully placed inside the trucks. All the furniture and the expensive silverware was taken. We tried, we really tried to take everything. But as we began driving out, we saw neighbours, friends and even strangers—Muslims who had no means of getting across—stranded on the streets, and slowly each precious item was thrown off along the way. The carpets, my uncle's great love, were discarded one by one. The furniture was thrown off to make room for people. And by the time we reached our destination, all I had with me were the clothes I was wearing: a white shalwar kameez with a baby blue floral design.

'And these pearls.' She gestured to the necklace wrapped around her neck. 'This one set that I had taken with me. These I slid into the folds of my clothes. That's all I had, *bass*. My mother would bring the rest of the maharaja's pearls with her from Jullundur and give them to me later, once we were reunited.'

She continued to run her fingers over the necklace around her neck, coiling sections of it around her fingers. I picked up the earrings from the velvet pouch. Three pearls set in gold created a triangle to be fastened at the ear, and from each pearl dangled a golden chain with more pearls woven through. They were not the most discreet earrings, but certainly small and light enough to hide within one's palm or tie within one's dupatta, without being seen or scrutinized.

'Did you come straight to Lahore, then?' I asked, still looking at the pearls. 'What did you witness along the way?'

She shook her head sadly. 'Terrible things happened along the way, terrible. I saw…' Then she stopped herself, breathed in deeply and, with eyes closed, she spoke, 'If you don't mind, I'd rather not talk about what I saw. I'm sorry, I cannot repeat those things. I cannot bring them to life again. I don't want to remember them.'

The pearl earrings were quickly forgotten in my hands. The trembling in her voice was the only thing that permeated the otherwise quiet room. I held my breath, not wanting to disturb that silence, not wanting to utter even a single word. I needed to know what she saw; my vivid imagination was travelling faster than her silence, but I didn't know how to ask … or what to ask. Given all the memories of violence and rioting I had already been privy to, it was hardly difficult to imagine what would have been the landscape of her journey.

'We tried to find a way to come directly to Lahore, but we couldn't. The roads were just too dangerous. And despite us being accompanied by army officials—these young Scottish guards—there was still the danger of being plundered along the way. In hindsight, it was perhaps for the best that we had to leave behind our belongings, since who knows what would have happened if we had encountered any riots. This way we were at least able to bring across more people. So we travelled from Dalhousie to Murree, a long and arduous route through the mountains where we were sure there wouldn't be any danger. Then for two weeks we were stuck in Murree with no transport out. No train, no cars, nothing left the mountainous landscape. We were stranded with no belongings and no news of the rest of the family that had set out from Jullundur. Finally, on 1 September 1947, we reached Lahore.'

'What kind of a state did you find the city in?'

'Lahore was devastated by all the gunfire. There used to be many beautiful monuments that had been burnt down amidst the violence. The Garden City had been pillaged, many people had been killed, bodies lay everywhere. Many Hindu and Sikh girls had been carried off by Muslim men. And if it happened on this side, it happened on that side too. Bobby, still in the army at the time, was involved in the evacuation of refugee camps. There were five camps in total in Lahore. And every day quite a number of trucks would go around the villages to extract Hindus, women especially, who had been abducted by force—dragged out of their villages, raped, abused, used. And the saddest thing was that many of these women refused to go back to their families across the border for fear of no longer being accepted.'

Her eyes were low, no longer looking at me, and her fingers fiddled with the edges of her kurta. 'This was their life now, for better or for worse. These women, when asked why they thought their families would no longer welcome them, said that they had now become, sort of, like … half Muslims: "Even though we may hold Hindu gods in our hearts, on the surface we too have become Muslims." Misfits, they were afraid of being misfits in their old lives, belonging on neither side of the border.'

An uncomfortable silence fell upon us. It had become, ultimately, a gendered partition. The female body, much like the landscape of Hindustan, had been massacred and abused. As I imagined the plight of women during the days of the riots, a feeling rose within me that I couldn't recognize. Was it sickness, disgust, or just bile rising within? It was difficult to tell. Then, taking me by surprise, the woman in pink gently reached out for my hand.

'It's okay to be upset by these things, my dear. That's what makes us human. The passing of years has smothered these events, but, as I said before, there are many things to remember if one really wants to. But *does* one want to? With the knowledge of the past comes the responsibility to take care of it. You *must* take care of it.' She squeezed my palm.

And then, for the very first time since the start of my research, a tear snaked down my cheek. It was as though this woman, unrelated to me, a stranger until today, had extracted a piece of herself from deep within, a dark place where she rarely ventured, and given it to me. That took trust. Here, she had offered. Handle this with the utmost delicacy, the action had whispered, make sure it is not repeated. I had come to sit in the presence of a string of lightweight pearls and was leaving with a weight heavier than I could bear.

Clearing my throat, though feeling rather numb, I asked with great effort, 'Where did you stay when you first arrived in Lahore?'

'We stayed with friends on Ferozepur Road for a few weeks until we could all stand on our own feet. In fact, that's where my husband and I got married, on 8 September 1947. In their home, in a new country, in an independent Pakistan. And from there on, life just continued…'

'Did you never think back to the Partition?'

'In the first few months, it felt quite strange. I would think about life in Jullundur often. I'd think about Mrs Bellamy and Mohanlal and Amma-ji, about the parties and gardens and puppet shows. As I'd take out the maharaja's pearls, I'd think about the summer spent in Bikaner. I'd remember how I carried them with me from Dalhousie, how scared I'd been to lose them, to lose even the memory of them. Childhood, they represented childhood for me.

'There was such a feeling of uprootedness. We had a completely different lifestyle now, with no ancestral house, no great fortune. It was not penury by any means, but it was a painful modesty that the family was unaccustomed to. And then, just a year later, both Abba-ji and his brother, my father-in-law, passed away within five days of each other. The family dwindled on both sides of the border. My dear cousin Begum Para had migrated across to Bombay, where she married an actor, Nasir Khan, who was originally from Peshawar and was quite the sensation in Bollywood!'

She then gestured to a photograph on the wall of a younger Azra, elegant and lithe, wearing a scarlet red sari, leaning gracefully against a low wall, her face turned to the left, seducing the camera. 'This was taken on my birthday, 17 May 1950, by the *Vogue* photographer Ronnie Chib, who was working on a feature titled, "A Day in a Pakistani Woman's Life". It was taken near Lahore's Assembly Chambers and later appeared on the cover of *Vanity Fair*. This red sari was sent to me by Begum Para from Bombay specially for the photo shoot.'[5]

I stood up to get a closer look. A grey sky in the background, similar perhaps to the sky on the day that Mohanlal had fallen from it, highlighted the contrasting brightness of Azra's red sari, the sheerness of its fabric showing a section of pale skin between the blouse and petticoat. The photograph had faded in places but was still, most certainly, a sight for sore eyes.

'The feeling of loss can often catch you off guard—arrive when you least expect it,' her voice floated out from behind me. She had put on the earrings as well now and they danced beside her long, slim neck. 'Loss came to me, along with a new shade of sadness, one evening when my husband and I were taking a walk on Mall

Road in Lahore. I was expecting my daughter, Scherry, at the time, and I remember myself with my big belly, counting all the cars— there were so few people rich enough to have cars in those days— and suddenly spotting an ice cream-*walla*. By then I had left the army. My husband too had just completed his assignment with the refugee camps and so everything in our life was extremely budgeted. This much for food, this much for clothes, this much for electricity, this much for the baby. I had never lived on a budget before and now anything *but* that seemed impossible for survival. The ice cream cost two rupees and I remember it pinching my pocket. I couldn't bring myself to buy it. My husband laughed and said that I must have the ice cream, but I couldn't do it. That was two whole rupees out of the budget.'

She gave a half laugh, instilling irony into her humour, and said, 'In India, I was living as an anchor … to my parents, to our ancestral wealth. But Pakistan put us through unimaginable struggles, days that I didn't think I'd see the end of, and ultimately taught us how to be truly independent.'

4

UTENSILS FOR SURVIVAL

THE KITCHENWARE OF BALRAJ BAHRI

THE PAST WAS NEVER as familiar as it was in those last few days. For most of his life, and all of mine, my paternal grandfather, Balraj Bahri, had hardly ever dwelled on times gone by. But it was at the end, the very end, that the past finally caught up with him, with newfound vigour and purpose.

'*Dilli*,' he would croak, holding on to my grandmother's hand tightly. '*Dilli chale?* Shall we go to Delhi?'

With tears in her eyes, and a heavy heart beating at the speed with which they had fled the land of their birth, she would say to him, '*Dilli mein hi toh hain*, *ji*, we are already here.'

Gradually, all the things that had once held him together now tore him apart. In the months leading up to the end, he often gazed at the handkerchiefs that my grandmother had carefully embroidered with his initials in their youth, refusing to leave home without one. When we found something aged in the house like a book, an old photograph or a letter, he would stroke it tenderly with his large fingers and flash a smile that had remained concealed for years behind his bushy white moustache. He held on to his outdated agendas, journals and notepads, and carefully noted down even the most mundane of details with a maroon fountain pen, in a tiny, illegible scrawl.

One day in the summer of my twenty-fifth year, as the family sat together after dinner, he, the head of the family, ritualistically sliced open two ripe *safeda* mangoes and distributed them among us all. There was a pause in our conversation as we bit into our slices, and he chuckled. 'These are no mangoes!' he said. 'In our

Qadirabad, mangoes used to be this big!' He opened his palm wide, forefinger and thumb extending to opposite sides to reveal a substantial hollow. 'This big, *inne vadde-vadde*,' he repeated in Punjabi, smiling at my grandmother.

Truth be told, for as long as I could remember, my grandfather had worn a veil of professionalism, and I only knew him as a diligent, dignified gentleman. Entirely self-made, he had carved for himself a niche in the world of bookselling in post-Partition India, having travelled from across the border with virtually nothing. But old age had unravelled him and the veil had finally come off, exposing the vulnerable skeleton of his success—the difficult past that had moulded a more-than-comfortable present.

* * *

'But what will you do after you know, what will it change?' he sighed, as if unable to understand. 'The past will still be the past. *Khatam*, gone, is it not? The tale of how and why we came to Delhi is not an easy one.' His voice was typically firm, yet something in it wavered, telling me that it was time.

'Bade Papa,' I said, 'I exist because of everything that happened before me. I need to know.'

The look in his eyes was not the same as it had always been, determined and resolute. My weeks of gentle prodding had softened the profound creases in his forehead and, this time, he succumbed to my request, eventually narrating the story of his life over the course of many afternoons.

Chewing the last morsel of rice on his plate one day, he wiped his mouth with a napkin and put down his spoon. Then, slowly, he took a long swig of water. I too pushed my plate away, drew in my breath, notebook ready, and waited. My grandmother came and occupied the seat across from me at the table. 'Let us listen, Balraj-ji,' she said to him lovingly, though she had heard it all before. 'Come, tell us your story.'

Clearing his throat, he plunged into the past, as if with no beginning and no end, landing somewhere in its middle, puncturing its very heart. 'Sometimes it would begin from one end of the *mohalla*. The stillness of the neighbourhood would dissolve into echoes, coming nearer and nearer, growing louder and louder. We would hide inside our houses under tables and beds, with all the lights out, and listen to the maddening rush of people screaming and chanting slogans. "*Pakistan zindabad! Pakistan zindabaad!*" they would bellow, lifting their arms, their fists balled up, their eyes wild. The men in these groups carried blazing sticks, burning everything in their way. We had never seen anything like that before. There are no words to describe that atmosphere. Something was in the air. An insanity, a thirst, a hunger for violence and freedom. Yes, there is nothing more precious than freedom. But freedom at the cost of others, what freedom was that?

'At the time, we lived in Malakwal, a small town in the Mandi Bahauddin district of Punjab, but our ancestors hailed from Qadirabad. Back then, under Mughal rule, many Sufi shrines, *dargahs*, were built across the landscape. After them, the Sikhs occupied the area, and then the British. The population in the countryside remained predominantly Muslim, and the towns cultivated a more Hindu community. There had always been mutual respect and co-existence between us. The Muslims tended to do more manual labour, working in fields and factories, and the Hindus usually worked in offices and banks. Things were systematic, people were cordial, life was simple. But with the announcement of Independence and Partition in June 1947, the entire nature of Malakwal was unforgettably mutilated.

'By night, mobs of Muslims from the countryside roamed our streets, which lay blanketed in silence and terror. Families hid together, seeking sanctuary wherever they could. With dawn came relief and gratitude that they had survived another night. But I should tell you, this was not one-sided, both Hindus and Muslims murdered each other. If one would strike, the other would retaliate. Many lives were cut short, *beta*, right in front of us.'

His flat palm sliced through the air like a sword. His deep voice was seeped in helplessness, coloured by defeat, as if all the air had been punched out of an otherwise fiery man, leaving him on the brink of apathy. His town had been pillaged before his very eyes, and he, a nineteen-year-old at the time, could do nothing but flee.

And I, living with the inherited knowledge of such atrocities, finally realized the reason for his self-imposed silence when it came to the Partition. He was right: nothing would change, the past would still be the past. Arduous to forget, yet even more so to recall. This experience was not mine, it was inherited. It was my responsibility to acknowledge it as a part of my history, a part of me. I had asked, after all. And so, unflinchingly, though my heart beat faster with each detail he divulged, I listened.

'Many of my ancestors had been in the police service with *angrez* officers, but traditionally we were landowners. It was my father's generation that began to move away from the family work and into the services. He chose to work at the local Malakwal bank, leaving the *zamindari*, the land holding, to my uncle. My elder brother, Devinder, also got a job at a bank right after his matriculation, choosing to contribute to the family income rather than studying further. So, though money was not plentiful, I became the first person to go to university in our family, moving to Rawalpindi about three hours away. I had come back home for my summer holidays when the riots began.

'One night, my parents, younger brother, sister and I packed a small bag with some clothes and essentials and, under the cover of darkness, crept out of our house to take refuge in a local police station. Many other Hindu families joined us as we stayed there, cocooned in the insufferable August heat for two days. Soon we heard that a local cotton factory had been turned into a camp for fleeing Hindus, and groups of refugees from the adjoining towns and villages had begun pouring in and were given food and shelter there. Rations were provided from the Hindu shops and granaries that had not yet been destroyed. Ten days we lived at that camp. We had been unable to get much from the house, having left in a rush, but my mother did carry some kitchen items. In the camp, over a makeshift *chulha*, she cooked simple food, dal and rice, but food nonetheless.'

'Did she manage to bring these utensils with her when you crossed over?' I asked.

'Yes, those were the only things she brought, actually. Brass utensils. Survival—that was her basic concern. To live, to survive, and for that we needed food. Rations would be provided but what would we cook them in? We couldn't eat raw lentils or rice, so she carried the utensils. Actually, many people took kitchen items when they migrated across the border. The journey to the other side would be long, and there would be no food or water. So the least they would do was take a glass so that, if the trains ever stopped near a body of water, a *darya*, they could quench their thirst, at least until their next stop. I remember a tall and heavy tumbler, from which my father would drink *lassi* every day. We still have it, don't we, Madam-ji?' he addressed my grandmother.

'Yes, it is in the kitchen upstairs. In fact, all these utensils should be there. *Jao*, go get them,' she said to me.

As I got up, excited at the prospect of what I would find, he called out to me, 'That's enough, *beta*, I have remembered enough for one day.' With both his hands, my grandfather massaged his head, and the memories within. 'My head has become quite heavy, I will tell you more tomorrow.'

I nodded, but ran upstairs regardless to search for my great-grandmother's long-forgotten kitchenware.

* * *

The next day, he picked up from the cotton factory. My mother joined us this time. The utensils sat in a big pile before us on the table. I had used the largest *kadhai*, a wok-like deep pot, as a makeshift carrier, filling it with two large plates, a smaller *kadhai*, two saucepans, a *pateela* pot, a blackened frying pan used to make chapati, and two long-handled, unshapely serving spoons.

'*Wah, wah*! You found them all!' he exclaimed with raised eyebrows, both pleased and surprised.

His gaze fell on the *lassi* tumbler he had mentioned the day before. Smiling, I told him that they lived at the back of a small cupboard in the kitchen. Pushing his chair out, he excused himself and came back a few minutes later with an old-fashioned magnifying glass. Then he picked up the tumbler and looked inside. Turning it around, he squinted and ran his fingers across its surface. Then, bringing the magnifying glass close to the metal, he peered through it, satisfied with his discovery. He held out both items to me and I too peered through. Small, delicate perforations on its brim set this tumbler apart from all others.

'You see this, these initials—D.L.M. Daryayi Lal Malhotra. My father. He would be the first to eat any meal, then us children, and then our mother would follow last. *Har savere*, every morning,' he said, repeating it in English to make his point, 'he would have a large breakfast of *puri-aloo* and *lassi*. He called this a *kade-wala* glass, why was that, Madam-ji?' he asked my grandmother, his syllables sweeping into each other in a particularly Punjabi way. When they spoke to each other, it was less in English and more in Hindi, Urdu and Punjabi. They conversed in these with an organic, leisurely ease of the colloquial that polished English could never provide, despite them both being fluent in it.

'It is called a *kade-wala* glass on that side of the border, and on this side it is a Patiala glass,' she replied.

He laughed. 'Yes, Patiala glass! Did you find a matching plate and bowl too?'

I rummaged around in the pile and sceptically extracted a large flat dish. Too large to be used for eating, I thought to myself, a *thali* for serving, more like it. But as soon as I placed it in front of my grandfather, his face lit up and he nodded. 'Yes, this is it. He would always eat in this.'

Then his own hands dove towards the utensils and he unearthed from the bottom of the pile a shallow, handle-less saucepan, in which we still warmed milk and soup over the stove. 'See this, this he would use as a *katora*, a bowl. A bread bowl.'

My eyes widened as I surveyed our own lunch plates and bowls, meagre in comparison. At least twice their size and far heavier, the old plate was made of coated brass, *kalai*. Similarly, the saucepan my great-grandfather had used as a bowl was larger than the whole length of my palm and as weathered as the plate. Its bottom had blackened completely due to the direct flame of the gas stove and its silvering was barely visible in the centre, where pools of brass shone through.

My mother remembered my father, my Bauji, eating out of those large utensils in the early years of their marriage. Nodding, my grandmother explained how the patriarch's utensils would always be the largest and often come as part of the wife's dowry, the husband's initials inscribed somewhere on the surface. Then, taking out a small quarter plate from the pile, she pointed at the inscription: B.M., my grandfather, Balraj Bahri Malhotra. She told me that at the time of their wedding her mother had had a set made for her new son-in-law. I grazed my pinky finger over the initials, my skin feeling the carved, rough depressions in the metal.

Each and every utensil would be made by hand, for there were no moulds in those days. Each curve, rivet and corner would be shaped individually and carefully. Every motif or design would be engraved painstakingly using special tools. Having worked on traditional engravings in a studio, I remembered the malleability of metal. When handled correctly, using their chemical properties to one's advantage, certain metals proved to be most receptive to welding and contouring, resulting in an array of beautiful wares. Upon closer inspection, I saw a small roundish pattern across the entire surface, evidence of the plate being hammered into shape. Its uneven ridges had now been occupied by rust and oxidation. The shiny, once-silver veneer was almost back to its original brassy colour. My grandmother picked up the plate and drummed her fingernails over it, creating a series of sharp metallic notes.

'Have you ever seen *kalai* being done?' she asked me, and then, without waiting for an answer, described the process. 'First the utensils are washed and cleaned. They are then heated to a fiery hot temperature and, using a pair of tongs, they are held and coated. A flat wire covered with this silvering metal is slipped in for just a moment to coat the pot, and then removed. Almost like depositing a little bit of paint inside. Then, with a soft cotton cloth, this metal is spread evenly over the entire surface. One second, it takes only one second, because though the coating metal melts very fast, it also solidifies very fast. We used to watch it being done as children because everything in the house was usually brass or copper. You see, brass,' she tapped the plate once more, 'is a very good conductor of heat but the minute it comes into contact with something acidic, it becomes poisonous. Copper doesn't, but it was coated as well. Now that these are hardly used in the kitchen, they are not cleaned properly.' Her hands traced the harsh water lines that decorated the aged glass. 'In the olden days, we would clean these heavy metallic utensils with coconut husk!'

My grandfather nodded in agreement. '*Yaad hai*, I remember that too!' Then, turning to me, he continued the story.

'My mother cooked in these utensils over an open fire at the camp. Ten days of tasteless food, but it didn't matter since we were alive and surely something was better than nothing. Policemen and guards even watched over us at night, lest we be attacked by those from the countryside. Then, gradually, in the course of our time there, the cotton factory came to stand on Pakistani soil and we did not belong there any longer. It was a peculiar concept to wrap our heads around, since we were still in Malakwal. Where else could we belong? Rumours flew around the camp that a convoy would come that very night to transport Hindus to the train station. With heavy hearts, we too made the decision to leave and travel across the border to Amritsar, the only city we knew, where my mother's brother was a police officer. We had had no contact with him, but with hope in our hearts that we would somehow find each other there, we packed up our miserly belongings and waited for nightfall.'

'You were all able to leave together and safely, Papa?' asked my mother.

'No, Devinder was not with us. His bank was in Rawalpindi and he would have to make the journey across the border by himself. So, again, under the cover of night, we arrived at Malakwal station, only to find it steeped in chaos. Hundreds and thousands of people from neighbouring towns and villages had thronged the platform, their eyes scanning the track for any sight of a train. Like all others, we too hoped to squeeze into one of its compartments. When a train finally arrived, we succeeded in pushing our way in. Under normal circumstances, these conditions would have been unbearable. We stood so close, almost stuck together, that we could feel the breath of the next person on our necks and faces. But there was relief at having found a spot at all. My mother and sister wept, worried for Devinder. My younger brother was still an infant and my father was trying to devise a future plan.

'For one whole hour, the train did not move an inch. The crowds of people packed into it were silent with anxiety and fear. Then, suddenly, we felt a jerk. The train began to move and there were many audible sighs and screams of relief and joy.'

He paused and took another sip of water. Three pairs of eyes and ears hung on to his every word, but he looked at me, eyes filled with sadness, as if asking whether I wanted to hear any further. I placed my small hand over his and, squeezing his palm, said, '*Phir kya hua?* What happened then?'

'*Phir...*' The word lingered long, waiting on consent. 'Then ... we thought that we were on our way to the border town of Amritsar, that we were going to be safe. We travelled for about an hour and pulled into the main junction of Mandi Bahauddin. Utter silence fell on the train. Then, suddenly, a whole mass of people clambered into the already overcrowded train, trying to get even inches of space for themselves and their families. Loved ones were separated, children flung across to a known face that was in a better position to hold them, women wept. Amidst all this, our family tried hard to remain united. But, again, the train remained at the station much longer than was expected or required. Gradually, the wailing of children, the sobbing of women and the loud voices of men died down to give way to only hushed whispers, starting at one end of the train and making their way towards us. It appeared that a group of men had climbed on and were looking for someone. As they came closer, we heard the hurried, fearful shifting of people begging for their lives, but the men were not interested. They stopped directly in front of our family and I watched the colour drain from my father's face. They were looking for him. Without a single word, they pulled him off the train and on to the platform. We followed, protesting, my mother begging to them to leave her husband, but they paid no heed to her.'

My hand stopped writing.

'I haven't thought about these things for such a long time now...' my grandfather said, and then, after a long pause, continued.

'It turned out that these men were his colleagues from the bank. Because my father had been the manager, no one else quite knew the inner workings, and now they needed him more than ever to train the new staff. Neither he nor we would be allowed to board the train, they threatened, if he did not help. My father protested, my mother screamed, holding on to him, folding her hands in front of the men, my younger siblings cried out of fear, and I—I tried to make sense of what was happening to us. We couldn't understand anything. Then, from the back of the group emerged a man I recognized. His son used to be in my class at school. Swearing on the boy's life, he assured my mother that my father would join us in India in six months—after he had helped the bank through this transition period. If the family wished to stay with him, we could, but he wouldn't guarantee our safety and advised us that it was best we continued our journey across the border.

'What could my father do? There was little choice in the moment. He said that if it were his destiny, he would be reunited with us. He assured my mother that he would find her in six months and bring Devinder with him. And then, just like that, we were separated. My mother, dazed, confused, reluctant, was put back on the train along with her children. In a single day, she was made to leave behind her husband, her son and her home, with no choice of her own. As we pulled out of the station, she stood at the edge of the crowd by the door and watched Mandi Bahauddin fade into the horizon, along with everything of our past lives.'

With a heavy sigh, he stopped recounting and nodded his head. '*Bass*, it was like this, the journey across the border. From then on, our situation seemed impossible to believe and the outcome of our journey difficult to predict. The absence of my father and elder brother meant that I now became the patriarch. In those first few moments of indefinite parting, a paralysis overcame me and I had the strangest feeling of sudden maturation, as if completely leaving behind my childhood and emerging across the border as an adult, disoriented and overwhelmed, needing to earn for and feed my family. Then, hours later, as the train finally pulled into Amritsar station, the sheer gravity of the situation dawned on us. Refugees. We were now refugees. What a dirty word, I had thought to myself even then, in complete disbelief. It felt like the end of our old life. As if we had died or left parts of ourselves in a strange land that was now called Pakistan. How had this happened, how had this become our predicament?'

Even now, sixty-nine years after the Partition, his voice bore the same disbelief he said it had had back then. When the family arrived in Amritsar, no one was waiting for them on the platform. They knew their uncle lived in the city, but with no address and no contact, how would they find him? Tired, broken, hopeless, they made their way across the chaotic station, attempting to build a new life in Independent India.

'When we got off at the station, we were all tired and hungry from the tumultuous journey. None of us had eaten, we had no food, and neither had we had a single drop of water in hours. From a tap at the station, using my father's *lassi* tumbler, we quenched our thirsts and washed our faces. My younger siblings no longer cried but were anxious and scared because of the new and congested surroundings.

'A camp similar to the one in Malakwal had been set up in the city, and we, following the other refugees from the station, made our way to it. All around us, people were talking about who had made it across, who was there, and who had been left behind—or even killed. None of us knew whether we would be reunited with our father or brother, but there was no point in looking back now. The only thing on my mind was leading my family to safety. We had survived and now we had to find a way to thrive, despite any and all circumstances. There was no looking back. Malakwal was now our past.'

As I listened to him talk about survival despite their miserable predicament, I wondered about the ineffable loss that would have grown within him and how desperately he had tried to resist it. Against all forms of remembrance, he had locked Malakwal away into the unreachable, dark depths of memory, refusing to retrieve it until decades later. In that moment, what I felt was something close to a proxy loss. I had had the luxury of education and distance from the Partition to feel a sorrow that my grandfather had not had the time for. While he was caught in the whirlpool of responsibility and need for survival, I had had the fortune of slowing down the past, picking it apart, scrutinizing and understanding the unravelling of events and their consequences.

'I wrote two letters from the camp in Amritsar,' he said, scribbling in the air. 'One to my father and the other to my brother, and sent them to the addresses of their respective banks. I told them our whereabouts, the situation at the camp, and the fact that we would wait for them there no matter how long it took. I doubted whether the letters would reach them, but I had to try.'

'Did you hear back from them?'

'Yes,' he smiled. 'My father wrote, telling us that Devinder was with him and they would meet us in a few months. So, while we were pacified that they were alive and well for the time being, we still didn't know what the future held. Both for them, and for us. The most crucial thing we needed was the very thing we didn't have. Money. Every day I would venture out into Amritsar city along with the other boys in the camp, in search of work. The residents took pity on us, wanted to know about the circumstances of our migration, all we had left behind, what kind of compensation we would receive, but no one wanted to provide us with any substantial work. And being the only earning member of the family, I couldn't deviate from my goal. I had learnt too much about survival since we left Malakwal to allow my pride to be my downfall. As a result, I picked up even menial or low-paying jobs. Then one day I chanced upon a familiar face—our uncle. He put me in his jeep, drove to the camp, picked up the rest of the family and took us to his home. This was the first time in months that my mother seemed truly at ease, crying with happiness. This showed her that if we were together, we could overcome any circumstance. We lived there for over a month. Then, finally, one day my father and Devinder arrived in Amritsar, safe as promised.'

With that, he placed both his hands on the edge of the table and helped himself up, subtly telling me that this chapter too had come to an end, and the rest, as always, would eventually follow.

* * *

'*Dilli*,' he said with finality, 'it was decided that *Dilli* would be our final destination, our home.'

'So you packed up and made your way to yet another new city?' I asked, by now becoming quite used to our afternoon storytelling sessions. I felt like a child again, listening to tales of a faraway time, and through them my grandfather finally began to visit his past. Once he started to remember, it was difficult to stop. It was almost cathartic, for the more he divulged, the less control the past held over him. The pain, displacement, anger and penury were replaced by all that he had learnt as a result: hard work, diligence, modesty and simplicity.

'We were used to being uprooted by then,' he joked. 'My father and brother applied for and were eventually given jobs as compensation for the ones they had lost in Pakistan. We also put in a claim for land in lieu of our property in Malakwal. We didn't know anyone in *Dilli*, but before we left Amritsar, our uncle told us about the many rehabilitation schemes the government had devised for those from across the border. *Dilli* became the city of our dreams, testing our limits, but also rewarding every single honest effort we made towards a better life.'

'If you didn't know anyone, Bade Papa, where did you stay when you arrived?'

'*Arey*, in the camp, where else!' my grandmother responded for him.

'Yes, she's right,' he nodded. '*Beta*, we lived in the camp for years. We have spent many years in different refugee camps. We took the train from Amritsar to *Dilli* early one morning. All the villages looked the same out of the train window and, as we passed by them, I imagined each and every one of them to be Malakwal, to be Qadirabad, to be home. A small word wrapped in a large, familiar landscape that I longed to see again. But soon the village greens gave way to the cityscape and we arrived in *Dilli*.

'If the station at Amritsar had swarmed with refugees, *Dilli* was the equivalent of ten such stations. So many people, huddled in corners, torn blankets covering their thin, rake-like bodies, children crying; the scene was pitiful and instantly we were afraid that we would become one such family.

'But this time we had the address of the camp where our extended family was and so, with only a small iron trunk containing our belongings, brought by my father and Devinder, we made our way to Kingsway Camp.'

'My family used to live there as well,' my grandmother said shyly. 'That is where we met, actually!'

My face broke into a wide smile. Even the most impossible circumstances of life give birth to the most sacred of unions, it seemed. In 1948, my grandparents met and fell in love at Kingsway Camp.

'The camp was much larger than the one in Amritsar, and the area still exists in north Delhi. It's no longer a camp, of course, but just another neighbourhood. *Chaar* lines *thi*, the camp was divided into four lines to accommodate refugees. Whether you could afford your own food rations or not, for instance, determined whether you would be assigned a canvas tent in the Edward and Outram Lines or concrete barracks in the Hudson and Reeds Lines.'[1]

'We lived in barrack #16 on the Hudson Line, and their family,' my grandmother gestured to her husband, 'was first assigned a tent in which they lived for many months, and then finally a more concrete accommodation on Reeds Line. Where Khalsa College is now, that's where the barrack was.'

'Your sister was one of the camp commandants, right?' I asked her.

'Yes, she had managed the camp in Meerut, where we spent our first few months after the Partition. That is why we were automatically assigned concrete housing at Kingsway Camp.'

'Bade Papa, what were the tents like?'

'*Beta*, they were like you see in films, I suppose. They were large tents, but usually shared by two families separated by a cloth curtain in the middle. There you lived, slept, ate, spent your days. Half a tent, just a *purdah* between us and another family … that was our life for many months. We received ration from the camp that my mother cooked for us in the same utensils that she had brought. That first night we located many of our relatives in the camp—Uncle Ram Lal and a few of my mother's aunts. After so many months of hardship, at last we experienced joy and the pleasure of seeing our parents laugh and smile freely. Together we shared a simple meal of roti and raw onion; that was all we could spare but we enjoyed it like a feast![2] You see, hunger really is in the mind, not in the body and, sadly, we had trained our minds to survive on even the most meagre of sustenance. It was not the most comfortable life, but with my father and brother finally by our side again, it felt as close to home as it could be. Devinder and I thought alike—we were just two years apart in age as well—and through our shared determination to find our bearings in this new city, we grew closer and stronger.'

'Did you ever think about life back in Malakwal?'

'There was no time to … and there was no use brooding over what could never be recovered.'

From makeshift stoves over an open fire outside their tent, my great-grandmother moved to using the camp's communal kitchen. Their relations, who had been there for months, helped them familiarize themselves with the camp—the shared latrines, ration and announcement systems—and, most importantly, guided them to find employment. An enterprising group of cousins told the brothers that they had found a way of making eight to ten rupees a day, a large and handsome sum at the time.

'Early in the morning, we ventured out with our cousins to the railway station, where we made our way to the open sheds where the trains were parked overnight for routine maintenance. Most of us boarded the empty carriages, two or three boys per compartment, and then stretched ourselves on the seats and waited. A few of us remained on the platform.' A mischievous grin spread over my grandfather's face. 'In those days, second-class seats couldn't be reserved and were sold on a first-come-first-served basis. Our cousins on the platform would secure offers for the seats we kept warm and sold them for the princely sum of five rupees! On the very first day, Devinder and I brought home an unthinkable sum of 16 rupees!'

His eyes shone with wonder, and for a moment it felt like he had gone back to his youth. Sixteen rupees, I made a mental note, what could 16 rupees buy me now? Not much, certainly no food fit to feed a whole family, but in those days, seven decades ago, it was more than enough.

'There was a free bus ride from the city to the camp, but that day we were so full of energy that we walked all the way, hoping to prolong the feeling of anticipation and pride when handing over our first day's earnings to our mother. But those last few kilometres from the gate of the camp to our tent, we could hardly contain ourselves and we ran, arriving breathless and elated. That night, in celebration of our first earnings, our mother, in addition to the daily staples of dal and roti, prepared a plateful of vegetables! It was still not the kind of special food we would have had in the past, but in those circumstances it felt like we were dining in style.'

Thus began their routine of life in the camp. True to their entrepreneurial Punjabi nature, the family never looked back and adapted to their new environment with a learned ease. The brothers worked hard, less for the sake of wealth and more to keep busy and to rebuild the family name. Along with comfort and security, the migration had also led them to lose hard-earned respect and credibility, and they were determined to earn that back. Always on the lookout for new opportunities, they worked delivering items on bullock carts, rented out rickshaws, and continued the reservation of train seats. It took many years before Kingsway Camp finally came to be known as their home.

'For me, yes,' my grandmother said softly when I asked whether it was love at first sight. 'For Balraj-ji, I don't know!' she said, looking at him. 'We would meet in the camp after work. For a while we were both volunteering at a social service camp and so we would meet there too. But we were not like the couples of today. Those were the days of courtship, we would just look at each other from afar—no movies, no dinners—that was not the norm.'

'And books?' I asked, referring to the family business. 'How did you come to work with books?'

He laughed. 'That is another story, for another day! So many questions! Are you not tired of listening to these old stories?'

Not at all, I wanted to say, not at all. The stories of his struggle infused my heart with a determination never to take a single moment for granted. His resolute single-mindedness to succeed and his need to continually look forward and have no regrets now inspired me to become the best possible version of myself. This is why I had needed to know. But I didn't say any of that. All I did was wait for tomorrow.

That night, unable to fall asleep, I lay awake imagining my great-grandmother's screams when they dragged her husband off the train. Sliding out of bed, I quietly walked downstairs to the dining table and picked up the *lassi* tumbler with both hands, grazing my thumbs over its surface. I brought the cool metal to my lips as though drinking from it and then placed its wide, open mouth against my ear, as one would a shell. Like the sounds of the ocean, what kissed my ear was the dull echo of air stuck in a vacuum. Closing my eyes and holding my breath, I listened more carefully to the low, eerie sound of a draft moving within a tunnel with no opening. A ghostly reverberation, impossible to ignore and difficult to un-hear, as if in a train compartment with no open windows, the hovering breaths of passengers, stagnant and recycled. As the small hair on the back of my neck stood up in unease, I let out my breath loudly, placed the tumbler down and scrambled through the dark house back into bed.

* * *

The next day, at what I knew would be the last lunch wholly dedicated to his story, my grandfather finally talked about bookselling.

'In 1950, we applied for and acquired a tender for printing and distributing government publications. A small shop was allotted to us in Lajpath Rai market opposite the Red Fort, which still exists today by the name of Bahri Brothers. My father sat there full time, Devinder came in the evenings after his work at the bank and I stopped in after work at the social service camp. Then I was offered a job selling pens at a stationery shop owned by a small-time politician in Chandni Chowk. Many months passed like this and in 1953 I heard of shops being allotted to refugees from the NWFP [North-West Frontier Province] in a newly constructed area called Khan Market, established in 1951 and named after Khan Abdul Jabbar Khan, the brother of Frontier Gandhi.[3] But I had neither the capital nor the experience to own a shop of my own and so I approached my employer to help. Impressed with my dedication and hard work during my time with him, he agreed to help me acquire a shop in the refugee market.'

'What was Khan Market like at the time?' I asked, keeping in mind the reputation of the infamous U-shaped market in the heart of New Delhi, one of the most upscale and expensive pieces of real estate in South Asia today.

'Oh, *beta*, the market was very small then,' he laughed. 'Modest in character, with only a few stores—two vegetable sellers, a grocer, a chemist, a cycle shop, two [sweet shops], a store for household items, an ice cream parlour, banks and two bookstores. If you take away the exorbitantly expensive exteriors of today, what will you find? At its core is still the humility and hard work of the refugees who originally populated it.'

Recognizing my grandfather's drive to establish his own business, his mother gave him a single gold bangle, which he used to pay the fee of Rs 200 to acquire the shop, one-third its size today. Along with that, and a handsome contribution of Rs 800 from another friend, Bahrisons became a reality camouflaged as an empty shop in Khan Market. Gradually my grandfather worked his way into bookselling, acquiring knowledge, directly and on the job, of a trade he knew nothing about. A friend of the family's, Prem Sagar, who owned Lakshmi Books on Janpath, was instrumental in helping my grandfather set up his collection.

'I knew nothing of books,' he stressed, smiling. 'I was a student of maths in Pakistan and was great at *hisaab*, calculation! But in the last few years, I had learnt plenty about survival and making the best of any circumstance. It was too big a shop to accommodate just a counter of fountain pens, and so when Prem Sagar offered to help me learn about books, I readily agreed. Bit by bit, I slowly understood the trade, people's reading habits and literary needs, and the business grew.'

'Every day,' my grandmother said, her index finger held up, making a point, 'every day Balraj-ji would sit at the counter with a notepad and pen. It's true he knew nothing of books, but I have seen him learn and absorb the knowledge from those around him. If a customer asked for a book he did not have, he would note down the title and make sure to have it the next day. He is very hardworking,' she beamed at him. 'The same qualities that he brought with him on that journey from Pakistan—determination, purposefulness and honesty—he has put into his work.'

'*Bass, bass*, Madam-ji,' he said to her, the colour rising in his cheeks, 'enough. *Beta*, the truth is, we have seen many hardships, much violence and upheaval. Life has not been easy, but it is never supposed to be. At every step, life has challenged us, demanded more from us. For so many years we lived in Kingsway Camp as refugees. For so many years, my mother cooked in these same *peetal bartan* before we could buy new utensils. For so many years, we saved every single anna to be able to afford our own house, our own transport, our own shop. For so many days in the beginning, we didn't have any money to our name...'

I had heard this line in passing many times, but only now did I grasp the heaviness of the past and the heartbreak that lay within. His deep voice was unnaturally hoarse with emotion. When he looked at me, the tears of the past shone in his eyes. Laughing sadly, he said, 'I told you not to revisit the times gone by, but now it is all before my eyes. Malakwal, Qadirabad, the cotton factory, the police station, Kingsway Camp. I know that it will never leave me, but there is no point in being consumed by the past.

'Honestly speaking, the comfort and life we achieved in *Dilli* could never have been found there. Never. Independence forced us to flee, made us refugees, but *Dilli* forced us to stand up on our feet. We had no choice. We have eaten the *anaaj*, the ration of refugees, we have endured the hardship married to that label, and we have risen above it. *Dilli* is responsible for that. It has moulded us into the people, the family, the business we are today. Never forget that in the blood of independent *Dilli* flow the unending and tireless sacrifices made by the refugees who poured into its landscape during the Partition. We have built this city, and it has built us.'

5

STONES FROM MY SOIL

THE *MAANG-TIKKA* OF BHAG MALHOTRA

'ASK ME QUICKLY BEFORE I forget,' she said to me as I went about setting up my recorder and camera.

I looked up, surprised by the urgency of her tone. There was little I knew about my grandmother's history, apart from the fact that she was born in a city now across the border. Except for that lone memory, brought on mostly by the elegant portrait of her mother hanging on the wall in her room, Bhag Malhotra never spoke of the tragedy that had caused her family to migrate to Delhi. So the alarm with which she uttered these words made me consider that perhaps age had caused the wall she had built around her history to slowly crumble away. Something had changed, something had stirred in her. Maybe she feared that if the past didn't surface now, it would fade into oblivion forever. Or maybe the reason she had never opened up before was simply that she had never been asked.

'Are you ready?' I smiled at her unexpected eagerness.

She nodded, sitting up and straightening her sweater as I turned on the recorder.

'All right, just begin whenever you want to.'

'But from *where* do I begin?' she asked. 'What about my life do you want to know?'

I thought for a moment and said, 'Begin from where you think is important.'

She hesitated and then, as if she had rehearsed this narration many times over, her diffidence fell away and she began in a composed voice. 'I never knew my father. He died when I was

115

very young. I don't remember the year and I never bothered to ask anyone either...' I was startled by this choice of beginning, having expected her to be a more conventional storyteller and to start with her birth. But the stories of one's past, I suppose, often tumble out of the unlikeliest of places, and so I welcomed this unusual starting point.

'His death left my mother all alone with six young mouths to feed,' she continued. 'She was married at twelve and widowed at barely twenty-five or twenty-six. We were five sisters,' she said, counting the names on her fingers, 'Kaushalya, Sumitra, Shakuntala, me and Dharam, and one brother, Madan Mohan. I think Dharam must have been just six months old when our father passed away.'

From the large plastic box of medicines on her bedside table, she took out an ivory envelope, from which she retrieved an aged, sepia photograph. Slowly and preciously, she placed it on the bed. Her father, separated too early from his family, looked up at me. With smooth skin and a dark and dense complexion, he was the original bearer of the sharp features passed down to my grandmother. He sat imposingly, dressed in a Western coat and white turban.

Tracing her fingers along the edges of the photograph, she shook her head from side to side. 'When I look at this photograph, I think to myself, yes this is what he was like. This was his face, this was the colour of his skin, these were his hands, this is how he wore his turban, this is the coat he owned. But from memory, I don't remember anything about him.'

'Where was this?'

And then it began. Gradually, with the utmost care, each solid layer that had congealed with the passing of years was pulled back to reveal a childhood I could never have imagined.

'A city by a river, a city known for its *khajoor* [dates], and *langra* mangoes! I was born in Muryali in the North-West Frontier Province in 1932 into a family of landlords. My father, Hari Chand, was the youngest of four brothers, and when he was alive he worked in Peshawar. One of his brothers, Diwan Chand, had gone abroad to a place near Iran to study horticulture and had brought back several instruments and new agricultural techniques, which he used on our lands. There used to be no water in the village, so he had wells dug, tilled the land and upgraded technology. From what I remember, the family business mostly related to land. We were *zamindars*. And on one end of that *zameen*, that land, stood our ancestral house, built and divided in such a way that each of the brothers could actually live with his family separately.'

'You remember the house—what it looked like?' I asked.

'Ah yes, of course I do, I remember it well. We were wealthy in Muryali, my child. We came from an old family called the Gulyanis. Our *haveli* was a very strong building—large, with long corridors and spacious rooms. There were separate quarters for women where no men were allowed. Like a *zenana*. Even if the women had to buy something, merchants would come home and display their wares. And the women would take care to keep their faces and heads covered completely, as was customary. In the main sitting area—and this I remember distinctly—there was a large *purdah*, a beautiful thick curtain that divided the room, and all the women sat behind it.'

As she said this, her hands gracefully cut through the air, drawing an imaginary curtain.

'Now the *haveli* has been converted into the local college and hostel, so you can imagine how large it was at one point. My cousin, Lakshman Bir, the son of my eldest uncle, visited Pakistan many years ago and went back to the house. He was amazed to see that all the living quarters had been converted into either classrooms or hostel rooms. Oh, the family owned a lot of land back then,' she said matter-of-factly. 'There were wide open fields with cows and buffaloes and hens. We lived in that house until our father died ... everything changed after that.

'We heard that he was poisoned and killed by his brothers because of a property dispute. After his death, we might as well have been foreigners in that *haveli*—isolated in our rooms, cut off from most family matters. My mother was refused our share of land—or rather what was my father's, and ours by extension. In those days only sons could inherit family property, and because my brother was so young at the time, my uncle became the legal guardian of our share, though in reality he started selling off the land little by little. But my mother was adamant to fight for what was ours and began a court case on the matter. "I want our share, we need it," she would say. "I have children to feed."

'For months she made frequent trips to the court. But the time, energy and resources the case required soon made her realize that there was nothing the family would do for her. She was not educated enough to work anywhere, nor were any of us children old enough to earn, so our financial situation worsened each day. Her mother-in-law, my *dadi*, was an educated woman, a nurse who treated the village children. She was close to my mother and understood her plight, but in those days a woman's voice was hardly heard in a house full of men. What I remember about my *dadi*, though, is that she was blind. It was said that after my father's death, she cried herself to blindness, confined forever in a self-imposed darkness.'

She sighed deeply and her shoulders slumped forward. As I watched her carefully return the aged photograph to its envelope, I felt a sharp pang of guilt for not knowing her past.

'Life had become very difficult for us in that house,' she continued. 'But I think as soon as my mother realized that there was really nothing her late husband's family would give her or her children, she took matters into her own hands. Having tasted the greed and bitterness of familial relationships first hand, she vowed that none of us would ever find ourselves in such a situation. She moved us out of the stifling environment of the ancestral *haveli* and into my grandmother's home in D.I. Khan city, where we continued our education. In fact, it became her absolute priority, and she made no distinction between girls and boys. We were all the same for her and we all had to be educated. She made sure that we would stand on our own feet, never rely on anyone. At the age of eight, I was walking two miles to school and back every day!

'The truth is,' she said, as a gradual smile spread across her lips, 'when she put her mind to it, my mother, she could do anything, you know. She empowered us all, she was powerful.'

'She was powerful,' I repeated, believing it.

'Yes, and then, on my grandmother's insistence, she left us children in her care and went to Lahore to complete her own education by doing a teacher training course. With that certification, she began teaching at a government school in D.I. Khan and life regained some of its normalcy. We were able to move out of our grandmother's house and into our own rented accommodation, where we lived for about eight years until...' Her voice trailed off.

Mentally calculating the year, I completed her sentence. 'Until the Partition.'

Batwara, she called it. Separation.

* * *

She pursed her lips, crossing both arms tightly over her chest, as if these small gestures would act as a barricade, preventing her story from spilling out against her will. But as I locked eyes with her, her body softened and she reached out for my hand. 'Sometimes I think that the story of my father's family imbues the memory of my birthplace with bitterness. But then I realize that those are two different things. No matter how much we suffered in that *haveli*, it has not been able to affect the affinity I feel for the place I come from.

'Truth be told, for us, the freedom movement began in 1942, along with communal riots. D.I. Khan had always been predominantly Muslim, and small fights would break out sporadically. But this time the violence continued right until 1947, which is when it became clear that we were going to be on the wrong side of the new border. In the years between 1942 and 1947, we saw ... we saw what was happening to the Hindu families around us. Many were not as lucky as we were to escape when we did.'

She paused.

'I think it was the beginning of '47, the early months, and we could hear some people proclaim on the streets, "*Iss saal, khoon ki holi khelenege*, this year we will play Holi with blood."[1] This was the year of Independence, the year that changed everything, and whether it was violence or intolerance, it was the year that saw the worst side of humanity. We were not allowed to leave the house except to go to school, and even then our Muslim helpers would always accompany us. They were loyal to us till the very end, and that I will never forget. Sometimes, on our way back from school, some of the villagers would call out to them, "Where are you going with these *kafir* children?" *Kafir*, that word stung us even then. We had lived among them all our lives and now suddenly we were *kafirs*!'

'*Kafir*?' I asked, having never heard the word before.

She had begun our conversation in Hindi, but as we ventured deeper into the past, her speech became abundantly peppered with Urdu; the words easy to distinguish, the transition effortless and natural. Their texture was smoother, more poetic, and she enunciated them with natural intention and comfort, as though the language was second nature to her.

'*Kafir*, it is an old Urdu word, which means non-believer. That's what they called us. And if it weren't for our helpers, I don't think we would have stayed alive. They were Pathans, and the most exceptional virtue of Pathans is that they will always remain loyal.[2] During the long nights of flaring savagery in the weeks leading up to Independence, they would stand guard on the roof. They watched over us when the riots eventually became uncontrollable, and then in the darkness of night brought us to a refugee camp for Hindu families. But before we go any further, I must tell you that in our community girls were given training of some kind to protect themselves during the riots.'

'What do you mean?' I asked, intrigued.

'One,' she said, holding up her index finger and looking straight at me, 'we were told to keep *mirchi* powder on us at all times and to fling it into the eyes of our assailant. Oh yes, it's very spicy chilli, so it stings!'

Her eyes danced.

'And two, to keep a small knife or blade to use either on our attacker or on ourselves. Now, this is before I was born, but what I have heard is that during the Raj it was normal for every house to keep swords or guns. Because we were *zamindars* who had to protect the land, our house in Muryali had both. Only later, when they were banned or one had to get a licence, did we have our swords melted down to create knives of different kinds. Some were made for the kitchen and a few small ones for the women of the house. We would hide them in our pockets and hope that a time would never come when we would have to use them … Actually, I think I might still have mine in a drawer somewhere…'

She got up and hobbled to the kitchen, from where I heard sounds of drawers being opened and closed, followed by the creaking of a cupboard door. Smiling, she returned to the room five minutes later and presented me with a small blunt knife. I stared at it, my mouth half open, amazed that my grandmother had kept it all these years. Something that had been so vital for her safety now sat in my palm, cold to the touch and seemingly out of context.

The first thing I noticed was that it was foldable, and when opened and laid flat, it didn't sit straight. The blade was completely swallowed by rust. The once-sharp edge was thinner on one end. On the other was a deeply engraved line and, curiously, the letters D-O-G. The handle was made of ivory, what she called *haathi daant*, literally 'teeth of the elephant'. Over the years the ivory had been scratched and had yellowed, and the bottom of one side had chipped, revealing the real colour beneath.

'This is made from really old *loha*, from the iron of those swords.' She sounded impressed herself.

'What do you use it for now?' I asked.

She laughed. 'When I go for morning walks, I take it with me so I can cut the leaves off the aloe vera plant.'

I stared at her, struck by the knife's fall from grace. How could something once used to protect one's honour at the most crucial moment of the subcontinent's modern history be reduced to such a mundane existence? It was almost unfair, I thought to myself, as I brushed my fingers along its smooth, once-grand surface. A sadness settled on me as I thought about what the innocuous knife stood for. This was the way of the world: all things have a time and place in our lives; they occupy exactly that period and purpose for which they are created. After that they may continue to live, if at all, in the shadow of their once-indispensable existence, appropriated for whatever use seems fit.

With a heavy heart, still caressing the knife's handle, I visualized my grandmother slipping it into her bag or pocket every day and immediately feeling a sense of safety. In that moment, the rusty old knife came back to life in all its former glory in my mind's eye.

'In those days of riots, we were told that it was better to sacrifice yourself than have your character tarnished—if it ever came to that,' she said with finality. '*Beta*, I want to explain this to you but I cannot find the right words.' She swallowed hard and audibly. 'The kind of things we were told to do to protect our reputation, the kind of things women did to protect themselves in those days ... those days were most unfortunate for women. Many jumped into wells, many were killed or wounded, their breasts were cut off and they were left to bleed to death, some were dragged away and abducted, forced to marry or convert ... too many acts of savage violence against women. *Izzat*, my child, honour. Always protect your *izzat*, no matter what. That is what we were taught.'

Her voice was firm and her eyes bore into mine unflinchingly. Drawing a sharp breath, I tore my gaze away. Holding my face in my palms, I carefully considered what she had said. There was a hunger that grew amidst the communal riots, and it was appalling to hear how gender violence seemed to satiate it to an extent.

'How long did you live at the refugee camp in D.I. Khan?' I asked, trying to rid myself of the images her memories had conjured up in my mind.

'A few weeks at least, if I'm not mistaken. We continued our schooling from there itself, and in May 1947 my brother and I took our final exams. Then, because we were old enough to travel alone, we left for *Dilli*, leaving our mother and two sisters behind. Our eldest sister was married and already living there, and so our mother thought it was best for us to reach *Dilli* as soon as possible. It took us two days and two nights by train from the Frontier.

'By August, though, the violence had spread significantly and my mother decided it was time for her to leave too. The main train station was in Darya Khan and no roads connected it to D.I. Khan. The Sindh river flowed between them, and my mother and two sisters crossed it using a small boat. Then they took a carriage to the train station and finally a train to Lahore. From there they picked up my third sister, who was studying medicine at Sir Ganga Ram Hospital, and arrived in *Dilli* on 14 August. We were all safe because we came early, I think. We didn't even know about the Partition trains with mutilated dead bodies and the terrible circumstances under which people came during and immediately after Independence.

'My eldest sister and her family lived in a two-bedroom flat in the Karol Bagh neighbourhood, and we had hoped to stay with her, at least in the beginning until we found our bearings. But their extended family had also arrived from across the border, and so space was tight. Two days after we arrived, my mother understood that they considered us a burden. After all, my brother and I had been living there for a few months already, and now there were four additional mouths to feed. A proud single mother, she was never one to overstay her welcome. She immediately packed up whatever luggage we had and marched us out of the house.'

'Did you understand what was happening, why you were leaving again so soon?'

'We talked amongst ourselves, of course. But we were just children. We would follow our mother anywhere, we trusted her,' she said with determination.

I felt my heart go out to my great-grandmother, amazed at the courage she must have had even to consider taking such a step. Delhi was practically a foreign land for her—she had never before ventured beyond Lahore, which now lay across the border. For a moment I considered how anxious she must have been not to have a shelter for herself and her children in this new place they had hoped to call home. And then, imagining a woman so proud and resilient, determined not to be a burden on anyone even in such a time of need, I felt pride in her ability to find strength in a moment when it seemed to have all but dissipated.

'So you were, in a way, homeless once again,' I said softly. 'First you left your house in Muryali, then the one in D.I. Khan, and then your sister's home in Delhi. Was it ever confusing for you and your siblings? Where did you go?'

She nodded. 'It felt strange. Of course it did. It was so difficult to leave our house in the Frontier. In the haste with which we had fled, it was as though we had left some part of ourselves behind. So much of us belonged there; so much of us remained there. Here we had nothing, we came with nothing. You could say we were like beggars.' Her face tightened and became stony. 'We had no clothes to wear, no place to sleep at night, no sheet or blanket to sleep in, no utensils to cook with and no money even to drink a cup of tea. We had nothing to our name.'

To describe their predicament to me, she used the Urdu word *mohtaj*—one heavy with shame and remorse that its English counterpart, dependent, is unable to capture. Even the way my grandmother spat it out in her polished Urdu tongue conveyed the disgrace that her fiercely proud and independent mother must have felt in those first few months. What they had experienced at the time was far more than dependency; it was pitiful what the family had suddenly been subjected to, reducing them to the lowest form of helplessness.

'When our mother walked us out of that Karol Bagh house on 16 August 1947 and took us to Old Delhi station, it was to take the train back to the Frontier. My mother had decided that if this was how we were to survive in India, without aid or respect, then it was better to just go back. All we had with us was one small bag and the clothes that we were wearing. I remember our mother standing in front of us on the platform, her body covered with a long shawl, trying to figure out what to do. That was the first time we saw a train full of dead bodies arriving at the platform. We were told it wasn't the first such train to have come from across the border, and that trains from this side too had met the same fate going across. I was sixteen years old and I remember distinctly that I had never been gripped with as much fear as I had that day. That grotesque sight was far worse than the riots we had witnessed in D.I. Khan. I remember wanting to look away as the bodies were removed from the compartments, but being unable to do so. One by one, mutilated and butchered, stained bright crimson, the corpses were piled up on the platform as the compartments of the train were washed down. But now, maybe for the very first time after all these long years, I find myself wondering whether a station across the border had a similar pile of dead bodies too. *Bass*, these were the circumstances of that time.

'We stood there, staring at the train, knowing full well that if we boarded it, it would most likely lead us to our deaths. That's what everyone was saying around us, begging my mother to think about the four young children who stood behind her. The stationmaster even took off his turban and placed it at her feet—a mark that he was willing to humiliate himself if only it would convince her to change her mind. But that didn't matter to her. Even if we died, it would be on our own soil. Dying in Pakistan was much better than dying in this unfamiliar, foreign place. Even as children we knew that; she made sure we knew that—the importance of one's soil.'

'After Pakistan was created, did you still think of it as home?' I asked. 'Oh yes, it was the same land, only now it had a new name,' she said with a sense of certainty. 'I say that even now. It was where I was born. The place you come from moulds you into the person you become. Remember that. You must never forget where you came from, because a part of that soil stays with you forever.'

She paused to let me absorb what she had said, something she believed in all her life.

'Much of what I grew up to be,' she continued with the same conviction, 'I owe to the land that is now Pakistan. The life, the respect, the *rutwa*—the importance, the status—that we had over there were lost when we came to India. Though it's true that coming here gave us the kind of freedom we probably wouldn't have had back in the Frontier, in order to gain that freedom we were pushed to our limits. We struggled to stand on our own two feet but we were stronger for it, because it taught us the meaning of resilience. It was as though we had started life for the first time all over again.'

She smiled sadly.

'So what happened that day at the station? Did you get on a train back to the Frontier?' I asked.

'Thankfully not,' she said. 'By a stroke of luck we encountered a man who was waiting at the station for refugees from the Frontier with nowhere to go in India.[3] He took us to Meerut, where we stayed for seven months at a refugee camp. Because she was educated, he gave my elder sister work as the camp commandant and provided the family with a means to live. Soon, our mother got a call from Delhi for a job as a teacher in a government school, and so we packed our bags yet again and followed her to the capital.'

'What was her name?' I asked.

'Lajvanti,' she said with pride. *Laaj*—*izzat*, honour. It made sense. 'Slowly we all learned to stand on our feet in Delhi. The city that had dealt us a bitter rejection only months earlier now held the promise of a future. My sister was transferred to Kingsway Camp as the camp commandant, and we were given housing in barrack #16. We lived there for years. The camp was exactly how you would imagine it, with refugees pouring in every day. It was one of the largest camps set up for rehabilitation and consisted of tents, barracks and small flats. We were lucky to get housing big enough for us all because of my sister's job. Soon, my mother too began work, as a teacher. Since I had been educated till grade ten, I started teaching a course in adult education in the camp itself. My younger siblings went to college. In those initial few months, my mother and elder sisters were our real pillars of support. To be honest, it's because of them that we never felt the absence of a father figure.'

There was a long pause and I knew she was thinking of them, of all the strong women around her who had shaped her—and me in turn.

'What was she like, your mother?' I asked.

'Well, you can see what she was like,' she said, pointing to her photograph on the wall. It showed a seated woman in her late thirties, dressed all in white, her dupatta covering her head. Her posture and expression made her look like a stern woman of principles, but her eyes gave her away. They were round, soft and compassionate. She was truly beautiful, with skin strikingly fair and features that were defined and delicate.

'Are you at all like her?' I asked, reaching out to touch the photograph. She laughed as if she had found my suggestion absurd.

'There was no one like her. No one can ever be like her. I can't even begin to fathom the kind of strength she had, to have raised us all at such a young age by herself.'

* * *

My grandmother smiled broadly like a child and closed her eyes, cupping her face in her palms. Then, her eyes flew open and, still smiling, she said, 'I showed you the knife. But I almost forgot that my mother brought one other thing with her all the way from the

Frontier. It was the only thing she made sure to take and now it is with me. But you have seen it already … many times.'

I instinctively sat up straight and braced myself. She got up from the bed, unlocked the cupboard and rummaged in the back for a while. From under a pile of clothes she unearthed a small plastic box and placed it ceremoniously on the bed. Inside it were thin layers of cotton, and within those layers, as if seated on a soft bed, was the most beautiful ornament I had ever seen. My eyes lit up and I smiled. I did know this piece of jewellery; I had even worn it before, completely smitten by its beauty. But I had no idea it was such a special heirloom.

It was a large pendant with a ruby flower at its centre. Leaves and branches set in gold formed a web around it, with a round border enclosing the ornament. It was a spectacle of blue stone, red ruby, dull garnet, dusty gold, pearl and diamond. It was handmade; one could tell that from its subtle imperfections.

She held it up to her forehead, placed it in the neat middle parting of her hair, and said, 'This was once a *maang-tikka*, something to be worn on the head. These stones are peculiar to the Frontier and are found only in that region. My mother received it as a wedding gift from her mother-in-law, and I believe it had been in my father's family for quite a while before that.'

She tried to calculate mentally how old the precious jewel was. 'My mother was married in 1919 when she was twelve years old. If it had been in the family even before that, I would say that it is close to or maybe even more than a hundred years old! But from what I remember, she never wore it after her wedding ceremony—just looked at it from time to time. Later, she converted it into a necklace, feeling it was too heavy to be worn on the head.

'When she left Pakistan, though, she made sure to bring it, because she thought she could sell it and get some money to raise and educate us. I remember her telling us how she had tied it within the folds of her clothes for fear of being robbed on the way to Delhi. It was precious; it would have brought us a hefty sum even at that time. But I don't think she could ever have parted with it. This is the only thing that reminded her of that house in Muryali, of her in-laws, of the bonds of marriage. Though they had rejected her, I don't think she had the heart to sever those ties. There was a sanctity to those relationships she wasn't ready to abandon. And, in a way, this piece of jewellery was the only thing that remained of her land as well; the stones were from its soil. It was born there, just like her.'

A decorative gold rope chain held it at the centre as I picked up the pendant and held it to my grandmother's neck. I let my fingers linger on its surface, noticing its brilliance against her soft wrinkled skin. The dusky brown of her neck magnified the vibrancy of the stones as the ornament sat heavily between her collarbones.

'Like my mother, I too wore it at my wedding, but of course as a necklace. She had shown it to me when I was a child and I had loved it, so she gave it to me as a wedding present.' She pointed to a framed black-and-white photo on the wall. It showed my grandmother in side profile, smiling on her wedding day, and round her neck was the beautiful ornament.

'Today is the second time I've ever worn it,' she said, clasping the necklace shut. This was an object that had survived the transitions of time, circumstance and geography. It brought them closer somehow, mother and daughter, and a part of my great-grandmother remained in it. I found myself wishing that I had met her, that I had known her for myself. But somehow, because I had worn the necklace too, it made me feel as though I was a part of someone I had never known.

Carefully, I took the necklace off her and put it back into its box, between the layers of cotton.

'No, no, no! Not like this, *beta*.' She took it from me and began placing the necklace back into the folds of its soft bed in an almost ritualistic way. 'She wouldn't have done it like this. She would have…' I said nothing, quietly observing the nuances of this relationship she shared with her mother. In that moment, I saw in her a keenness to be one with her mother. In some ways it amazed me that she felt this way, because, ever since I was a child, I had felt the same way about her. For as long as I could remember, I had wished for a part of her to somehow make its way down the generations and find its place in me. I would admire each fold of her soft skin, each wisp of silver hair that escaped the bun on her head, each wrinkle that decorated her arms, wishing that one day I too would be this graceful. That she would always live in me.

With the necklace now locked up safely again, she sat tucked within the folds of her blanket. Her eyes were far away, her smile slowly fading into sadness, and I could tell that she was thinking of her mother. Of all the siblings, she was the one closest to her, and I could see so much of Lajvanti in her just then. I turned off my recorder and watched her as she sat in the warm yellow light, caressing the side of her teacup, lost in thoughts that had for decades been banished to the remotest recesses of her memory.

6

STITCHES AND SECRETS

THE *BAGH* OF HANSLA CHOWDHARY

I SAT AT THE EDGE of my seat, surveying the wad of rolled-up newspaper in her lap. Our eyes met and she began to unroll it slowly. With inherent familiarity, her nimble fingers loosened the jute strings at either end. Taking the string between the thumb and forefinger of her right hand, in a single sweeping gesture she untied the bundle and laid it on the couch beside her. Nestled in the crumpled newsprint sat a thick red bundle, similar in shape to a small log, surrounded by a bed of black peppercorns.

'Somehow, the ink from the paper repels termites and other insects. Same for the peppercorns,' Hansla Chowdhary said knowingly. 'I don't know how true that is, but it's what my grandmother used to do and the habit has found its way into me. This is called a *bagh* and is much larger in size than a scarf or a dupatta.'

I reached out slowly for the bundle. The outside was red fabric, with the threads and seams clearly visible. My fingers moved unevenly across the rough surface and found two kinds of stitches—a wide tack made with several threads, which bound sections of the base fabric together, and a finer, more delicate stitch stippling the entire surface in angular diamond shapes. The threads of both stitches were yellow—the dull yellow of winter sunshine, the muted yellow of desert sand. 'This base fabric is usually made with raw cotton called *khaddar*, or *khadi*, woven on a homemade wooden loom. But it's quite versatile, cool in the summer, warm in the winter, and is often starched to give it a stiffer feel. It can afford to be rough and raw, as it is never meant to be seen or displayed to anyone but the wearer.' Her fingers grazed the rough brick-red surface. 'But the skeleton is always the most important part of anything, isn't it? These threads you see on the *khadi* simply demarcate the outline of the pattern, but I like to think of them as narrations of how each stitch will eventually be embedded into the fabric.'

Her voice was dreamy, the smile on her face matching the one in her eyes and, before I knew it, her hands lifted the bundle and unfurled it. Like a magician, her fingers deftly grasped opposite corners of the delicate heirloom. As I watched the fabric settle gently onto the sofa, her hands now supporting it from beneath, its corners spilling over onto me, I was reminded immediately of the Kashmiri shawl-*wallas* who visited our house each winter to sell their wares. Their fingers too would effortlessly find the corners of heavily embroidered textile and, like whirling dervishes, they would fling them through the air and onto our shoulders: exquisite shawls that would have taken months to meticulously create.

'Now this,' she said as her voice filled with pride, 'this is the front!' The coarse red had disappeared to the bottom to reveal the regal golden outside. The garment was indeed much larger than a scarf, comparable to a full-size shawl. 'This was made by my maternal great-grandmother, my *nani*'s mother, in Rawalpindi, which is now in Pakistan. It was brought to Delhi by my *nani* in 1947, when they migrated across during the Partition.'

Compared to the dense maroon inside, the outside of the *bagh* bore a feeling of luminescence. Threads of gold, canary yellow, orange and white embellished its surface.

'The handiwork done on this piece is called *phulkari* and is a traditional embroidery technique from the Punjab region. *Phulkari*…'—her tongue jumped across the 'oo', elongating the 'aa' and 'ee'—'*phulkari* means flower work, *phul* meaning flower and *kari* meaning craft in Punjabi. I've been told that the earliest mention of the word *phulkari* can be found in the love story of Heer–Ranjha, written by Waris Shah, where Heer wears many outfits with such embroidery.[1] It depicts the blossoming of flowers, the lightness, the spring. A piece this large is called a *bagh*, and the word translates to garden. These are densely embroidered pieces in which the base cloth is no longer visible. A garden of various varieties of flora covers the entire body. Do you feel its heaviness? That is the weight of all the embroidery.'

My hands slipped under it, lifting it to feel the heaviness.

'They were considered an auspicious item of clothing, ancient in their form and sacred in the time it took to create them. The fabric would transform—blossom—from a piece of simple raw *khadi* to a heavily embellished, silken tapestry, and as such it was made for the occasion of one's blossoming, like a wedding or the birth of a child. So often, in the olden days, all the women of the family would get together to weave such a piece to include in the trousseau of a young bride. If you think about it, it can be considered a means of socializing, for when these women got together, they would talk and share cups of chai and stitch the fabric. Special songs were sung—songs of marriage, the solemn sadness of having to part with one's daughter, or songs of happiness at the birth of children, the flowering of a womb—and the energy from these would flow subliminally into the work. *Phulkari* became a language of the women, decorative and beautiful, and every stitch appeared on the fabric as a rendition of that private dialect.'

A *bagh*, I mused, a garden of good wishes on the cusp of a new life that would get sewn into the cloth each time a needle pierced through the rough *khadi*. Goosebumps appeared on my arms as I thought of the secrets that women poured into the objects of their affection.

'This piece, however, was made singlehandedly by my great-grandmother and she finished it over the course of three or four years, working on it in between household chores. After she gave it to my *nani*, it was used mostly as a throw over the sofa—just something decorative. But many years have passed since it was completed in 1931, and now it is one of my most prized possessions. An antique.'

'Tell me about her, the maker of this *bagh*.'

'Well, I only met her when I was very young. But I do have a picture to show you.'

She excused herself, returning minutes later with a large wooden photo frame, inside which sat a black and white portrait. At first glance, if not for her wardrobe, the woman in the photograph could easily have been mistaken for a Romani,[2] a gypsy, for her strikingly simple beauty spoke clearly of nomadic features. She had an angular face, a sharp nose, small, delicately shaped lips and big eyes that looked into the distance. On her head sat a dupatta, which covered her right ear and was draped across the chest. Her neck was generously embellished with several necklaces.

'Her name was Sardarni Sundar Kaur Sabharwal. Her name, Sundar, means beautiful,' she said, lightly touching the face in the frame, 'but we all called her Beji. She was a very liberal woman, believed in educating all four of her children—three daughters and one son—of whom my *nani*, Gobind Kaur, was the youngest, born in 1923 in Jhelum. She was also the most spoilt and spent a lot of time with her mother, far more than any of her siblings did, and they had a wonderfully deep connection. In the years that she was growing up, she became her mother's shadow, and all the habits, values and traits that Beji possessed were naturally passed down to her.'

I imagined a young girl sitting beside her mother, the striking Punjabi woman, and watching as she kneaded the dough for chapatis, or ground the spices in a mortar and pestle to make fresh masala, or chopped up vegetables to make pickles. I imagined her small fingers learning how to sew, slowly and hesitantly, as they tried to mimic her mother's deftly mechanical and practised hands. I imagined the child's small eyes following her mother as she moved around the house, tending to her chores.

'Now the process of making *phulkari* is long and repetitive.' A voice brought me back from the Jhelum of the past to the Delhi of the present. 'It is made on the reverse side, from the centre, as one works one's way gradually across the entire cloth. Traditionally, the handspun *khadi* was the most popular base for *phulkari* as it would have been most inexpensive and could be dyed in several colours. You see these larger stitches?' She turned it over and pointed to the seams. 'These are called *jor*, the joint, and show that several panels of *khadi* were joined together first to make a large enough surface area for the *bagh*, and only then did the embroidery process begin. In this case, three panels were joined together with great care. If you take a closer look, you will see certain imperfections, not every stitch is exactly the same size; but that is the beauty of the handmade versus the machine-made. It has aged now, and some threads are loosening, but this is truly how one can tell that someone spent the time and effort to create this with their two hands.'

With that, she turned it over and, using her hands, her body and her heart, delved deep into the history of her family to explain to me the process of each silken stitch.

* * *

'As I said, *phulkari* begins at the centre of a cloth, flowering its way to the outside. Always done from reverse, its fine skill requires mastery so that none of the background material is visible and also the reverse side remains neat and tidy. A wooden embroidery hoop is often locked in place, the small section is embroidered completely and, in the same way, it migrates across the entire expanse of *khadi*. The darning stitch—you see this simple running stitch? It is the very basic unit of *phulkari* and the work is graded according to the length and density of each stitch, which usually ranges from one to one-fourth of an inch.'[3]

Her thumb and forefinger measured the length of one stitch, long and uninterrupted. The chevron pattern spread across the length of the *khadi* in yellow and orange threads and stopped at the border.

'The work is done entirely with soft, glossy silken threads. And though it is simple and repetitive, it requires practice, patience and great eyesight, since any mistake in the symmetry of the motif and pattern will immediately be visible. These colours—

the reds, yellows, mustards, oranges—these are very typical of *phulkari* as they signify celebration and happiness.'

Suddenly the mechanical tone she had used to describe the process of *phulkari* dissipated and her voice became softer. It became the kind of voice that recalled a faraway dream. 'Sometimes I tell myself that my great-grandmother made this *bagh* to commemorate the relationship she shared with her youngest daughter, my *nani*. Because they would often stitch together. Maybe this was her way of teaching an age-old traditional language, the dialect of stitches, silken threads, history and customs. Maybe this was her way of imparting the importance of patience, perseverance, practice and perfection—traits that my *nani* would need later in life. Maybe that's why she made this singlehandedly, so that only her singular thoughts could flow into this piece of elaborately embroidered fabric.'

She was no longer speaking to me but more to her memories. And though her thoughts were heavily coloured in nostalgia, I too fell prey to their affection. For the second time that day, I found myself thinking about the unspoken secrets that women shared and whether it was possible for an inanimate object to carry those secrets through time and the generations of a family.

Life is long, my child, a stitch would lovingly be placed into the cloth, *but I am with you every step of the way. Here, this is my love*, a stitch, *this is my compassion*, another stitch, *here is my patience, my diligence, my dedication. And this*, the several threads that bound the base fabric together, *this is your union with your husband. May it be strong like the strength in this* khadi. *May your temperament be as smooth as the texture of these silken threads*, she eases the gorgeous gold through the eye of the needle, *may the many phases of your life be as consistent as the patterns that decorate this* bagh, her hands graze the embroidered surface. *May you learn to be resilient*, a stitch, *as accommodating and malleable as the folds of this fabric*, another stitch. *May you remain grounded*, her hands fold the embroidered *bagh* and roll it into the shape of a log with the coarse red *khadi* visible above. *And may you always pass these traits along to the generations of women born from your womb.*

* * *

'My *nani* received it before her wedding, along with a promise,' Hansla Chowdhary said, 'that the *bagh* be bequeathed as a treasured heirloom down the family tree.'

'Your *nani* was married before the Partition took place?' I asked.

'Yes, my *nana*'s family hailed from Lyallpur, also in Pakistan. But he had moved to Quetta for a clerical position, after which he began a trade of importing dried fruits from Iran. He had been engaged once before, but his fiancée passed away in the earthquake of Quetta in 1935. When my *nani* was in class eleven, they were introduced and married in 1939 in Rawalpindi. She finished her schooling after their wedding, as he too came from a very well-to-do family that encouraged the education of women.

'If she learnt resilience, hard work and humility from her mother, then from her mother-in-law my *nani* learnt social etiquette and elegance. Nana-ji's family were *zamindars*, landowners, and quite wealthy. For instance, even when she was home, his mother dressed in finery, complete with a *maang-tikka* and a four-string necklace. My *nani* would tell me stories of their home in Rawalpindi and the decadence they lived in.'

'Did she ever tell you about the Partition? Why and how they chose to come to Delhi, anything of their journey along the way?'

'Just once, I think. Rawalpindi had suffered gruesome acts of communal violence in the early months of 1947—February, March—and during the days of Partition, the princely state saw a great exodus of Hindu and Sikh refugees making their way across the border to safety. Amidst the murder, pillage, rapes and mutilations, my grandparents travelled from Rawalpindi to Delhi on a train that stopped in Amritsar. They had left in haste, unable to carry many belongings, but my grandmother carried this *bagh*. How could she not? She had to wear it throughout the journey, though, despite the August heat, just so that no one would try to

steal it. From Jhelum, Nani-ji's family—her parents and siblings—also migrated.

'Delhi was where they all chose to come. My *nani*'s brother
was a businessman and at the time had owned properties in Delhi,
so it seemed the most logical destination. His family first moved
to Karol Bagh and, later in the 1960s, to the southern part of
Delhi. My *nana* used to have a very close Muslim friend who lived
in Delhi before the Partition, in a luxurious grand mansion on
Prithviraj Road in Lutyens' Delhi. When talk of the Divide began
to gain legitimacy, this gentleman and his family chose to leave for
Pakistan, but not before contacting my grandfather somehow and
proposing an exchange of property. His house in Delhi for their
house in Rawalpindi. Unable to believe this serendipitous offer of
a home in a city unfamiliar to them, my *nana*'s family gladly
accepted, and essentially swapped houses with all their belongings intact.

'Thankfully, no one in our family suffered during the Partition,
but the unthinkable acts of violence that they saw along the way
were enough to shroud their memories in silence. Apart from
fleeting mentions of it, I don't think that my grandparents, or
even my great-grandmother Beji, ever spoke of the Divide, or
even of their land that then became Pakistan. There was no need
to remember, and maybe it was because we never asked, either,
that there was little talk of the Partition in our house. The truth
was that when they came across, albeit safely, they made a conscious decision to look forward, always to the future—which, I
think, was something many refugees who crossed the border did.
They had lost their homes and, in most cases, their businesses and
properties too. Caring for their families, building a new life was
of prime importance. My grandparents would always say, "We
have paid our dues, we have paid the price, and now we can start
afresh, enjoy the life we have built for ourselves." And now if I
really think about it, which I haven't really ever done … I think
maybe what they meant when they said "the price they paid" was
the Partition. They had sacrificed their homes and would never

get to see them again. The Partition had been the price for freedom, for Independence.'

Her eyes glazed, and for a moment she closed them and sighed deeply.

* * *

'This *bagh*,' I began, 'this is the only thing that remains from your grandmother's life in what became Pakistan. How did you come to have it, how did it skip your mother's generation altogether?'

Clutching the edges, she brought the fabric close to her heart. 'I think in some ways my relationship with Nani-ji mirrored her relationship with Beji. She was my friend more than a grandmother. I picked up so many habits from her. Like, for instance, when we went vegetable shopping, she would always teach me about the ripeness of fruit, or how the lemon shouldn't be too yellow or the lime too green...' Her voice trailed off into a smile.

'I remember everything about her. She carried herself with the utmost elegance and grace. Every evening, before my grandfather came home, she would dress up in her best clothes, even if they weren't going out anywhere, wear a tiny bindi and do up her hair just to welcome him home. The romance, the love, the dedication they had to each other and to their family was truly remarkable.

'Like my *nani* I am also the youngest in the family, and so I was around the longest while everyone else moved away or got married. One day when she was quite old and unwell, she called me to her bed and told me that she wanted to give me something. It was sudden and unexpected. A parting gift, she said. I think she knew that it would soon be time for us to say our goodbyes. I told her I didn't want anything, didn't need anything. She offered me her jewellery, which I politely declined because I knew I'd never wear it. "If there is something you must give me," I told her finally, "then let it be something that will always remind me of the more intimate moments we shared. I want your essence near me, your blessings, your warmth." She told me she had just the thing and from her cupboard took this out and presented it to me. Along with it, that day, she gave me my history, she gave me the knowledge of how the *bagh* was made and, lastly, she gave me the promise that she had made to Beji—to continue to pass the *bagh* along through the generations of my family.'

She picked it up delicately and placed it across my shoulders. Almost instinctively, I drew my breath in and sat up straighter, wanting my posture to be worthy of the beauty and fragility of the treasured piece. Despite the light summer colours, the fabric itself was heavy, and the heat emanating from it crept up to my cheeks, warming them. Slowly, Hansla Chowdhary ran her hands across my shoulder, from the collarbone to the blades, and, sighing deeply, stood back and admired the sight.

'Beautiful.'

But something didn't feel quite right. Beautiful though it was, on my shoulders it sat awkwardly and out of place, devoid of its genealogy and history. The strangest feeling crept over me, as if I were privy to a secret that didn't belong to me. I felt like a trespasser on a family's ancestry. Slowly and carefully, I removed it and placed it on the shoulder of its rightful owner.

'Now it is truly beautiful.'

She smiled warmly. 'Here, look at the border. It's different from the rest of the *bagh*, more intricate and colourful.'

Indeed, compared to the rest of the embroidery, the border of the *bagh* was more embellished. It took up nearly a foot of the fabric from the edge and was embroidered in fine diamond shapes of green and maroon. The pattern was more playful, less organized, yet consistent. Shapes grew organically from one another. Geometric lines of dark and light shone through their silken threads.

'These silk threads make it very warm and perfect to wear in winter. I consider this my *suraksha kavach*, my armour, against the cold. I wear it rarely now as it is quite fragile.' With that, she removed it and began folding it in halves, then fourths, then eighths, and then rolling it into the log shape. 'I would never use this as a throw or a rug. It's far too delicate. You see, even when I pack it, I roll it. But each time I change the side so it doesn't acquire hard folds or sharp creases and eventually crack.'

I watched her in silence as she painstakingly placed the log on a sparse bed of black peppercorns, smoothening out all the edges, and then wrapped it in newspaper and finally in a new plastic bag.

'I wonder,' I said, breaking the silence, 'how do you feel when you wear it now?'

She paused for a moment, surveying the neat roll covered in plastic. Then, very slowly, as if infusing every single word with her memories of the past, with nostalgia and exceptional affection, she spoke. 'Well, like you said, it is the only thing that remains from my *nani*'s life in a land that is now across the border. I thought for a long time of framing it, but it seemed too impersonal. Wearing it means keeping it close to my body, my heart. So sometimes it feels as if I am living in history, as if I can trace the direct lineage of my family through this one fabric. I am a part of all the women who wore this *bagh*, those who owned it before me. Those who poured themselves into it; who let their habits, memories and teachings envelop its surface; who let their perfumes and bodies, fingers and gestures add to its delicacy. I am a part of them, and they are a part of me.'

7

HEREDITARY KEEPERS OF THE RAJ

THE ENDURING MEMORIES OF
JOHN GRIGOR TAYLOR

'I THINK WHAT I REMEMBER best is laughter…' said the Englishman as he sank comfortably into the beige armchair, by a window overlooking a street in the heart of London. 'Perhaps I'm just cheating myself in saying that now, but it is always *khushi*, happiness, that lingers in my mind when I think of my childhood in India.' John Grigor Taylor looked at me and smiled and, charmed by the thought, I smiled back. We sat in a room that seemed inspired by the colours of India: saturated in the golden sunlight spilling in from the windows and the crimson paint of the walls. At one end was a large, soft couch and at the other were alcove shelves with objects displayed on them—decorative china to the right and old leather-bound volumes to the left. In front of each alcove sat rust-coloured armchairs. Several works of art adorned the walls and a red Persian rug ran along the length of the floor. By the windows sat the Englishman, surrounded by small footstools and tables, each disappearing under the weight of newspapers and books. Making myself comfortable, I sat cross-legged on the floor next to him.

'Ah, I used to be able to do that!' he laughed. 'Not any more, I'm afraid. Back in India, that is how I used to sit.'

The simple act of sitting cross-legged on the floor had triggered in a ninety-four-year-old man the memories of a childhood in a distant homeland. 'So then, tell me about your India,' my voice filled the air with curiosity.

'Well, let's see. I was born in 1921 in Ahmednagar, near Bombay. My parents had only me—I'm a solo product, an only child. My mother was a schoolteacher named Dora Ducé and my father a soldier named John McCleod Grigor Taylor—or Jack to most. He was born in 1884 in Singapore because his father was working with the company Cable and Wireless, laying telegraph cables all over the world. Jack was raised in England, joined the army, and was sent to India at the age of about twenty in 1904, after which he was posted to Hong Kong as part of the British garrison there during the Russo-Japanese War...'

His voice trailed off for a few minutes and then he continued, rather hesitantly, 'Now that we are talking about India, I should mention that though I believe very much in keeping links with the land of my birth, I don't believe in justifying things that went wrong there. Indeed, Independence Day came with such speed and in the midst of such turmoil that there was little opportunity for either preparation or reflection.[1] It's difficult, even now, to untangle the events that occurred at the tail end of the Raj, but so many years have passed and, to be honest, I'd much rather remember the India of my childhood.'

I wondered if it was even possible to detach the beginning from the end, view them as entities independent of each other in the course of a person's life, but nevertheless I agreed.

'Certain families,' Kipling once said, 'serve India generation after generation as dolphins follow in line across the open seas.' The descendant of one such family sat before me now.

'So, where was I...' he said. 'Oh yes, my father began his military career with the Multan Regiment and retired with the Rajputana Rifles—as did I—where he rose to command the 2nd Battalion as a lieutenant colonel. My mother had come to India to visit her sister, who was the wife of an English judge, when she met my father and fell for him!'

'Darling, it was mutual,' his wife's warm voice floated across the room towards us.

'It was, it was,' he replied leisurely.

Sophia walked in, dressed in midnight blue, her short silver hair falling around her face. Taking the armchair across from her husband, she said, 'But in those days, there was quite the culture of "husband-hunting", you see. The men outnumbered the women by about four to one in India and as a result, young women would travel across the seas from England to look for these eligible bachelors serving the Raj, fearful of being left on the shelf.[2] These were called the "Fishing Fleet" and they came usually around Christmas to stay through the cold weather. Some were lucky enough to find love on the ship itself, while others met their mates—a handsome young officer or a rising ICS [Indian Civil Service] man—through endless rounds of parties, dances at clubs, hunting outings, or through family and friends. Those who failed returned to England in the spring and were known as the "Returned Empties"!'[3]

My eyes widened with both horror and amusement.

'That's right,' she laughed, handing me a half-torn black-and-white photograph of a group of English men and women perched atop a mound of earth, men in hunting pants and sweaters with rifles in their hands and the women in flowing skirts and tops, holding binoculars and shielding themselves from the sun. 'That's Dora and Jack shooting crocodiles in the Punjab in the 1920s.'

'Crocodiles?' I asked.

'Oh yes, *magarmachh*!' nodded the Englishman.

I took the photograph from her and peered closely as she pointed out the couple. Dora, fashionably dressed and hatted, sat at the left edge of the image, delicately positioned against a rock, gracefully holding an umbrella with her left hand. Jack was a slim man with a long face and dark moustache. He was dressed in light-coloured trousers, a sweater and a tie, a pith helmet atop his head and a rifle casually placed in his hand.

'They also went pig-sticking,' he said. 'Quite barbaric, actually—a sport essentially involving riding cross-country on a horse while chasing a wild pig.' He handed me another monochrome photograph from the 1920s: a group of Englishmen, dressed in presumably khaki hunting uniform, holding long spears and standing in front of the carcasses of three wild pigs. The landscape in the back was barren and flat, sparse in vegetation.

'They married on 26 February 1921 in Poona,' he added.

'These photographs…' I gestured to the photo album from which the two quaint images had been extracted. 'How do you still have these?'

'When my parents moved back to England in 1935, they brought back some belongings to remember India by.'

'I will bring a few things out to show you,' his wife added. 'Most of them, though, are not my husband's, as he couldn't get anything of significance back with him after the war. What we have all belongs to Dora and Jack.'

I smiled gratefully and then turned to her husband.

* * *

'Do you remember it much—the land of your birth?'

For a moment, the question was met with silence. In his hands still lay the thick photo album belonging to his parents, opened to an image of a hockey team of Englishmen and Indians from March 1906. His fingers lingered over the figure on the far left, fair-faced and dark-haired with a centre parting and a bushy moustache. In the border of the image was a notation in dull black ink: 'JMGT, then a 21 year old, is sitting at the ext. left. This must be from 119th (Mooltan) Indian Infantry.' The border had all but been destroyed by weather; the black ink had faded to a light dusty brown in places. The handwritten text at the top read 'Winners of the Hong Kong Tournament,' and each player's name was listed at the bottom, in order. The men sat in chairs in the first row, Mr Taylor's father included, all holding hockey sticks.

He pushed his glasses up his nose just as they slid dangerously to the tip, cleared his throat and, still clutching the album, said, 'Well, I'm British, but I do remember India at times. And I am proud of my birth there, it's a second home really…'

'First home, actually,' I corrected him softly.

'Huh?' He looked up at me, his tone almost a bit disoriented. 'Yes, right. It was my first home. So naturally I have strong feelings about it. I told you I was born there in India, in…' For a moment, his face drew a painful blank, as if the thread of his thoughts had been abruptly cut, then finally he finished the sentence, '… Ahmednagar.'

I nodded, and the lump in my throat nodded with me. Sophia looked at me helplessly. 'Age,' she said sadly. 'This is what happens with age: your memory begins to fade little by little. First the edges soften, eroding away the most recent years, and then slowly age gnaws its way till it reaches even the seemingly impenetrable, the nucleus of our lives—our oldest and dearest memories.

'For many years he would tell me about his India, but it's difficult now for him to remember cohesively. Let me tell you something, though. The voices, they have stayed with him. The familiarity with the accent, it has stayed. We go to many lectures and he often finds them very hard to understand unless the speaker is very clear. About a month ago, we went for a book reading by a Pakistani man here in London. He was talking quite fast and with a very heavy subcontinental accent and I thought that my husband wouldn't be able to grasp a thing. But when I asked him after, he said it was absolutely fine and he understood every word because it was an accent he was familiar with and used to. Imagine that, the sounds of words have stayed with him, even though the memories of physical places are now blurred.'

Then, from under the window, from atop the plush armchair, came a voice submerged in nostalgia, sudden and unexpected: 'I was in D.I. Khan as a young boy.' From the album, his frail hand extracted a torn photograph of a child and his father, the

inscription on the back reading 'JGT with his father at the Fort
DERA Ismail Khan, NW Frontier.' He handed me a pile of
photos from their time in the Frontier and I leafed through them.
A hazy monochrome image—the surface of the film was
scratched and badly worn—showed what appeared to be a tank
in the middle of a street, with stones and other items scattered
around it, as if the scene were from amidst a riot or protest. On
the right could be seen multi-storey buildings with ornate
jharokha balconies. 'Khan Abdul Gaffar Khan, 1930 riots,
Peshawar,' the back of the image read.[4] Another image showed a
very large procession of men—all donning identical white
turbans, some beating drums, one holding a large dark-coloured
flag—walking alongside a small body of water, rowboats tied all
around the docks. 'India, probably Khan Abdul Gaffar Khan
demonstration, 1930'.[5]

'My father was posted to the Frontier Province at the onset of
World War I and then to Mesopotamia for the rest, where he
was wounded. I was born there … no wait, I was born in
Ahmednagar, I told you that already!' he chuckled, uniquely
aware of his repetition, now even somewhat conscious of the
breakdown of his memory. 'But we didn't live there for long.
We moved to Nasirabad, and then to D.I. Khan when I was about
four years old. In those days, the whole army just sat on the
frontier [with Afghanistan]! They were spread out across the
whole land, like icing on a cake, Indians and Brits, but the Brits
often died too young. The average lifespan of a British soldier
posted to India was about eighteen months. Then they died.'

'What do you mean?' I asked.

'Well, if you go to any old British graveyard in India—there's
a famous one in Calcutta—they are all littered with tombstones
of so-and-so died at twenty-one, so-and-so died at twenty-three,
all young men! There were rarely any old people among the
British in India. Because of the climate, diseases, accidents and
such, officers died young and suddenly. That was something one
had to become accustomed to, the sheer suddenness of death, the
mourning and burial. And to think that the footprint of the Raj

still exists today in the form of all the soldiers buried in English cemeteries in former English colonies, so many years after the dissolution of the Empire.'

'I see…' My voice trailed into the memory of a radio broadcast transcript I had once read about an old English cemetery in Calcutta, and I wondered if it was indeed the same place. The broadcast spoke of a place where many English men and women were buried, most unknown yet glorified by their overarching tombstones and pyramids. It spoke of the dust into which they had eventually transformed through these burials overseas in various lands—so mixed were they with the dust of the wide world, as no people had ever been before.[6]

'Dust,' the word involuntarily escaped my lips, as I thought of becoming one with the land. To my surprise, the Englishman found within it a curious memory.

'Yes, dust… In the soil of our garden in D.I. Khan, the *mali* who tended to the flowers would help my father and me build a trench. My father spent a lot of time in the trenches of World War I and so he tried to show me the battlefield—where to put the little toy soldiers…'

'So, in a way, you had war strategies ingrained in you!'

'Naturally, because I was the son of a fighting soldier.'

'And what were his views about the Raj?'

'He was quite keen to defend India. Nearly all of them, the men and women who were sent to India, were keen to defend it and be some part of it. But if ever there was a clash of interests between British and Indian, they would always be in favour of the British. Though my father would often try to retain the balance. I don't think we ever consciously thought of "the Raj", but rather accepted it as a fate we were born into and had to live with. My destiny and the destinies of my ancestors were amalgamated into the land of Hindustan in a way that wasn't necessarily always considered exploitative.

'When my father was commanding his battalion, I remember there being no difference in his attitude towards an Indian or a

British officer. He was equally interested in and responsible for both—he often knew where they came from, perhaps had even met their families and visited their villages. The army represented a very distinct bond of fraternity and brotherhood, regardless of the several castes, creeds and ethnicities it included.'

Just as he finished his sentence, Sophia handed him a large wooden photo frame. Within it, on faded ivory paper, was a caricature of an English officer and his Indian subedar sticking their tongues out at each other. 'Personal Example,' the text in the top left corner read. Mr Taylor held the portrait erect in his lap with his left hand and brought his right palm to his lips. A small smile bloomed on his face, widening gradually until he let out a laugh.

'This ... yes ... come, look at this!' He beckoned me closer.

'What is it?' I asked, also smiling.

'That's my father,' he pointed to the Englishman dressed in formal uniform, now much older, his hair thinning, but moustache just as bushy and black, 'and this chap is his subedar—a Jat, you can see from the way he's tied his *pagdi*, the turban on his head. Some men would wear them such that the fabric trailed behind them like a *dumm*, a tail! So anyway, the story goes...' He narrated in a unique blend of crisply accented Hindustani and English. 'One day, the subedar, who had been sick for a while, greeted my father with a "Good morning, *sahib*" and the *sahib* in return said, "*Subedar, aapki tabiyat kaisi hai ab?* How are you feeling now?" And the subedar replied, "*Sahib, abhi bhi dukh aur bohot dard hai hume*," motioning that his body still hurt quite a bit and he was still very unwell. So my father said, "I don't believe you. Stick your tongue out!" and so he pulled his tongue out so my father could examine it, and for comparison my father stuck out his own tongue. Just then, a man, an artist who would draw funny pictures, happened to stumble across this hilarious scene of two officers and drew it! The subedar had a very long tongue, as you can see here, though the artist might have exaggerated a little. Anyway, what is interesting is that though my father was his commanding officer, the two were quite good friends, both the same age, old men who both retired at the age of sixty!'

'And your father brought this back with him?'

'Yes, I suppose that for all the keenness with which he travelled back to England, my father unknowingly brought with him the most earnest parts of his Indianness, or whatever he had acquired of it over the years. These bonds of friendship, the familiarity with language and land, his love and attachment to all the peoples of India—these are the bits that remain with us, those that have been passed down to me, and will perhaps…' He paused for a moment, then said, 'Perhaps be lost after me, given the rate at which our history is being forgotten.'

'But not if you don't let it,' I said softly. 'This is why your memory is so important—so that *we* don't forget. Now tell me, you too were in the Indian Army. When did you join and where were you posted?'

'Before that, you must know that as a child I left India…' he began, and then stopped, as if trying to remember.

'Darling, you left India around the age of eight or nine years to go to school in England,' Sophia offered, and then turned to me. 'Meanwhile, his parents remained in India and his mother visited every year, which was rather indulgent as most women visited their children every two years!'

'I didn't know anything about England. My whole life had been spent in India until then,' Mr Taylor said, picking up now from where his wife had left off. 'As a young boy, when I was told I'd be going off to school, I would have bad dreams. And when I finally arrived here, I didn't like it. It was too cold and sparse, and I used to wake up at night saying, "Take me away, back to India! Rhubarb! Don't give me any rhubarb!"' He laughed.

'He started university at the beginning of World War II,' Sophia continued, 'and just halfway through he reached call-up age and, because he had Indian connections, he opted to join the Indian Army.'

'Yes, it was all quite familiar, actually, as if I'd never left at all. I already spoke the language because I'd learnt it when I was young. You couldn't communicate with the servants or anybody otherwise. The only people who spoke English were the Anglo-Indians and the British. In fact, I can still speak Hindustani…'

'Yes, I know,' I smiled, remembering the local words that had slipped into our conversation. Then, out of nowhere, the dignified Englishman—dressed sharply in a tweed coat and laced suede shoes, his thick glasses perched on his nose—began humming an old Indian jingle, very much to my surprise.

'Vicks *ki goli lo, khich khich door karo*!'[7] He swayed from side to side as I burst into laughter and joined him. He then continued on to an even older tune, from the black-and-white Bollywood film *Shehnai*. '*Aana meri jaan, meri jaan, Sunday kay Sunday…*' He spread his arms as the Chaplin-esque hero had in the film and continued in a slower, more melodious tone, '*Tujhe Paris dikhaoon, tujhe London ghumaoon, tujhe brandy pilaoon, whiskey pilaoon, aur khilaoon murgi ke murgi ke andey andey, aana meri jaan, meri jaan, Sunday kay Sunday*!'[8]

My eyes were wide open with shock at how accurately he still remembered the words, how the tune had still not left him. I laughed, clapping as he finished his performance.

'Anyway,' he said, catching his breath, 'this was life. These were the songs of my days!'

'He was about twenty years old when he returned to India in 1941 in a luxury P&O liner that had been commandeered and converted into a troopship.' Sophia recalled with ease and promptness the details that she had become so familiar with over the years. 'It carried several thousand soldiers going to India or Singapore, and conditions were extremely cramped. All the cadets were on the lowest deck, sleeping in hammocks. The deck was open-plan, about the size of a tennis court for 200 men. There were about a dozen ships in the convoy, with four or five destroyers protecting them. Though fortunately they were not attacked, the convoys before and after them both had ships sunk.'

Then she looked at him, his frail face illuminated by the spring sunshine, and continued, 'The journey took six weeks. He always says the atmosphere was tough but jolly, with lots of camaraderie among all these young men. Once in India, he was taken, with several others, to the training ground at Mhow, Indore and then to Burma, serving first in the 2nd Battalion and then in the 8th.'

I nodded and then turned to him. 'In your regiment of the Rajputana Rifles, were there soldiers of all communities, much like in the time of your father? Hindus, Muslims and Sikhs?'

'My father's regiment...' His voice trailed off. 'And my regiment...' He attempted to untangle the specificities of the military experiences of father and son, who had served the same unit in the two wars that had changed the contemporary history of the world.

'Yes,' he said finally and affirmatively. 'Yes, and we took that diversity absolutely for granted. In my regiment, we had in our company British, Hindu, Sikh and Muslim men. The Subedar Major was an Indian, a very grand figure who always wore his uniform very proudly, like a turkey. And apart from our overt differences, when we joined the army, we became one unit and fought for that one unit, regardless of our ethnicities. What you're perhaps trying to understand—as well as what I'm trying to say, very confusingly it appears—is that there was a friendly relationship between Indians and the British, as well as between Hindus, Muslims and Sikhs. Not all the time, but most of the time. There were only few disputes. For instance, when a commanding officer retired or took leave from his post in India, he'd often make it a point to visit the villages where his men came from. *Bara khana* it would be, a big feast. So it was quite amicable.'

He then turned to Sophia. 'The playing cards...'

'Ah yes.' She got up and went to the other room, bringing back a set of cards, mounted inside a stiff cardboard frame. There were five in total, each bearing the image of a soldier from a different regiment of the Indian Army: 10th Gurkha Rifles, the Burma Rifles, Bahawalpur State Forces, 6th Rajputana Rifles and British Honduras Defence Force. The text at the top of each card read 'PLAYER'S CIGARETTES'.

'Cigarette cards were very common between the late nineteenth century and World War II, and then they were discontinued to conserve paper,' Sophia explained. 'They covered all sorts of subjects, from butterflies to military uniforms, and many people, both children and adults, collected them. All the big cigarette companies included them in their packets of cigarettes, and they were obviously a marvellous marketing tool!' I inspected the card frame. Each soldier stood proudly, donning the full military uniform of his particular regiment. Fourth in line stood the Rajputana Rifle, resplendent in deep forest green, a turban atop his head, poised in front of Delhi's India Gate, which was built to honour the lives of the soldiers lost in World War I.

The Englishman's gaze was upon me, and he told me to turn the frame over. Each card bore a short description of the regiment—'MILITARY UNIFORMS OF THE BRITISH EMPIRE OVERSEAS'—along with information on the company itself: 'JOHN PLAYER & SONS, BRANCH OF THE IMPERIAL TOBACCO COMPANY CO. (OF GREAT BRITAIN & IRELAND), LTD.' Each card, it appeared, was from a series of fifty and the Raj Refs bore a small No. 19.

'Before 1945, we were known as the 6th Rajputana Rifles because it was formed by merging six previously existing British Indian Army regiments. When parents came home with a new packet of cigarettes, the children would immediately ask for the card in the hope that it would be one they did not yet have. I remember collecting them from my mother's cigarette packets!' Mr Taylor told me.

I smiled, still admiring the majestic uniforms of each regiment. 'So were you in Burma till the end of the war?'

'No, I developed health problems, actually, and was sent to a hospital in Delhi for treatment in 1943–44. After that, I was sent to work in an administrative capacity as a staffer within Lord Mountbatten's office. At the time, he was the supreme commander of the army, air force and navy in India.'

'You used to dance with his daughters, remember?' giggled Sophia. 'Ah yes, how I remember,' he smiled back.

'So what were the British saying about Independence—both the officers deployed to India and the people back in England?' I asked.

'Well, a declaration was made by Muhammad Ali Jinnah and the Muslim League for a separate state. Pakistan. But it was all sort of brushed aside because, first and foremost, everyone wanted to win the war and this was a secondary concern.[9] Also, the British government didn't want Partition. They had no interest in breaking up the subcontinent. Not to mention, the largest contingent of the British Army came from India! But, that being said, the masses in England didn't know much about what was happening in India. They didn't realize the extent of the Empire, nor the intensity of its struggles there, both to exercise control and to subsequently retain it in one form or another. Sadly, the doings of the British in India made little impress upon the daily lives of countrymen at home. Their imagination remained untouched by it.'

I nodded slowly and intently. How was it possible, I thought to myself, that a small section of people from an island that raised an empire on which the sun never set could exercise control and sovereignty over such a large subcontinent? And, despite all that, that these actions hardly seemed to sway the lives of their people at home?[10] Did the years of the Raj—recorded extensively in laws, letters, journals, books and papers of British officers in India—having shaken the very foundations of Hindustan, not create even the slightest tremor in the English terrain?

'I left just after the war. Went back to England with only my army trunk by my side. I know you have travelled far to see the objects that remain from our time in India, but I'm afraid, apart from my parent's belongings … and my memories—which, to be honest, are now crumbling away—I have little else to show you. Soldiers had few possessions in those days, anyway…

'Meanwhile, the English judge, Sir Radcliffe, was sent to divide India. I gather that he strove to find a balance—rather unsuccessfully, though—but such a task would've been too large for anyone. But then, I must say, all said and done about the stature and luxuries we had as part of the Raj, Independence was a necessary step and was indeed inevitable. Even though our time there, according to me, wasn't completely exploitative, one must never overstay one's welcome. Perhaps this is where my father and I differed in our opinions. He was more generational and political, a conservative soldier. Most of his time there was fraught with communal tensions, which made him believe that India was far from ready for Independence, and without the British to keep order, there was an unending risk of chaos. I, compared to him, had more radical views as a young man: that even though there were communal problems in India, Independence was inevitable. Yes, it was complex and the movement and struggle towards it was never fully a unified one amongst its many peoples. But it was inevitable. The situation had turned to utter chaos, with innumerable instances of communal disruption all across the north of the country. It wasn't an ideological move for the British, but more an act to retain some civil order. The real fear was that all order would dissolve into anarchy. And so with the departure of the British came Independence and looming Partition.'

'Yes, but not every Englishman necessarily wanted to go back,' smiled Sophia, 'and some certainly lingered on for decades after.[11] But all the Indian Civil Service officers of English origin had no choice but to leave; those in the army were given transfers and several other officers were made to find homes in an England they didn't quite recognize any more. England after the war was almost in a state of penury, the war had cleaned out the treasury and the situation was similar to that of a depression.'

'And did you ever come back to India, then?' I asked the Englishman.

'Oh yes, I had joined the diplomatic service and immediately after Independence was invited to set up the first British High Commission in Delhi.'

'How interesting!' I exclaimed. 'Did you feel as though you were going home?'

'Well, he was quite English by then, and a diplomat no less,' said Sophia. But after a moment of quiet reflection, she added, 'You see, he was going to fulfil a role. During the time of the Raj, the British were, in some ways, both British and Indian, as my husband told you earlier. But it was not so straightforward to live with such a duality because, at the end of the day, though they were emotionally attached to India, they belonged to England.'

'Even though for him,' I gestured to the armchair, 'England would have been an adopted country, a second home in the course of his life?'

'Yes, absolutely.' Her voice was firm, but then suddenly she smiled and added, 'But his British passport will always say, "Born in Ahmednagar, Undivided India".'

I sighed and closed my eyes. In my mind, the dusty roads of Delhi slithered into the earthy rugs under our feet; the leather volumes stacked on the bookshelves smelled of the old libraries I had grown up frequenting; the fabric on the sofas was block-printed Rajasthani; miniature Mughal paintings and maps of Kashmir and Undivided India graced the walls, confirming that, in this home, there would never truly be an exile from Hindustan.

'How much had India changed in those two years that you had been away?' I asked.

'Well, I felt the same way about Delhi then as I do about England now: there was just no room! The city had changed so much since the end of the war. There had been such an influx of

Hindu refugees. So many Muslims had fled to Pakistan, and many had gone deeper within the alleys of the old city. Large refugees camps had been set up in places, with populations larger than the infrastructure of the camps could handle. Families living on the streets, in tents, in barracks. Naturally, the number of Englishmen had dwindled tremendously as well, almost countable now as they gradually wound up their jobs. During the war, you wouldn't be able to walk a moment without bumping into another Englishman, and now, if you went to Old Delhi, you'd be the only one for about 20 yards...

'I arrived there in December 1947, and I recall going to the prayer meets organized by Gandhi-ji. Nehru was constantly afraid of rioting breaking out again, especially since so many refugees were still making their way across the new border. One day, at the end of January 1948, I was with a friend, Narender, a Hindu, both serving our respective governments, though both not in uniform at the time. We were at this open *dhaba*-type restaurant in a Muslim neighbourhood and it was evening time, around 5 p.m., so we stood around the *tandoors* waiting for our food. And then suddenly, out of nowhere, there was a deafening crack in the air.' He brought his hands together in a loud resounding clap that startled both Sophia and me.

'An unmissable sound, after which all the shutters of the stores in the markets began coming down, one after another ... BANG, BANG, BANG! At 5.17 p.m., during his evening prayer at Birla House, Gandhi-ji had been assassinated. For a while, there was utter confusion and we were all scared, not knowing what had happened. Narender and I went home and heard on the radio that a Hindu had gunned down the Mahatma.'

'Nathuram Godse...' I whispered.

'Yes ... I think we had all feared it was a Muslim.' He turned his head from side to side, very slowly. 'I will never forget that day.'

* * *

As we dwelt on his memories, Sophia broke the silence. 'Our granddaughter is doing a project—a film on people's concepts and memories of home as part of her university degree—and she came over last week to interview my husband.'

'And ... what was it, his memory of home?' I asked, expectantly, looking at the photo album and the caricature we had abandoned to one side of the living room.

'Smell,' she replied. 'He found smell particularly evocative.'

'I told her the two things that remind me of home, of India, were both smells,' he said with a distant look in his eyes. 'The first is the scent of *geeli mitti*, wet soil, like in the garden after it had been watered by the *maali* or, even better, after it had rained.'

I nodded. Of all the ways to remember, I, too, trusted my senses the most, like the man sitting in front of me. Touch, the feel of things; taste, the freshness of moist air, the earthiness of the *tandoor*; sound, of the crowd, of rickshaws, of voices; and smell, the enveloping nature of smell triggered memory like nothing else. *Geeli mitti*—the very smell the Englishman had evoked, the very smell we were both so far away from at that moment.

'No other land will ever smell that way ... as earthy, as heavy, as dense and somehow as light as the soil after the rains in India,' I said.

He nodded, animatedly.

'And the second thing I remember is the smell of my father's leather boots when he'd come home from work in D.I. Khan. The mustiness of leather, mixed with earth and sweat and heat and the fatigue of the day. That smell, that particularly Indian smell, is unforgettable.'

8

THE LIGHT OF A HOUSE
THAT STANDS NO MORE

THE STONE PLAQUE OF MIAN FAIZ RABBANI

'THIS IS MY FATHER,' he said, tapping his index finger softly on a sepia-toned photograph. The dulling paper showed a shadowy figure standing by a latticework stone railing, on the terrace of a magnificent-looking three-storey building. Given the distance from which the photograph was taken, none of the man's features were discernible, except that he was tall and broad-shouldered, wearing dark clothes and a turban, with his hands likely by his sides.

'It was taken in 1935, when I was only four years old. I have wondered many times how we still have this photograph; who brought it across with them; or even who took it, in those days. But this is how I remember him.' For a few seconds, Mian Faiz Rabbani gazed at the sole surviving image of his father, and then handed it to me.

He ran his hands over the smooth skin of his handsomely angular face, and then, grazing the neatly trimmed white beard, he said, 'Bauji, everyone called him *bauji*, father. He married three times but had no children with his first two wives. No one could understand why. The family tried all kinds of remedies; they even travelled as far as Ajmer Sharif Dargah to pray. Then finally, after twelve long years, his third wife—my mother—gave birth to not one but six children in the years that followed! And I was the last one, born in 1931, which is why I never spent much time with Bauji. I only remember him as an ageing man with Parkinson's disease whose memory was slowly fading. He died not long after this photograph was taken, actually.' His low voice

167

dissolved into silence, until a sudden knock on the door brought him back to the present.

'Please excuse me,' he said. He stood up, straightening his tall physique and smoothening out the creases in his indigo-blue kurta, and slipped out.

As he left, I began to fan myself with my hands for some respite from the brutal Lahore heat. Fleetingly I thought of the sun blazing down on my old-fashioned white house in Delhi, which made me glance down at the photograph of the house from the past. Peering at it more carefully now, I noticed how breathtaking the building was. The sprawling mansion boasted of elegance and regality. There were three storeys, each with its own distinct character. And just as I was looking closely at the architecture, my host walked back into the room.

'*Jee*, where were we now?' he asked.

'Tell me about this house.' I placed the photograph on the sofa cushion between us.

He smiled. 'During the Partition, we left the house [on the other side]. But we certainly have its memories with us here, that is all of it that remains alive. It was in Jullundur.' The name of his birthplace sprang softly off his tongue with a musical Punjabi lilt. Curling his lips into a sad smile, he continued, 'It was the house I was born in, the one I grew up in, and the one I fled from as a sixteen-year-old at the time of the Partition.' He leaned in and pointed to the part of the house visible in the photograph. 'This is only about one-eighth of the whole structure. Such a splendid building it was, it was palatial. It was built in 1909 by my grandfather, who named it Shams Manzil after my uncle. It was in a predominantly Muslim neighbourhood of the city.

'The front courtyard was this big,' he said, opening his arms wide. 'At that time it was one of the largest homes in Jullundur city and would host the festivities of the *mohalla* (neighbourhood); it saw weddings, Iftar dinners, Eid gatherings and many other celebrations! Okay, let me tell you another interesting thing. Very near to ours was the home of Muhammad Zia-ul-Haq, who went on to become the sixth President of Pakistan. Theirs was a small house that my elder brother would probably have remembered better than me. Had his marriage taken place in Jullundur before the Partition, the celebrations would have likely been in our courtyard! We belonged to a predominantly agricultural community called Arain that had a large presence in Jullundur.'

He smiled widely. The longer he recounted the memories of his childhood, the more the sadness from his voice dissipated and the more vibrant his tone became. I was amazed by the precision with which he described every nook and corner of a home he had left behind nearly seven decades ago. The parts that were not in the photograph came alive, and I imagined an ageing house whose every brick had absorbed the history of its occupants.

'At the entrance to the courtyard were these beautifully arched open doorways. And above them…' His voice trailed off as he picked up the photo and squinted at it. 'Ah, you can see it here! Above them were these inscriptions, which would have been common in those days. These were stone plaques, either painted or engraved and fitted right into the outer walls. The text usually commemorated the house and the family. These stones plaques too have a story of their own … but I will tell you that later.' He smiled knowingly and continued the virtual tour.

'On the other side of the arched doorways was a large central room where the men of the family and neighbourhood would gather. This was the first room of the house. There was no electricity in those days, so we had to come up with creative arrangements in the summer. The floor of this central room would be covered with sand and then sprinkled with water. Several *manjis*, low jute beds, would be laid out across the floor, and there was a strict rule against opening any doors or windows during the day. The only openings would be covered with *khus* curtains sprinkled with water every few hours.[1] From the ceiling hung a large fan, a *punkha*, tied to a long string held by the *punkha-walla*, a man who sat outside the room slowly pulling at the string to fan those within.' He chuckled.

As we made our way to the second floor of the house, he described the filigree windows constructed towards the back of the open verandah. The borders of each landing were adorned with carvings, and ornate railings ran the length of the floors. A slim staircase led to the topmost level, the *chhatt*, memories of which evoked in the eighty-three-year-old man happiness beyond measure.

'Now look,' he told me, 'we used to live in a Muslim locality and go to an Urdu school, so I didn't have the chance to make any Hindu friends. But our route to school cut through Hindu localities. There wasn't much difference between the two communities back then, there was no such distinction. And, perched up on this *chhatt*, we would watch the Dussehra celebrations, which would culminate in a fiery arrow piercing through the large wooden structure of the demon-god Ravan, and we would cheer as it went down in flames! The skies would be filled with fireworks—I still remember them! Then soon the Diwali processions would begin and the streets would be as crowded as during [the sacred Islamic month of] Muharram. Everyone would be clothed in extraordinary costumes and the *jaloos* would stop at a square, where they would enact the *Ramayana*. The props were so beautiful, and earthen lamps would be lit up all around the city! As a child it was difficult to understand the connotations of such occasions, so we often took them at face value and treated them as days to celebrate and rejoice, regardless of religion.'

He paused, putting down the photograph. 'There was peace when I was young. I remember there being peace. Jullundur was a quiet place, and in those days we had little exposure to things outside our immediate circle. As a result, I actually remained quite oblivious to communal strife or the nationalist struggle while growing up. It was only when I finished my matriculation and moved to Aligarh to be closer to my brother, who was serving in the air force and working with the Quaid-e-Azam [Jinnah], that the reality of the world unfurled before me. I was at the Aligarh

Muslim University for one year, in 1946. The students of AMU were enthusiastic supporters of both the League and of Pakistan, the new country on the brink of creation. And, in the wake of Independence, the small town on the Gangetic plains became a vortex of communal attacks and violence.[2]

'The city became alarmingly polarized—Hindu *mohallas* demarcated clearly from Muslim *mohallas*—and people began to live in fear against the backdrop of violent riots and religious and political sloganeering. We had rented a nice house, but its boundary wasn't quite secure, and so, in the middle of the night, we along with other families would assemble at certain safe houses around the city. There was a woman named Begum Abad, hailing from a prominent Aligarh family, who would open the doors to her home—called Neeli Chattri, Blue Umbrella—every night for the Muslim families of the *mohalla*.'

'So, how did you first hear about the Partition?' I asked.

'Radio *pe*,' he replied. 'We all heard it together one night in the summer of 1947. That's when I knew I had to go back to Jullundur.'

'And what did you think was going to happen when Partition did take place?'

'Number one, we would gain our Independence. And second, the country was to be partitioned; it would be divided. This much we were all aware of after the announcement on the radio. But nobody ever thought that they would have to vacate their homes. You see, when I returned to Jullundur at the end of the summer after taking my exams, I was told that there had been massive riots in the city since the beginning of the year. Sikh leaders had marched down the lanes shouting slogans against the Muslim League and Pakistan. "*Jo koi maangega Pakistan, ussko milega qabristan*"[3]—those who demand Pakistan shall be sent to the graveyard. But even after all this, we really thought that these uprisings would die down eventually. We never even imagined that we would have to migrate to someplace else, that we would have to leave our home. We thought that we were Indian then, and after the Partition we would become Pakistani, for we were certain that Jullundur would be part of the new country.'

'How could you have been so certain when the exact border had not yet been announced?'

'Well, in Jullundur city, Muslims were in a majority. And not just there but also in the areas around, like Ferozepur and Zira sub-districts, the princely state of Kapurthala, Batala and Gurdaspur sub-districts,[4] and so logically it just made sense,' Faiz Rabbani said simply.

'What happened then?'

'Our palatial home that had once hosted weddings and parties turned into a camp for Muslims during the riots. People came from faraway districts and congregated at our house. My cousin was the municipal commissioner of Jullundur and so naturally our residence was deemed safe. And because my own brother was still with the Quaid, I became the patriarch of my family, having to take care of a widowed mother and sisters. And,' he scoffed, shaking his head from side to side, 'the day we finally learned of our Independence, it was not in an ambience of jubilation and celebration, but in the courtyard of our home, where an entire Muslim *mohalla* was seeking refuge, fearing for their lives. What sort of freedom was that? Then, much to our surprise, we learnt that Jullundur was now in India and we were on the wrong side of the border.'

Again, he shook his head and pursed his lips. Placing his hands on his knees, he sat up straighter, exhaled deeply and continued. 'For a while we thought it was safe as long as we remained within the house, but then Hindus and Sikhs from West Punjab [now in Pakistan] began pouring into the city with stories of atrocities caused by Muslims, which further worsened the riots.[5] One night, the military came and asked us all to vacate the house. They had come so suddenly that we didn't have a chance to take anything, everything was left behind. The families that had gathered in the courtyard slowly trickled out into the darkness. Anyway, because my cousin was in the government, he was able to arrange private transportation for us—a *ghoda-gaadi*, a horse-drawn carriage. At that time, travelling in a carriage was a matter of prestige,' he said, smiling softly, 'and even in situations as dreadful as those, the stature of the family had to be taken into account.'

'Where did it take you?'

'Considering how safely we left our house, our journey after that was anything but. At first we went to a place called Basti Guzan, where we stayed for two days in locked premises, praying for safe survival. From there we tried to move westward. The agriculture minister in Kapurthala state took the whole family in as my cousin had a cordial relationship with him. We thought we would be safe there, but little did we know that disturbances had begun everywhere, and yet again we had to flee. The minister was made to vacate his position, but he did make sure that we were escorted out of the state by military guards. I was later told that we were the first and last convoy to leave Kapurthala safely. From there we had no idea where to go, how to get across, where it was safe, and so we went back towards Jullundur and found shelter in the refugee camp that had been set up.

'But the conditions of the camp were terrible. So much dirtiness, so much contamination. There were hundreds of people cramped together. Given the unsanitary conditions, there were outbreaks of diseases like cholera and smallpox. The officials provided little information about whether or not we were even going to be transported safely across the border. There was little regard for social customs and law and order, women were taken advantage of[6] ... the conditions for them were terrible, unthinkable ... and my cousin decided that for the safety and dignity of the family, we could no longer stay at the camp. Across the road from the camp was an area called Ghara, but due to the riots a curfew was imposed there.'

'What was the curfew, how long was it?' I asked.

'It would change depending on the situation. Sometimes it was during the day, sometimes during the night, and sometimes for twenty-four hours. It was imposed so that the authorities could control the violence. Anyway, we stayed in the camp all day, and then at night, when the curfew was lifted, we went across the road to Ghara. My cousin's in-laws lived there and we stayed with them for one week.

'In the meantime, my brother, who had by then travelled from Aligarh to Lahore, found transportation and came to Jullundur to pick us up. But we were no longer at our old house—it had become a shelter for people coming in from West Punjab. My brother was unable to find us. But our hosts in Ghara made arrangements for the ladies of their family to get across safely, and they agreed to take some of us too. By the grace of God, the women—my mother, aunts and sisters—all arrived safely in Pakistan.'

'And what about you?'

'Well, they didn't have room for us all in the convoy, so they took whomever they could. Most of the men came later, trickling in one by one after a few days, and we were all reunited in Lahore, where my brother finally joined us. We had abandoned our life, our home, our history ... but we had crossed over safely and at least we were alive, and in those days that was enough. We had relatives on Mall Road who had vacated their flat for us and gone to stay elsewhere, so we even had safe accommodation. Then, a few days later, my brother made another attempt to go to Jullundur with a military convoy—this time to recover some of our possessions from the house—and my cousin and I joined him. But there were already new occupants living there! We couldn't even go inside and returned empty-handed.'

'You were able to travel back across the border so soon after the Partition?' I asked, surprised.

'Oh yes, the border was open! There were no gates or fortifications, in the early days it was a border in name only. And because it was so open in those first few weeks, many people risked their lives by travelling across to retrieve their belongings or find someone they had left behind. They had left all kinds of items in their houses because they'd thought, like us, that they would return after the riots! Not many people had bank accounts and so they embedded their most precious belongings into walls, or underneath floors or in the ground of their gardens and fields. Many succeeded in retrieving their belongings and many didn't, many things were lost forever.

'So we went and came back by Wagah, but the border didn't look like what it is today. No arrangements had yet been made, on either side. Pakistan was a new country, and the government had much larger issues to deal with in those days, which took precedence, and so the border remained a nominal line. Just a line. And when you found out that you had crossed that line— that you had left India behind and were now in Pakistani territory … oh, people would kiss the earth with gratitude!'

* * *

'What did you feel while moving from place to place before you finally reached Pakistan? And were you not afraid? You were only a teenager, after all… You lost everything that was familiar in a single moment, but then to have the chance to go back to Jullundur so soon…'

He remained quiet for a few moments and then, with great effort and melancholy, said, 'If you uproot a sapling from its natural habitat and try to plant it elsewhere, the chances of it growing and thriving are slim—and perhaps it may not live at all…'

I nodded, slowly transcribing these simple words, which spoke volumes about the uncertainty that most refugees would have carried in their hearts during the days of migration.

'Things born from a certain land belonged to that land alone.' Repeating his words under my breath, I looked up from my notebook, eager to know more. But the gentle face of Faiz Rabbani was looking through the window into the distance, far away from where we were sat in Lahore and far, far away from the present day. Tears laced his eyes, and for a moment I thought I had crossed a line in my attempt to cross the physical boundaries between our nationalities and generations. I asked him to forgive me for my inexhaustible questionnaire.

He brought his hands to his eyes and massaged them. Then, smiling sadly through his tears, he said, 'Sometimes the most important moments of our life—those that required incredible strength, those that defined us—get enfolded within the tides of time. Years accumulate over them and they become faint and eventually dormant. It's not that I have forgotten our journey to Pakistan; it's just that I don't think of it often. I have the memories, but one must actively remember them. So you are right in asking your questions, for the questions need to be asked.'

And with that he sat up straight. 'You had asked if I was scared when we were moving from place to place. I was not. You're scared once your mind has the chance to imagine the worst. But while it's happening, while we were fleeing, there was no fear. I couldn't afford to feel fear. Yes, I was only a teenager, but in those days I was also the head of the family and so I knew I needed to get us to safety. We had to find a way to survive. And when we went back to Jullundur, to be honest, it was too soon, and we were disheartened about not being able to look inside our house—not to mention that it was no longer our house—so I don't think I felt anything.

'Then from Lahore, we moved again. My mother didn't approve of living in someone else's house for so long, and she insisted that we travel to our ancestral lands in Lyallpur, which is now called Faisalabad. That was the only place that was still ours, though it was not as if Lyallpur were much safer than anywhere else. Muslim families in need of a place to live were fighting over homes that had been abandoned by Hindus. But my mother insisted, so we moved to a primitive house on a primitive road. It didn't come close to the mansion where we had lived in Jullundur; this house was small and frail and needed maintenance. But it was ours. After travelling for weeks, we finally made Lyallpur our home.'

'As the years passed, did you not miss your life in Jullundur?' I asked delicately.

Though he laughed, his eyes betrayed their sorrow. 'More than you can ever imagine,' he replied. 'If I now think about the time when we went back to Jullundur after the Partition, I wish I had cherished it more, even if we came back empty-handed. As a young man I thought of that a lot, and so after nearly twenty-five years I decided to go back and visit the house.'

My eyes widened and I smiled.

* * *

'Since the Partition we had made several friends in India, and I went to see a family called the Tandons in Amritsar. Because I was so close to Jullundur, I took a train by myself to visit the city. When I got off the train, the first thing I noticed was that the station, though unchanged, seemed tiny in comparison to how I remembered it. Anyway, I walked out and hired a rickshaw and gave him the address of my *mohalla*. He must have driven for barely a few minutes before we were there. Confused, I insisted he was wrong: "*Nahi, nahi*, I remember it used to be this far and take us this much time…" But then I looked around and recognized my sister's college. That was the place, so I paid the man and got off. The municipal garden close by, which at one point used to be famous for its beautifully manicured trees and flowers, had now been converted into a football field!

'Actually, what I was looking for were the graves of my father and eldest sister, who were buried there, and so I began walking around asking people where the *qabristan* was. I found out that the graveyard had been converted into a complex … they had ploughed the land and built houses. It happens everywhere when the population increases and the city needs land. So I went there and paid my respects in general to the whole plot. Then I set out to find my old house.

'Everywhere I looked there were new places I didn't recognize, so I kept walking for a few minutes, and suddenly I was in front of my house! The long distances I had walked in my childhood seemed so short now; the bazaars and lanes seemed so small. I stood at the side entrance of my house and knocked on the door.'

Then he leaned in closer and, with a smile on his face, added, 'It so happens that this story is exactly the kind of connection you've come to Lahore to unearth. What I will tell you now is at the heart of your research, so listen carefully.'

I inched my recorder closer to him and drew in a breath.

'The house looked exactly as it does in this photograph from 1935, except that rooms had been built where my father is standing here in this empty verandah. And as I was looking up at those rooms, a Sikh gentleman opened the door. I explained to him that I was born in this house and had come from Pakistan to see it, and he promptly opened the door and welcomed me in. "But first, breakfast!" he exclaimed.

'After we ate, he showed me his section of the house, which was the front portion where the men used to gather. We used to call this the *baithak*, and it had a few rooms, bathrooms and a kitchen. I was almost surprised that nothing had changed; time had been kind to this house. Then he brought me out into the courtyard and pointed to the space above the arches where the stone plaques were still fixed. The main plaque with the name of the house was intact. Jokingly, he told me that his mail still came to this address—Shams Manzil. We then went up to the *chhatt*, and from there we got an extraordinary view of the city. It was far removed from the days of Dussehra and Diwali in our small Jullundur. This was a view of a modern city, populated, sprawling and bustling.

'Then he said he would show me the section that used to be our living quarters. You see, the house was very large, and so after the Partition it had been divided into four portions. The ground-floor front portion was inhabited by the Sikh gentleman's family, and the rest of the house—the area above the garage, the living quarters of my family and those of my cousin's family—were allotted to three brothers of a Thakur family. The brothers had partitioned off their part of the house by building a wall inside and calling their section Durga Bhawan. We walked inside Durga Bhawan to where my family used to live, and what the Sikh gentleman said on the threshold of the house I will never forget.'

For the second time that day, there were tears brimming in the old man's eyes. Wiping them, he continued in a lilting voice, '"*Thakurain, ghar de maalik aa gaye ne*." He was calling out to a widow, the oldest member of the Thakur family, telling her that the original owner of the house had returned. I was so emotional, tears ran down my cheeks … just as they are now!' he smiled. 'I was young, perhaps just forty, but all my memories of childhood and the house rushed back on hearing the Sikh gentleman's words and I was overwhelmed. My heart filled with emotion.

'Anyway, the old woman was very unwell, but asked me to come inside and see her. I wiped my face dry and walked into her bedroom. By then everyone from the *mohalla* had gathered around to see what was happening, who had come and from where. As I sat down at her bedside, she held my hand and the first thing she asked me in Punjabi was whether we had reached Pakistan safely. She said she had heard stories of people from Pakistan coming back to the *mohalla* to see their old homes and retrieve belongings. But no one had come back to that palatial house. She had wondered what had happened to its owners.'

'She had been waiting for you, all those years?' I asked.

'*Jee*,' he nodded. 'She was waiting and then, still holding my hand, she asked me tenderly what had taken me so long. "*Beta*, you took so long to come…" Imagine that, she had been concerned for our safety. Those were the values of those days. This was the kind of love and compassion people had for one another, regardless of religion. So I told her how my family had made it across during the riots and what everyone was doing now.

'When I was taking her leave to go see my old school, she told me to come back to have lunch with them. She even arranged for the neighbour's son to take me around the city on his scooter! My school had been converted into a girls' school, but some of the old staff were still there, so I went inside and looked around. I told them that I remembered the courtyard being flooded during the monsoon, and they all laughed and said it was still the same. After that, the boy took me to visit the shrine and then back home, where the family had prepared a grand feast in my honour. When I finally left, everyone from the *mohalla* gathered around Shams Manzil to say goodbye. To be honest, I wished that they had given me some time alone because I really wanted to walk through the old lanes of my childhood, but I didn't get a chance!' he laughed.

Then suddenly he stood up. '*Chalo*,' he said, 'come, I will show you Shams Manzil.'

Confused, I picked up the photograph from the sofa and held it out to him, but he shook his head and beckoned me to follow him up the stairs.

'For many years after we left Jullundur,' he reminisced as we climbed slowly, 'I would remember the streets of our *mohalla*, the colours of the buildings, the spaces where we used to play and, of course, our house. As I grew older, I felt such a connection with the city of my birth—especially after that trip—that I wished I had brought some of its soil back with me. But fate works in mysterious ways sometimes…' We reached the landing. Bright, golden sunlight flooded the room.

'*Aao*, come,' he said, leading me to a bookshelf that held nothing but an old stone plaque propped up between the shelves. The text was in Urdu and I attempted to read the words written in the centre with my functional knowledge of the language. The index finger of my right hand traced in the air the fading curve of a graceful half *shin* with its three dots overhead—the *nuqte*—as it merged into the barely visible round-headed *mim* and finally ended in the arch of a pale *sin*.

'Sh-m-s,' I read out slowly and then turned to him with wide eyes as realization dawned. 'Shams Manzil?'

'*Jee bilkul*, Shams Manzil. You are right,' he said, smiling.

'But how is this possible? How could you have this?'

'That's the whole story!'

He walked closer to the plaque and cleaned the dust off its surface with his palm. 'You already know about both my visits back to India, but this story I am going to tell you relates to my niece Samar and her husband, Air Commodore Kaiser Tufail, who is an aviation historian and wrote a largely unbiased book about the Indo-Pak wars.[7] Now, this book was so well-received on both sides of the border that he was invited to India in 2008 to talk about and promote it. So he and his wife travelled to India and toured the country a little after all the book events, including a visit to the ancestral home in Jullundur. Samar was born in Pakistan and had never been to Jullundur, but she had always heard fond stories from her elders and so was naturally quite curious. The couple had searched the area on the Internet before arriving, and though some of the names of roads had changed, finding their way around wasn't difficult.

'They were greeted by the Thakurs, who showed them around the house. But, much to their surprise, the *haveli* was being broken down to build shops in its place. The main portion had not yet been torn down, and this slab was still holding on securely. Later that day, the couple phoned the Thakur and requested him to let them have the stone plaque. He agreed and said that they could collect it the next morning. When the couple arrived and the plaque was handed over to them, they realized it was heavier than they had imagined: 15 kilos, perhaps more than the weight limit for flights! So they went to the outskirts of the city where the marble cutters sat, hoping to slice its depth in half, making it thinner and easier to transport. It was deduced that the plaque was made out of a rare Rajasthani stone, and no one had the proper tools for it. They would have to take it to Rajasthan!

'They decided to take a chance and walk across the border with the plaque—Wagah *se*, taking the same route that we had in 1947, and that I'd taken again twenty-five years later. But even then the risk of being held up by a customs officer—as the plaque bore old Urdu writing and hence could be considered an antique—was high. There was a long conversation at the border, as expected. The date on the plaque was as per the Islamic calendar—1331 AH— and when they translated it, they too were shocked to discover that it was ninety-nine years old, built in 1909 AD. They were precariously close to violating the Antiquities Act, which can penalize someone for taking items older than 100 years out of the country![8] But thankfully they were able to leave India, walk through no man's land and enter Pakistan, all the while carrying a sliver of Samar's ancestry and my childhood.'[9]

By now, both of Faiz Rabbani's hands were caressing the cracked surface of the plaque. 'Imagine how I must have felt to receive this plaque from them. It was as if a long lost part of me had been returned. We had resigned ourselves to the Partition. But on touching this stone again after nearly six decades, whatever the Divide had managed to destroy within me came back to life. It didn't matter any more how far Jullundur was, or how many borders I would have to cross to get there; it didn't matter because Jullundur was already here with me, in this house, contained in this rectangular stone plaque. That home, that part of my childhood, that courtyard, those summers and winters, my father and mother, the celebrations and the crowds of refugees—the plaque had absorbed the memories of everything.' Taking out a handkerchief from his kurta pocket, he wiped his eyes. Then, clearing his throat, he said, 'It was perfect when it arrived but unfortunately it remained sealed for many months, and the lack of moisture made parts of the stone weak and crumbly. That is how these cracks came to be...' He pointed to the far corners of the stone.

I looked up at him, speechless. I reached out carefully to touch the plaque, not wanting to disturb the already loosened parts. It had a thick black frame, and a painted border ran vertically on either side. The surface of the stone was not glacial like marble but smooth nonetheless. It had a warm, light mustard hue, and the black inscriptions had dulled over the decades. Two prominent gashes ran diagonally through the stone, interspersed with scores of smaller ones. Towards the bottom corners, chunks of the stone had fallen off.

'See there,' my host said, gesturing to the words. 'These verses on the plaque are written mostly in Urdu but with certain words of Farsi and Arabic—which was, in fact, quite the norm at the time. Some of these words are still commonly used, so you might be able to read them, but in places the writing is illegible due to the cracks.'

He traced one of the deeper cracks gently with his index finger. Then, clearing his throat, he began reading and explaining the verses, weaving a complicated tapestry of familial history, prayer and poetry.

'*Kya khoob ho gayi hai tauqeer Shams Manzil. Tauqeer* means dignity, the writer is describing the dignity or honour of the house. *Aur Qasr-e-Iram hai goya … Iram* means *bagh*, a garden, and *Qasr* means a palace, a fort, *mahal*—so a palace with a garden inside. And the word *goya* means perhaps. *Aur Qasr-e-Iram hai goya tasveer-e-Shams Manzil.* You understand the word *Tasveer*—photograph, image? So it says that the image of the house perhaps resembles a *Qasr-e-Iram*, a palace with a garden. *Ho naam Rehmat-Ullah aur Sadruddin ka roshan.* These are two of my ancestors, Rehmat-Ullah and Sadruddin, and the writer wishes for their names to be known far and wide. *Qayam rahe hamesha tanweer Shams-Manzil*—may the light of Shams Manzil burn bright forever.

'Now this next part is interesting, so listen carefully. *Fikr-e-bina*—this originates from Farsi and the phrase means the thought of laying down a foundation—*buniyad daalne ki soch, daalne ki lagan*, the determination to lay down the foundation. When is a house built? When we lay down the foundation. In Farsi, that is called *bina*. So the complete line is *Fikr-e-bina thi dil mein bola kalam se Hatif.* Now, Hatif is also an Iranian poet, but over here the word is more complicated. *Hatif* is a Farsi word, which means a *farishta*, an angel, a transcendental being. In Urdu we would call it a *Ghaib*, someone who is invisible, mystical, but whose words one can hear loud and clear in one's ears. The writer is saying *buniyad ki fikr thi dil mein*, there was determination in one's heart to lay down the foundation, *toh hatif se awaaz aayi*, the voice of a transcendental being said…' He paused for a moment, squinting at the letters that had all but faded, and then recited the final line, '*Likh bebadal hui hai tameer-e-Shams Manzil*. Write this down, that the architecture of Shams Manzil is unparalleled. *Tameer* means construction, the building. *Bebadal*, the word *Be* comes from Farsi and the word *Badal* comes from Arabic, and together they make *Bebadal*, which means that which cannot be replicated.'[10]

I listened intently to his explanation, enamoured by the complexity of the languages the family had amalgamated into the plaque, which represented the very spirit of Shams Manzil: everlasting, incomparable, a garden within a palace. Though the building stands no more, the happy survival and migration of its last remnant—the plaque that bore the family name—means that one part of the structure will at least last forever.

As I began photographing the plaque, feeling fortunate to have encountered such an incredible piece of family history and heritage, Mian Faiz Rabbani, drawing in a deep breath, began to recite the whole thing from memory—an homage to a home across the border:

Kya khoob ho gayi hai tauqeer Shams Manzil. Aur Qasr-e-Iram hai goya tasveer-e-Shams Manzil. Ho naam Rehmat-Ullah aur Sadruddin ka roshan. Qayam rahe hamesha tanweer Shams-Manzil. Fikr-e-bina thi dil mein bola kalam se Hatif. Likh bebadal hui hai tameer-e-Shams Manzil.

9

THE INHERITANCE OF CEREMONIAL SERVINGS

THE *KHAAS-DAAN* OF NARJIS KHATUN

NARJIS KHATUN WAS a woman of few words. Her raspy voice rarely filled the air, as if she only spoke when absolutely necessary. She scrutinized me quietly when I arrived at her home in Lahore, but said nothing until we sat down across from one another at the dinner table. She waited till midway through the meal, her gaze shifting between her plate and me, and then, clearing her throat, she pierced the silence with a single word.

'Patiala.'

Five pairs of eyes belonging to the members of her family turned towards us.

'Have you ever been?' she continued.

Slowly I shook my head; I'd never been to that city in Punjab. 'Are you from there?' I asked.

Her smooth, bare face broke into a smile. 'Yes, I was born in Patiala in 1937 on the first day of *saawan*. We lived with my maternal grandfather, my *nana*, who was a tax collector, in a large *haveli* with fourteen rooms. Sometimes he would even set up a local court in some of the rooms!'

Her grey eyes danced with joy.

'How come you lived with the maternal side of your family?' I asked. Our conversation had brought the dinner to a pause; no cutlery clanged, the heaps of rice, meat and potatoes lay untouched on our plates. All that unfolded now was family history.

'You see, my *nana* only had daughters, and so when they got married, their husbands moved in with them. It was quite an unconventional set-up, but he couldn't bear to be separated from his daughters. My mother, Zubeida Khatun, married my father, Mustafa Haider Naqvi, who was originally from Samana in Patiala district. That is where we went during the days of the Partition to escape the riots in the city.'

Her son-in-law, Justice Shabbar Rizvi, was sat at the head of the table. He told me that, coincidentally, his family too had migrated from Samana at the time of the Partition, but it was mere fate that had brought the two families together in Lahore.

'I was ten years old in 1947, but I remember everything about Hindustan,' said the old woman.

* * *

After dinner, we retreated into the living room. The eldest grandchild, Bano, slowly led her grandmother to the sofa by the window. We both sat down close to her, and her daughter, Lisa, sat by the door. In the bright light of the chandelier, Narjis Khatun's cloudy eyes, looking straight into mine, resembled a storm brewing in an overcast sky, which was exactly how she began her story.

'In the days of the Partition, there was something heavy in the air, dark and dense, and our life in Patiala fell prey to that darkness. At the time, the population of the state was about 1,800,000, half of whom were Sikhs, and the remaining half were Hindus and Muslims in an equal ratio.[1] We had heard that there had been mass genocides in Calcutta and then in Bihar. By 1947, when the riots reached Rawalpindi and other parts of the Punjab, the Maharaja of Patiala invited large numbers of Sikhs and Hindus to seek shelter and refuge in the state. We would keep living together, remain united regardless of religion—that was the hope. A relief committee was formed with a relief fund for refugees,[2] though little did we know that the accommodation of these refugees would be at the cost of our own homes and lives.

Again and again we were told that no harm would come to the Muslim population.

'But slowly, riots, abductions and looting began in the farthest corners of the state and finally reached us. There was much bloodshed in Patiala, in all the communities, but eventually it was we [the Muslims] who had to flee. Our family was full of young children and women, so naturally the elders feared for our safety. We decided that we could no longer live in Patiala. My *nana* was a powerful man, the tax collector, but that position came with the risk of being targeted during the riots. The future had never been as uncertain as it was in those days of August. We packed a few boxes with only the essentials—some clothes, some utensils, a few valuables—and we left in the middle of the night. We left behind almost all our belongings for fear of being attacked or looted on the way. And under the cloak of darkness, we travelled to Samana, only 16 miles away but somehow calm, despite the imminent Partition.'

'You went to your father's house?' I asked, and she nodded.

'Bari Amma, show her the things that were brought with you from Patiala,' Bano urged her grandmother. Smiling, Narjis Khatun gestured for her to bring them out.

As we waited, she continued the story, and it became clear that her mother tongue was from the other side of the border. She spoke in a low voice, and very quickly, so at times the words were barely audible. There were few clear demarcations between words and so, though it resembled Urdu, her language had a rhythmic lilt seemingly borrowed from a more rural Punjabi. The words and phrases she used were coarse, as some dialects of Hindi could be. The texture of each sentence was gritty, utilitarian and unadorned despite the intonations, and far removed from the glacially poetic Urdu spoken by the rest of her family.

'Our relations arrived in Samana from various parts of the Punjab. In the early days, I remember playing with our cousins in the fields, sometimes quite late into the night. It was a nice place and it was quiet until the riots reached there as well. Compared to the luxuries we had in Patiala, Samana was different—not a city, but more like a small town. There were unevenly laid alleyways leading to brick houses; there was no electricity or modernity. It was small and rural but many Sayyid families had arrived there during that time. Eventually, once we migrated to Pakistan, everyone dispersed across the country, so in hindsight Samana feels like a special place.'

'Samana has a very unique history,' added Lisa. 'It is a town where several Sayyid families, who are direct descendants of the Prophet through the twelve Imams of the Shia faith, had settled down. Archives tell us that Imam Sayyid Mash-had Ali—a grandson of Imam Ali Raza, the eighth descendant of the Prophet—fled to India from Iran and colonized the area, naming it after his mother, Samana. He was buried there about 1,200 years ago, and after the visit of my husband in 2003, his tomb and other shrines came into prominence again, and the town has now become a major pilgrimage site for Shia Muslims. Historically, Samana has always been a place of saints and scholars.'

Nodding gravely, Narjis Khatun continued, 'At night, we would hear people scream warnings—"*Sikh aa gaye, Sikh aa gaye*," the Sikhs are coming—and we would all rush to our imambargah hall to pray. The Sikhs were never able to come close to our homes because of our *dua*, the prayers that saved us.'

Just then, Bano walked into the room with two metallic objects and placed them on the small side-table next to her grandmother. Using the corners of her sea-green dupatta, Narjis Khatun wiped the heirlooms that had been in her family for three generations, making sure to clean even the tiniest crevasse.

'These are the objects they brought with them from Patiala,' said Bano, 'and for as long as I can remember, they have been lying on the shelves of our homes, so I never actually thought of them as having any sentimental value.'

'Do they hold sentimental value?' I asked the old woman.

When she answered, it was with carefully weighed words that seemed to have been uttered for the very first time. 'When we left Patiala, it was to eventually make our way to the new country of Pakistan, a land we believed we had earned, we had gained. But little did we know how much we were going to lose in the process, how much of our life would remain on the other side of this border. I told you that we left our home as it was—full of valuables and decadent objects. But, before we left, my mother filled a big *tokra*, a metal basket, with the utensils from our kitchen—pans, woks, *lassi* glasses. I think within that pile she placed these two objects as well…' Her voice trailed off. '… These objects that would come to remind us of the everyday traditions and customs that we had grown up with in Patiala.

'You see, my *nani* was very fond of *paan*, a digestive made with betel leaves, and every day she would sit and meticulously prepare it for the members of the family. But hers wasn't the kind you can buy today. According to her, making *paan* was an art that one had to acquire. It took time, patience and practice to understand the correct consistency of the ingredients that made up the perfect digestive.'

Lisa came closer to the sofa and crouched down near her mother. 'Ammi had seen her *nani* make *paan* every day, and so it became a habit of hers as well,' she said. 'When they came to Samana and then migrated to Pakistan, they couldn't keep up the same lifestyle, nor did they have the means, so this extravagant habit was somewhat lost…' Placing her hand over her mother's, she continued, 'Ammi has never really admitted this, so I'm quite surprised at the conversation we are having today, but one can tell that these two objects are subconsciously of nostalgic value for her.'

'*Achha achha*, listen to me,' said the grey-eyed woman, firmly clasping her daughter's hand. 'When my mother got married, this utensil came as part of her bridal trousseau, her dowry. But she was never interested in *paan* and so eventually it became part of my trousseau. This would have been given to every girl. It is called a *khaas-daan*.'

She held in her palm a beautiful dome-shaped object, once a standard inclusion in every bride's trousseau. At first glance it looked almost like a smaller Eastern version of a French cloche. But on closer inspection I could see that the dome was not quite semi-circular; rather, it was a rounded oval. Its top was tall and pointed, similar to those of mosque domes. It was cast in bronze and intricately hand-carved to create a pattern of foliage around the outer body. The bottom plate was equally magnificently embossed, with a rounded braid-like pattern and foliage at the centre of its flat surface. Despite its years and the air of the different places it had been exposed to, the heirloom was in a surprisingly good condition, its bronze darkening only at the very top or within the carved crevasses.

'What is a *khaas-daan* used for?' I asked, holding it up to the light and studying it from various angles. It was heavier than it looked but smooth to the touch; each and every flower and leaf had been handcrafted with precision so as to retain the softness of its look.

'Whenever there was a special guest at home, the *paan* would be made and served in this. It was *khaas*, special, for a special occasion.' The old woman took the *khaas-daan* from my hands and demonstrated how it would be served.

'But why would such a thing be included in your trousseau?' I asked.

'Because, in those days, it was part of one's culture,' said Lisa. 'It used to be considered a quality of delicacy that a lady should know how to make and serve *paan* to the family's guests. Feeding guests like this was an art, as Ammi said.' With a discreet smile, her mother added, 'One was expected to make a beautiful small *paan*, tightly wrapped so that none of the ingredients fell out, and then present it. The guest would accept the *paan*, pick it up and say *"Adaab"* in return, bowing their head politely.' She then picked up a rectangular silver box, resembling a jewellery box, from the sofa next to her and opened it. This was her *paan-daan*, and its little compartments contained the different ingredients for making *paan*.

'*Khayengi aap?*' she asked me. Would I like some?

An ardent fan of the sweet *paan* I often devoured at home in Delhi, I accepted her offer excitedly. Bano crept up and whispered in my ear, 'This isn't the kind of *paan* you are thinking of!'

Confused, I looked at the process of preparation unfolding before me. A medium-sized betel leaf was cleaned and the ingredients lathered onto it carefully. I was walked through the list of condiments. 'I will make a simple *paan* for you,' said Narjis Khatun, 'but when I make it for myself, it will be exactly how my *nani* used to make it, with *supari*, areca nut, and *zarda*, tobacco. This white paste is an edible mixture of slacked lime, called *choona*. This brown paste is called *kattha* or catechu, often used in Ayurvedic medicine.'

Then, she skilfully extracted one silver-coated cardamom pod from a small green glass bottle, crushed it onto the pastes and folded the betel leaf into a triangular shape, enclosing the mixture tightly within. She then picked up the *khaas-daan*, placed the *paan* on it, and offered it to me. I smiled and accepted it, followed by "*Adaab*", and then popped the folded leaf into my mouth.

Immediately I realized that Bano had been right as I saw her giggle out of the corner of my eye. I was used to ingredients like *gulkand*, a preserve of rose petals, or *mukhwas*, a mixture of fennel, sesame and anise seeds and coconut, all of which sweetened the *paan*. The burst of flavours in my mouth was not sweet; on the contrary, it was … highly unusual for my palette.

As I chewed the bitter concoction and slowly swallowed it, Narjis Khatun began preparing a second *paan* for herself. She picked up an odd tool from the table, something that resembled a metallic nutcracker. It had two prongs: one attached to a D-shaped carved frame, which was likely made from either bronze or an alloy; and the other to what looked like a knife blade. When the two prongs were brought together, they would cut whatever was placed along the blade—in this case, a round areca nut. She cracked it with the iron blade and proceeded to cut it into smaller pieces.

'This too came from India. It is called a *sarota*, but you will not find many like this today. It belonged to my *nani*. Look, see how much it's been used, it has darkened on the inside. Now these are the only things left from our life there.'

'Bari Amma,' Bano said, 'why did you leave India?'

'*Beta*, leaving was the only way to survive.'

'Did no one tell you that you might survive even if you stayed there?'

'No, no one did, because no one believed it; the chances of that happening were slim. And because we had fled our home in Patiala in such haste, we had only taken the things we thought we would need immediately. But we stayed in Samana longer than we had expected, and the season turned from monsoon to winter. We were completely ill-prepared. But my father had a close friend in Patiala, a Hindu man named Ram Dutt, who came to Samana and brought us all warm clothes. It was then that we bequeathed all of our valuables, or whatever little we had left, to Ram Dutt. There was a box of fine silk clothes with glittering brocades that had somehow ended up with us and, along with that, we gathered up all of the jewellery we had brought and gave it to him for safekeeping. There were these enormous gold *patriyan*,' she said, gesturing to her feet, showing us the size of the gold anklets, 'there were bangles and necklaces, a *maang-tikka*, rings and so many other valuables. The only thing we kept was some money. But the box of precious items was accompanied by a small request from my father: that if we were able to cross the border safely, we would contact Ram Dutt for these items, which would help us begin a new life. And if by chance we were not so lucky, he should keep and use them as symbols of his friendship with my father.'

As she paused for a moment, I thought about the friendship of Mustafa Haider Naqvi and Ram Dutt, sealed with such heartbreaking promise.

'How did you come to Pakistan then, Bari Amma?' asked Bano.

'One day, a fleet of buses arrived in Samana and transported us all to the train station. From there we were to catch a train to Pakistan.'

'Were you scared? You were only ten years old.'

'I was not scared because we were all together. But I suppose you could say we were all nervous. Because I was quite tall and attractive for my age, I was made to wear a burqa all through the journey to our new home. I don't remember whose I wore but I was swimming in it! When we arrived at the station, the train to Pakistan stood before us, manned by Pakistani army guards, who told us not to eat or drink anything, for it could be poisoned. Those were bad days, you had no idea what people were capable of.'

'So, where did you think you were going, what was happening?'

'I was ten! I had some understanding of it, I knew where we were going and was so happy about it. We were on our way to Pakistan, to safety. At the time, the main aim was to reach Pakistan any way we could. When we got on the train, its conditions were worse than we could imagine. People were crammed and pressed against each other, with no space to move or even breathe. There were people hanging on to the doors and windows, and then there were people sitting on top of the train with their luggage and children and even small animals like goats or dogs. My brother fell sick on the train and we planned to get off at the first station in Pakistan.

'But the strangest thing was that we never realized when it happened, when one country ended and another began … when India stopped and Pakistan started. There were no obvious differences between a land and its conjoined neighbour, and so I suspect that we gained our new citizenship in a moment curiously lost on us. Tucked away in a corner of an overcrowded train, we had quietly become Pakistani.'

She sighed, her grey eyes heavy with memories.

'Multan, we got off at Multan. We didn't know anyone, so we scrambled through the land until we came across an abandoned *haveli* that might have belonged to a Hindu family that had migrated to India. In those days of riots and uprootedness, everything was allowed and every empty house was a potential home. After all, we too had left behind two such homes in two cities across the border, likely to be inhabited by those who found them. We lived in that house for a while, buying whatever food we could and trying to establish some form of normalcy. My brother's health also recovered. But our money wasn't going to last forever and this worried Abba-ji. One day someone told him that we should move to a city called Alipur, where land was being allotted to refugees and where living was not expensive. My father agreed, and so yet again we packed whatever belongings we had and left for Alipur.

'The people there were very kind and supportive. They gave us food and water, welcomed us into their homes and helped us get on our feet. We were even allotted two kanals of land and a buffalo. After that we would drink kingly cups of sweet tea every day.'

'Alipur is an eight-hour drive from Lahore,' Bano told me. 'My *nana*'s family is from there and that is where they met and married, nine years after the Partition.'

The old woman nodded. 'When we had settled down in Pakistan, my father wrote to Ram Dutt. And, would you imagine, he had remained faithful all that time, safeguarding our valuables. He travelled to the Indian side of the border and my father was on the Pakistani side to receive our belongings. Everything in those boxes was intact—all the jewellery and even the clothes with silk brocade.'

'Do you still have those things with you?'

She scoffed. '*Nahi*, in the circumstances we sold it all. Everything.'

My eyes widened with sadness at what she had said. There was such crassness in her words, yet I knew that it was the only way they could have survived. Their conditions had been so dire and their need for survival so desperate that the family had literally eaten into its old life by selling, one by one, each piece of family jewellery, each brocade-bordered cloth.

Bano looked at her grandmother's downcast face. 'Bari Amma, when you arrived in Pakistan, were things really as bad as you've described?'

'We had nothing left, *beta*. The papers for the properties we had left behind came much later, and only then could we claim some land. But, before that, the Partition reduced us to penury.'

'Did you not remember India, wish that things hadn't turned out the way they did?'

'I would remember it and I still do. But how much can you afford to think of a life you have left behind? There was no point in thinking about it; we could not go back there. But the truth is, even though I might try to forget—and trust me, I have been successful in doing so for many years—I know that I can never truly get over what the Partition did to us. Even though it was our decision to leave, and we made the choice, I will never forget the Partition of Hindustan, the *taqseem-e-Hind*. [3] How can I forget my land, my Patiala, my Samana?'

Her moist eyes looked around, searching the room for answers that did not live there. Then she turned to me and, placing her right hand over her heart, lips barely moving, she said, '*Ab bass, beta*, enough.'

* * *

Later that evening, when it was just Bano and me sitting on the floor of the living room, I picked up the *khaas-daan* and caressed its smooth surface. Holding it out to her, I asked, 'Does this hold sentimental value for you?'

'Before tonight, I don't think we knew that it held sentimental value for anyone,' she smiled. 'I saw a completely different side of my *nani* today, and because of it I suppose I view these heirlooms differently now. But, truth be told, my associations are more with the physical place, India, than with these objects.' She bit her lower lip pensively and then, knitting her eyebrows, asked, 'Did you understand everything she said?'

'What do you mean?'

'Her language, did you understand it?'

'Of course!' I laughed. 'Didn't you?'

Swallowing hard, she nodded. 'She was speaking in a language called Samanishahi. It becomes more pronounced when she's excited, as she was today.'

'I have never heard of such a language,' I fumbled. 'I don't speak it, so how could I...? But I did, I understood everything.'

'Samanishahi is essentially a mix of Hindi and Punjabi, but unless someone is fluent in both languages, they don't quite pick up the nuances of the tongue. You would understand it all because you're a native Hindi speaker. Her tongue is a little coarser; it's more raw, as if made from the soil of the land. Comparatively, Urdu is softer; its idiom is a little sweeter and more polished. At the dinner table, when my father spoke to my *nani*, it was in Samanishahi. In fact, when my parents' union was formalized, that was one thing that connected the two families—that they could speak each other's native language.

'When I was young, my two grandmothers would speak to each other in Samanishahi, and I remember thinking that it was a language they just made up so they could talk in private! At some point, I even associated its primitiveness with the fact that maybe they weren't well-educated and that's why they spoke this way. It was not that I was judging, but it sounded so crude that I felt for them ... I never made the connection as to why the older generation from both sides of my family spoke the same way.'

I nodded in fascination, still not quite grasping how I could understand a language I had never even heard of. I thought back to our conversation in order to extract words or phrases that had sounded unfamiliar, but I couldn't. And then, still holding the *khaas-daan* in her hands, Bano began her third-generation tale of the Partition's lingering effects on her family.

'It wasn't until 2003 that the border between India and Pakistan really began opening up,' she said. 'That was the year my father went to Chandigarh for an official conference and from there managed to travel to Samana. Before that, Samana had been a sort of fantastical place for us, only alive in the memories of my grandparents. My father, who is essentially from the first generation of Pakistanis, had heard stories of the family's affluence there, the land they used to own, the childhood they had, the struggle they witnessed when they came here. But because I had never been there and nor did I have any tangible connection to it, Samana remained just another word in my vocabulary. I associate it more with my father's family than with my mother's, probably because my paternal grandfather was the only person before my father who had gone back to India, in 1986, to retrieve some papers for their land claim.

'But, in 2003, when my father went across for this official visit, he requested that the Chief Minister of Punjab let him visit his family's ancestral town. Very kindly, the government arranged a visa for him for two days and a minister even accompanied him. Because the border had just been opened and having a Pakistani official in India was such a novelty at that time, the event garnered considerable interest in the media.

'When he arrived, he received a welcome I don't think any of us expected. No one was obliged to receive him, but from what he described to us on his return, the whole town had come out to welcome him. Banners reading "The son of Samana has returned!" were hung in the streets, and they took pictures and even had an official photographer make a video of the half-day he spent in the village! They even had the footage processed quickly enough for my father to take with him. And when we saw that video, and when we heard how excited my grandmothers, their siblings, and my aunt and uncles were because my father had crossed the border and gone back to their Samana, well, it just made the whole thing...' She paused, thinking of the right word. 'It just made the whole thing real. Samana became real for me. Since then, my family has made so many friends across the border; they visit almost every year. My father once took about seventy members of his family to visit the ancestral graves and shrines.

'And then something else very interesting happened. Over the course of his visits, my father told the Punjab government about the existence of an ancient shrine in Samana. Little did the people of the town know that the land where they once let their cattle graze was the very site where Imam Sayyid Mash-had Ali, who founded Samana, was buried! When they cleared the area, sure enough, an inscription appeared confirming it. That is the only Shia shrine in South Asia belonging to a direct descendant of the Prophet Muhammad.'[4]

Bano tapped her fingers against the *khaas-daan*, creating a dull, hollow sound. Smiling to herself, she continued, 'My grandmother is old now; she cannot walk very well and that makes her nervous while travelling. She was so certain that she would never be able to see India again, and so this video of my father's visit became a real treasure for her. It returned something to her, something that she had lost. It might seem silly but these videos returned to her the feeling of being there as a child.'

'Have you ever been to Samana yourself?' I asked.

'I have. I was in Chandigarh for a friend's wedding and, to be honest, I didn't think I'd have the time to go to Samana, so I didn't make any plans. But then, towards the very end of my trip, I decided to visit, because I knew how disappointed everyone would be in me otherwise. So I went and I think surreal is the best way to describe my experience.

'I travelled there with my father's friend, a Sikh gentleman, Nainy Uncle, who had been there before and was aware of our family history. At first glance, Samana looked like those typical dusty small towns that one sees in films. On one side, there were *chhoti-chhoti galiyan*, alleyways like my grandmother described, children playing on the street with tyres and goats, people sitting under banyan trees on woven *charpai* beds and just talking to each other. It was very idyllic and kind of sleepy and backward-looking. On the other side of the main street was a small graveyard, basically the first thing you see when you enter the town. That was our first stop.'

As Bano described the town embedded in the hearts of her family members, she did so with great care and delicacy, making sure to leave out no details.

'The graveyard has only three tombs and these belong to my family: one is my father's great-grandfather, the second is his wife and the third we do not know yet. That they were fully intact was close to a miracle. And what I saw on them left me even more shaken. When my grandfather came back to Samana in 1986 he had visited these graves, and because there were no headstones on them, he had created a makeshift plaque with wet mud. He carved out each name with his finger. When my father went in 2003, he got the graves cleaned and proper stones erected, but this handwritten plaque my grandfather had put up is still very much there. I think that was the first time I felt like I was a part of something much bigger than myself.'

With that, she let out a deep sigh.

'Just as we were leaving the graveyard, we saw a group of people coming towards us. Somehow they just knew that someone had come from Pakistan. I tried to explain to them who I was—the daughter of a man who often travelled here from across the border, from Lahore. They knew immediately who I was. "Oho, judge *sahab*'s daughter! Judge *sahab*'s daughter has come!" They had seen my whole family, and they also knew that I lived abroad, which was why I had never visited. All the townspeople suddenly wanted to come and meet us, and knew everything about our family, like we were a part of that town. It's difficult to explain, but there was just so much familiarity and love, and I remember feeling so drawn to them all.

'Samana didn't feel like another country any more; it felt like the very essence of me. In that moment, the pain of a Partition I had never witnessed, the pain of my grandparents when they had crossed the border, the pain of "othering" those we didn't know or understand, the pain of conforming—all for the sake of survival—became more real for me than I could ever have imagined.'

She took a long pause. 'The people of the village took us to the tomb of one of my ancestors, Mir Aman Ullah Hussaini, after whom our ancestral village in Pakistan is named. Our family tree had been enshrined there on a plaque on the wall, and my father's name was inscribed at the very bottom. At the end of his name they had added "Samanwi", to denote that he hailed from that town. Justice Syed Shabbar Raza Rizvi Samanwi. Though this continues to amuse us, I have never encountered anything more endearing; the sense of belonging and acceptance was so mutual. They took us to the main shrine, which housed the grave that my father had helped the government locate. Even though I had heard stories about people from various religions coming to pray there because they believed in its energy, this was the first time I saw it for myself.

'This was a proper enclosed shrine with a durbar and some graves on one side. On the other were rooms where one could go to pray and light candles and lamps. In the very centre was an open courtyard with a huge *Alam*, the symbol of the Shia faith. The day we visited was a Thursday and pilgrims from all over—Hindus, Muslims, Sikhs—had come to pay their respects and pray. It was incredible for me to witness this because we come from a generation that claims to be secular and open to pluralism and multiculturalism; but to see the same facets in a place my grandparents came from, a place where they had left parts of themselves behind ... well, it filled my heart with pride. I think, during that trip, many things just came together for me.'

'Did you hear people speaking Samanishahi?' I asked.

'Yes, and that was another very surreal element of the trip.' Her face broke into a big smile. 'I had lived my whole life in the midst of a language I did not speak but had unknowingly inherited. In this small town, on the other side of the border, that very language thrived. If we stopped to ask for directions, people would reply in Samanishahi. If we asked about the graves and tombs, they would explain the history in Samanishahi. But with that came a heartbreaking realization—that there is just one generation after my grandmothers that speaks this language. No one else will know it after my father is gone. And so, when I tell my children the story of where their ancestors came from, and if

I want them to hear their own language in its truest form with all the nuances and intonations, we will have to cross the border, because it's really only available in Samana.'

'Could you not learn it now?' I asked. 'Or at least teach yourself to be more attuned to it?'

With a sad smile she replied, 'I don't think I can because it's difficult to adopt, not having spoken it since birth.'

I nodded, and for a moment we were both quiet, lost in the thoughts of forgotten languages.

'Anyway,' Bano said, breaking the silence, 'it was very strange to be in Samana because I had never thought I would have any affiliation to it. But being there, even just for a day, made me feel like that place was a part of me and I was a part of it. I realized why my father was so attached to this place and why he wanted his children to have the same attachments. It felt like homecoming.'

I wanted to say that I understood, that being in Lahore with her, on the soil of my own ancestors, I could relate to how she had felt when she travelled to India. But before I could say anything, Bano looked up at me.

'I had always wondered why my grandparents had never spoken to us about the Partition or how and why they came across to Pakistan. Perhaps they were too young to understand what was going on, or maybe they were brainwashed by the politics around them. They were just so certain that they were going to die amidst the riots, and then they miraculously survived and arrived here. Then, I suppose, they didn't know what to do with all the memories they had accumulated of this place called home that was now beyond reach.

'Tonight, after listening to my *nani* speak to you about her life, and realizing that she had never mentioned any of those things before, I feel as though she believed that if she didn't speak about Patiala or Samana any longer, the memory would fade and disappear. As though it had never existed. And I feel really sad now, knowing that they tried to bury that history and didn't make an active effort to keep it alive, maybe because it was too painful. The very same history that I now feel so proud to have inherited.

'I cannot imagine what it must have felt like to flee your home in the middle of the night because you feared for your life...' She let the sadness in her voice fade into the expanse of the room and waited until it surrounded us, unshakeable and heavy as a boulder. 'But surely it must be the most heartbreaking thing to force yourself to forget your own past.'

10

THE HOCKEY FIELD I LEFT BEHIND

THE PHOTOGRAPHS OF NAZEER ADHAMI

'PARTITION,' HE SAID, AND his hands broke away from one another, motioning the Divide. 'At the time of the Partition, my parents were staunch followers of the Muslim League, but despite that they stayed on in India. Strangely enough, they chose to. *Beta-ji*, child, life is a long and complex tale. If you will listen, I will tell you about it...'

Eagerly I nodded and Nazeer Adhami cleared his throat. The pale lemon yellow of his shalwar kameez stood out against both the maroon sofa he sat on and his own soft, sand-coloured skin. In many ways, his face reminded me of my *nana*'s, equally soft, kind and wise. He straightened the wire frame of his spectacles, brushing aside his bushy grey-white eyebrows. Then with a deep and heavy sigh, he began.

'The truth is that my whole family, including me, worked for the Muslim League. Hardoi—that's where we are from, where I was born in 1930. It is a small district near Lucknow in Uttar Pradesh. My father was born in a family of *zamindars*, landowner–tax collectors, but studied to be an advocate. In 1920, he joined the combined efforts of the Khilafat Movement and the Indian National Congress under Gandhi, seeking to impose pressure on the British—a combined Hindu–Muslim movement of peaceful resistance.[1] Due to these associations, my father was rusticated from the Aligarh Muslim University, after which he travelled to Calcutta to finish his degree. Then he returned to Aligarh in 1926 and, while continuing his education there, joined the Muslim League with full force and dedication. Right from the beginning,' he swept his hands through the air to show the passing of time, 'my father's mindset was political. My mother was born in Bilgram, also in Hardoi district. As she grew up, she too found meaning in political work and did mostly propaganda, creating awareness among young men and women.[2] She would organize debates, lectures, and often travel around the town in cars, making announcements on the loudspeaker, encouraging people to join.'

'Join…?'

'The League, of course! Working towards the creation of a separate Muslim homeland, independent of India. I was sixteen when I first joined in 1946, working within the student bodies, encouraging young Muslims to vote. I considered it my duty. In those days, we were inspired by the very idea of Pakistan…'

As he released the word into the room for the first time, allowing it to settle and join the conversation, he did so with a sense of pride. He was no longer reclining on the sofa, but sitting bolt upright, his hands placed on his shalwar-clad knees and his eyes full of belief and purpose.

'Look, *beta*,' his wife added, as she too sat up straighter next to him, 'at the end of the day, there was and still is a difference, *farak toh tha*, between Hindu and Muslim.'

'*Farak*,' I repeated softly, feeling the sharpness of each syllable against my lips.

'Yes, without a doubt,' said the man who resembled my grandfather. 'Even though *we* considered ourselves equal to the Hindus in every way, there was no denying the inherent differences. Though Muslims had been a dominant power in India for centuries, and were the only people apart from the British who ever gave India a semblance of unity, that was all in the past.[3] We were certain, given the way the political situation was unfolding, that with the dissipation of the Raj and the dawn of Independence, there would be no intention to give equal rights and representation to both communities. And maybe it was to regain some of the lost glory of the past, or perhaps for adequate political space in the new, democratic order emerging in India ... but the concern was not to get drowned in an unseeing, uncaring sea of majoritarianism.[4]

'That was, in our opinion,' he gestured to himself and his wife, 'the basic cause for the demand for Pakistan: that we were living in a world of difference. And it was not merely about religion, though that played a role; the differences were intrinsically cultural. Our diet, our prayers, our clothes, our language. Everything was different.' He spoke in the past tense, as if Hindus and Muslims no longer existed in the same thought.

In March 1940, barely seven years before the Partition, when Muhammad Ali Jinnah put forth the proposition of Pakistan in his presidential address to the Muslim League in Lahore, he said that 'it was but a dream to believe that Hindus and Muslims could ever evolve a common nationality, that it was a misconception as they belonged to different religions, philosophies, social customs and literature[s]'.[5] The first time I read this address, I couldn't understand the vehemence, perhaps due to my own naivety, liberal upbringing or lay approach as an ordinary citizen. Or perhaps it was the fact that thousands of Muslims still lived in India, which made me question the drastically separatist notion. You or me, the text had clearly elucidated, us or them. When Gandhi protested during their discussions in 1944, pleading with Jinnah to consider how the independent states envisioned by the League would benefit from the split, and the potential menace they might cause themselves, Jinnah inflexibly responded that this was the 'price India must pay for its independence'.[6]

And that day, for the very first time, seated in front of a Lahori couple whose origins could be traced to a centrally landlocked province of India, I became exceptionally conscious of my perceived otherness. 'How different are we?' I asked hesitantly, in a voice I didn't recognize as my own.

'Very intolerant, Hindus can be very intolerant,' came the assertive reply.

'But I am also Hindu…' I began softly, looking into the man's eyes, my fingers wrapped nervously around the ends of my dupatta. 'I am also Hindu.'

'It's okay, because you are like our daughter,' smiled his wife, patting my cheek.

My eyebrows knitted together in confusion, and the man, sensing this, said, '*Beti*, on an individual basis, everyone was and continues to be good. But as a community, *farak toh hai*.' There is a difference.

'When we arrived in Pakistan after the Partition,' his wife cut in, 'we thanked Allah for our safety. Only after setting foot in this land could we breathe freely again.'

The man nodded sharply. 'It is crucial to understand the historic lineages of these differences that led to the demand for a separate state, for what is common knowledge is not always true. Sometimes, we need to believe things to see them, need to unlearn our subconscious biases to learn the truth.

'Quaid-e-Azam [Jinnah] mentioned once that it was important to differentiate the politics of the Congress from the Hindus as a community; his position did not arise from ill will towards any Hindu in particular. Rather, his cause had always been to fight the British, not the Hindus.[7] When he first returned to India from England, his aim was to lead a unified force against the Raj. In fact, he played a key role in preparing a draft constitution for India and getting it adopted by both the Muslim League and the Congress. The Lucknow Pact was a result of this constitution, where the Muslims of the League agreed to work with Hindus towards freedom, in return for the Congress conceding to separate electorates for Muslims.[8]

'But it was at the first Roundtable Conference in 1930–31 that Jinnah *sahab* realized he could no longer remain in the middle ground between the two communities he was attempting to unite. Muslims thought him to be too pro-Hindu, Hindus thought him to be a Muslim communist…[9] A profound line had been drawn between the two, and Jinnah *sahab* stood on that very line.

For both communities, this position was unacceptable. In 1938, years before I joined the Aligarh Muslim University, he addressed a gathering of students, to whom he confessed that the Roundtable Conference had led him to conclude that no hope remained for unity in India. He felt so depressed and helpless that he left India to settle down in London.'[10]

Attempting to unlearn, I asked him about the transformation of Jinnah into Quaid-e-Azam, the Great Leader.

'Ah,' he said softly, 'the circumstances that compelled him to transform from an all-India nationalist leader into a "Muslim" one, despite his very liberal lifestyle, are both complex, and a true microcosm of the political landscape of that time. Jinnah *sahab* returned from England in 1934 to find a persistent absence of political harmony in India, but also that the Muslim community was somehow divided within itself. And the same men who had earlier rejected his unifying values now invited him to represent the Muslim cause. And he, who had returned to India with forlorn hope, resisted the idea of separatism between the two communities right up until it was the Congress that made it clear that there could be no cooperation with the Muslim League.[11] This is what finally made Jinnah the champion of Indian Muslims, the sole spokesperson for Pakistan, our Quaid-e-Azam.[12] It is unfortunate, though, that the only way we could carve a substantial identity for ourselves was through separation, but it was inevitable. And we were only fighting for our rights. We earned this land.'

My head seemed to nod affirmatively, independent of my desire to do so. Perhaps his perspective was one version of the truth; perhaps a United India would not have been possible. But the simple fact was that I had not been alive in the days of the struggle for Independence to witness the political and social atmosphere of the time. So my understanding of it would always remain a collage of inherited memories and secondary academia, once removed from the 'reality'.

'*Beti*, this is reality and I don't blame anyone,' he said, bringing me back to the present, 'It is what it is. We had our own aspirations as Muslims, and *they* had their own.'

And with that, the word 'difference' found its place in the room, next to 'Pakistan'.

* * *

'So why did you not come to Pakistan in 1947, right after the Partition? If you had fought for it for so many years, why wait till 1953?' I asked curiously.

'I had to complete my education! Obtain my degree.'

'And so, through the Partition, you remained in India?'

'Oh yes. At the time, my mother was working in the refugee camps set up in East Pakistan [future Bangladesh], my father was campaigning in Uttar Pradesh, and I had just gained admission into the Aligarh Muslim University, one of the most sought-after institutions of the time, and enrolled myself first in engineering and then in geology.'

'And what was AMU like at the time? And the city of Aligarh? I have never been there…' I knew that the institution had played a significant role in fanning the flames of separatism. In 1946, nobody doubted the intensity of such feelings within that city, situated between the rivers Ganga and Yamuna, many, many miles away from the current border. The word 'Pakistan' was daubed on front doors, pictures of Jinnah could be seen pasted on walls, and green-and-white Muslim League banners were suspended across the narrow alleyways of the old city.[13] Needless to say, I expected exactly such a description from Nazeer Adhami.

'Aligarh in those days was … let me show you.' He lifted himself suddenly from the sofa and wandered out of the living room. When he returned, he held in his hands three large framed photographs, generously sheathed in dust. 'This is a rare piece of Aligarh I have carried with me through the years,' he proclaimed proudly, holding out the first wooden frame to me. 'Look at this,' he said as he pointed at an older man wearing dark glasses. 'Do you recognize this man? *Yeh hai* Dr Zakir Hussain.'

I squinted my eyes and indeed there he was, the third President of Independent India, seated in the second row among a group of young boys from AMU. The black-and-white photo had now faded to a vintage patina green. It was framed by a thick black border, which was further framed by parchment discoloured with weather stains. The typewritten text on the top read 'AFTAB HALL HOCKEY CLUB', followed in the next line by 'M.U., ALIGARH'. The bottom of the photograph was torn in places along the black border. The back row was of five uniformed boys standing with their hands folded across their chests; the middle row comprised the faculty seated in chairs, their hands nestled in their laps; and the front row showed three lanky boys on the ground, their knees propping up a large tournament cup.

'… And where are you?' I asked, my eyes searching.

'You tell me,' he smiled. 'Have a look.' I shrugged my shoulders and then, wiping clean his spectacles, he peered down at the frame. At first he looked at the photo in its entirety, from corner to corner, and then began focusing on each of the boys, as if he had forgotten where he was. Then he pointed at the boy sitting in the middle, on the ground, with the tournament cup in front of him and no hockey stick in hand. His dense, wavy hair was parted down the centre, revealing a sharp widow's peak. His angular jaw, thin lips and wide eyes stared up into the camera in a stoic manner, both hands resting on his knobbly knees.

'*Yeh*, here I am!' he exclaimed.

'He was a wonderful hockey player!' his wife told me.

'How come you still have these photographs?' I asked, gesturing to the one in my hand and the two remaining frames: 'AFTAB HALL HOCKEY ELEVEN 1947–48', showing the seven team members standing, arms crossed, Nazeer Adhami first in line from the left, a demure expression on his face, and the faculty seated again, along with the hockey team president; and 'AFTAB HALL COMMON ROOM, M.U., ALIGARH 1948–49', showing five young students, the young Nazeer Adhami in the very centre, all of them clad in either a smart Western suit or fitted *sherwani*, with the faculty seated in front of them. Both frames were in pristine condition; there was not a single tear in the photographs, nor a single crack in the glass. The text was still as crisp as on the day it was embossed off the letterpress.

'Now, this is the only memento I have from that time,' he said, his tone suddenly nostalgic. 'After all the years, these are my most memorable belongings. I brought them with me from AMU. Before I left in 1953, I took them off my common room wall and packed them in that single suitcase. Whether I brought any clothes or not, I don't remember, but this I would never have forgotten.' There would have been no chance of him leaving behind his most beloved possessions, these photographs from his days at AMU.

'The Aligarh of that time was a university town. On one side were the main residential settlements, then a train station, and on the other side of the tracks lay AMU, resplendent and grand. I chose to remain in India even after the Partition to be able to finish my education there rather than anywhere else. It was my choice.'

'But was it safe, as a Muslim, living in India after the Partition?' I asked.

'Of course, it was safe. My parents were still living on our own property. We had quite a bit of land, and before I moved to Aligarh, life, for the most part, remained unchanged for me. But during the months leading up to the Partition, there were constant riots in Aligarh and we would stay up at night to keep ourselves safe. We were scared, yes, of course, but we survived. In those days, the disparity between Hindus and Muslims opened up like a wound, cavernous and dense.'

He paused and again his hands separated, indicating the largeness of the gulf that grew between the two communities. 'My parents continued to work and both my sisters were married into Muslim families living in India. But, in 1948, my father died of a heart attack and my mother decided she could not leave her daughters behind and go to Pakistan, even though it was the land she had fought for. So she remained there until the end, unable to tear herself from the land of her birth. And I, in turn, throughout my degree, kept the thought of Pakistan alive in my mind. But I do remember there was one single incident that shook me and made me think, however fleetingly, that perhaps our lives as Muslim in India weren't entirely safe after 1947.'

I held my breath.

'During and even after the Partition, trains of slaughtered men and women were sent from one country to another. It was December 1947, my winter holidays had just begun and I was coming home from university to Hardoi. There is a small town called Chandausi, which derives its name from the moon, *chaand-si*, and it falls between Aligarh and Bareilly. The townspeople knew that the train I was in usually carried Muslim passengers and they often lingered at the station, ready for both attack and defence. That evening, a sudden breeze blew past me and I closed my window, blocking the platform's view of my seat. Just then, a Hindu boy on the platform caught sight of the man sitting in front of me and, through his open window, hacked him to death. It left me thinking that if I hadn't shut my window, if I hadn't felt a chill for that single moment, I too would have been dead. In those days it had become difficult to travel by train. It was a terrible time, the fear of death or riots was always palpable.'

'Did you not feel then that it was time for you to leave? To go to Pakistan?'

'*Nahi*, not at all. I knew I had to go someday, but it was not yet time. My education was more important and took precedence. Pakistan was a new land yet to be given an administrative structure. What would we have done once we came here, how would we have survived, where would we have lived? The least I could do was finish my education in a prestigious institution so I could come to my promised land a capable man.'

His views were definitive and clear. Even whilst studying in India, he had had thoughts only for Pakistan, the land he had fought for. But was it that easy, then, to give it up—India? Was there no sense at all of duality, of existing simultaneously in two places? Could his years in India from 1947 to 1953 have been those of unbelonging, unlearning? Had he taken that time to slowly and entirely scrape the land of his birth off his back, remove it from every fold, wash its every residue from his mind, wring out each memory into a receptacle of the past?

'Was it easy to leave when you knew you had nothing on the other side?' I asked. 'Was it easy to leave it all behind?'

'It was not money or material prosperity that brought me here to Pakistan but inspiration. I was inspired by the idea of this land and aspired to become something for it. I worked honourably in and for this country for over forty years, until retirement. I have given it my youth, my life. It was born as an idealistic notion but we had fought for it and earned it. And it deserved the best from every single citizen.'

There was a fire in his voice, a youthful zeal uncharacteristic of a man his age. His eyes showed not a single regret, not a single indication of loss, and just when I was about to submit to the fact that perhaps identity was more malleable, more adaptable to circumstance than I had imagined, he spoke again—suddenly, and in a voice no longer laced with zeal. Rather, slow and painful nostalgia oozed out of his every word.

'But a man can never forget his home country…'

* * *

My eyes shot up in disbelief. I had not expected this—this accidental surfacing of an emotion he must have felt in spite of himself. It caught me completely off guard. How deep down was it buried, how much had it weighed on his mind, and for how long had it not found a release? His voice now warmed up, and he spoke to me as if speaking to a child, simply and directly, attempting to dissect and explain the complex topography of the idea of 'home'.

'*Apni paydaaish*, one's birth. *Bachpan*, childhood. *Dost*, friends. I miss these things a lot. They are impossible to forget.'

216

He patted the photographs from AMU lying on the sofa. 'Sometimes at night when I close my eyes, I can still feel that air around me. I am able to smell the earth of India, of Hardoi, of Aligarh. I studied geology after all, the study of land, its history, its component structure and making. How could I ever divorce myself from it?'

Then laying out the three photographs before him, he caressed them slowly, memorizing each and every face he had shared his years with. 'The hockey field. The campus. The classrooms. The library. The books. The lectures. I remember it all. We have an association here in Pakistan called the Aligarh Old Boys Trust, under which we have set up three schools to promote higher education. One day, at one of those centres, there was a presentation on Aligarh Muslim University, its history and evolution. That day, watching the film, I thought about my days as a student there and just couldn't help myself. Tears began flowing from my eyes…'

When he looked at me, it was with the same moist eyes. It was in that moment of silence that I ventured to ask the unaskable.

'Home. Where is home? Is it the India you lost, or the Pakistan you gained?'

For a moment he said nothing, and I feared the remembrance had all been too overwhelming. But when he spoke again, it was with the same softness. 'No one can ever take away the love I have for my homeland. But there is a place for memory and then there is a place for ideals. Pakistan was my inspiration and became my ideal. India is my home and became my memory.'

Then, with his left hand resting under his chin in deep thought, he said, 'I took a flight. I think it was 23 June 1953. I had just completed my degree, and with a single suitcase in hand I boarded a flight from Delhi to Lahore. I can never forget the date. After all, I was the only member of my family to cross the border. *Beti*, I came to Pakistan six years after the Partition with one suitcase containing all of my India. Apart from memories, I brought nothing with me. I left my home, my land, my family and my alma mater. I brought no clothes, no shoes, no money, just my education and these photographs. I have lived my life through the faces in these photographs, and then slowly, as the years passed, I have buried them in the recesses of my memory.'

He then gestured to his wife, who had been listening intently the whole time. 'When her family migrated to Pakistan from Dehradun, she was only eight years old…'

'I barely remember anything,' she whispered.

'But I know how it pinches to be separated from your roots.' With a deep sigh, he gathered his most prized possessions, his parting slivers of AMU. He wiped a stain off the glass frame with his kurta sleeve, and as he piled the pictures one on top of the other, he smiled wide and said, 'If I really think about it, I wonder … as I have many times since 1953 … if it's possible ever to be completely separated from the soil of your homeland, even if that homeland is now inaccessible and isolated from your physical being. Can somebody truly be severed from the land of their birth?'

THIS BIRD OF GOLD, MY LAND

THE HOPEFUL HEART OF NAZMUDDIN KHAN

'Let me tell you something about India,' he said, drawing close. 'This land, this very land that you stand on right now, was once the greatest land in the world. *Sone ki chidiya*, "Bird of Gold"[1]—a country of riches and wealth; of countless jewels, gems and gold; of trade routes; of ancient civilizations; and of discovery. It was once a country of powerful ideals, where people lived in peace and life flourished. It was once the greatest country in the world.'

He spoke passionately, animatedly, stressing each word, a fire blazing in his sunken eyes. His voice was soothing—deep and husky. His tongue was Urdu, littered with words of English. It wasn't the glorified, delicate Urdu that I had heard in films or around Old Delhi, but a curt dialect. It was an everyman's Urdu, a utilitarian Urdu. It too possessed its own subtleties, but overall it was far coarser and more ordinary than I would have expected.

'During the time of King Poros, Hindustan was a vast, vast land—one nation.[2] Then slowly, with various battles and annexations, we lost Afghanistan, Burma and Pakistan, and then Bangladesh was created. India became smaller and smaller. Over time, she lost herself, her essence, her magnificence, and just look at what is left of her now! The truth is, it is we who have broken her into bits; we sliced her borders, dissected her time and time again.' He smiled sadly.

I studied his face. Nazmuddin Khan was an ordinary-looking man. He had smooth dark-brown skin, high cheekbones and hollow cheeks. A long kurta and sweater, worn over old cotton pajamas, covered his frail frame that hunched forward when he walked. A woollen cap protected his head from the cold. He had long fingers and clipped fingernails, yellowing with age. Overall, there was little distinctive about the man who sat across from me, except for the solemn sadness that accompanied him.

It enveloped the room and suffused our conversation. But mostly it prevented me from saying anything and compelled me to listen, for if melancholy had a sound, it would resonate in the long lingering silence between his sentences. Many of the things he described were not seen or witnessed by him, but he seemed to feel them all the same. The sadness seemed to be inherited, but also nurtured and cultivated and expanded within him. From his eyes it was evident this was not a sadness he had recently chanced upon, but one that had aged well beyond him—a parasitic pain that fed on old, invisible wounds. Each time I opened my mouth to say something, anything that would comfort him, I was at a loss. No words I could say would diminish the truth in what he had said.

We were seated in a dimly lit room of a humble two-storey house in the Hauz Rani neighbourhood of New Delhi. The demeanour of the old man seemed to resemble the walls around us, which were vacant, save a small bookcase stacked with leather-bound volumes on the Indian legal system. There was a desk, and two rather uncomfortable chairs placed on either side. The floor was covered in a slightly faded Persian print carpet and the curtains were of a functional-looking shade of cream. This scanty room served as the home-cum-office of his son, who was a small-time lawyer. I was seated cross-legged on a cane chair and the old man leaned back into the hard sofa by the window. On the desk sat two small steaming cups of tea.

'My father used to say to us—Hindustan is our *vatan*, our land. It didn't matter that we are *Musalmaan*; what mattered was that we were born *here* and here is where we would die. We didn't belong anywhere else except on this soil. And ever since we were very young, he made sure that we knew the importance of being loyal to the land.'

This he said with conviction, both palms flat and pointing deep into the ground to emphasize the reality of his physical belonging. Each word embodied the values his father had instilled in him. And it was not that he was attempting to divulge a fact of great significance or philosophy. In fact, whatever he told me that afternoon was so candid and uncomplicated that to my jaded ears it sounded impossibly mundane. He described what, in my opinion, was the purest way to understand the essence of secularism in regards to India.

'Our Hindu brothers,' he began, 'are born in Hindustan, they grow up here, live their lives here, they die here. And when they die, they are cremated and their ashes are immersed into the holy waters of the river Ganga. Within her tides they flow, even if it is eventually into foreign waters. But look at us *Musalmaans* … we are born in Hindustan, we grow up here, we live here and we die here. And when we die, we are buried deep into the ground and, eventually, when our bodies decompose, we become one with the land. *We become Hindustan.*'

Then slowly, still seated on the sofa, he bent his stiff, wiry frame halfway to the floor and patted it. Straightening himself back up, he heaved a loud sigh. 'We become Hindustan. Our bodies mix into its soil. How could we ever leave this land, then? Our home, our life—how could we ever leave it? We are within the very land.'

All of my two and a half decades of life looked him straight in the face as his notions sent shivers down my spine. My father had once told me that sometimes religion precedes nationalism and sometimes nationalism precedes religion. This was an instance of the latter. Within his earnest words lay a poignancy that struck the deepest chords of my heart. It was a product of something exceptionally rare and pure, drawn from experience and evident lament. The truth was that it had been a long time since I'd met someone who possessed such an undeniably strong relationship with India. But the most extraordinary thing about this relationship was that it was reciprocal. Here was a man in love with his country and he truly believed his country loved him back, wholeheartedly. Here was a man content with his love for his land. A lover of Hindustan, a patriot in his own way.

People don't think like that any more, I thought, and allowed myself to be inspired by the passion of the man with sunken eyes.

'My father used to live and work as a high-ranking security official in the Viceroy's House, what was later converted into Rashtrapati Bhavan [the presidential residence] when India became a republic,' he said, 'and he was privy to the official visits of various leaders and pioneers of the nationalist movement. He would tell us that Jinnah *sahab* had never really visited Delhi much before 1940, until the formal demand for Pakistan was made. It was only when he began making these frequent trips to the capital that he purchased Number 10 Aurangzeb Road, a lavish white colonial mansion with lush gardens. At the time, the Nehrus were staying on Motilal Nehru Marg, and Gandhi-ji was living in Birla Bhawan. In 1947, when the atmosphere became very tense, Jinnah *sahab* left for Lahore, and Gandhi-ji would call him every day, trying to persuade him against the Partition.

'He would say to him, "You are the most senior barrister among us, Mr Jinnah. Please think of our nation, of India and its people. Consider what I say, consider the offer to become the home minister."[3] The *wazir-e-dakhila*, we say in Urdu. They would discuss this often and at length, Gandhi-ji hoping that he would be able to dissuade him from the idea of creating the nation of Pakistan.[4]

'The two men were so different. Gandhi-ji was simple and unembellished, and Jinnah *sahab* a *pakka* Englishman. He was so handsome and always impeccably dressed. In those days, we would hear stories that he never wore the same silk tie twice, and his closet was full of tailored suits. *Pakka* English gentleman he was. Then later, when he began wearing *desi* clothes, it was with the same aristocratic flair: a fitted *sherwani* encased his body and a Karakul topi perched on his head. When the weather was pleasant and breezy, you could see him riding along the wide roads of central Delhi in those fashionable cars—you know, the ones with the tops that could go down when the weather was nice and up when it rained…'

'A convertible?' I offered.

'Ah, yes! Exactly. Such a grand sight he was!' His eyes twinkled at the memory and he reached for the cup of tea on the table, taking a long swig, savouring its strong cardamom taste.

'Anyway, as you know, these discussions about coexistence were in vain. India did not remain undivided. Pakistan was created in 1947. And then 1948 bound these two great men together. In January, a Hindu nationalist assassinated Gandhi-ji on the grounds of being pro-Muslim, and in September Jinnah *sahab* passed away due to illness, each leaving behind a legacy. But everything that happened during the days of Independence—the Partition and the departure of the Raj—we saw it all unfold before us. Sometimes I wish I hadn't, but *jo dekha, woh dekha*. What has been seen cannot be un-seen. But I said it then and I say it now: it was wrong. Partition was…' A sudden commotion outside interrupted him. Craning his neck, he looked out the window to see a group of children playing in the street. Then, as if in slow motion, he straightened his body and stared at me. With his sunken gaze still holding mine, he said, 'One after another, great cities fell to a vast and violent tragedy. The unthinkable. The unimaginable. And then we saw a great exodus. Hindus arriving on unfamiliar soil, and Muslims leaving in vast numbers for the "promised land" that was Pakistan. We saw them leave their homes, their belongings, their lives…'

He paused and closed his eyes. Then, opening them slowly, he leaned in close to me and asked in a grave tone, 'Tell me, *beta*, weren't *Musalmaans* also born here? Isn't this our country too? Don't we have the right to live here, where we were born, where we grew up? Aren't we part of this soil? My father told us that this was meant to be a secular India, but I'm losing that vision now. He used to paint a beautiful picture for us and we believed it. But now I think perhaps that was not the truth at all, just something we had wanted to believe. Because, right up until today, something new always continues to disturb this land.'

Silence.

His ghostly quiet crept around us like a lurking shadow. No matter how much I wanted to, I could not look away from him, and yet I could say nothing either. I felt stuffy in this uncomfortable silence and guilty for feeling so. My eyes desperately scanned the vicinity for objects he had brought out for the occasion of this meeting. I imagined him breaking the silence by extracting from his worn kurta pocket his father's old security papers from the Viceroy's House, fraying at the edges but still preserved, his name and position still legible in cursive handwriting. I imagined him unfolding an old newspaper displaying Jinnah's angular face, regal in his pre-presidential glory, looking ever the gentleman in a long *sherwani* and Karakul topi. A photo of the elusive convertible, a newspaper clipping about the grand new capital of New Delhi, *something* that irrevocably bound this man to India. But there was nothing.

And then suddenly his words filled the air again.

'But you don't want to hear all this, an old man talking about forgotten virtues, do you? The Partition. Yes, that is why you are here.' He drank the remainder of the now-cold tea and placed the cup on the floor with a clink.

I felt my head nod at the prospect of listening to his story.

'Now, as I told you, my father lived at the Viceroy's House due to his work. When the governor general—you know the last governor general, right? That tall Englishman…? Yes, Mountbatten, yes, when he would be in Delhi, he sat at the Viceroy's House. When the country was going to be partitioned, he called my father [and the other Muslims on the security force] and told him to join Jinnah *sahab*'s guard in Lahore as a senior officer. "Leave immediately," he said, "there is a plane waiting for you and your family at Safdarjung airport."'[5]

He paused, coughing and clearing his throat.

'But my father … my father said, "No, sir. I will stay in India." Mountbatten told him that when Pakistan was officially created, all the *Musalmaans* would leave India, and as my father was in the official guard, it was their responsibility to send him to work for the new Islamic government that was to come into power. But my father just looked at him and said, "When all the *Musalmaans* leave, only then shall I go." He was adamant about staying in India as long as he could. But not all the *Musalmaans* left during Partition and so my father decided that our family would also not leave. This was our country—why would we go anywhere else?'

'How old were you at the time of the Partition? And your childhood in Delhi—what was it like?'

'Oho! I have never even calculated!' he chuckled. 'Well, I was born in 1929, I think. So I would have been around eighteen years old. We were five brothers and two sisters. Now they are all gone, except one brother and me. My childhood ... my childhood was great, all of us brothers would wrestle. We were fit and healthy, not interested in all this *chori-chakori*, all this stealing, cheating and creating ruckus. Children should not have these bad habits!'

'And where did you live at the time?'

'Right here in Hauz Rani! We have always lived in Hauz Rani. Of course, the area was quite different then. It was a simple neighbourhood. The houses were not made of cement but were rougher—made of mud and straw. All the land around here—Hauz Rani, Begum Pura, Chirag Dilli, Malviya Nagar—these were all small villages. There was no light or electricity in those days, and at night we all slept together in the same room or on the roof on straw mats. Hardly anyone owned a business, back in those days; they would all just do simple jobs, manual labour mostly. They would go to Dhaula Kuan, about half an hour away from here, to find work. There were large mountains there, and the men would spend the day breaking down stones so they could be used to make roads and houses. That's what I did too. We would get *sava rupaiya*—one rupee, 25 paise—for the whole day's work.'

Then suddenly his face softened for the first time, as if a sudden wave of nostalgia was passing over it. He smiled and spoke fondly of how Delhi once was—smaller in size, more glorified in its architecture.

'Sometimes I revel in the beautiful childhood memories I have—full of pure, joyful, untainted happiness. Other times I lament the impossibly high standard they set for the future. Now, when I was young, Delhi only extended as far out as Safdarjung airport. All of the area around it—where the hospitals now are— that was all fields of corn! Can you imagine? South Extension, Defence Colony, Greater Kailash—all fields! No buildings, no urbanization. Just by the airport there used to be an old railway line; now there is a flyover there!' he exclaimed, laughing and slapping his hands jovially on his knees.

'Lutyens' Delhi was so new at that time, so grand. Now that was the time to see the city, the real New Delhi. Not this diluted version of today. The magnificent new roundabouts, the tall columns of the colonial buildings, the pristine walls, and smooth, wide roads … they were all so majestic when they were first built. Go to Connaught Place, to parts of central Delhi—you will see remnants of it still standing today.'

Then suddenly he asked: 'Are you Hindu or *Musalmaan?*'

'How does that matter?' I laughed.

'It doesn't matter, but I just wondered.'

'I am Hindu.'

He nodded. 'And you are from Delhi?'

'I suppose my family is now from Delhi, yes; I was born and raised here. But my grandparents are from different areas that are all now in Pakistan. They came to Delhi during the Partition.'

'Who is really from Delhi?' he scoffed. 'Everyone is a refugee here! We are too.'

'What do you mean? You are the original Delhi-*wallas*! Your ancestors were born here!'

'Well, we too had to leave Delhi for a while during the Partition. We were forced to run away in order to save our lives, but then after a while we came back to the same place. Whatever we have now is what Allah has given us.'

Gently, he threw his hands up to the sky, eyes following.

'So, what happened here in 1947 … in Hauz Rani?' I asked. 'How did you hear of Independence, of Partition? Why did you leave?'

He sighed deeply and, with a slow movement, brought the fingers of his right hand up to stroke his drying lips, as if in deep thought.

'All these fights between religions are not a good thing, let me tell you that,' he said. 'They only break up our society. Before the Partition, there were no differences between any religions here in Hauz Rani. We were like brothers, Hindu–*Musalmaan bhai-bhai*. But then we began to hear talk on the street of the British finally leaving India, of complete Independence, and these were followed by rumours of a possible partition: Hindus on one side, *Musalmaans* on the other. You see, radios were not common at that time. All kinds of news went around just by word of mouth. And because my father worked at the Viceroy's House, we came to know from the peons in offices and the security guards of government buildings.

'Today, Hauz Rani is mainly a *Musalmaan* area, but at that time many, many Hindu families lived here. Oh, there was such uproar in this area in 1947. There were riots everywhere.[6] In Munirka *gaon*, the village just next to Hauz Rani, there was a man who was so against *Musalmaans* staying back in India that I remember him throwing petrol bombs, setting everything in our area on fire. And that fire spread violently. There was a small hill nearby, to which people fled, running hurriedly away from the fire, trying desperately to save their families. But there were rioters waiting for them there, so whoever made it safely to the hill was eventually killed. Thousands of people, just inhumanely slaughtered. Their bodies lay there for days—weeks even. Their bones lay there for decades, maybe even till today.

'Then, in the other nearby areas—Sheikh Sarai *gaon*, Chor Minar—all around what is now Laxman Public School, people were killed there too; their bodies were cut up and a huge pit was dug where they were piled up on top of one another and buried.

This I saw with my own eyes. People were yelling in the streets about how there was a mass burial of *Musalmaans*. We had to go see for ourselves. It happened so close to us we couldn't help but think that we were next. It would soon be us in those trenches.'

He shook his head slowly, and his dry lips pursed in disgust with the foul taste of an unpleasant memory. 'This is all true; I saw it with my own eyes. These are things I have tried to forget time and time again, but let me tell you, I cannot forget them. No matter how many years pass, I cannot forget them; I cannot bury these images. I remember them just as clearly, as vividly, as the day they happened before me. Those people stuck near the hill, those people nearly buried alive in the trenches, the cut-up masses of flesh and organs, the pile of bones, the corpses laid out in line—I cannot forget them. My heart beats so fast when I speak of that time ... and I cannot fall asleep for hours after.'

The old man with sunken eyes didn't embellish his words; he didn't decorate his language or curate his thoughts. They were as they were, just as he remembered them. His tone was matter-of-fact, and in the strangest of ways it seemed like he was not narrating his own life story but rather something he had once watched on the news or read about in the paper. He was distant and removed from it, from his memories, from his own life. As if the scene were playing in front of him as he stood on the side-lines, watching himself and his surroundings unravel during the Partition.

He stared ahead, right through me to the empty wall behind. There was a long pause, and during that pause a hard lump formed in my throat. Just listening to his vivid descriptions made my blood curdle. What kind of madness was this? How could we do this to each other, how was it even possible? I remembered what he had told me about Muslims ultimately becoming the soil of Hindustan and it saddened me to think of the manner in which some of them had decomposed into the land during the weeks of violence in 1947. I felt an inexplicable wave of guilt for my religion, and the merciless acts of violence committed in the name of that religion. I clenched my jaw and balled up my fists so tight that my knuckles turned white and the ends of my fingernails dug into the insides of my palm.

Taking a deep breath, I swallowed the lump in my throat and asked him how he had escaped from the bloody riots in and around Hauz Rani.

'It was only then, when the circumstances truly became unbearable, that we realized it might actually be unsafe for us to continue living in Delhi, and so we ran away as fast as we could. I knew we had no choice, but it was a heartbreaking move, nonetheless. That day we fled from our own home in a way that felt so cowardly. Yes, we had no choice, but the weight of that action bore down on us all.

'So one night, under the cover of darkness, the Viceroy's House sent military cars to the house, which drove us out of Delhi and into what is now Uttar Pradesh, where we stayed with our relatives for a few weeks. People thought that we had left to go to Pakistan but we always knew that we would return; there was no question of not coming back. We waited till the madness of the Partition died down, and then, frightened and cautious, we came back to the city, again under cover of darkness.'[7]

His jaw now tightened; his breath became heavier and his voice raspier. 'Nothing of our old life remained. When we returned, all those who had once lived in our neighbourhood had disappeared and what had settled in their place was a heavy, foul stench. An unimaginable mixture of rotting and burned flesh. A transfer of matter had occurred, our neighbours now existing in a new and horrifying form. Stagnant, dense and lingering.

'No matter how hard I try, no matter how many years pass, I can still smell it, I can feel it surrounding me as vividly as I could when I first experienced it. In the first few years, I would even wake up in the middle of the night, as if from a bad dream, and imagine that I, my body, my hands were soaked in the smell. Tell me, can one touch a smell, can one feel it, can it seem physical and alive? I didn't think so, but there it was. My deathly companion. My silent, invisible, looming reminder.

'The house had also been burned down; *all* the houses in Hauz Rani were demolished. The whole neighbourhood had been consumed by the riots. Even the cement blocks from the foundations of solid houses had been stolen! And we had left in such a rush that we had only packed clothes, no other belongings. So, our house and any possessions that were in it were now gone. Even our land had been occupied by the refugees who came in from across the border. So, with the help of our family in Uttar Pradesh, we began our lives again. Eventually, we did get back the deeds for the land, but never the land itself! Just an official letter that demarcated what land was ours, just a piece of paper … but what good is the paper without the land?' He laughed bitterly.

He was right. It was a souvenir, at best. A memento of the Partition, of the country's chaos and the family's flight.

He told me how he wished they hadn't left, that they should have hidden somewhere, anywhere. But at that moment, amidst the riots, there was no choice. Even though they had never left India, they had to rebuild their lives in Delhi as if they had arrived as refugees from across the border, with only the promise of help from the government.

Here, the authorities had said to them, here is the deed to your land.

But where is the land, they had responded, where is one to live?

* * *

I thought about a different piece of paper: the one that had declared the division of the country. Documents were often seen as powerful instruments of change, depending on the conditions they laid out. The paper that re-allotted the family its land was never going to live up to its promise in the disarray of post-Partition Delhi. But in the case of Undivided India, a piece of paper had changed the fate of millions. Lines drawn on a map and swift signatures of the officials involved had divided India into its respective parts: Hindu, Muslim; Friend, Enemy; East, West; Mine, Yours.

I asked him whether he still had that piece of paper, the land deed, my thirst for a tangible object from the past still not satiated. In response, he scoffed and shrugged his shoulders, as if it would be the most absurd thing to have kept. I couldn't help but wonder, then, exactly what the attraction to Delhi was for him and his family. What was this unexplainable patriotism? Why remain?

'I have seen this country get ripped apart by that one single event. I have seen it. But despite all that, it is my country,' he said firmly, not really to me.

'But didn't you ever wonder what it would have been like if you had moved to Pakistan, especially after you were made to leave Delhi once?'

'No, the thought never even crossed our minds. At the time we had envisioned it to be a small country. We didn't know anyone in the areas that had become Pakistan. We didn't know what kind of *mulk*, what kind of country, it would be, what respect we would get there, what our conditions would be like, what our plight would be after the journey there, how we would survive. We didn't know anything and it was all just too foreign to even think about. Coming back to Delhi was the only option; this was home. It was familiar.

'It's true that we were just laymen in India; no political leaders or important public figures ever decorated our family tree. We were labourers, our work could be done anywhere. But it was the layman, the common man—Hindu, Muslim, Sikh, Isai, it didn't matter—it was people like us who made up the population of secular India. *Secular India.*

'Yes, Pakistan was created from Hindustan, carved from within. But in my opinion it was born in the midst of loss. Hindustan lost an integral part of herself in the violence, in the bloodshed, in the politics, and that part became Pakistan.'

Suddenly, his eyes grew wide. 'Ah, but you know, I have visited Pakistan once—in 1984. I went on a passport with a visa! During the Partition and in the years following it, some of our extended family did eventually move there, and so I went to visit them. The society, the people are not so different from here, but it is no Delhi!'

I smiled widely at this lover of Delhi. I thanked him for his time and gathered my things. Just as I was about to leave, I heard him call out to me. Turning around, I saw him standing by the front door. His demeanour seemed different all of a sudden— lighter, softer—from what it had been throughout our conversation.

'Don't think I have not served my country,' he said, almost whispering. 'We all do it in whatever way we can.'

His voice grew louder now, infused with an unexpected conviction. 'We, my family and I, have done it by staying here, staying true to this land. India is my country, regardless of my religion. I live in unity with its people; I don't create disorder or initiate violence. I respect it. And so I have served it all these years in my own way.'

Unsure of how to respond, I just nodded softly in agreement. I gave his thin frame one last glance and walked away from the house.

I wandered through the narrow streets of Hauz Rani, trying to find my way back to the main road. The area didn't feel like the Delhi I knew at all. It resembled nothing of the capital's chaos or noise. On the contrary, the neighbourhood was a discreet pocket at the city's core that had retained some of its old-world charm and tranquillity within its deep, narrow lanes, which did not admit cars. Colourful shops adorned both sides of the street; old men with long, grey beards and crocheted prayer caps sat together in clusters, sipping tea from small glass tumblers; children played on the paved pathway without fear of traffic; two goats strolled by leisurely. An old village in a new city. I smiled to myself, feeling almost like a tourist in Delhi for the first time.

I had said nothing when I left his house, but now my mind was occupied only by Nazmuddin Khan's parting words. He had come back to Hauz Rani after everything. Despite every act of violence he had witnessed, and every massacre he had seen with his own eyes, he had returned. He had chosen to rebuild his house in the same area. He had begun again from scratch. He had acquired belongings over the years: the house, the objects that existed in it, social status, the wisdom of age.

I had visited him with the intention of talking about any material remnants of the Partition that he had with him, anything that had survived the event—any object at all that was a memento, a souvenir of a time gone by. But he had nothing. Somewhere in the middle of our conversation, I had wondered what I was doing there, and now, walking away from him, I suddenly felt small and insignificant for obsessing over the tangible. Though the purpose I had come for hadn't been fulfilled, I found myself feeling fuller, more satisfied. Little by little, every part of me felt renewed. I had come, as it appeared, to listen, to learn and hopefully to live his tale with him.

His family had taken nothing with them except clothes when they left their house. You might say Nazmuddin Khan had had no say in the matter. But, seen another way, it had been his choice to keep nothing that would serve as a reminder of what had happened to the country. He hated the fact that Hindus and Muslims were no longer brothers, and he didn't need physical evidence to remind him of that every day.

Perhaps what had remained with him, though, was something entirely intangible: an abstract entity that cannot be held or touched or caressed as an heirloom or a treasure. The remnant of the past that Nazmuddin Khan held on to was an emotion of brotherhood and unity; the feeling of secularism that he was trying so desperately to keep alive even today. He had said it so simply, so elegantly. There was no deliberating over the facts. In his own way, he had indeed served India his whole life.

12

THE BOOK OF EVERLASTING THINGS

THE COLLECTION OF PROF. PARTHA MITTER

'THERE ARE TWO THINGS that I have never understood about the past,' said the professor, his arms resting on a pile of books wrapped in brown paper and tied with string. Holding up his right index finger, he continued, 'The first is the reluctance to revisit it, either consciously or subconsciously, and the second is its immensely transient nature. But, for me, these two things are complementary.'

He gestured to the books, old treasures inherited from his ancestors, and smiled, 'To revisit the past is to relive a time gone by and learn from it. No moment lasts forever, but it's the sheer ephemerality of time that makes it so important. Maybe it's because I am a historian that the past has always seemed more alive than the present, but more and more, I have come to wonder at its relevance. There is a loss of memory, an unwillingness to unearth the past, especially in younger generations…' Professor Partha Mitter trailed off and looked over at his wife, Swasti, as the sunlight illuminated her in a halo of gold.

'When our generation is gone,' she began sadly, her accent a quaint combination of English and Bengali, 'it might be difficult to piece together your past.'

I noted how she said *your* past, not *the* past. How, because of our shared ethnicity, though we were generations apart, their past was also my past, and momentarily I wondered about this colossal collective memory that we inherit from our ancestors. I put down my pen and closed my notebook, looking at the Bengali couple who had graciously welcomed me into their cosy Oxford home. 'That's true,' I found myself nodding. 'For me, the past has become a strange and almost unrecognizable word now. One that comprises borrowed experiences and memories, things I was not yet alive to witness but which have shaped me nonetheless…'

We sat in silence for a few minutes. Sunlight poured in; the day was beautiful, though spring had not yet blessed the English countryside. Cool, crisp air floated in from the open window, and I warmed my feet by rubbing them on the thick Persian rugs that covered the wooden floor. Shelves of books and other objects adorned the room; the tables carried similar piles of files and papers.

The interior was tastefully simple, as if it wouldn't dare to compete with the most important element of the house: the art. It graced every inch of wall space, and for a moment it was difficult to imagine this house belonging to anyone but an art historian. Modernist pieces sat alongside Mughal miniatures, curiously complementing one another. The house was full of different time periods of literature and art alike, colours and forms, yet it didn't feel crowded. There was a lightness, an airiness to it, and that came from those who lived in it.

'Do you remember the past, then?' I asked the professor.

'But of course. My earliest memories are of my *mama bari*, my mother's home, in Calcutta. These books,' he said, again gesturing towards the brown paper, 'they are hers, from her childhood. They were brought out of what was left of my grandfather's home after it had been ransacked and destroyed during the Great Calcutta Killings in 1946.'

I nodded but said nothing, hoping that it would prompt him to continue. My eyes looked at him expectantly as I made myself comfortable, sitting cross-legged on the carpeted floor. His wife got up and headed to the kitchen to brew fresh coffee. I offered to help but she promptly refused. 'No, no, you must listen,' she said. 'So many momentous things happen in our lives and somehow time just swallows them whole. We forget the things that we should never forget. And now that you have come so far to archive these things, you must listen.'

The voice that ultimately narrated the past was glacial and beautiful. Despite the conditioning of his profession, Professor Mitter became the most effortless storyteller. There were no hints of Bengali in his English; his accent was smooth, diplomatic and trusting. Words slid off his tongue with a touch of hoarseness—the right amount of rasp to make his expression that much more endearing. And he began, most classically, at the very beginning.

'I was born in 1938 into one of the leading families of Calcutta.' His pronunciation of his birth city was sharp, as the British would have said it, the double 't' precise rather than soft. 'Actually, we originated from just outside—from a place called Dum Dum, which has now been incorporated into Calcutta proper. The family was, on one hand, very English and, on the other, very Bengali, and some of what I tell you might seem contradictory. But keep in mind that to have both nationalist and colonial associations wasn't unheard of, and they aren't exactly polar opposites of each other either.'

His narrative followed the path of his methodical thinking. Names, dates and appointments were stated as empirical facts, drawn from years of personal and scholarly research and interest. He curated and presented to me episodes from his familial past in the same way he would an exhibition of art. He drew effortlessly from memory, extracting the colours, textures, sounds and feelings of things that he and those around him had witnessed. He spoke of an empire on the brink of dissolution. In his chronicling, it became evident that he depended entirely on the visual and sensorial. And through his reading of history—first at the University of London, then at Cambridge and finally at Sussex, from where he had now retired—he had honed the skill of historical storytelling.

'My family comprised intellectuals and lawyers for the most part. One of its oldest known members—who lived from 1841 to 1870 and who was related to my great-grandfather [by marriage]—was Kaliprasanna Singha, the first person to translate the *Mahabharata* into Bengali. Though he lived a short life, he achieved a remarkable amount. Aside from his literary pursuits, he also advocated the Widow Remarriage Act, declaring a reward of Rs 1,000 to every man who married a widow!'

From a file close by, he extracted a pixelated sepia photograph of a young man, printed on bond paper. He wore a light-coloured shawl embroidered at the ends; his face was clean-shaven save for a sharp moustache; his hair was parted to the right and in his hands he bore a piece of paper with an illegible scribble on it. I squinted at it but was unable to read it.

'The family owned land, fruit orchards mostly, but it was hardly cultivated. Most of it was sold off eventually for a pittance—a small percent of the price. It was my great-grandfather who decided to break away from *zamindari* [land holding] and enter the world of business, a landscape unfamiliar to him. His name was Tripundreshwar Mitter, but let's call him Tipen, it's easier! So Tipen Mitter, in the 1800s, founded a very successful building and architecture firm, where he collaborated with English architects who provided him with the design blueprints for their projects. Soon he was commissioned to build several very important public buildings … I have some photographs of the more prominent ones.'

From the same file he extracted several sheets of paper and placed them on the table. 'Tipen Mitter built the Alipore Central Jail, where Sri Aurobindo wrote his famous *Tales of Prison Life* when he was imprisoned there after the Alipore bomb case of 1908–9.' The photo showed a brick-red building with minarets around the top for guards.

'He also built the Senate House. Here, see, his style was Neoclassical, a response to the Baroque and Rococo forms, which were theatrical and decadent. This, on the other hand, was uncluttered and elegant, clean and definitive, simplistic like most of the English buildings that still stand in India.' His finger traced the exterior of the minimalist Senate House, which, at first glance, almost resembled an old illustration of the Temple of Zeus. 'These columns all around are used to actually hold the structure up. Now, this elegant building was designed by a Victorian architect, Walter B. Granville, and erected in 1872. It was the first habitation of Calcutta University. They would have meetings and seminars in here.'

Picking up the final sheet of paper, he said, 'And this is Belvedere Estate. It has a main building, Belvedere House, and on the grounds surrounding it is the former palace of the lieutenant governor of Bengal, which was converted into the National Library. Tipen Mitter built that palace.' It was an idyllic image, very English in the rendering of both colour and architectural form. Though the estate could be dated back to the late 1760s, the palace was newer-looking, albeit in the same style. In the centre was a staircase leading to an entrance with four ionic columns, flanked by six graceful arcs on either side.

'Apparently, when the palace was completed in Alipore, he was invited by the governor to come and meet him. Despite all his English airs and connections, my great-grandfather refused to wear European clothes and went in his … you know, semi-Mughal formal dress. We also had a massive oil painting of him, this man of elegant, old-world fashion, smoking an *albolah*, a hookah.' His arms danced in the air to show the size of the painting. 'So this is what I mean. It was just never one or the other, never just Bengali or English.'

'How does it feel to have your family leave behind such grand, physical traces of themselves? Rather than private heirlooms, you've inherited a unique legacy of communal spaces, public and utilitarian.'

'When you grow up with it, it becomes second nature. Almost habitual, in that one doesn't necessarily ponder upon it, rather just takes it for granted, especially as a child. But, you see, even the school I went to, not far from our home, was built by Tipen Mitter.' He chuckled.

'But it's quite a weight to bear on one's shoulders, then, isn't it?'

'The beginnings of all things pertaining to my family were wonderful and decadent, but it continuously went into decline. By the time my grandfather passed away, the wealth and financial assets had all but been spent and the family had become quite…' he paused, searching for the right word, 'well, common.'

Then, giving the photographs on the table one last cursory glance, he continued, 'But life was different then, in the Calcutta of Tipen Mitter, from when I was growing up.¹ It was difficult to assimilate into the English circles if you didn't belong to the Indian aristocracy. Remember, this is all happening just after the Revolt of 1857. The English Crown has officially taken over from the East India Company as a result of the sepoy mutiny, and now the brand of Englishmen in India is different. They are no longer merchants or traders but a governing body, reorganizing the financial, military, administrative and, naturally, social aspects of Indian life.

'But I do feel that if you look at a lot of the old Calcutta families, they possess these ambivalent twin aspects. In part, they worked for and even with the British, but the attitudes they harboured were also deeply rooted in Bengali culture. It was not always so simple as to say that they, the British, were masters and that was that. The situation, especially with the more elite Indians, was complex. For instance, my great-grandfather's brother, the famed Ramesh Chandra Mitter, was appointed the first ever Indian chief justice of the Calcutta High Court. These were the early days of the Raj and racism was highly prevalent, but Lord Ripon, who was quite a liberal viceroy of the time, went through with the appointment. Ramesh Mitter was also one of the earlier members of the Indian National Congress. Though, interestingly, he and both his sons, B.C. Mitter and P.C. Mitter, were knighted. All lawyers, all brilliant, and all living against the backdrop of the first partition of Bengal in 1905.'

And thus, much to my surprise and fascination, as the afternoon wore into evening, the professor wove the story of his family into the story of the Partition.

* * *

'The first nationalist movement with India-wide implications was born out of the partition of Bengal by Lord Curzon, which separated the largely Muslim eastern areas from the Hindu western areas under the pretext of better administration, as Bengal was a large province. But what lurked in the shadows of this decision was the British policy of divide and rule, as they feared the two religious groups joining hands in a war against them. What followed as a consequence was a national anti-British campaign, involving riots, protests and the second phase of the Swadesi Movement, a boycott of all foreign goods and practices. Tilak was one of its chief architects and Sir Ramesh Mitter was often supportive of him. The partition was finally annulled and the two parts of Bengal were unified in 1911, barely half a decade later, though it sowed the first seeds of Hindu–Muslim disharmony, making them distinct communities.

'By 1919, at the end of World War I, the nationalist movement in India had grown to a considerable degree, leading to the outbreak of many anti-British activities. The government passed an act called the Rowlatt Act to curb the growing nationalist upsurge in the country. As part of the emergency measures, Indians involved in such "political terrorism" could be detained without trial or judicial review. The act enraged many political leaders, including Gandhi, but was passed. On the committee were six members and Sir P.C. Mitter was one of them. In the same year, two other iconic events took place: first, separate electorates were created for Muslims, Hindus and other communities, encouraging Muslims to develop as a socio-cultural group; and second, the Jallianwala Bagh massacre in Amritsar, where General Dyer opened fire on thousands of men, women and children who had gathered on Baisakhi Day.

'In 1920, rioting still continued in parts of India and, perhaps to escape from it, my father, Rabindranath Mitter, left home to study law in England. Accompanying him were his two brothers, who eventually moved to Germany. So, we are in the 1920s, where the world is recuperating from the war, and my father sees Adolf Hitler at a train station in England. Things were just beginning then, he was not as well known, but they were momentous times nonetheless.

'While my father was away, in 1928 the Simon Commission was put together to determine the future of India's constitutional reforms, though not a single Indian was included on the committee. On 26 January 1930, Jawaharlal Nehru called for complete independence, *purna swaraj*. This was followed by Gandhi's Dandi March, the salt *satyagraha*, a protest against the British tax on salt, which was further followed by several bouts of civil disobedience against the Empire.

'It is 1939 now, the year of World War II, and Viceroy Linlithgow declares India's entry [into hostilities] without consulting the provincial government, causing all the Congress leaders to resign en masse. This creates a complete political vacuum in India, and with the major local party off the political landscape, it's the first time minority powers come into play. As a result, Jinnah transforms the Muslim League from a moribund, old-fashioned party into a powerful political machine. And finally, in 1940, the official demand for a land called Pakistan is made at the Lahore Resolution of the League.[2]

'Now, of course, I have given you a very quick and simplistic unfolding of events, though in truth the Indian independence movement is far, far more complicated. But growing up against the backdrop of these changing political times were my parents, balancing their uniquely dual heritages.'

I nodded, noting down as much as I could, as fast as I could.[3] Then, looking up, my eyes fell on the brown paper-covered books. 'You've told me about your father's family, but what about your mother? What was her family background, and how did you come to inherit these books of hers?'

'Ah yes, my mother.' His voice turned suddenly dreamy and his lips curled into a soft smile. His wife, seated on the sofa, also smiled. 'You would have liked her.'

'My mother, brought up in the Park Circus area of Calcutta, was one of the two children of B.C. De. He was a lawyer, educated at Cambridge, a member of the Indian Civil Service. Very popular among his peers, though he was also well known to let off many revolutionaries. He was the only lawyer to ever give a judgment completely in Sanskrit, owing to which he was given the title of Siddhanta Sindhu, he who gives great judgments. He died young, of pneumonia, I believe, and without being able to do the one thing he had longed to—write a critical biography of the Marquis de Sade. You see, B.C. De was very interested in erotic literature and had a massive collection of such books. I have inherited some of them, though not many remained after the Partition. But, while writing my book, *Much Maligned Monsters*, I came across a torn fragment from my grandfather's books, which spoke of one of the first pieces of erotic Indian art and was authored by a British historian, Richard Payne Knight.[4]

'So, from her father Pushpa Lata De, a beautiful young woman, inherited the love of languages, picking up Polish, French, English and, of course, Bengali. She played many instruments and was taught classical music by none other than Kazi Nazrul Islam, who even wrote a poem for her on her birthday—I must find it! She was very cultured but unfortunately belonged to a period when her parents disallowed her from doing many things: for instance, singing or performing publicly, despite her lovely voice, or going to university. And so she'd be tutored at home—by the finest, mind you, but still within the confines of her home. She used to write very well and her work was accepted into an important literary magazine of the time called *Prabasi*, founded by Ramananda Chatterjee in the early 1900s. It was one of the first magazines that encouraged women to prove themselves as serious writers. The word *Prabasi* means a Bengali living outside Bengal, but can also be translated to mean a sort of exile or, as in my mother's case, a duality that was ingrained in her. Chatterjee once very famously wrote, "In truth, we are Indians first and Bengalis next."[5]

My lips rounded to the shape of the word *Prabasi*, pronounced as 'Probashi', with the gentle Bengali 'o' and the purposeful shadowy 'sh', and I considered how relevant Chatterjee's words still were over a century later.

'Of all the subjects my mother studied, English was her favourite, and English poetry closest to her heart. That is what these are—books of English poetry.'

Picking up the wrapped parcels, we climbed up the stairs to his study, where a few more books belonging to his mother and grandfather lived. At the far end of the carpeted first-floor corridor was a brightly illuminated room with a large wall-length shelf mounted on the back wall. Not a single inch of space was left bare: slim paperbacks, fat volumes bound in leather and cloth, and piles and piles of papers covered the desk and floor. The computer was the only thing that stood out in the otherwise antiquated decor of the study. It somewhat resembled a mad scientist's laboratory, only with books. Upon seeing my wide eyes, he laughed.

'Come on in, yes, yes, this is how it always is. I moved a few things around to make space for you.' He gestured to the soft green armchair. 'Otherwise, this is also stacked with papers!'

Gingerly, I sat on the edge of the green chair, eager to see what the packages held inside. Placing them on the black-coloured desktop, he began to unwrap them. The crinkling sound of wrapping paper filled the air. Paper and twine were discarded on the carpet and treasures of old were extracted.

Bo-Peep's Bumper Book, read the inscription on the first book, black ink in careful cursive handwriting, the Bs and Ps romantically classical. The yellow hard cover was protected with brown paper, which, it seemed, hadn't been changed since it was first put on. The front was faded and torn in several places, and the brown bore only faint traces of its original deep shade. 'Miss Pushpa De', written in the same cursive hand, sat below the title, her first name underlined with intention. The years had weathered the book, and the pages fell out as they had come free of their binding.

Opening up another package, he revealed his mother's favourite, *The Book of Everlasting Things*, a magical title for the magical contents within. She had been a fan of Romantic poetry, the collection filled with the works of Keats, Shelley, Byron, Browning. The book opened with an old and dusty crack. In rather graceful fashion, a stray page of a different colour fell out of the book, and I picked it up and placed it on the table. The inside pages of the book were thick and handmade. My palms grazed them, and the sound of it was heavy and deliberate. Handset metallic type was embossed on the page in pale black ink.

'Roll On, Thou Deep and Dark Blue Ocean, Roll,' wrote Byron on page 204. Either side of the spine was torn beyond repair. A large and violent rupture in the heart of the book slashed through Byron's zealous ocean, revealing words from pages beneath, as if a curtain opening into another world:

A shadow of man's ravage, save his own,
When for a moment, like a drop of rain,
He sinks into thy depths with bubbling groan,
Without a grave, unknelled, uncoffined and unknown.

I read Byron's famous words, attempting to hold within them the loss man felt when faced with the boundless, powerful ocean. I thought of man's defeat by the mighty forces of nature and wondered about the powers that one man could possess over another. What did it take to dominate a people, a country, a civilization?

'She always covered all of her books.' The professor shook me out of my bleak reverie. 'The brown paper hasn't been changed since her, but the book itself, well, it isn't in such good condition, I'm afraid. Moth-eaten in certain places.'

Turning its frail pages, I imagined a young girl reading the poems and stories inside. My hands explored the texture of the brown paper, its crinkly and crumpled sound, and again I imagined Miss De carefully wrapping the book, folding the edges into triangles and securing them with pieces of tape. The pages inside were water-stained and faded, and picking up a torn fragment of paper, I asked, 'Were these books at her house in Park Circus?'

'Yes, you're absolutely right. They were. Shall I move into the 1940s to tell you about these books, then?' he asked systematically.

I nodded.

* * *

'With the background of World War II, 1942 brought the Quit India Movement and 1943 the Bengal famine. Now, as I told you before, my family had been going into decline for many years. But the year that really changed everything was 1946. The Great Calcutta Killings, Direct Action Day, 16 August 1946. There are three things that have changed my perception in life, and this is the first.'

His voice, no longer melancholic, took on an ominous tone. 'Park Circus, where my mother's family lived, had always been and still is a Muslim area. At the time, the house was occupied by my grandmother, my uncle, his young wife and their baby girl. If you recall, my grandfather, B.C. De, the ICS officer, died early. Now, since I wasn't there, this is a story I have only heard repeatedly and what you will receive today is perhaps another rendition of it—mine. So, in the early evening, a mob was seen making its way towards the grand striking house. Breaking the gate, they came inside, threatening to kill everyone. A Hindu family living in a Muslim area. And this was wartime. There are no explanations for that kind of bloodlust. How people killed and massacred their neighbours and friends and acquaintances will always evade me.[6]

'Because they had a large house, the ground floor had been rented out to a tenant, a Hindu from the Punjab, whose name was

Shantilal. And it was he who came to their rescue. 'I am a Muslim man and this is my family,' he claimed, safeguarding the Des. The mob refused to believe him, so he recited the Kalima. I don't know how he knew it, but perhaps that was enough for the rioters. They weren't the most educated folk anyway. So the family was rounded up and pushed outside, though no one was harmed. Then the mob went around inside the house, breaking the furniture and setting rooms on fire. My grandmother watched her life crumble before her eyes as she sat on the pavement, grateful only to be alive. Not a single person helped, not a single English convoy stopped for the widow of an ICS officer. No one stopped.

'Meanwhile, their possessions were carried out with briskness and little care: the pivotal instant when all of their most precious belongings, which had taken years to accumulate and curate into a collection, were diminished to the status of mere *things*. Things that could just be discarded and easily fractured; surfaces of tables and counters scratched and vandalized; beds, sofas and shelves broken; a family branded as "the other". "Hindu," this madness, this hasty intrusion declared.

'That day, the mob took away many things—the musical instruments that my mother owned, objects and artefacts of importance and value, and...' (he said the next words with a heavy heart) '... the books. They destroyed all the books. My grandfather's great library, his collection of English, French and Bengali books, my mother's collections of poetry—they were all mostly destroyed. When they realized that they didn't have enough time to tear or set fire to all the books, they filled the grand bathtubs with water and immersed them.'

His fingers traced the marks that water had left on the book I held in my hand, *The Book of Everlasting Things*. The mystery of the water-rings had been solved, but had created a new whirlpool of emotions within the professor's heart.

'Whatever books could be salvaged were taken out of the house when the mob had left, but my uncle doesn't remember them being very many. The family walked around the two floors, among the rubble of what had once been their life, and collected whatever had not been made off with. There was a table that my cousin now owns, I believe. And these books were returned to my mother.' He patted the pile.

Picking up the half-torn fragment of a page I had placed on the table earlier, he said, 'This is what is left of my grandfather's copy of Emile Zola's work.' *La Terre*, the title read, The Earth. Perforated and worn, the page held a strangely apt set of dialogues. '"I've given them everything," cried an old man,' the professor read to me. '"You're well served out," came the wicked response.' He sighed. 'That evening, we heard it on the radio. It was official. Park Circus was all but destroyed.'[7]

'Where were you at that time?' I asked.

'Well, I was at my house with my parents. Tipen Mitter had also died at the early age of forty-two, after which his business had been taken over by my grandfather. But, before he passed, he had built a beautiful palatial home on Harish Mukherjee Road, a Hindu area. When the lieutenant governor's house was rebuilt and the old fittings discarded, he installed many of them in this home. I remember there was this wooden musical staircase called a musical deck. What a lovely sound it would play when you walked over it! We also had a beautiful pool with goldfish at the front of the house. The very interesting coincidence is that, as the goldfish died, the stature and wealth of the whole family died with them. In a rather melancholic way, they symbolized the family's decline. My Swasti always feels so sad when she thinks about it,' he said, referring to his wife. 'But things didn't remain bleak. Independence brought a new dawn, everyone began to do better.'

From the many piles of papers on his desk, he drew out a thick piece of card, a sepia print of an old colonial home. In the bottom left corner, true to the nature of his profession, was an archival note: 'Built by Tripundreshwar Mitter in late 19th Century.' To the right were the following words: 'Our House 53 HARISH MUKHERJEE ROAD, BHOWANIPUR.' A black border surrounded the entire image; the left side was torn and the bottom was completely discoloured, as though that part of the photograph had been left out in the sun for too long. Dark orange stains peppered it, and the edges were frayed. The top three-fourths of the image, though, were in good condition, though small random white patches could be seen across the entire surface.

The house was built in Mitter's signature neoclassical style, but with a twist. Into the façade of this grand ancestral home he had embedded his ambivalence—towards the twin aspects of Indian and English—by adding traditional local elements like the intricately embellished *jharokha* balconies. The lower level of the house was almost completely concealed by the tall trees in the garden.

'The riots lasted for three days, and I remember everything about those days. It was 16 August 1946 at 5.20 p.m.—of this I am sure. Yes, these are the things we need to be sure of,' he said, as if confirming the details to himself. 'This is the second momentous thing that changed my life. I was standing here'—he pointed to a window at the front of the house in the photo, nearly camouflaged by the trees—'and I happened to look outside. A woman, a neighbour, was being dragged out of her home onto the street, where she and her child were beaten to death. Beaten to death in front of me and everyone else. I was only eight years old, I didn't understand what was happening, but I saw the whole thing from the window.

'When you looked out, the sky was smoky and dark, and in the distance, as if at the end of a dark and horrific tunnel, were unfurling flames, wild and untameable … Calcutta was swallowed by savagery. But that incident with the woman and the child left a deep impression on me, and in my later years at university and while teaching I became very interested in the Armenian Genocide, the Holocaust and, of course, Partition violence. Race, representation, dominance, subservience, prejudice, I became very concerned with how one should perceive these concepts, and I believe the seeds for that concern were sown in me in 1946.

'When the riots began, my father got very worried for all the Muslims who lived nearby or worked in our house. I think it was the second or third day, and under the cover of darkness he told them to get into his car and lie low on the floor, not making a sound. Then he drove them out and dropped them to safety in the Muslim area. When he came back, the neighbourhood had heard of what he had done and a mob of about fifty people came to our house, wanting to burn the place down. "You've betrayed Hindus, you Muslim-lover, have you no shame?" they were saying, and we could hear them from inside the house.

'My father and one of his brothers went to the gate to pacify the mob but they wouldn't listen. You see, in those days, all houses had back entrances, and it was likely that anyone could come in, loot and plunder or even kill, or set the house on fire. So my father didn't want to enrage them further and he sought the counsel of a Congress party member who lived just a few houses down. She intervened and a compromise was reached. The Mitters were to open the ground floor of their house to the refugees who came in from parts of East Bengal. I was an only child and so was only too overjoyed to see the house full of people all the time. Little did I know that our house had turned into a makeshift refugee camp!

'The Direct Action Day riots in Calcutta also saw, for the first time, a large-scale participation of the upper and middle classes of the population. That is what made these riots such an important event in Partition history.[8] And it only got worse from then on. The riots continued in various parts of the country; people continued to pour into the already crowded city of Calcutta until Independence and even more so as a consequence of the Partition. 1946 led the bloodbath into 1947 as we emerged a wounded yet independent nation. But I must tell you I did not witness Independence in India.'

My eyebrows shot up quizzically. 'What do you mean?'

'Well, I was on a ship with my parents on our way back to India from England when "India awoke to life and freedom". This was the third thing to have a great impact on my life. Right after the 1946 riots, my parents couldn't bear to be in the city. My father's temporary appointment as the food commissioner had come to an end and he wondered what to do next. He was interested in the world, in travel. He longed to go back to England and so he decided that our family would embark on a world tour for a whole year!'

His eyes lit up as he said these last words, as if it was the most delightful idea. But I, in turn, was conflicted. What would it mean for the youth of the nation to leave it at such a critical time? The Mitters' ambivalence was clearer than ever.

'It was immediately after the war and foreign exchange wasn't that easily available,' he continued. 'Anyway, he got together some money and applied for the tour. But rather than Europe, he was more interested in America. Now that was the new and exciting foreign land. However, to obtain a visa and foreign currency, one had to present a reason to go—trade, business, whatever that may be. Oh, but my father's mind was set, so much so that he actually created a small business, a company called AmerIndia, and was promptly granted permission for a business trip! My mother, of course, said she wouldn't leave me alone for a year and I was only too overjoyed to not have to attend school, so there we were. The three of us set sail across the oceans to America.

'The trip was from Bombay to San Francisco. We travelled via Colombo, Hong Kong, Shanghai, and finally arrived in San Francisco. The ship was wonderful, very grand, even though we were just travelling tourist class and not cabin class, which was the finest. Of course, the children were separated—we had nannies to look after us in the nurseries, far away from the adults. From San Francisco we travelled by the RMS *Queen Mary*, one of the largest and fastest North Atlantic liners of that time—that's to say 33 knots per hour—to Hollywood, Washington, New Orleans, New York, and then spent five days in New Hampshire. From there we went to Europe, staying in England for a month. It was around mid-July to August, and I must tell you England in 1947 was terrible.

'My mother hated it, but my father, having spent time in London at the Bar, insisted on visiting. Though it wasn't the England he remembered. 1945 had seen Britain emerge triumphant from the war. Triumphant, yet bankrupt, which was one of the reasons for such a hasty decision to grant India independence months earlier than planned. If the Empire's condition was unfortunate in India, in England it was just as bad, if not worse. I remember the environment being drab, impoverished and depressing. The only things in abundance were rationing coupons for meat, butter, lard, sugar, tea, cheese ... the list was endless.[9] This was not the way my mother had wanted to spend a vacation, rationing food and supplies, and so naturally she was miserable. Men and women would line up for miles outside shops for even the most basic of goods. There were power cuts and the electricity stations were closed due to a shortage of coal. One would have thought that it was still wartime! And the streets, oh, London was filthy, the houses unkempt, the gardens untended; the situation was morose.'

I stared at him, my forehead creased, my eyebrows knitted together, confused as to how to respond. I had only ever wondered about the months leading up to Independence in India itself; I had never considered the state of affairs in England. In the descending days of the Raj in India, there was seldom talk of the goings-on in Britain, except at the political or governmental level. I had read somewhere that Sir Radcliffe, the architect of the Partition lines for Punjab and Bengal, had once said in a radio broadcast: 'It was amazing that the lives and doings of the British in India should have made so slight an impress upon the lives and imaginations of their countrymen at home.'[10] I wondered, for just a fleeting moment, if the same could be said in reverse.

'When we left India in 1946, the news of Independence was not yet confirmed,' the professor continued. 'Indians were still very much citizens of the Empire despite the strong negotiations of the local political parties. But, as the months went by, we received news of India in every port where we stopped, thanks to the BBC and several foreign presses. It is even said that in 1947, months before Independence, the majority of foreign presses like the Associated Press of America, the *New York Times* and Agence France-Presse had been encamped in the Imperial Hotel in Delhi.[11] And so, gradually, far away from the landscape of home, we learnt of impending Independence and then of Partition.

'When we left England to sail home for India, Radcliffe hadn't yet announced his boundary awards. Trains had not yet begun to cross into new countries, hordes of people had not yet begun to flee their homelands. India was still undivided, and we were still citizens of the Empire. And my parents, having spent the year abroad, had become more and more cosmopolitan, their ambivalence seemed reduced. They had always been polished, attended parties, [gone] dancing, seen the world. It was all very much a part of their liberal upbringing. But to return to India was to return to their undecidedness. Two distinct halves of a whole: not English and not Bengali enough, always balancing the colonial and nationalist elements they had each inherited from their respective families.

'But it was a strange end to an otherwise splendid trip—to return to an independent India pregnant with promise, yet overcome with brutality and communal madness. Now, there are things I still remember from the journey back home. It was the rainy season and the passengers on the ship were often unwell. I myself was seasick several times. Coupled with that was a feeling of sadness as the trip was coming to an end and I realized I'd have to go back to school.' He chuckled. 'You know, the things that children worry about!'

He grew suddenly quiet and, when he spoke again, his voice had lost even the shadow of its earlier chuckle. 'Broadcast via the BBC was the news of India's Independence, both in England and to foreign countries, to all ships at sea, and eventually throughout the British Empire…'[12] His gaze wandered to outside the window, beyond the garden and into the distance. I followed it, my recorder recording only our breaths.

'Such a strange place to learn of one's freedom,' I mused.

And after just a moment, as if silence had evoked the memory of reading *The Book of Everlasting Things* and Byron's great, infinite ocean, untethered and ungovernable, he said, 'Actually, I think it's rather befitting!'

13

LOVE IN THE TIME OF NATIONALISM

THE POEMS OF PRABHJOT KAUR

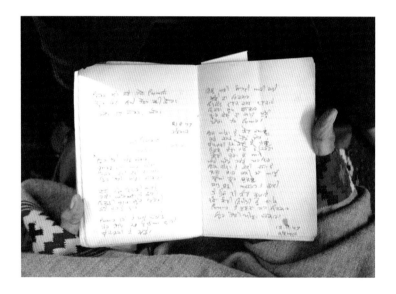

IS THERE ANYTHING MORE beautiful than a winter's sun in Delhi? Amidst the fog, soot and unexpected chill of a bleak January sky, a sighting of the sun was rare and its warmth ever rarer. Yet, there it hung, bright, luminous and welcoming. Smiling, I stretched out my left arm and watched as the rays bathed it almost immediately in a rich golden colour. I was sitting in a charming little garden at the front of an old house, waiting for an award-winning poet to join me. A few wicker chairs and a table were placed in the middle of the grassy patch, a clothesline hung towards the far end, bearing the weight of freshly washed laundry, and along the front wall stood pots of small flowering shrubs.

Hearing footsteps, I turned towards the house. There she was, dressed in a brilliant jade salwar kameez and a cream cardigan. Her silver hair was twisted into a neat bun, secured with white clips. On her ears sat jade earrings and on her fingers were stacked multiple rings.

Her younger daughter, Nirupama, also a writer, accompanied her. In her hand was a thin book. 'I hope you are not cold, Mummy,' she said, placing the book beside her and draping the jade dupatta around her mother's shoulders as they sat down. 'The sun feels so nice at this time of day.'

The poet nodded, her gaze still fixed on me. Small wisps of silver escaped her bun and crawled down her neck. I inched forward to greet her, but before I could say anything, she spoke, depositing between us a fact which has since propelled my belief that the accumulation of time and of stories go hand in hand.

'I am ninety years old,' said Prabhjot Kaur.

And then, as if this were not a conversation between us but rather an old, old legend she was recounting, she continued.

'Many years before I was born, a woman was widowed at the age of sixteen in a town called Andarkot, situated on the banks of the river Jhelum in Kashmir. She was beautiful—short but beautiful—with fair skin, blue eyes and the typically north Punjabi, Kashmiri hooked nose. Her husband used to work in the Indian Railways and passed away suddenly, but not before his wife gave birth to a baby girl. They named her Rajinder. After her husband's death, his family refused to give her any property or money, but they were obligated to feed and clothe her.

'With great difficultly, she raised the baby girl in one room of the ancestral house. The child grew to be taller and even more beautiful than her mother; her nose became longer and sharper and her eyes were bright and curious. Within the confines of the lonely room, her mother educated her as best she could, complementing academic knowledge with lessons in humility and social etiquette, and so the girl learned to be respectful and polite, even to the family that had cast them away. Whenever she left the house, she was made to cover her head with a dupatta and a chadar, and then her whole body with another thicker, larger chadar. And when she used to go out, the *tonga*, the carriage itself, would be covered completely. So striking were her features that no man was allowed to lay eyes on her, her mother made sure of that.

'When she turned fifteen, Rajinder was married off to an eighteen-year-old, who would, two years later, be employed by the Indian Military Farms. The couple lived in matrimonial bliss and soon the young wife was pregnant, giving birth once every year to about fourteen children, only eight of whom survived.

'Because of her husband's work, the couple was transferred from city to city, and the old woman, the girl's mother, would visit them wherever they were posted. She would travel all the way from Andarkot on horseback, sometimes changing two or three horses throughout the journey. She would take care of the children, spend time with her daughter, and then return home. One day, the young man told his mother-in-law, "You can no longer travel back and forth on horseback; it isn't safe and you are getting older. Stay here and let us take care of you." By this time, the couple lived in his family's village in district Gujrat, located between the rivers Jhelum and Chenab. The woman said she had property and belongings back home but he wouldn't listen; they didn't need any of it. Her safety was more precious than any property. So it was settled: she would stay with her daughter.'

For the first time in her story, the poet paused.

'This is how my mother married my father and my *nani* came to stay with us,' she said, having unfolded the history of her ancestors as though she were reading it from a book. True to her art, she had drawn her past out into the air, and grand images swam in my mind like the scenes from a long lost novel: a woman galloping on horseback across the hilly northern terrain, a young girl with a perpetually swollen belly, and a beautifully hooked Kashmiri nose.

'I was the second of those eight children,' she said, clearing her throat. 'We were seven sisters and one brother, who died young. I was born in 1924 in a small village called Langrial in district Gujrat, which is now in Pakistan.'

Slowly she spelled out the word, pausing between each letter. L-A-N-G-R-I-A-L. When she said it, the word glided out in an amalgamated accent that had once been Punjabi; her glacial 'la' and knotted 'ga' and 'ra' were remnants of the language's authenticity. Noting it down, I repeated it, and she nodded in satisfaction.

Then she placed her soft palm over my mine, closing my notebook. Nodding her head, she told me that life was a tale, a story where our past, present and future are all entwined, and to be able to listen to such a story unravelling was the greatest gift of all. Hesitant and fearful of missing even a single detail, I set aside my notebook and simply listened. She smiled, cleared her throat and, just as ceremoniously as before, began.

* * *

'Langrial was a lonely place,' her story opened, slowly filling the space around us with longing. 'When I was a child, it was an isolated village, desolate and remote. Fields of [millet] surrounded us, and when I sat on the roof of our *haveli*, looking out beyond the horizon, it seemed as though the mountains began where the fields ended. An endless landscape of lofty ranges that served as passage for both traders and invaders. Some came to sell the produce of those barren mountains, like large cucumbers, white radishes, white and black salt. Others brought stones like lapis lazuli, firoza and amber from Afghanistan. Some, of course, came just to raid.

'My grandfather, my *dada*, was the *chaudhary* of the village, Sardar Gyan Singh. He had had the settlement constructed around our *haveli*, which was at the centre. The population of the village was more Muslim than Hindu or Sikh, but *farak nahi padta tha*, it never mattered. Once, a plague suddenly spread through the village, killing many, including a Muslim family, whose daughters then became orphaned—Noora and Chhoti. My grandparents adopted and raised them as their own. My *dadi* was named Salakhani, which means someone who is very skilled. She would often sit at the threshold of the *haveli* with a huge canister of grain beside her, and doled it out to whoever came home. Along with that, she would give glassfuls of buttermilk because it would be churned at home every day. As a couple, they were certainly wealthy but also very generous to those around them.

'Surrounding the entire village were tall walls designed to prevent the Rashas, tribal dacoits who used to raid the villages near the frontier on horseback, from penetrating its interior. One evening, such an attack took the villagers by surprise. There was much shouting and screaming as the horsemen galloped through the village, claiming whatever they wanted. The women and children were told to stay inside the houses, and we hid, silent and fearful. I must have been five or six years old, but I remember my heart beating wildly. I didn't know the implications of such an attack, and so instead of dread I had felt excitement, for it seemed like a film or a play!' she laughed.

'This is how my stories grew, this is what they grew from, this is what their subject matter was. The landscape, the sky, the romance with nature, the desolate quiet and almost eerie silence that enveloped the village. I began by telling stories in the form of songs. I would spend hours on the swings outside the house, imagining that a fairy came to me and said, "You are now flying alongside me and you will be cursed if you don't keep flying your whole life."

'This turned out to be a blessing rather than a curse, for as I flew on those swings, I would compose ballads and poems and sing them to myself. While my elder sister readily helped my mother, I showed little interest in household chores. The stories inside my head captivated me far more. If I wasn't on the swing, I could be found lying in bed, with my feet outstretched and propped on the wall, talking and narrating to myself. Gradually I began writing these stories down and then my mother would often say, "*Kagaz kale kar rahi hai*," urging me to study rather than dream up tales and blacken pages with my words.

'But this was my world, the only thing I understood. I didn't know where the words came from, but they would visit me in my head and I would be compelled to write them down. Writers must succumb to their thoughts, their words; they must be consumed completely. *Kitabein meri jaan hai*, my books are my life. And I am lucky that the practice of storytelling sought me out at such a young age, because it demanded that I translate the world around me into narrative. Langrial moulded me into a writer, taught me to string words together, *kahaniyaan pirona sikhaya*,' as she put it in Punjabi. 'I still have all the stories written down in old notebooks,' she said with pride.

I nodded. A translation of her surroundings was how she described the process of writing, one that consumed her completely. Perhaps this was how myths and fantasies so entwined in our culture were born—from the soil, from the land. Stories were carved out of experiences—be it tales of villages, nature, brotherhood, kinship or the essence of Mother Earth—and passed down orally through the generations, grandmothers narrating fables of picturesque hamlets in lands and times far, far away.

Seeing me nod, she placed her hand—soft, aged, wrinkled—over mine once again. I felt the beat of her pulse, regular and timely, pass through my hand—a poem running through her veins, mixing with her blood.

'When I was seven years old, we moved from Langrial to Peshawar, where we lived until 1941, when I turned seventeen. After that, we lived in Lahore until the *batwara*, the Separation, in '47. We were allotted a grand house on Infantry Road in Lahore, large enough to accommodate all of us—children, parents and grandparents. I was in the middle of a BA degree in political science at Khalsa College, and two other siblings were studying as well, when my father was put in charge of the Dairy and Grass Farms in Kalyan, near Bombay. Leaving the three of us in the care of our *nani*, the family migrated to Kalyan in 1946. They took a significant portion of the household with them, leaving only the essentials for us. *Kuch kuch hai abhi bhi*, some of those things are here.' She gestured to Nirupama, who nodded and slipped inside the house. She came out a few minutes later, arms laden with utensils from the kitchen, and placed them on the table.

My finger ran over the uneven, crooked edges of a *thali*, visible proof of the handmade. The years had not just discoloured the platter's once-perfect *kalai* coating to reveal the copper beneath, but weathering had also expanded the metal, the *thali* bowing upwards in the centre. The coating of silvering mixed with copper hues gave the utensil a splendidly aged aura. Within its centre, the area used to place the food, darker, more circular lines had set in, presumably water or cleaning stains after years of scrubbing. Two larger, long-handled serving spoons bore the same imperfections. Their flat handles had now all but lost their silver sheen and the copper slowly inched upwards to their bowls. A flat spatula sat distinct from the two spoons, in terms of both its broad, flat blade and its ornately shaped handle.

'We still use these in the kitchen,' Nirupama said, 'but they are long overdue for *kalai* now … as you can see.'

'*Arey*, no one does *kalai* any more! Have you ever seen it? *Aise-aise, jaldi-jaldi*'—the poet's hands moved in swift, round motions across the *thali*—'the *kalai-wallas* would coat the inside of the *bartan*. In our days, they would come right to your doorstep! My mother would take out all the *bartan* from the kitchen and he would sit, heat the surface of the plate, pot, ladle, and coat it. All of these are from her *dahej*, the dowry from her wedding.'

'So these were brought by your mother to Kalyan?'

'And many more items. She moved the whole household! This is just what I have with me.'

She stroked the long spoon lovingly, her short nails tracing the scratched surface of the handle where the copper had bled into the silver in soft, frayed lines. Then she called out towards the house and a young girl, presumably the help, came out. She picked up the kitchenware and took it back inside.

* * *

'*Toh kahan the hum…*' she paused, remembering where she had left off. 'Yes, 1946, when we were in Lahore. But before that … in Langrial, communal riots began spreading as well, and we heard stories of our *dada* and *dadi* trying to prevent them. There was one radio in the entire village, but they were educated people, they could sense the impending Independence. There had been rumours flying around, *havaiyan udti thi*, of a partition based on religion … And because the religious landscape was heterogeneous in Langrial, people began fearing for their lives and land.

'So my *dada* assured them that the land in the village belonged to them all, and there was nothing and no one to fear. He might have been the *chaudhary* and, yes, he was Sikh, but there was no village without its people, no matter what religion they believed in. He brought out the papers of his land holdings and urged others to do the same. Then, in a large bonfire, they torched every last proof of what land belonged to whom and, by extension, to what religion. *Saare kaagaz jala diye uss din*, they burnt all the papers that day, and erased all the differences between them. The Muslims of the village would usually wear black turbans, and soon every man, regardless of religion, began wearing a black turban. These were discreet yet encouraging gestures for the village folk because, if they were united, no external force could eradicate the love.

'Meanwhile, in Lahore, my siblings and I continued to live in the grand house with our *nani* until the situation around us became absolutely unbearable. Then we moved to a small three-room flat near the local gurudwara in Badami Bagh.'

'What do you mean by unbearable?' I interjected.

'Well, from one side, we would hear cries of "*Allahu Akbar*" and from the other chants of "*Bole so nihal*" resounding in the air all day and night, like battle cries. Lahore, a city that had once been the nucleus of culture and amity, became the site of bloodbath in the months leading up to Independence. Our hearts would sink with fear, *dar baith gaya tha dil mein*,' she repeated. 'We would lock our houses and climb up to the roofs with bricks and stones in case there were riots in the neighbourhood. If we ever left the gurudwara vicinity, on our person we always had a *kirpaan* and a small bag with ID papers and some money. Most girls carried *mirchi* powder or poison, just in case.'

'Just in case of what … death?'

'Or something worse.'

'Or something worse…' I whispered.

'*Je Chenah vich zor hai nahi, te eh chal phir Sindh vich mar jayengi kudi Punjab di*,' came her reply, strong, subtle and poignant, the words she wrote decades ago still imprinted in her mind.

'If the flow of the Chenab is not strong enough,' Nirupama translated, her voice laced with sadness, 'then let me, a Punjabi girl, jump into the Sindh, for its current is fast and fierce. It is better to die with honour and on your own terms, than to fall into the hands of perpetrators…' Turning to her mother, she asked, 'Mummy, did you ever think that Lahore would remain in India?'

'*Beta*, I think, till the last moment, we all did; we all hoped at least. Given how many Hindus and Sikhs lived there, given the cultural character of the city, we were all sure that it would remain. But then the riots just kept getting more and more out of hand. There would be announcements on the loudspeakers set up on top of street poles, warning us not to buy vegetables for fear of being poisoned: "*Sabziyan vich zeher hai*," a voice would ring frequently through the day. But we were lucky. Because of my father's government job, we would get packets of lentils like *rajma*, and we had stocked up while our parents were still in Lahore. By the summer of '47, the streets of Lahore were drenched in the blood of all religions, the skies were heavy with dark slogans and I … amidst all of this, I would try to write.'

'You continued to write during the Partition?' I asked.

'Yes, of course! The need to write—the inspiration from my landscape—was heightened more than ever. I had grown up in the midst of the struggle for Independence, so it was all but natural that the momentous happenings all around would inspire me to write. During the Quit India Movement in 1942, I, along with many people, burned all my clothes in a public square in Lahore. Oh, *aur woh Dhaake di malmal…*' she sighed, 'the soft, dreamy fabric we had worn all our lives was never to be touched again once we came to know of the weavers in Dhaka who had their hands cut off by the British, preventing them from weaving the *malmal* and forcing people to buy it from the Lancashire mills in England.[1] From then on, I wore only *khadi* and nothing else until 1949, much after Independence.'

Her words had woven their way into the seams of the nationalist tapestry, spreading across the Punjab with both purpose and fervour. She would often attend local meetings, and was once caught by a police officer who warned her about being involved in such seditious activities, but that hardly ever deterred her. In the wake of the rising freedom struggle, she penned her first book of poetry, *Lath Lath Joth Jage*.

'The Lamp Burns Bright and Brilliant,' she translated the title, 'was devoted to the sentiments and aspirations of a new dawn, a new era. To an independent India!'

Nirupama and I smiled. Prabhjot Kaur joined in, a mischievous grin spreading across her face, and then she finally said, '*Bass*, listen to me … after that, also in 1946, I published two more books, *Kujh Hor*, Something Else, and *Azal Toh*, From the Beginning, both nationalist in theme. But this first book, *Lath Lath Joth Jage*, was purchased in large numbers by the military and was shipped and distributed to all those places in the world where Sikh regiments were fighting for the British in World War II, hoping it would inspire them. A young officer posted in Syria received a copy, read it and wrote to me at my college address in Lahore, printed behind the book. He wanted to marry me, all based on my writing! He also sent a formal letter home, to my father—this is before they had moved to Kalyan.' At this, both my eyes and my smile widened, and I wondered whether it was possible to fall in love with someone because of the words they wrote. Words could seduce, they could poison, they could even coerce, but could they prove to be the essence of a person? Could one be distilled, wrung dry, squeezed out completely into a string of words that another could love?

In April 1946, one Major Narenderpal Singh travelled from Syria to Lahore to see the poet whose words had enchanted him, to whom he had written a letter full of both admiration and growing love. Armed with his offer for marriage, he visited her home.

'I remember distinctly,' Prabhjot Kaur's love story began, 'that he pulled out a pin from his turban and asked me, "May I?" Both confused and surprised, I nodded, and then he did the strangest thing. He reached over and tapped my teeth gently. Then, laughing, he said that they were so lovely and pearly white that he had wanted to check whether they were real! Our lives were like this. Filled with these small, sweet, somewhat strange romantic gestures. Our relationship grew not just out of all the words that were said, but all the unsaid actions as well.' She smiled wide, revealing, sure enough, her pearly whites.

'*Phir agle din, college mein intezaar kar rahe the*, he was waiting for me the next day in college. "*Tere saath baat karni hai*," he wanted to speak to me, and jokingly I asked why he hadn't done so the day before. He asked me to accompany him to the canteen, but I was apprehensive—it wasn't the most private place. So we went to Mr Khosla, the principal, to ask what the proper decorum for such a meeting was. Since he was a major, a distinguished officer, the principal actually vacated his office for us, *daftar khali kara*! We sat, drank a cup of tea and spoke. For many years, Mr Khosla used to joke *ki meri shaadi unhone karayi*—that he was instrumental in getting us married!'

'What do you think it was about your mother's work that drew your father to it?' I asked Nirupama.

'It was the romantic in her!' she smiled. 'Whenever she wrote—and she continues to write to this day—it is always to excavate something, to go beyond the meaning, within the word. Always to reveal a denser emotion, be it about love, or nature, or the freedom struggle. And even when she speaks normally, it is in poetic phrases. The music, the words, they swim in her mind. I think he found that irresistible. It was the same things that drew her to him as well, you know. He was a charmer, very romantic, would read to her often—stories, poetry, Ghalib in particular.'

The poet giggled, listening to us talk as though she weren't in the room. 'The day after he came to the college, he asked me to marry him,' she revealed, 'and this time, I agreed. He had wanted to officially ask my father for my hand, but not before he had asked me. We couldn't get married so easily or so soon, for he had to return to his post. But during his time in Lahore, we went out for chai and walks, I introduced him to my friends, and there just seemed to be a new air of hope around me. Then, once when we were dining at Elphinstone Hotel,[2] he gave me a gift. A beautiful, hand-painted, mother-of-pearl bracelet seated in an ivory carved box. I have kept it safely my whole life and still have it.

'Soon, our time together ended and he left for his new posting in Baghdad. A few weeks later, while I was reading a gazette, *The Punjabi Sahitya*, I came across his name signed at the bottom of a poem. So he was also a writer, I discovered that day, and with great interest and keeping his proposal in mind I read the poem again. It was a love ballad, melancholic and full of longing. *Rohini and Bir Singh*, about a young couple at the cusp of separation.'

Again, the Punjabi accent slipped into her speech effortlessly, and a name—Rohini—which I would have pronounced crisply and carefully, with each letter intact, from her spilled out in a twisted liaison: Rohni, the 'ni' said with a rolling yet deep click of the tongue.

'I have it here,' Nirupama offered, handing her mother the slender book.

She nodded and placed it in her lap but did not read from it. Yet.

'The work, passionate and alive, had sadly felt incomplete. Sharing it with my sister, Surjit, I decided to add a verse to my young officer's poem. And so the next edition of the gazette carried a continuation of the ballad, and obfuscated within its words were, I think, my feelings.' I held my breath, unable to wait to hear the poem. My typically impervious heart seemed to both open up and dissolve simultaneously. The old-fashioned, discreet nature of the act led me to imagine how unknowingly bonds of love begin to grow. I thought of the young officer, dressed in uniform against the Baghdadi landscape, opening the monthly gazette and finding within it a continuation of his poem, and knowing subliminally that within those very public words was a secret, just for him. Decades on from that day, as I listened to the poet read the words of her beloved, I was convinced that the invisible awakening of affection, the gradual unfolding of warmth and desire, and quiet, private gestures had inspired but the grandest of love stories.

Slowly, she picked up the pamphlet from her lap. 'He replied to my reply and I further replied to his, making it a six-poem serial, a *naatak*, which was finally published in a book in 1947.' Opening it to the first page, which was torn at the bottom right corner, she read from the publisher's note: 'Surjit Singh Sethi, 19th January 1947. 4 Muzang Road.' Then she held out the book to me. 'It is titled *Kaafile*, which means caravans.'

The book was small, barely forty pages, fastened tightly with rusted staples that created small pools of dark orange where they sat securing the spine. The paper itself had dulled over the years, or perhaps it had always been of an aged hue. A simple screen-print of a woman against a backdrop of mountains adorned the cover: Rohini, her gaze distant and pensive. A dull pink highlighted certain areas against the bold black illustration. In my hands it felt smooth, and because I couldn't read Punjabi it seemed to hold an otherworldliness that I couldn't ever possess. Taking it from me, she began to read:

> *Bir Singh: ja, murh ja Rohniye! Shapa peh gayi hain.*
> *Tenu shayad koi udeekda howe*
> *Aah, aaj di raat kinni swadi howegi*
> *Mere dil andar dhundhkar hai, bahar Kali raat di*
> *Siyahi hai, sian han meriya bhawikht dia aasan.*
> *Par tenu ki Rohniye! Ja murh ja Rohniye!*[3]

The story unravels the indecipherable distances that grow between lovers. Bir Singh and Rohini stand inches away from each other, yet separating them are tides of uncertainties. Bir Singh has stripped their relationship of trust, *yakeen*, and infused it instead with doubt, *shakk*. While Rohini trusts too much, Bir Singh doubts too much, believing himself to be unworthy of Rohini's love. Doused in his own insecurities, he says it is now time for her to go, someone might be waiting for her. The night is beautiful, delicious even, but the inside of his heart is as foggy as the night is inky black.

'*Rohini: Haneri raat vich apne chan nu gawa ke kithe murh ja, pritama?*'

Our heroine questions this forced severance; in the darkness of night, how can she go and leave her moon behind? Bir Singh, wracked with self-doubt, leaves his beloved with the rather inconsiderate promise that, one evening, when the sky is similarly dark, she will hear the hooves of his horse: '*cheere pe savar*', she said in Punjabi, and then translated for me. Bir Singh would return for her any day in the coming 365 days, at the very time of their parting a year ago, and if he found her waiting for him, then he would know that their love was real. A perplexed and dejected Rohini waits day after day at the same spot at the same time for her Bir Singh, but he never comes. Then one day our hero appears to see a frail shadow of what had once been his beautiful Rohini. All this time, though life has begun to leave her, she has waited for him. When he comes for her, she lays her eyes on him one last time, intoxicated still by his love, and then, unflinching, falls at his feet and dies. His departure marked the beginning of her suffering, and his arrival its end.

As she read the internal dialogues of both Rohini and Bir Singh on why lovers do the things they do, I assumed these to be representations by extension of Prabhjot Kaur's own thoughts on love and separation. Through the misgivings of Bir Singh, both she and her future husband seemed to vow a holier commitment in love. I was surprised by the end of the narrative, as many parts of it, though written decades ago, still held relevance. Sacred relationships can be torn asunder even by the slightest doubt, if they are not tied with the secure and honest strings of love. '*Pyaar di mazboot dori naal*,' she smiled, tying an imaginary knot in the air.

'So your love survived the distance?' I asked her.

'Oh yes. We would be together eventually, that was certain. But we also knew that we wanted to get married in an independent India. So, until then, we wrote letters and he visited when he could.'

* * *

'Now…' she said, suddenly grave, 'in June, there was an announcement. A date for Partition had been set. Barely two months away, 15 August. Only then did it dawn on us that a *batwara* was truly going to happen. Politicians, of course, were ready to warm their seats, unconcerned about the common man. Governments change, but people don't.' She repeated this sentiment: '*Sarkarein badalti hai, par log ghar chhodke thodi jaate hain.* How were people expected to move from one part of the country to another? Would there be an exchange of population at all? Like so many others, we too were determined to stay in Lahore. But we couldn't. The riots became [u]ncontrollable, every day someone was murdered or raped or some house was burnt down. Not just of one religion but all: Hindus, Muslims, Sikhs, they all contributed to the insanity. With the announcement of Partition, the floodgates of violence opened and a terror spread across the entire north. Families were divided, children died, husbands and wives were separated, universities were closed. Was it worth it?

'And what was the rush to divide us, I ask, to separate us from our land and loved ones? And if we were going to be divided anyway, then there should have been a better compromise. It was an unholy rush. Mountbatten and Edwina and Nehru and Jinnah, they were all responsible for the crumbling of India.'

Silence.

'In the heat,' she continued after a pause, 'in the godforsaken heat of August, my mother travelled all by herself from Kalyan to Lahore to pick us up. When she reached the gurudwara at Badami Bagh, she was crying. "The land is drenched in blood," she said to us. "I barely recognize it." She was weeping as she got off the *tonga*. Unable to control or calm herself, she told us about all the death she had seen on the way. Independence had been declared, but we felt anything but free. Rather, we became strangers to the city we called home.

Disheartened and petrified of what lay ahead, we packed whatever little we had—I brought mostly my notebooks—and got ready to be transported to the train station. My *nani* and my mother dressed us all in black chadars, dark as the night, and then we waited.

'Suddenly, without warning, from the inky black night, a convoy arrived to take us from Badami Bagh to the train station. We scrambled in, leaving the house as it was. We had all been eating dinner, I had been making the chapatis on the open *chulha*, and with the confusion of the convoy arriving, I even left the *chulha* on. I remember thinking, only much later, about the fate of the chapati left over the open fire.

'At the station, we stood for two hours before a train arrived. And for just a moment, the only sound that was heard was the talking and shuffling of refugees lugging their lives and their homes onto the compartments of the train. No one attacked us, no one set the station on fire, no one even stopped the incoming train. Instead of the deafening chants of "*Allahu Akbar*" and "*Bole so nihal*", what filled the air was a crack of thunder, followed by a torrential downpour. As if the violence had not been bad enough for humanity, nature added to our misery as refugees, soaked in sweat, tears and now rain, boarded the train to India. But even then, we were safe. The worst was over, or so we thought, for another surprise awaited us on board.'

I drew a sharp breath, my eyes anxious, my imagination wild. The poet turned suddenly quiet, and brought her hands up to her temples. With closed eyes, she shook her head from left to right, her mouth contorted into the shape of sadness.

'Mummy … what happened? What happened on the train?' Nirupama asked, concerned.

In a small, feeble voice that hardly sounded like her own, Prabhjot Kaur said, 'An unthinkable horror. When we got onto the train, it was silent and still. Not a soul lurked in the corner, not a sound was heard, and that was because everyone was already dead. Those who had boarded the train at the previous stations had all been murdered and their bodies lay cut up and mutilated before us.'

I was unable to move. All of the afternoon's earlier romance and poetry had dissolved into a pool of blood on the floor of a train compartment full of murdered refugees.

'Then what happened?' I heard myself ask.

'*Phir kya*, then, we had to push the corpses aside and make room to sit. We sat next to them, we sat on top of them, *saath saath hi baithe*. Pools of their blood seeped slowly into the thick cloth of our chadars, staining them. It was so sickening; first, we were slinking away like thieves or robbers in the middle of night, dressed in black clothes for fear of being seen. There was no dignity in such flight. And then, to sit among the dead, it was sick. The stench of blood, the body parts, the hair, the idle suitcase...' her voice trailed off and retreated into silence.

After a while, Nirupama spoke. 'I have been told that a train brought them directly to Delhi, where they stayed in a *dharamshala* sanctuary inside a temple for a while. Then they took the train to Kalyan.'

'About the Partition, about that train, do you remember it?' I asked the poet.

'Before today, I have never thought or spoken about that train. Never.'

Nirupama nodded sadly in affirmation.

In the lingering silence, I tried to put myself in Prabhjot Kaur's place on the train. Having witnessed that sort of horror, would I ever have been able to speak about it, or write about it, or even unthink it, unsee it? Even later, as I left her house, the rotting corpses lived with me for weeks, haunting my nights. Impossibly resonant for a borrowed experience, they reminded me that a whole generation of the subcontinent had witnessed unthinkable horrors that had now been classified, allocated and essentially entombed, so deep under the sedimentary years and months and days of new lives, homes, families, marriages, children, jobs and old age that, when and if they were extracted and narrated now, seemingly out of context, they seemed almost inconceivable.

'I was an idealist back then,' came a remark that almost surprised me. 'I think we all had to be in order to survive. After everything we had witnessed in those days, one had to remain positive somehow. As the weeks went by, the smell and feel and memory of the people on the train gradually faded into forgetfulness. I never thought about it—or maybe I just couldn't, there was no time to.

'As soon as we reached Kalyan, I began working in the refugee camps. I couldn't dwell on my own migratory experience when more and more Hindu refugees were pouring in from parts of Sindh. They came by ship and, believe me when I say this, they came with nothing.' She said it again, this time in Punjabi: '*Kuch bhi nahi*. I heard that before they boarded the ships, they were searched and stripped of all their belongings: books, furniture, utensils, household items, money, jewellery and their homeland. *Hindu Sindhi yahan aa gaye*, they came to India, and Sindh remained in Pakistan. My family and I did *seva*, community service, in the camps. We were educated, so we taught in makeshift schools.

'Life went on. Freedom became a reality and nationalism its by-product. And, very quickly, like a deep internal wound that is left unexamined, the Partition became an unmentionable and invisible memory in the public sphere, reserved only for rare private discussions. Gradually, then, even at home, we stopped talking about Lahore, Peshawar and Langrial. Maybe we began forgetting them as well. My parents had a good life here. My husband and I got married in an independent India, as we had hoped to, in 1948. His position in the army rose and we were transferred to many, many places. Over the years, we have lived in Paris, Afghanistan and all over India, and I, of course, continued to write.'

I nodded. 'So when did you finally come to Delhi?'

'After travelling the whole world!' she laughed.

* * *

Then slowly, adjusting her dupatta, she got up, with the help of her daughter. 'Come, let us show you her notebooks,' Nirupama said.

Eager, I followed them into the last room of the house. A tubelight was on. I looked around. At the far end on my right stood a large bookcase with three shelves and a sliding glass door, half open. Against the wall was a large wooden *almirah*. In front of the bookcase lay a small single bed with white sheets and a forest-green velvet bedcover. To the far left stood an old-fashioned dressing-table with a long, rectangular mirror and three shelves. By the door was a writing desk. The poet sat down in her chair, sighing. On the wall in front of her hung frames: one of the couple, a handsome turbaned man and a beautiful woman smiling and looking into the distance; one of her in her youth; one sepia-toned group photograph; and two paintings.

'This is from the Lahore home as well. It was brought to Kalyan,' said Nirupama, watching me admire the vanity. 'Come, sit down on the bed. I will show you the books and notebooks.'

Gingerly, I came and sat at the edge and watched as book after book was selected off the shelf and placed on the bed. *Pabbi*, a book of poetry, was laid out in several editions: *Plateau* in English and French, *Light and Shadows* in Bulgarian, *Shadow* in Danish, *Lala* in Persian and others in Greek, Arabic, Russian, Hungarian and various regional Indian languages. As I skimmed through the pages of the poet's books, Nirupama told me that her father too, who finally retired as a colonel from the Indian Army, became a prolific novelist.

'My parents remain the only couple in India who have both won the Sahitya Akademi Award. My mother won it for *Pabbi* in 1964 and my father for his novel *Baa Mulahaza Hoshiar* in 1976.'

Then, a sea of blue and black notebooks was taken off the shelf and placed before me. All of them were leather-bound, though the front of each notebook was different—some with lettering, some with perforations and some completely blank. Most of them held folded notes within their dog-eared pages and yellow post-its peeking out like bookmarks.

'These are very old, some are even from her childhood. So just be careful with the pages.'

I selected one at random and picked it up, slowly and carefully, in the same way I would a national archive. Pale blue and ripped at the top and bottom to reveal the thread binding of the spine. Opening its pages, I smelled them deeply, closing my eyes. When I opened them, the poet's gaze was upon me. I picked up another. Black with perforations like polka dots across the front cover. I flipped through its pages until my gaze landed on the dates: 21.8.47 … 12.11.47.

'These are…' I began.

'Yes, these are from the days of the Partition. Remember … she continued to write during it,' Nirupama said.

The poet smiled now, also nodding.

Nirupama took the notebook from me and handed it to her mother. '*Yaad hai*, mummy? Do you remember writing this?'

I picked up all the other notebooks and placed them on her desk. We turned on the table lamp and brought it closer so she could read. Putting on her glasses—rectangular, with clear plastic frames—she placed her ring-laden right hand on the page. Under her thumb sat the aged paper, and a black ink stain close to the bottom of the page bled into the number 11 of November. Written in her clear script with blue-black ink and a sense of immediacy and purpose were Punjabi poems of nationalism.

Standing behind her chair to be able to photograph the pages, I asked her to read out the poem, but she didn't respond. After a few minutes, Nirupama called out, repeating the request, but also in vain. Surprised, she checked the hearing aid on her left ear and, seeing that it was in place, a knowing smile spread over her face.

'She cannot hear us. You see, she is here, but she is not. She hasn't read these in a while…'

As if rediscovering herself through her words, her forefinger drew invisible lines on the pages she had blackened so many years ago. Her lips moved in a soft, inaudible babble and her head nodded from time to time, as if some words still held truth. Her eyes were glued to the pages and she appeared completely removed and unaltered by the movement in the room around her. Was this what it felt like to slip back into your former selves, I wondered. The keepers of journals and notebooks live forever in duality, inventing and reinventing realities. They tread the fine line between the world in their mind and the world on their page and hope that which they pour out remains the truest form of life.

As I watched the poet unearth her different selves that she might have forgotten over the years, just like the incident on the train, I realized that eventually, and inevitably, one does forget. A new self grows seamlessly and quietly over the old one. Experiences become memories that become history that becomes story.

And she was writing the definitive story.

14

MEMORY OF A NATIONALIST

THE PASHMINA SHAWL OF PREET SINGH

WE HAD BEEN TALKING for about an hour when Preet Singh excused herself and went into her bedroom. She returned with two shawls. One, a light beige bordered by magenta, she draped round her own shoulders; the other, soft and fawn-coloured, she placed across mine.

'For you, my dear, before you catch a cold. The sun is very weak today,' she said, distractedly. 'It was always weak in the winter ... barely peeking out from behind the clouds, straining its rays for only a few minutes at a time on our house in the valley between the mountains...'

We were sitting in her living room in Delhi. There were no mountains or valleys around us, yet that's all she could see. The sun was indeed weak that day, not atypical of the kind of winter the city experiences, but within it Preet Singh found something of another sun she had witnessed decades ago. Dreamily, her fingers moved across the delicate gold rim of the teacup that lay before her on the table. And though she turned to face me, I knew the sun still held her attention. She existed in a place of the past, a house in the valley between the mountains, the weak sunshine teasing her playfully.

'But even then...' she continued, returning to the present, 'even then it was never this yellow, never as vibrantly gold as it is here in Delhi. It was a muted kind of sunshine, Quetta's.' She smiled, as if relishing the memory of sombre yellow in a cloudy sky.

'Tell me more,' I said.

She smiled again, shyly. Watching her closely I noticed that her elegance resided in her small movements. It was in the way she smiled before she spoke, or how her posture was so naturally poised. It was in the way her short, dark hair fell neatly beside her face, not a strand out of place, and when her hand reached up to tuck it behind her ear, it was with a nuanced composure. It was in how graciously she played the host, and how even the air around her seemed somewhat calmer.

She wore a maroon sweater with smartly fitted dress pants. Her face, though now aged, still showed signs of beauty and emanated a sort of glow. She spoke in refined colonial English, seated in a carefully curated living room displaying works by famous artists and beautiful antique furniture that complemented the typically grand layout of the homes of Lutyens' Delhi. Yet, in that moment, she transformed immediately into the young girl who had grown up in the valley.

'Quetta is in the Balochistan region at the pass to Afghanistan. I remember it being a beautiful place—full of fruit orchards, and surrounded by mountains on all sides that naturally fortified the city. There was a vastness to it; the landscape seemed unending. The air was crisp and clean, and most of the year the weather was very cold.[1] The city of Quetta housed many, many Englishmen as the Command and Staff College was situated there. But we lived mainly among Muslims, though there was a substantial Sikh community of very tightly knit families and a very large gurudwara within the city.'

She paused for a moment.

'… Or perhaps it just looked very large to me, since I was so small at the time!' She laughed and then continued. 'Anyway, I spent most of my childhood there, apart from the holidays, when we would go to Sargodha or Karachi to visit family. I still think of those long, long train rides, crossing the mountains, trees and endless acres of land until we reached the bustle of city life.'

'What kind of life did you lead in Quetta? What were the houses like?' I asked, as a city slicker who would never give up urban life, yet found comfort in the anecdotes of mountain trails.

'Well, we had a modest house with rooms on three sides and a courtyard in the middle. At the front of the house there was a very long room that was never used since it was too cold, and next to that was a room used just to store coal during the winter months. Apart from that, there were bedrooms and the kitchen and pantry, where we would store mostly vegetables like onions, potatoes and garlic. In the courtyard there was a little cornered-off area with a hand pump and above it grew grapes. The best thing was that the grapes hung low from their vines and attracted bees, so the courtyard was always buzzing softly.'

I smiled at the things she remembered—an idyllic life that belied the tragedies to come.

'In 1935, there was a large earthquake in Quetta, probably the largest ever in South Asia.[2] My grandmother died in that quake. It left the city in ruins, and it was then that the Japanese came and helped rebuild and make the housing resistant to natural calamities. But somehow due to the technology they used, the new houses became more prone to fires. One would have to be very careful in the winter months when lighting wood fires to keep warm...' She trailed off.

'How cold would it get there?'

'Oh, the summer months were very pleasant, like any hill station. The sunshine, bright blue skies, it was lovely. But the winter was long and bleak, and would envelop the city for the better part of the year. Before going out to play in the winter months, my siblings and I would be bundled up in layers and layers of warm clothing. Our mother would give us fistfuls of dried fruit and would cut up the pockets of our coats, so when we put the dried fruits in, they would fall right into the inner lining. We would reach into the recesses of our pockets and munch on almonds, raisins, cashews and pistachios.

'During those months, men called Kabulis would come down to the valley from the Afghan mountains. Their timing would be fixed, as would the houses they visited. It was these men who would bring us our coal, vegetables, dried fruits and meat. They would do odd jobs around the house like melting ice for bathwater in the *hammam*. Due to the extreme weather, all the water in the pipes would freeze during the winter and we could not bathe every day. So, once a week, they would fill the *hammam*, and each member of the family would take turns to bathe. That was it—one icy bath per week!

'I remember the floor of every room of our house was covered with layers and layers of carpet to protect us from the cold. But these would never be placed directly on the floor; the Kabulis would weave a fairly loose matting of jute as per the exact measurement of the room and lay the thick carpet on top of it.'

Smiling wide as if she had just remembered something, she spoke excitedly, 'The carpets! Oh, the room at the front of the house—the cold, long room—actually had nothing but carpets in it! Rolls and rolls of wide, beautiful Persian carpets!'

'How come?'

'Well, during World War II, there were a number of people who invested in ships laden with goods. My father—Papa-ji—was a simple man who ran a supermarket of high-end items. He had a friend next door who ran a carpet store. Since they were close, he borrowed money from my father to invest in one of the ships. However, the ship sank and so did all his investment, and since he had no money to pay back my father, he suggested we take the equivalent in carpets.

'It must have been a significant amount of money since our house definitely had many more carpets than we needed! The most amazing thing was that none of the details of this transaction were ever written; it was just his word. And in those days you kept your word. He was Muslim—my father's friend—but that didn't matter then, you know ... it was all the same: Hindu, Muslim, Sikh. There was no distinction like there is today. When we left Quetta at the time of the Partition, it was impossible to take all those carpets with us, and so eventually my father left them in the possession of the same friend! They were so beautiful—impossibly intricate hand-sewn patterns, luscious rich weaves and dense colours. They adorned all our floors and walls and kept the house cosy through the year.'

I smiled, imagining a house full of carpets.

* * *

She fiddled with the embroidery of her shawl. The sun had set completely, the room was cooler now, and Preet Singh pulled her shawl more tightly around her. Her fingers grazed the delicate pink needlework. 'My mother gave me this shawl, you know,' she sighed. 'I wore it a lot when I was a young girl. I almost never wear it now.'

I studied the fabric as her fingers continued to smooth out the stray pink threads. It was pure pashmina, soft and comfortable. The carefully done Kashmiri embroidery created a beautiful floral-patterned border of magenta over the dull beige background.

'How come you wore it today?' I asked.

'It reminds me of my mother. Given what we are talking about today, I felt it was appropriate to wear. Objects have a way of inspiring the mind to remember things it might have forgotten. I had put this away at the back of my closet and nearly forgotten about it! But when I look at it closely now, I see this edge has been hemmed in.' She pointed to an uneven side roughly sewn with brown thread. 'This is where the shawl was cut in half ... it was so wide that my mother cut it down the centre. One half she gave me and the other to my sister. But, as far as I know, she never wears her half either.'

The object slowly excavated the memories from the recesses of her mind. I watched as she first touched the fabric near the hem, and then spotted a dark patch near its edge.

'Look at this stain!' she exclaimed, alarmed. 'This stain probably won't even go away now … it's so old!'

I looked at the dark stain on the otherwise flawlessly clean shawl, once just a footnote in her history. It suddenly became so much more with the discovery of a small blemish on its surface. I wondered about its twin. Unexpectedly, Preet Singh looked up from the stain. Her attempt to lighten it by rubbing it with the tips of her fingers had been in vain. She laughed, as if feeling silly.

'Look at me, an old woman worrying about an old stain!' She put down the edge of the shawl and sighed. Then she looked up at me.

'I was born in 1939 in Quetta to slightly older parents and was the youngest of four siblings—eighteen years younger than my eldest brother, Waryam Singh, whom I called Bhaji; sixteen years younger than my second brother, Manmohan Singh; and eleven years younger than my sister, Bir. The year I was born, my eldest brother left for medical college in Lahore. My second brother soon went to law college and my sister also to medical college. So, for most of my childhood, it was just my parents and me. I was very close to them, as girls usually are, and indulged—by my father mostly.'

She settled more comfortably into the sofa.

'When I think of him now, I can only remember him in his later years—with a long, grey beard and a warm smile. I recall this little daily routine that he and I shared. When he drove home from work, he would honk in a specific way when he was right outside the gate. I remember waiting for it so eagerly! Then, when I would hear it, I would run out and stand on the little foot pedestal of the car. As he rolled down the window, I would hold on to the door. And every day he would drive into the garage with me hanging on to the door. It was our thing!'

I smiled. 'And what about your mother?'

'My mother—she was a good-looking woman, though fairly short and petite. Mentally, though, she was very strong—would never let anything break her spirit or bring her down. When we left Quetta, I think it was her strength alone that kept us going.

She rarely thought of the past, of the way life was before the Partition, and never once did she complain about the things we had left behind. Throughout her life she taught us that if we were together, circumstances would never be as bad as they seemed. I can't explain it, but she possessed some sort of incredible inner strength. She had faith, she was resilient. There were times when we didn't know what the future held for us, but in all those moments there was her voice assuring us that things would be okay. She trusted my father and the decisions he made, and I think that took courage—to simply say "I trust you" and to genuinely believe that, whatever turn our family took, it would be for the best. I think that took immense courage.'

She paused. Her folded hands held the edges of the shawl, almost as though she were being reassured by her mother.

'You said you left Quetta at the time of the Partition—how? And where did you go?' I asked.

'When we left, there were no riots in Quetta. It was quiet. But still we left, on my eldest brother's insistence. A year before the Partition actually took place, he had begun his internship at a hospital in Lahore. That was also the time he had joined the nationalist movement. He would come home for the holidays and Independence was all he spoke of. He quoted the famous speeches and slogans of freedom fighters, talked endlessly of the rallies and movements happening in Lahore. He always carried these pamphlets with him, the kind you were forbidden to keep according to the British government, and he would distribute them to people to inspire patriotism.

'When I was younger, my siblings and I would go to watch a lot of films together. My second brother would always gesture towards me and say to Bhaji, "Why do you take her with you? She is too young. And she walks too slowly!" Bhaji would laugh and say, "If you don't want to come, don't ... but I am taking her!" He was very fond of me! After the show the lights would come on and everyone was expected to stand to 'God Save the King'. But Bhaji would sharply hiss at us and tell us to keep sitting. By then the nationalist movement had affected many across the country, and this was his small way of protesting. Sure enough, every single time, gurkhas would come with their *lathis* to make us stand and pay our respects to the Crown.

'But my brother—he had this mischief in his eyes. "Run! Run!" he would say and all four of us would dash out of the theatre to save ourselves. I was so young and, as I told you before, apparently I walked very slowly, and so he would pick me up and carry me on his shoulders until we were at a safe distance from the gurkhas. He was never embarrassed to have to run from the law. It was not so much about defiance of the British Crown, but about taking a firm nationalistic stance.'

'Did you ever feel the same sense of patriotism as your brother?'

'Oh no, dear! I was far too young. I would have only been seven years old then. But I do remember the things he would say or do when he came back to Quetta during the holidays. I used to have this bicycle, and in those days everyone had the Union Jack at the front. So did I. It sat on my handlebars and fluttered as I rode around the neighbourhood—until my brother came home one day and ripped it off! He looked at me straight in the eye and said, "Don't you ever put this on again!" And after that I never did. I had seen that fire in his eyes, and I think that was the extent of my understanding of it all. I didn't know what was happening, but I knew he was fighting for something he believed in.'

I nodded.

'After World War II was declared, a lot of Englishmen had left the country, selling off the possessions they couldn't take back with them. My father had bought a number of large, beautiful oil paintings of women posing in carriages and quaint views of the English countryside, which he displayed along the walls of our living room. One day my brother just came and took all of them down, and in their place hung two big portraits: one of Rabindranath Tagore and the other of Mahatma Gandhi.

'That was his favourite room in the whole house. He would often lie down on the carpet in front of the fire and read. He read a lot, even when on vacation—always surrounded by books as he lay under the two majestic paintings. When I think of this nationalist drive now, I understand that he did whatever he could. His smaller, quieter protests—the pamphlets, not standing during the anthem, ripping off the Union Jack—they all amounted to something. He believed deeply in the cause of our freedom, and fuelling all these acts was a desire to be part of something bigger than himself—the struggle to free India.'

My heart swelled with a proxy pride as I listened to the stories of her brother. It wasn't anything I hadn't heard before; many young men and women had fought till their end for the greater cause of Independence. But what struck me was the sincerity with which he had done whatever little he could.

'So you heard about the Partition from your brother, then?' I asked.

'Yes. He was working as a surgeon in Lahore, and that's where the riots first began. They hadn't spread to Quetta at the time, but he came home for a week and insisted that we leave immediately. Lahore was getting bad and he was sure that the violence would quickly spread to other parts. My father thought he was just being paranoid but Bhaji's mind was made up. There was no arguing with him; his word was final. He had arranged for us to go to Mussoorie … we didn't even know where Mussoorie was! I have no idea how he found out about this place or how he arranged a house for us there, but all I remember is that he was adamant we leave Quetta at once. After that it all happened so fast, there was no time to sit and consider the situation. He simply arrived and told us to pack lightly and board the train.'

'And that was it?'

'That was it,' she said, hardly believing it herself. 'It was the end of the summer months in 1947, could have been early August. My sister and second brother were home with us as well, so we all left Quetta together. Really, we just thought we were going to a nice hill station for a short holiday until the riots died down and it was safe to come back home. So we packed accordingly, not taking many clothes or belongings. This shawl, however,' she stroked the soft fabric covering her small frame, 'I was wearing it when we left and I think that is the only reason it survived.

'But if I were to be honest, I doubt anyone ever thought the country would be divided. I promise you, we never imagined it. From a distance, it looked simply like communal riots that would fizzle out after a while. No one ever even considered that they would go on and on and would destroy the lives of so many people. On an individual level, it didn't make any sense. Muslims, Hindus, Sikhs had all lived in harmony once, so what had changed? It seemed, in some ways, completely removed from reality.'

At first, there was disbelief in her voice about the events that had unfolded. It gradually gave way to a tone of conviction, as if trying to convince me and, in turn, herself that the Partition did actually happen. I wondered what it would have felt like for her at the time.

'So, you travelled by train to Mussoorie?' I asked, interested in her journey of migration.

'Yes. Everyone except Papa-ji and Bhaji travelled by train, first to Khanna, which is in the Punjab, and from there on to Mussoorie. Because we thought this would be a short trip, my father didn't join us. Khanna, where we stayed with his eldest brother, was a market town.[3] The railway station was always busy with trains bringing in different vegetables and fruits from all over the province.

'The roof of our uncle's house overlooked the station. One day, from atop that roof, we saw a train arrive, carrying no vegetables or fruits, but a cargo of the dead. Those who had boarded the train alive from our land that was to become Pakistan had arrived in India dead. I can remember to this day the pile of bodies extracted from that train, the mountain of flesh, the smell of burning limbs and bones, the dark cloud of smoke that covered the city after, and the river of blood that drenched the tracks. The stationmaster had to clean the inside of each compartment with a large hose. I remember it all like it happened yesterday. I can see myself sitting on the roof, staring down at the station, and even now, when I fleetingly land on the thought, it's as though it is playing out in slow motion in front of me and I can do absolutely nothing.

'I was disgusted. This was the first time I realized the riots were real, the violence was real, the country truly was going to be partitioned. And that was the very moment when, even as a child, I was thankful that my brother had made us leave Quetta when he did.'

'Where were they—your father and eldest brother?'

'My father was still in Quetta, closing up the business and selling some land. He then journeyed to Karachi, and though it was very rare those days, he was able to take a flight to Delhi, where he put all the money in a bank. If I think about it now, I have to say he had incredible foresight to do that since that money came in handy when we were getting back on our feet in India. From Delhi he came to Mussoorie to join us.'

'And your brother?'

She sighed deeply. 'Well, after we left, my brother went back to Lahore, where the situation had gotten from bad to worse. The riots were spreading fast and violence engulfed the nation, especially around the border areas, and this included Lahore. He was still working at St George's Hospital and wanted to leave to come join us in Mussoorie. But he couldn't, as he was responsible for fourteen Hindu and Sikh patients who had no way of getting across the border. You see, he always worked for the greater good. From ripping off the Union Jack on my bike to not abandoning his patients in a time of need, his concern was always for something greater than himself.

'In those days, he had a close friend called Saifi. When the Muslims got to know of a young Hindu doctor and his fourteen patients, they came to take him away. Saifi's mother was the one who hid him in her house and stood in front of the door. She refused to let any of the rioters in, saying, "I am a Muslim mother. If you want to get past me, you will have to kill me first." In doing so she saved his life. She was the one who helped my brother get his patients on a truck and across the border into Amritsar.

'I suspect he had to bribe his way into the country, because when he arrived in Amritsar in the middle of the night he had only five rupees in his pocket and no place to stay. He walked across the street from the medical college—where he had dropped off his patients—to a restaurant called Crystal and knocked on the door. When the owner answered, he told him what had happened, how he had just crossed the border, how he had no food, no money, no place to stay and no means to get to his family in Mussoorie. The owner was kind, he invited him in, gave him food and a place to sleep and even lent him some money so he could travel to come see us.'

'Did he find you, then?' I asked, my eyes wide.

'He did. He knew we would be in Mussoorie but didn't know exactly where, so it took him a while, but eventually he found us. But there were several weeks in between—after he left us in Quetta and before he joined us in Mussoorie—when we had no idea where he was, whether he was even alive or not. It was hard to get any information in those days. The radios didn't report anything from across the border, and we never stayed at any refugee camp, so there were no lists to refer to. We just had to wait. There was an anxiety that lived in the house with us. Every day my father would go to the post office to try to make a phone call to Saifi's mother. Every day he would be unable to get through. Every day he would return home with red eyes and an expression that could only be described as helplessness.

'The silence began to gnaw away at him. Sometimes I wondered why he put himself through that every day, how he endured it. But, in fact, it had become his ritual. That was what kept the thought of his son alive, the possibility of finding out what had become of his son. You see, Bhaji meant the world to my father. Somehow he was the best part of him. He was the best part of us all, actually.'

She shook her head sadly.

I considered what she had said. How does somebody go on living, knowing that an important part of them might be dead? How does a parent live with the fear of having to cremate his or her own child? Or, worse, of never seeing them again—of forever being in limbo? There is no easy way to confront that sort of grief, and so we wait. Waiting is a painful comfort, demanding no acceptance of any fact or future, allowing us to retain even the smallest possibility of hope.

* * *

'He finally found us in late September 1947. Our house in Mussoorie was built on top of a small hill. I was playing outside with my ball when it rolled downhill and, as I followed it, I saw him walking aimlessly on the road below. I nearly froze. He looked up at me, and I don't know what got into me then. Instead of running up to him and hugging him, I ran back up the hill to the house and yelled to my parents, "Bhaji is here! Bhaji is here!"'

She laughed—an almost child-like laugh.

'On his return, he spoke mostly about what had happened to him: the riots in Lahore, the violence, the fires, his fourteen patients, the owners of Crystal and his journey to Mussoorie. We couldn't even fathom the kind of violence he had seen; we couldn't believe the country had been divided. You never imagine something like this can happen until it does and you are there in the midst of it, witnessing it like some surreal dream. But what is amazing is that, despite all the communal violence that we heard about, there were still good people like Saifi and his mother. That thought gives me comfort.

'I think, for us, the saddest thing was when we realized we would never go back to Quetta again. But, regardless of that, Bhaji was proud that India had gained Independence, and the way he spoke about it made us feel proud of him, momentarily easing our pain.'

'You were fond of him…' I began.

'Oh, very much,' she replied. 'We were very similar, you know. I was inspired by his passion for life. He is the strongest person in my memory … and now he is no more.'

She said this slowly, her voice drenched in incurable sadness.

'Do you still think of him?'

'All the time,' she smiled. 'All the time.'

'I wish, after hearing his story, that you had something of his. Something to remember him by.'

'Oh, my dear, memories really are enough sometimes. With my mother I need this shawl because in a way it's a physical connection. It was what I was wearing the day I left Quetta. It's the only thing I can say is from my home. But with Bhaji it's different. I don't need anything to remember him by. His memory is so strong, and he is etched so clearly in my mind, it feels like yesterday that we were together. His face, his laughter, the way he picked me up on his shoulders when we ran from the theatre, when he hung the oil paintings of Tagore and Gandhi in the living room, his endless piles of books … I remember it all. And I hold it close to me in my heart.'

She began clearing the dishes from the coffee table, piling our teacups and saucers onto a tray. Her body was still wrapped in the beige pashmina shawl. I observed the dark spot she had tried to wipe off earlier. It resembled the stain on our history: the Partition. Much like the blemish on the fabric, this event was impossible to erase. It was too old now, too set in its character, too ingrained in history. It had carved a place for itself, and there it lived. A tangible memory.

Yet, I found myself smiling at the thought of her intangible memory of her brother, one too strong to need the aid of an object, and how he had saved his whole family from the stains that decorate our history with blood.

15

THE LEXICON OF MY LAND IS
DEVOID OF EMOTIONS

THE BATTLE-HARDENED MEMORABILIA
OF LT GEN. S.N. SHARMA

'LANGUAGE IS A STRANGE thing,' he smiled. 'Urdu, no, Hindustani, actually, was the language when I was growing up. I could write the Urdu script just as well as Hindi. But it's not that way any more. Even the south could speak Hindustani, despite all its different languages and dialects. Back in the day, people could understand it as far down as Kodaikanal!'

I raised my eyebrows.

'But as a young student from 1932 to 1942 at Sherwood College, Nainital, I remember being taught proper enunciation, diction, poetry and elocution as part of the everyday curriculum. We had British teachers who insisted that along with all that we must also learn Latin. And so it was thrust down our throats. I disliked it, but I could see there was an art to it. You see, if you wanted to study engineering back in those days, you had to do Latin. They wouldn't let you enter Cambridge or any other college, even to study engineering, if you hadn't done Latin! Now, of course, Latin is very archaic, just like Sanskrit.'

Lt Gen. S.N. Sharma's speech was refined, with the slightest tinge of a lingering British accent. The ends of his sentences rolled off the tongue, lighter and airier, his Ts and Rs crisp and his diction smooth. It was evident that even the public education of his day had aimed to polish a pupil's character.

'I was in Bangalore in 1944 as a cadet with the Madras Sappers, who have existed as a continuous unit since 1780—over 200 years so far! They recruited anybody from the south and so you got a mix of Tamils, Telugus, Kannadigas and Malayalis! And they spoke their different languages, but these were the British days, you see. So what did we do to unify ourselves? We all sat in a circle around a big metal tumbler filled with water. And one by one everyone took a sip from it and said, "From now on, our caste is Madras Sappers, and we shall speak the Madras Sappers language!" It was a mixture of all four languages, with English and Urdu and Hindi thrown into the mix! But I don't think they're doing it any more. In fact, slowly we are getting rid of all these good things that unite our country. "I" is gradually replacing "we". It wasn't like that in our time.'

'It's fascinating how our preoccupations change with time, isn't it?' I commented.

'Well, there's really nothing extraordinary about that,' said the distinguished-looking man. 'Throughout history, people have been born, they have lived their lives and they have gotten old. And when they get old, they are always different from the youngsters of their time.' He crossed his left leg over his right, placing both hands firmly on his knees.

'Yes, I suppose,' I offered, silently mulling over his words.

'You know,' he said, interrupting my thoughts, 'I'm alive today thanks to a Pathan who saved my life in 1946 when I was doing something very foolish as a soldier. This was before the Partition. And long after it, while fighting in Kashmir, we found ourselves shooting the same Pathans. And when peace was finally declared, we exchanged cups of tea and gave sweets to each other. You see, as a junior officer, I had once commanded a platoon of about fifty Pathan soldiers.'

'But how do you justify such actions to yourself?' I asked.

'Well, it's the battlefield,' he replied curtly.

'What do you mean?'

'You train dogs, don't you? A dog will do what you tell him to do. If you train him as a fighter, he will fight another dog, regardless of how different or similar they are.'

'And where does the self, the mind, factor in?'

'Your self stays separate from the work you do. It's human nature,' he said, his words the product of a certain conditioning. 'Men from India—Hindus, Muslims and Sikhs—who fought together for the British Army during World War II on foreign soil had to fight each other at the borders of their own homeland. But that is duty demanded on the battlefield: first for your country, then for your fellow soldiers, and then you live for yourself. Anything else, anything less is unjustifiable.' His words hung heavily in the air between us. I looked around, almost to escape them, and was met with tasteful, minimalist decor. The windows, overlooking the main road of New Delhi's Defence Colony, were large and wide, allowing the entire house to draw in natural light. From where I sat, though, I could see nothing of the road below—only the trees outside—and, as a result, was faced by his shadowy silhouette surrounded by a warm sunlight.

'You have a beautiful home,' I said suddenly, cutting the silence. He looked around and smiled. Just then, a thin girl appeared at the door and put down a tray before us: two cups of light-coloured tea, biscuits and *pohe*, a delicacy made with flattened rice and vegetables. 'So I understand that you joined the army a few years before the Partition,' I said as she walked out with the empty tray. 'But was it what you had always wanted to do, or did your interests lie elsewhere?'

The lieutenant general's face broke out into a wide smile. 'What I'd really wanted to do was become an aeronautical engineer.'

'Really?' I asked.

'Oh, yes! I was at Sherwood College in 1941 when I received a letter from a university in America, asking me to join. I was all ready to go but then the Japs went and bombed Pearl Harbour in December '41, and then when the war started I couldn't go! But I told myself there would be other chances and continued my studies, graduating at the age of twenty-one with a Bachelor of Science from the University of Allahabad in 1944. Mind you, by then we had been through the 1942 Quit India Movement led by

Gandhi. I was in my first year when we students were shot at in Allahabad by the British-led police.'

'Why?' I asked, shocked.

'Oh, we got rallied into the movement. We were yelling slogans around the campus: *"Inquilab Zindabad,* long live the revolution, *British Raj Murdabad,* down with the Raj!" You know how it goes. Anyway, I was young, I was a student, I was told that the British wouldn't learn or leave unless we had a gun in our hands, and so soon after graduation I joined the army with the Madras Sappers in Bangalore.'

The retelling was precise in its details. Not once had he faltered, not once did he stop to think. His memory was sharp and accurate, as if he were living those moments once again. To complement his narration, a series of old sepia photographs showed the lieutenant general as a young cadet during his training in the south. Cadets standing by a bridge—'Mysore Road, 1945'; him seated in an old Singer Roadster from the early 1930s with two colleagues—'1945 to Nandi Hills'; a dog-eared print showed a group of Indian and English cadets at a training camp near Bangalore in 1945, all dressed in khaki uniforms, donning sola topis, jungle hats and helmets, each one's name inscribed on the photograph in permanent marker, the young engineer sitting cross-legged on the ground, his face obfuscated by shadow; three young cadets, Sharma in the centre, standing against a backdrop of forestry, names inscribed along the bottom of the photograph: 'Cleaning up the Camp, SHIMOGA, 1945'.

'Ah, yes,' he said, looking at the last photograph. 'In 1945, we were training outside of Bangalore in a forested place called Shimoga. A top English cadet named Simpson and I were huddled up somewhere, cursing like hell because it was raining. Monsoon season! Anyway, this chap turned to me and said, "When the hell are you going to take over this bloody country?" So I looked at him, shocked, and said something like, "What do you mean ... it's King and Country ... the sun never sets on the British Empire ... the flag flies twenty-four hours..." and he said, "We are no longer making any money in this country. You bet your life we're pulling out as soon as the war ends!" And that's exactly what happened. The end of the war marked the fag end of the Empire in India. Then that same year I travelled to Surabaya, Indonesia, as part of an engineering unit with the Bengal Sappers. A whole lot of Allied soldiers were detained there and were only later pulled out. We also had lots of Indian soldiers in Malaysia, Singapore, Indonesia…'

Within a large rectangular frame were two rows of medals. He pointed to the one in the bottom right corner. 'Here, this one.' A beautiful silver disk depicted the face of King George VI, with an ornate clasp bearing the inscription 'S.E. ASIA 1945–46'. 'This is a General Service Medal and it would have been made with several clasps. See, mine says "S.E. Asia", and even the colours are particular to the area one was sent to: green in the middle flanked by purple on either side. It was awarded to all British personnel involved in South-East Asia after the Japanese surrender post–World War II—for activities such as guarding prisoners of war, maintaining order and rebuilding and rehabilitation efforts.[1] The British medals of that time were something else—heavy and regal!

'This one right next to it—red, blue and white, the colours of the British Union Jack—is the War Medal we received at the victory of World War II, as subjects of the Commonwealth having served full time in the Armed Forces or the Navy for at least twenty-eight days during the war. At the front, as you see, is the profile of King George VI, and on the reverse side is an engraving of a lion standing on the body of a double-headed dragon— whose one head, I believe, is an eagle and the other a dragon—to signify the occidental and oriental enemies during World War II.[2] It is important to understand that every single aspect of a military medal has meaning. Its every inscription and every colour hold significance.'

He drew my attention to a similar frame hanging on a wall in the room, bearing identical, scaled-down versions of the medals. 'Those are my father's. These are original-sized'—he gestured to the row of large medals stacked above his—'and those are the miniatures. If you look closely, you will see that only two are from Independent India and the rest are all British. His name was Major General Dr Amarnath Sharma, and he qualified as a doctor from the King Edward Medical College in Lahore in 1915, just when World War I started. Most of his graduating class joined the army. Why, it was considered the finest opportunity!'

In an impressive row of fifteen medals, only a General Service Medal from 1947, with a neatly inscribed 'JAMMU AND KASHMIR, 1947–48' clasp, and an Indian Independence Medal, bearing the colours of the *tiranga*, were awarded in an independent India. The rest were bestowed by the Crown. As my eyes scanned the row, two medals caught my eye: a Silver Jubilee Medal from 6 May 1935, commemorating the twenty-fifth anniversary of the coronation of King George V, his profile shadowed by that of Queen Mary; and the second, dated 12 May 1937, issued at the coronation of King George VI and Queen Elizabeth.

Above the framed miniatures sat two elegant portraits of army officers: his father, wearing a dark-blue ceremonial uniform, his medals overlapped as per custom; and his father-in-law, wearing a warm service dress of a deep khaki colour.

The lieutenant general's gaze returned to me. 'Where was I…? Ah, yes, after coming back from Indonesia in 1946, I went to Ranchi with the same engineering unit and then travelled to Rawalpindi to train to be a paratrooper. There was an air transport liaison officers' course at the Army Air Transport Support School in Chaklala which taught us everything, from how to put a jeep on an airplane to how to drop a jeep with a parachute … Oh, it was such a ball! You see, my real passion was parachuting. I didn't want any money for it. I was just happy to be able to do it at all. In fact, I am one of the oldest paratroopers, having completed my last jump after the age of eighty-five!'

'After the age of eighty-five?' I repeated in disbelief.

'That's correct.' His eyes lit up mischievously. 'This was never for the money. It was for the sheer exhilaration, the freedom.'

I listened as he recounted his life phase by phase. And for a while it seemed that age really was just a number, for the energy with which he spoke made it seem like he was still in his youth. As he spoke, I scribbled down in my notebook his gestures, posture, the nuances in his speech. He sat at the edge of the sofa with his back erect and his eyes keen and knowledgeable. A handsome man in his youth, he had aged gracefully: white-grey hair and eyebrows, sharp features and smooth skin. In typically military fashion, he was sharply dressed in grey trousers and a fitted jacket with an army pin fastened to his lapel.

He talked categorically about his various posts around India and the world. He talked about the various skills one is taught in the armed forces, the conditioning and adjustment to whatever circumstances come up, the absolute discipline that becomes second nature. He talked animatedly, with his hands and his eyes. He painted images in the air, describing the nature of war, the geography of the different locations he parachuted to and from. All these things he recounted with pristine accuracy in the same way one would recite facts learnt at school. Accustomed to the sacrifices of army officers, he told tales of witnessing companions die in service to the nation. His voice reflected pride; his stature, confidence; his face, pragmatism.

'Emotions,' he concluded calmly, looking me straight in the eye. 'No emotions remain after one has seen war. Over the years I have learnt that if a man dies in the trenches, you bury his ashes in the trenches with dignity. You might think that's disrespectful, but that's how it is in the army. In war, the trench is your life, your everyday. That's where you sleep, it's where you relieve yourself. If you have to live there for days on end, you get used to things you would never have to see in civilized society. That is how war is,' he said with finality, and no hint of sentiment coloured his voice.

Then, his wife finally entered the room—and something wonderful happened. Almost instantly, the air around us became somewhat lighter. Lt Gen. Sharma's face broke into a wide smile, and the detached army man was replaced promptly by a lover.

'Kumu,' he said affectionately, welcoming her.

Standing at the door was one of the most beautiful women I had ever seen. She wore a long maroon shawl over a beige salwar kameez. Her face was round and her skin flawless and fair. Her white hair was tied into a neat bun and her lips were painted a deep red. On her ears and nose sat small diamond studs. Her eyes were a captivating grey. But her most endearing quality was that she carried with her a rare, unexplainable calm, and I too found myself smiling widely as she sat down next to her husband.

'Kumu was born in Quetta,' he said.

'Yes, but I don't remember much. I was only born there, and being from an army family meant that we kept moving,' she said, also gesturing to her father's portrait.

'Tell me about your family before the army,' I said to her husband. He laughed.

'From the beginning, you mean. All right, but the army is interwoven in it all...'

He sat back comfortably and began. His wife listened quietly, only adding what was most necessary.

'I was born in 1923 in Srinagar because my father got posted from place to place. At the time, both my grandfathers were working for the ruler of Kashmir, a man who ruled the state for forty years: Maharaja Pratap Singh, the uncle of Maharaja Hari Singh, who is the father of Dr Karan Singh.'[3]

The page I was writing on soon became an exact record of names and dates.

'My *nana*, Pandit Daulat Ram Vasudeva, was the chief accountant for the maharaja. And as soon as he died in 1925, my *nana* resigned as well. This much I remember. My other grandfather, my *dada*, Pandit Mohan Lal, was a *hakim*.'

'A medicine man?' I asked.

'Yes, that's right. Yunani medicine. That's his picture right there.' He pointed to a painting hung high on a wall. 'He died in 1923. And next to him is his wife, who passed away in 1936 in the North-West Frontier Province. Some time in the '30s, long after my grandfather had died, an American artist took their photographs from my father and, using them as references, made these two paintings. They probably cost about 50 rupees, and that was a lot of money in those days, but my father was being paid as an officer in the army and lived a comfortable enough life to be able to afford them.'

'Your *dada* died the same year you were born?' I asked.

'Yes, that's right. I never got to know him. But her,' he said, pointing to his grandmother, 'my *dadi*, I knew very well. We used to call her Ma-ji. She was very rigid, old-fashioned, tough as a bloody nail as all Punjabis are! I used to hear this story from my parents that my grandmother was a vegetarian and my grandfather loved to eat meat. Now she, being the diligent wife, believed that it was her duty to cook whatever her husband liked. And so, outside their house in Kashmir, even in the bitter cold, she would cook a big pot of meat for him over an open fire. He would come home from work and be fed outside as no meat would enter the house. When he was finished, she would empty out the pot, wash it under the tap outside, and then, fully clothed, she would purify her body. Mind you, this was not every day, but whenever he wanted to eat some meat.'

The two paintings hung side by side on the wall facing the window. Walking closer to them, I saw my own reflection in the fitted glass of the uniquely oval wooden frames. The polish of the frame had chipped in places, revealing the lighter wood beneath. On the top and bottom, along the very outer ridge of the frames, was a floral pattern engraved in the wood. On the left, his grandmother's serene, bespectacled face stared back at me: delicate features, a sharp, pointed nose, sunken cheekbones and soft eyes. Over her head sat the *aanchal* of her regal, plum-coloured sari, weighed down by an ornate grey border. Delicate brush strokes adorned the sari folds; the light and shadow on her face bore a likeness to reality. The back of the painting, a bare wooden surface, had an inscription handwritten in red marker: 'HUKUM DEI, my grandmother as we knew her, died 1936—

age not clear—about 60? In Abbottabad where father was posted to the Mil Hosp.'

Next to her sat the portrait of her husband, the lieutenant general's *dada*, a man with handsome features and a neutral expression. A resplendent white turban covered his head, the colour of the fabric almost merging into the white-grey of his beard close to the ears. Dressed in a majestic black *bandh-gala*, a close-buttoned jacket, he looked every bit as esteemed as his grandson who now sat before me.

'He looks like a descendant of the Mughals. A mixture of Mughal and Sikh, perhaps.'

'Yes, well, the Mughals had a lot of Punjabi blood in them. Back in the day, it was all a mixed race: Pakistani Punjab, Indian Punjab, Himachal and Haryana were all one territory after all.'

'There was a lot of mixed blood between Indians and other races too,' his wife spoke for the first time. 'My own mother was born in Neuchâtel, Switzerland. She was called Eve Yvonne Maday de Maros. Her father was a man named Oberleutnant Andre de Maday, who did his military service from the Hungarian Hussars regiment and had served in World War I. When she was sixteen years old, she met my father, a Konkani Maharashtrian, Vikram Ramji Khanolkar, in Chamonix. He was a young lieutenant then, on his term break from the Royal Military Academy in Britain. They exchanged letters for a while before she arrived in Bombay and they got married. Later, she took the name Savitri Bai Khanolkar. He died a general in 1952, just when he had been approved for promotion to lieutenant general, but during his life he had the honour of being the first Indian colonel of the Sikh Regiment.'

Another sepia photograph showed a slim, stunning woman whose dark hair was held in a low, elegant knot. She stood in profile, hands entwined in front of her, resting against the silky fabric of her floor-length gown. In the bottom right corner, unmistakably written in fountain pen, were the words 'For Vikram'—his name written neatly and carefully in the Devanagari script, and 'With Love, Eve'—hers, written in the same style. A similar photograph showed a handsome, clean-shaven officer, a profile in full service dress, hair parted fashionably to one side, eyes looking longingly into the distance. 'With Love,' said the inscription in cursive in the bottom right, 'Vikram.' A present for a beloved.

I studied the features of the woman sitting before me, who bore an almost identical resemblance to her mother: porcelain-like skin and light grey eyes. Though they were all features reminiscent of people from Quetta, part of her heritage was also clearly European.

'You will hardly see any photographs displayed around the house except for these,' said the officer.

'And why is that?' I asked with curiosity.

'Survival, mostly. These have survived the times.'

'Not memory, not nostalgia?'

'Oh dear no, I'm afraid I've been cured of nostalgia over the years. Compared to my contemporaries and even my own brothers, I haven't seen as much battle, spending many of my field years in the wild, building roads, airfields and things like that. But when you've been in battle at all and seen fellow soldiers die in the field, or spent time in dangerous places like the depths of forests and insides of mountains, away from your family for months on end, then what is nostalgia to you? I have lost many valuables over the years—people and things—and I have learnt not to dwell on them. This is life. So I keep these portraits not for memory but for their survival. My father brought these along with him from Rawalpindi, either during or just before the Partition.'

Then, after a pause, he laughed. 'It appears we have gotten side-tracked; you had asked about the beginning…'

I smiled.

* * *

'We were five siblings. My elder brother, Major Som Nath Sharma, then me, then my sisters, Mrs Manorama Sharma and Major Dr Mrs Kamla Tewari, and lastly my youngest brother, General Vishwa Nath Sharma, who retired as the Chief of Army Staff in 1990. I grew up all over the country but, as I mentioned before, was sent to boarding school at Sherwood and then went off to university and then the army.

'In 1946–47, when I was in Chaklala, my father was posted in Rawalpindi, just four kilometres away. Pindi was a very old cantonment station and at the time he was a full colonel, a doctor from World War I. When the Empire dissolved in August 1947, his appointment as major general came directly from the War Office in England. At Independence, what had once been the mighty British Indian Army now suddenly lay barren, due to not just the loss of English soldiers, but also the Partition, which, like the land, divided all government entities, including the Hindu, Muslim and Sikh soldiers, into their respective new dominions. There were vacancies in every rank. My father was made major general, and I was made captain after barely one year and four months of service! My father's new posting was in Delhi and he brought these portraits of his parents across.'

'During the Partition, you were still across the border?'

He nodded. 'Oh yes. And what border? There was no fortified border in those days like there is today. The land remained the same as it had always been. The real truth is that even the British didn't expect Partition; it happened quickly and hastily. One day I was an instructor at the Transport School in Chaklala and the next day Chaklala happened to be in a new country called Pakistan. All the courses were stopped, but I continued to stay in the Rawalpindi area until November '47. I was waiting for a train but, mind you, I wasn't the last Hindu to come out of there. I was a captain and, sure enough, I continued to head my unit despite the fact that I was Hindu and they were now mostly all Muslim Pakistani soldiers. We were put in charge of rescuing refugees and those who had been abducted.'

Then, suddenly, the highly animated lieutenant general grew quiet and gave way to a more pensive officer. 'There is an incident I remember from that time, one I have tried to forget many times since. One day a few of us were driving around the city trying to keep the peace, and we heard a baby's cry. The drains were all open in those days, and so we stopped to find this one-year-old child abandoned in the drain.' He looked at me, then at his wife, and then once around the room before finally continuing with great difficulty. 'The boy's hands and feet had been cut off, maybe by the rioters or whoever, don't ask me. These were good Indians, and by that I mean good Indians, good Pakistanis, good Bangladeshis … they're all the same. But when they begin rioting, when they begin looting and raping and killing the innocent, under the spell of unexplainable bloodlust, then they're the worst people in the world. It was such an unthinkable act, and the boy's body must have been bleeding for a while since it lay in a pool of blood. He hadn't died yet, though; he was just screaming in pain. A limbless baby, I can never forget that sight.

'So my *hawaldar*, the constable, who was a Punjabi Muslim from the north, pulled out his sten gun and asked, "*Maar dey, sahib*? Shall we kill it?" and when I said no, he responded with, "*Kya zindagi hogi iski*? What life will the boy lead now, with no hands and no feet?" But I couldn't do it. Regardless of how many soldiers one might kill on the battlefield, something from within wouldn't let me take the life of this suffering child. Who was I to make that decision?' His head shook from left to right, his eyes were distant. 'So we put him in the car and took him to the civic hospital, where thankfully there was a captain who took charge of him.'

'Do you know what became of the boy?'

'I have hardly thought about it since. Here I am speaking to you so I might wonder out of sheer curiosity. But I must tell you, over the years, as a soldier, something inside you hardens and you begin to believe that no matter what happens—sickness, accidents, wars, injury—life goes on. Life goes on…'

And though he spoke of the grave, battle-hardened nature of a soldier, the only thing that permeated his voice then was an expansive sadness. Accustomed though he might have been, he had also felt helplessness, humanity and pain. Perhaps more pain had existed in that moment of holding the limbless child than any gunshot wound could have inflicted upon him. And what could I say in such a moment, what could I ask? Had I seen such a sight, had I felt such powerlessness, such disgust towards perhaps my own fellow countrymen? Would I, after hearing this gory memory, be able to vacate my mind of it? In my head, there were only questions, to which there were no conceivable answers.

* * *

For what seemed like an interminably long time, my recorder picked up the silence in the room, which was finally broken by his wife.

'Three months after the Partition, he travelled to India by train and got off at Ambala station. There, someone told him that one Major Sharma had been killed in action in Kashmir.'

The colour drained from Lt Gen. Sharma's face as he looked at me. 'My brother was killed on 3 November 1947. I heard the following day that one Major Sharma had been killed, but there were no initials provided and Sharma was such a common name that we didn't know for sure. We didn't even know battle had begun and that he, serving in the Kumaon Regiment at the time, was summoned to Kashmir from Delhi.

'Kashmir was always going to be a bone of contention between the two new dominions and perhaps the most peaceful thing would have been to partition the state of Jammu & Kashmir altogether. The population was diverse enough, yet restricted to specific areas.[4] The valley was mostly Sunni Muslims with a small population of Shia, but there were also Sikhs and Kashmiri Pandits. Jammu was predominantly Dogra Hindus, and Ladakh was Ladakhi Lamaistic Buddhists.[5]

'There was a Standstill Agreement that Kashmir, as a kingdom, had signed with both Pakistan and India. But when Pakistan launched a forcible accession, Maharaja Hari Singh turned to India for help and troops were sent up to fortify the border. There were large-scale massacres in the frontier areas of Poonch and Mirpur. My brother, fighting with his regiment in the battlefield at Badgam, trying to stop Pakistani infiltrators and raiders from attacking the airfield in Srinagar, was heavily outnumbered and killed. In the last radio message he sent to the brigade commander, he said, "The enemy is less than 50 yards from us. We are heavily outnumbered and under devastating fire. I shall not withdraw an inch…"[6] There is a memorial erected in Badgam at the exact location where he died.'

I could feel the ineffable loss spilling out of his heart, crawling up his body and, through his voice, into the air around us. 'Eventually, things do come full circle—from womb to tomb,' he said, the memory catching up to his years, his tone assuming the final rank of a wise, experienced lieutenant general. 'Jammu and Kashmir welcomed his birth, and then, twenty-four short years later, ushered [in] his death.'

'Major Som Nath Sharma was the first ever recipient of the Param Vir Chakra, posthumously, when it was established in 1950 as India became a republic,' said his wife. 'The foremost military award, given for the highest degree of valour and self-sacrifice.'

Literally meaning the Wheel of the Ultimate Brave, it was introduced as a counterpart to the British Victoria Cross. A bronze disc with the state emblem sitting in the centre on a raised circle, the medal also bore four images of *vajra*, the mythical weapon of the Vedic god Indra. It boasted a royal purple ribbon and carried within it the weight of a family's entwined history.

'Incidentally, the medal was designed by Kumu's mother,' added Lt Gen. Sharma. 'After she married Major General Khanolkar, she devoted much of her time to studying Indian languages and history, likely to acclimatize herself to the new life in India. Soon after Independence, there was an acute need to replace colonial gallantry awards and campaign and general service medals, and General Hira Lal Atal, the first Indian

Adjutant General, was responsible for this task.[7] He requested her to design these medals, as she had a deep and intimate knowledge of mythology, Sanskrit and the Vedas—which he hoped would give the design a truly Indian ethos.[8] Kumu is also an artist, just like her mother.'

Then he turned to me. 'You told me I have a beautiful home,' he beamed. 'Well, it's all because of her. Everything beautiful in my life is because of my wife.' He smiled deeply at her and the pink crept up her fair cheeks. I looked around the room once more and my eyes caught the medals on the wall. 'When you travelled to India from Rawalpindi, what did you bring with you?' I asked.

'Well, we brought our military trunks, in which were all my uniforms, decorations, certificates, IDs, photographs. That's about it.'

'And personal possessions?'

'None. When you have to move from posting to posting, you learn to be quite frugal when it comes to material possessions. Ah, but yes, I was very fond of books, and since the early years of my army life I have lost three libraries. When I went off to university, I left a box of books at home. The library I made in university had to be left behind when I joined the army. And then, finally, when I was posted in Ranchi in 1946, I had a small collection of books, which I again had to part with when I went to Rawalpindi. But there was one book I had with me, a Gliding Log Book, which I have now donated to a Museum of the Bombay Sappers in Khirki, Pune. Anyway, yes, apart from books, I only brought my military trunk.'

As his familial possessions sat before us, confined behind glass frames, hooked carefully onto smooth velvet backdrops, I wondered about the very public nature of these personal possessions. One family's mundane efforts at keeping its own official records in pristine condition spoke to the preservation of the often hereditary nature of the defence service. In intergenerational military families, to study such decorations was no different from reading old letters or journals packed away in dusty boxes. To trace the engraved lines of each medal, revealing the particularities of rank and war, was to trace the social and professional chronology of a life. These seemingly public awards conferred for extraordinary military service were testimony to the intrinsically personal characteristics of the officer.

Though his father's miniature medals were hung on the wall here as tangible symbols of pride, the retired lieutenant general told me that his own medals usually stayed at his son's house. His son and grandson, collectors of military memorabilia, were far more interested in these artefacts of old than he was. Perhaps it wasn't lack of interest, though; perhaps the fact that they weren't within sight meant that they could be put at the back of the mind, along with the memories of a war that many an ex-serviceman wished to forget.[9]

Then, almost as if to unexpectedly validate my assumption, Lt Gen. Sharma spoke. 'You can ask your questions and you can look at the remnants from that time: our medals and certificates, these paintings of my grandparents from before the Partition, from an Undivided India. And though they will help you piece together the society and ethnography of the land, they will not help you understand its syncretic culture. I am a military man, someone who has been at war with men who became Pakistanis, but I am also someone who has been *to* war *with* the men who became Pakistanis.[10] There are some passages in time whose horrors should never be repeated. The Partition was one such horror. I don't want to remember it, there is no use any more. But I do want to remember the important things.

'I spoke to you about the psyche of a soldier when on the battlefield—how during wartime we fired at the same men with whom we'd later share cups of chai. That was war. That was what war was like. It bound you to your duty, there was no room for emotions. The trench became your life, your honour, your vow. You obeyed it, you were trained to obey. But, off the battlefield, you must realize that things were different, relationships were different. To be honest, relationships, especially those between the Hindu, Muslim and Sikh soldiers who had fought together before Independence and had to fight against each other during and after it ... those relationships are very difficult to explain to or be understood by those who were not there at that time.'

He looked at his hands, turning them over, studying them, and then finally said, 'It is not religion, it is human nature, it is power that drives madness. Christians have killed more Christians in the name of Christianity than anything else. That's what history tells us. In India, all the way from the north to the south, the east to the west, as people, we were reasonably peaceful—until the quest became for power. The Empire dissolved, leaving us with an aching need to affirm our own nationhood—both India and Pakistan. It was power. Not religion. The hunger for power and authority is what drove us to madness.'

16

A HEART OF MORTGAGED SILVER

THE ASSORTED CURIOS OF
PROF. SAT PAL KOHLI

'LAHORE,' THE WORD ESCAPED his lips, as ephemeral as the dreams in which it was the main character. The afternoon was ending in Delhi, the evening light overpowering an already weak winter sun, and in the south of the capital, a story was unravelling of a twin city across the border. 'I was born on 9 August 1926 in Lahore.' Neatly dressed in shades of beige and brown, Professor Sat Pal Kohli sipped his tea and took a long pause. In the professorial tone he had internalized over years of giving classes, he asked me, 'Do you know why 9 August is a significant day in our history?'

Then, answering his own question in the same breath, he painted a chronological picture of the political events that had led up to Independence. 'Historic day. It is a historic day. The Quit India Movement started on 9 August 1942. Earlier that year, in March, Sir Stafford Cripps had been sent to India to present a proposal for a new constitution, which was found unsatisfactory.[1] In May, Gandhi-ji said his famous words, "Leave India to God. If this is too much, then leave her to anarchy." In July, the Congress approved a resolution that declared the immediate end of British rule as an urgent necessity. Finally, in a historic session of the All India Congress, which began on 7 August and was concluded after midnight the next day in Mumbai, a resolution called the Quit India Movement was passed. It electrified the atmosphere in the entire country.[2] Gandhi-ji gave a brilliant speech and, merely twenty-four hours after that speech, on 9 August, all the top political leaders were arrested.

'That day, the struggle for our freedom was at its zenith. I was only a school student then, sixteen years old, but I remember we were fired with enthusiasm, with passion. Agitation ruled the streets. Schools, colleges were closed and we threw ourselves headfirst into the freedom movement. *Azadi*, we wanted freedom. *Jung ladh rahe the*, we were at war, fighting for our independence, and with signs in our hands we would just march and chant, "*Chal chal naujavan, rukna nahi tera kaam, badhna teri shaan, badhna teri shaan.*"'

I was hardly surprised, given the zeal with which he spoke, that he remembered the exact slogans chanted decades ago. As he spoke, I watched the muscles of his face move softly in the organic shapes of his syllables. His words had no definite ending. They simply lingered in the air, half enunciated, half nasal, with an effortlessly Punjabi veneer. '*Shaan*,' I heard myself repeat softly in a similar fashion, disposing of the 'n' altogether. Dignity, pride, brilliance.

'That's why, *beti*,' he addressed me affectionately, 'I am proud to be born on this day. And not just born anywhere but in Lahore. In my beloved Lahore.' He placed both his hands over his heart and looked at me, a wide smile spread across his face.

'Situated on the banks of the river Ravi, Lahore was founded by Luv or Loh, one of the twin sons of Lord Rama. The other son, Kush, is said to have founded the neighbouring town of Kasur. The very word Lahore means the fort of Loh.[3] It is one of the oldest cities in the world and, if I may say so, one of the greatest. It is the city of gardens, of sin and splendour, of Rudyard Kipling and Amrita Pritam. The city of forts and palaces and history and age. The city of my birth, separated from me now by a border, by wars, by religion and by time.' Then, with a deep, prolonged sigh, he concluded, 'That is Lahore.'

'Do you remember your life there?' I asked.

'Yes, at this juncture, I am still able to remember everything. I was the youngest in the family of two brothers and two sisters. My eldest sister died during childbirth much before I was even born. There were complications in the delivery, and my grandfather was told that she should be taken to hospital but he never agreed. He was orthodox. "My granddaughter be taken to hospital? By no means!" He was adamant, and so ultimately she passed away. But though I had never met her, I was told that she was a paragon of beauty. A paragon of beauty…'

As he narrated the story of his life, his hoarse voice was overcome by a slow, sincere nostalgia. 'I should also tell you that I have never seen my father. Or, if I have, I have no recollection of him. I'm told I was two years old when he died of asthma. Imagine that, asthma took his life at the age of just thirty-nine. My mother, Shiv Devi, who was a couple of years younger than him, brought up the family single-handedly. Brave lady—none of us are any match for her. None of us. Since I was the youngest, I spent most of my time with her. She was the only daughter and heir of very rich parents and so inherited all their property and wealth, which was why we were quite well off.

'After my father died, she decided to open a small moneylending business. Imagine that, a female moneylender! It was almost unheard of in those days, perhaps even now. She started it to pass the time. At first, mostly Muslim ladies would come to her to mortgage something small like jewellery or heirlooms. Later, it grew to include much bigger items like furniture.' He explained that this pawnbroking service allowed women in particular to borrow money for a specific need that had arisen in their lives. His mother had started it because she had the wealth and wanted to share it.

'Soon the locals gave her the title of Shah-ni. Shah-ni, you understand, like the Shah. Big heart, she had such a big heart, and her motto was always that whoever came up the stairs of her house must not leave empty-handed. They must have come with such hope, [she reasoned,] I must fulfil their need. Naturally, she gained an enormous amount of respect, and our house became less of a home and more of a space that housed other people's belongings!

'In Lahore we lived in a predominantly Muslim neighbourhood in a tall double-storey building. We occupied the ground and first floors, which in total consisted of a salon, a storeroom, three bedrooms and a kitchen. The second floor was occupied by tenants. My grandfather used to own a lot of land—he was a *jagir*, a feudal lord—and that land was in a place called Garhi Shahu. It is one of the oldest towns in Lahore and has now become a part of the modern city. Many decades after the Partition, I went back there with my son and went straight to the *lambardar*'s house and introduced myself. He remembered everything, said he had heard the story from the locals over the years of a Hindu woman moneylender in the years before the Partition. He called out to the people of the neighbourhood: "*Shah-ni ka beta aya hai*, Shah-ni's son has come back." We met many old Muslim families who remembered her. He took us through the alleys and bazaars and I showed my son all the land that had once belonged to us. In those days, my grandfather would have rented out the land and the *havelis* on it.'

'How much would the rent have been at the time?'

'*Arey*, let's see … *yehi kuch* two to four rupees per month,' he laughed. 'Nowadays such a paltry sum will get you nothing. But, for those days and for the size of the small *havelis*, it was ample. In the first week of every month, I went around the *mohalla* to collect rent from all the tenants living on my grandfather's properties and it would take me the whole day. The total rent was never more than Rs 500 and the highest that anyone paid was just 10 rupees a month!

'Garhi Shahu wasn't in the main city of Lahore, as I just mentioned, but on the outskirts. Whenever my grandfather went to Lahore *sheher*, the city proper, he would use a *tonga*, a horse-drawn carriage. It was a distance of no more than one mile, but it would always take him over an hour to get to the city because of all the people who would stop to greet him on the way! Oh, he was very sociable, and I think I've inherited that from him!'

He flashed me a warm, boyish smile, and then his face grew serious. He leaned in close and said in a soft voice, 'Now people don't have the time, do they? The pace of life seems almost foreign to me at times. I look around and I see there is little intimacy left in the relationships we build with one another. Even this, what you are doing, sitting with an old man and talking about his life—who does this any more, *beti*? But let me tell you'—these next words he said slowly, savouring each syllable—'that was an age of integrity; people spent hours talking to one another. We had community, kinship and kindness. Modern man has gained the world but lost his soul.'

His last sentence, the truth in it, sat like a stone over my heart.

'What else do you remember of that time?' I asked.

His lips curled into a boyish smile again. '*Sab kuch*, everything,' he said, meaningfully.

'Your land, your home, is it ever possible to forget where you came from?' His warm eyes looked into mine and I knew without a shred of doubt that there was Lahore in the deepest recesses of his being. 'I remember everything. The most beautiful memories of my childhood are times I spent in the company of my friends. One of whom I lost, at a very young age, to fever. Bal Kishan was his name. Fever, *bass*, that's it. He died of a fever. In those days, hospitals were far away and there was little cure for things like asthma and fever.' The same disbelief coloured his voice now as when he had spoken of his father's death. 'There was no one to examine him in Garhi Shahu, and though we brought him all the way to Lahore city on foot, he had lost consciousness. He didn't survive.'

I watched him as he swayed his head sadly from side to side. 'Didn't survive,' he repeated, and then, after a short pause, continued. 'Look, in the *mohalla* where we lived, there was no telephone and only one radio. *Ek* radio *tha*,' he repeated. 'And we never thought it was going to be any different. Like I said, at that time, it was difficult to imagine that the *raftaar*, the pace, of life would ever change. We would ride around on our bicycles, and if we wanted to listen to songs or the news, we would go to the gurudwara. They had the one radio. The news of the *batwara*, the Separation, came from that radio. I was twenty-one years old at that time, in the second year of my BA. We had read about it in the papers, of course, and we were involved in the Independence movement. But the news of a divide startled us all.'

* * *

'How come? Was it not expected?' I asked.

'Not at all, *beti*. I told you there was harmony and kinship between the people of all religions. It's true that there were isolated instances of violence in Lahore's past, but nothing like the kind of riots that erupted during the Partition. You see, Lahore was the most important city of north-western India, having been a provincial capital under the Mughals, the capital of the Sikh kingdom, and again the provincial capital of Punjab under the British, and for years it had enjoyed great economic, political and military significance.[4] When the news of the division was announced on 3 June 1947, we were told that the partition line would be the river Ravi, putting the entire city of Lahore within Independent India. "Lahore is an invaluable part of India," we were told. And so we never imagined we would have to flee the way we did…'

'What happened in your neighbourhood after the announcement?'

'Well, we were one of only ten Hindu families living in a predominantly Muslim locality. Our house was the first to be looted, and it shocks me to say this but it was the neighbours. Mob mentality—there is no justifiable explanation for it. The violence that unfurled after the announcement of the Partition was terrifying, and Lahore burnt in its wake. Gone was the beautiful city of my childhood and what remained was a city entirely unrecognizable, coated in fire, blood and destruction. The relationships that had been fostered over years, a life, were forgotten. I speak proudly of kinship, but even that was not enough to keep the peace.'

He stood up with his hands on his knees, straightening his stiff legs slowly. Then, smoothening his brown Argyle sleeveless jumper, he gestured for me to wait. '*Ruko*,' he said and went into the bedroom. When he emerged, his hands bore silver.

'We left our home amidst the darkness of night, during the riots in June. Many Hindus and Sikhs had left, many had shifted their businesses from Lahore to other cities, but still we heard of dead bodies found in homes and on the streets after nights of looting and plundering around the city. Murders continued to happen in the areas of Mozang, Shahi Mohalla, Garhi Shahu and others, and finally we decided to leave. My brother was already in Delhi at the Ministry of Defence and my elder sister was married and living in a Hindu neighbourhood of Lahore, so my mother and I went to her.'

Suddenly, he held his head in his hands and said, 'Such an old tale, it's been years since I thought about it, as if the memory had disappeared from my mind completely. The things we saw during those days I'd never wish for anyone to see.'

In that moment, I thought to myself how unjust it was for people to have to recollect their most traumatic memories, consigned to the farthest ends of their minds, for me. Because I had asked, because I had wanted to know. I was overcome by a strange guilt, and I felt myself reaching out to touch his hand. Soft and wrinkled with deep-set lines, his hand, like his memories, felt like a gift.

'I'm sorry for making you remember things from the past,' I heard a small voice escape me.

'*Beti*, if you do not ask, how will you know? How will anyone know what happened, what we saw, what we sacrificed? How will the younger generation ever know?' He smiled and, wiping his eyes, continued his tale.

'Before we left that night, my mother went around the house packing up her jewellery and collecting items of value—things that had been mortgaged with us. There was no time to pack clothes or other belongings, the streets were burning, the slogans could be heard in the distance. "Only items of value," she told me, and so, one by one, we picked those things—small and discreet enough to be put in a small *baksa*, a box that we brought with us, and still valuable enough to be sold later. These are those items.' He led my gaze to the table.

Before us sat the last remaining traces of a Lahori woman's life. Ironically, none of them truly belonged to her. And yet, in some ways, they were the perfect metaphors for the migration, because, much like the land to which the refugees had fled, the objects too were borrowed. And they carried within them the promise of a new life.

He picked up the first object and handed it to me. A silver cigarette case. I felt its sleekness against my palm and, holding it between my thumb and forefinger, I studied its body. It was approximately two and a half inches by three and a half inches, and in excellent condition. The top and bottom had a bubbled pattern—space for the cigarettes to lie within the box. Around the edges, my fingers traced a highly exquisite and detailed traditional design, engraved with a fine needle. A small clasp in the centre opened the case, revealing the smooth finish inside.

'For the first time, during World War I, society was introduced to mass-produced machine-rolled cigarettes, which were not as tight as the hand-rolled ones. And so cases were made to protect them, especially during the war. Solid silver cigarette cases came to be produced during this time,' the professor informed me, squinting at the object, 'and these became obvious signs of personal wealth. The silver is durable and does not damage the cigarette. And here, look at the craftsmanship, the sheer elegance. Many people had left such cases in our care. They were worth a good sum of money, too!' His fingers traced the pattern, taking the case and holding it up to the light. Then, putting it down, he picked up the next object, a quaint silver dish.

'A silver soap dish,' he giggled, and I raised my eyebrows. Indeed, it was a soap dish made entirely out of silver. Rectangular with rounded edges, its outer rim was simple and unembellished.

In contrast, the dish itself was decadently embossed with geometric and floral patterns. The more deeply embossed areas had gathered a layer of rust and patina, standing out against the otherwise polished artefact.

I smiled, imagining the kind of lavish life one must have led as a moneylender if the mortgaged items consisted of household banalities like cigarette cases and soap dishes made from solid silver. As if reading my mind, the professor chuckled. 'It was a different age, *beti*, people lived differently. Now, here, this you must have seen before…'

He picked up the third item, a silver drinking glass. 'Patiala glass, that's what we call it. It was quite common in most families. This sort of glass usually came in the *dahej*, a woman's trousseau, and on it were engraved the initials of her husband-to-be. There would have been a similar plate, a set of bowls and cutlery. In those days everyone had their own utensils, and the man of the house, especially, drank and ate only from his own dishes. Though this is a common item, look at the beauty, the sheer smoothness, of its craft.' He held it out to me.

Holding it up to my face, I saw my reflection in its highly polished surface. The dark red of my sweater against the shining silver of the glass reminded me of the blood he had said Lahore was bathed in at the time of the Partition. I swallowed hard and, turning it upside down, admired the darkness of its oxidized bottom. I looked for the sharp dotted lines that usually formed the engraved initials, but found none. The top edge was uneven and not perfectly round, betraying its handmade nature. Instead of initials, here there were fine yet noticeable lines around the glass, and I assumed that years of cleaning with steel wool had erased any claim to its original ownership.

'There were more things. She brought an intricately carved *gulab dani*, a sprinkler used to shower guests with rosewater as they arrive for weddings and prayers. She brought all her jewellery, which we were forced to sell little by little in the years following the Partition. And … this, she also brought this, which was perhaps the only thing that truly belonged to her.'

* * *

From beside him he picked up a pair of scissors and held it out to me, much like a jeweller proudly and delicately displaying his most precious wares. The sheer metallic weight of such an antique, which would have gone unnoticed had he held it the correct way, appeared much more pronounced as he cradled it in both his hands like a child or an offering.

'This was my mother's,' he said. 'She was a hardworking and determined single mother, made all of our clothes at home. Meticulous, both in business and in housework, exceedingly meticulous. I often wondered why she brought these—they weren't really of any monetary value—but if I think about it now, it makes perfect sense. These were so banal, but an integral part of her everyday life and hence precious to her.'

He smiled, offering them to me. I accepted the scissors into my hands and ran my forefinger over the blades, still sharp despite their age. The entire surface had succumbed to the air and moisture of years, and was now coated in a thick layer of dark brown oxidation. The handles were darker than the rest of the body, almost blackened, and I slipped my fingers into them, holding the scissors now as if I were ready to cut through fabric. As I opened them, the insides of the blades revealed themselves to be even more worn than the exteriors, and I smelt rust. I recalled my grandmother having a similar pair somewhere in her drawers at home. I remembered her sitting in the bright sunlight, peering over the markings on a length of cloth, and then confidently and effortlessly cutting out patterns with sharp snips of her trusty pair of scissors. My memories of such days dissolved into the mechanical sounds of her Singer sewing machine, stitching the pieces of fabric together.

'The company that made these has been manufacturing scissors and knives for over three centuries, I believe,' Professor Kohli said, suddenly drawing me out of my childhood. 'They are forged in *loha*, iron, and nowadays are used mostly only by tailors. If you look closer at the centre near the screw, you should be able to read the word "Meerut", unless time has swallowed it whole. I don't know how she got this pair in Lahore, but the company was quite popular and perhaps exported them to different cities across India. It's still quite sharp, as you can see. Let me remember their slogan...' his voice trailed off and he closed his eyes in concentration. 'Ah yes! I do still remember it. "*Dada le, potaa barpe*,"[5] which means, "A product bought by the grandfather can still be used by the grandson!"' he laughed.

I looked closer at the scissors in my hand, peering at the screw. Looking up at me, still sharp despite its age, was the incomplete word 'M.AEV', the rest of which was dulled and unreadable. And right underneath, as crisp as the first cut into virgin cloth, was the word 'MEERUT'. Beneath that was engraved the number '9', likely the size or length of the scissors. I looked up at the professor and, meeting my gaze, he nodded, smiling.

'When I visited Lahore, I was told by the *lambardar* that, after we left, our house was first looted for all the precious mortgaged items inside, and then it was fed to the flames. Burnt to the ground, he had heard.'

'When you left, did you ever imagine that you would never go back and live there again?'

'To be very frank, at the time, *nahi*. It just hadn't registered. Neither my mother nor I had thought that far. We were only concerned about leaving safely. Only when we got to my sister's house, which was in an enclosed Hindu locality, did we realize how far the situation had worsened. And only then did the thought cross my mind—the vast and impossible truth that, as a result of the Partition, Lahore might not be a part of my India.'

'Why do you say impossible?'

'Well, because that's how it felt. Impossible. Despite all the systematic negotiations with the British Crown so that Indians could gain Independence, we found ourselves supremely underprepared for the sheer loss and displacement that accompanied this freedom. After all, one is not raised with the knowledge that perhaps one day, in the distant future, everything familiar will be irretrievably lost forever.'

'And so when did you finally cross over?'

'Before the date of the Partition, we travelled from Lahore to Kartarpur in district Jullundur because my mother's extended family lived there. My elder sister and her family migrated with us too. Though the trains were nowhere near as bad as during the days following Partition, hordes of people had already begun to leave their homes. And so the train we boarded was packed to the brim, with people even climbing to sit on top of the compartments. I still remember, the distance between Lahore and Kartarpur is approximately 100 km, and the same journey that we had undertaken innumerable times as children seemed altogether different that day. As if the distance had suddenly expanded and the train trudged along its track, more slowly and cautiously than usual, magnifying the time it took to cross that otherwise short distance of two or three hours.'

'And when you arrived in Kartarpur…'

'*Beti*, when we left Lahore, I had given two final exams, but two still remained. So when we reached Kartarpur, I enrolled in Punjab University and completed my BA degree. But my brother was still in Delhi, and so, after I finished, my mother and I planned to join him there. Delhi extracted the last remains of whatever little wealth we had carried with us from Lahore. Piece by piece my mother sold off all her jewellery for a total of Rs 25,000 and purchased a home in Karol Bagh for Rs 20,000. Gradually, over the years, we received property through the claims we made to the Ministry of Relief and Rehabilitation in lieu of the land we had left behind in Lahore.

'In 1947, Punjab University opened Camp College as an evening college in Delhi. It was later dissolved and DAV [Dayanand Anglo-Vedic] and Dyal Singh Colleges came up.[6] I obtained an MA in English and graduated second class, which made me eligible for the post of lecturer.'

He went on to tell me about his various jobs teaching English, and how, even today, at the age of ninety, he continued to give lectures at the Delhi College of Art. He spoke about the foreign tongue we had inherited from the British, one that he had honed so carefully over the years. He attributed his love for the language to his brother, who had a wonderful command of it.

'It's true I teach English, but my love for languages extends to Urdu as well, as I opted for it as an additional subject in college. There's something to be said about the way words sound when they are placed next to each other. The syntax, the poetry, the enunciation. At times, I read something in a book—a line, a word—and it is so beautiful that I'm compelled to write it down. I have made a small diary of such things … come, I will show it to you.'

Leaving behind his past in the living room, I followed him into an inner room. In the far corner sat a small wooden writing desk. Books, framed photographs and stationery were all allotted their place. From the top of a small pile of books he picked up a notebook.

'As a young student,' he said, 'I was very fond of reading Omar Khayyam, a Persian philosopher and poet whose most popular work was translated by Edward Fitzgerald and titled *Rubáiyát of Omar Khayyám*.' Then, gesturing for me to sit down, he too made himself comfortable in a chair and, in a tone deep and professorial, began reading: '"The moving finger writes; and, having writ, moves on: nor all thy piety nor wit shall lure it back to cancel half a line, nor all thy tears wash out a word of it."'

He closed the notebook intently and, as if he were leading a class, looked at me and explained, 'Whatever one does in one's life is one's own responsibility and cannot be changed. "Nor all thy piety nor wit shall lure it back to cancel half a line." Life cannot be changed, no matter what we do, "the moving finger writes…" In the context of the Partition, too, these words hold true. Indeed, the moving finger writes. Things cannot be changed. It is impossible to go back to the past, but what was done at the time, as the prose clearly states, was the assumption of responsibility. We had demanded Independence and we received it. Though the consequence of that Independence was unimaginable, we took responsibility for it, we learnt from it.'

With that, a silence fell over the room as he placed the notebook back on the pile. From the bottom he picked out a slim volume and handed it to me. *Lahore*, its title read. As I leafed through its pages, I wondered whether the anatomy of a city could be adequately compressed into a codex.

'How do you feel living in today's society?' I asked softly.

'Quite out of place,' he laughed. '*Beti*, that time was different. Now, people's perceptions have changed. Society is different. Let me tell you an anecdote from my Lahori days. We lived in a Muslim *mohalla* and women mostly observed the *purdah*. Now, on our way to college, sometimes we would attach our bicycles to the back of a *tonga*. Now, if by chance there was a girl sitting in the back seat of the *tonga*, and if by chance, even by mistake, we got a glimpse of just her hand, oho, our day was made! Our day was made!' he laughed. 'Just the hand, imagine that. I have so many such stories, I will tell you some day. So many stories…'

'Stories from Lahore?' I asked in anticipation, remembering the beautiful objects left in the care of an entrepreneurial Lahori woman in the wake of the Independence movement.

'Stories from Lahore,' he confirmed. Then, smiling widely, he quoted Syed Asghar Wajahat's famous words: '*Beti, jis Lahore nai dekhya, o jamyai nai.*'[7]

17

STATELESS HEIRLOOMS

THE *HAMAM-DASTA* OF SAVITRI MIRCHANDANI

'ALL THE NEWSPAPERS REPORTED the same news; the radios played the same bulletins over and over again,' Savitri Mirchandani recalled, putting on a newsreader's matter-of-fact tone: '"The birth of India's freedom … the two dominions of India and Pakistan … murder and arson … these many killed in Lahore … these many displaced … fires blazing…"The months following Independence—and Partition—were just flooded with accounts of communal violence.'

'Where were you when India became independent?' I asked.

'We were still in Karachi.'

'Even after the Partition?'

She shrugged and nodded. 'I remember my father-in-law giving us lectures,' she said, her voice suddenly rising to impersonate him. 'He would say, "We do not have to leave Sindh. It was ours and it will always be ours."' Although Sindh was majority-Muslim overall, most of Sindh's middle class at the time was Hindu, and Hindus formed a majority in four of Sindh's five major cities.[1] She echoed her father-in-law's words again: '"All this is only political; we will not leave." And so naturally we remained.'

As she dived into her memories of that turbulent period, I noted how charismatic the old lady was. She was dressed in dark purple trousers and a floral button-down shirt. Her white-grey hair was cropped short in a chic way, her ears bore simple diamond studs and a small *til*, a beauty mark, adorned her right cheek. She was graceful in her movements and generous with her story; she drew me in with her feisty and endearing humour.

'You were married before the Partition?' I asked, as her daughter Shobha laid out plates of biscuits and bowls of salted peanuts on the low table in the centre of the room. Her granddaughter Maya, a senior New Delhi journalist with a keen interest in her family history, listened in closely as she poured chai from a teapot into four ornate cups.

'Oh yes, in 1941,' Savitri Mirchandani replied. 'Well, I was born in 1922, so I would have been nineteen years old at the time. My husband, Sunder Mirchandani, was a lawyer when we got married. But after two years of practising, he left the firm to join the Sindh police force—a better-paying job—acquiring the title of Direct Deputy Superintendent. It was a high post in those days.' She gestured to Shobha, who was sitting on the other side of the room. 'Shobha was born in November 1946, and my son, your father,' she said to Maya, 'was born in July 1945. My third son was born a few years later. So at the time of Partition, I was married with two children, living with my husband and in-laws in a comfortable house in Karachi.'

'Was it relatively safe, given that you didn't move immediately?'

'There was no violence in Karachi in August 1947.[2] Hindu and Muslim Sindhis always had good relations. We read about the riots and violence in other areas like the Punjab and that scared us, but Karachi was still relatively safe. As far as I remember, only the telephone service had collapsed in the city.'[3]

'So just to put it in context,' Maya said to me, 'at the time of Independence, the Hindu Sindhis from Karachi, who were mostly in business or held positions in the government, did not leave, since the riots had not spread there yet.' She methodically unfolded for me an unfamiliar Sindhi tapestry of belated and forlorn exodus. Between August and October 1947, the Hindu Sindhis were still tending to their businesses, homes or lands with no intention of migration as such. However, the sudden influx of about 2 million Muslim refugees from parts of present-day Gujarat, Uttar Pradesh, Bihar, Hyderabad, Rajasthan and other provinces of India led to terrible riots and violence. The Hindu Sindhis then had no choice but to flee. Now a stateless people, their homeland was suddenly situated within a new nation and tied to a new and distinct citizenship separate from their own.

'I remember sitting on my verandah one day a few months after the Partition,' Savitri Mirchandani continued, 'and my maid, who was a Muslim, came running outside and told me to get back inside the house. When I asked why, she said there were gangs going around the neighbourhood, looting houses, killing people. But before that, this was unheard of … and even then, as I told you, my father-in-law told us repeatedly that this was just political.'

'So what happened that led you to migrate eventually?' I asked.

'Well … towards the later months of 1947—in October and November—the riots finally reached Karachi. We lived in a good neighbourhood that was quite safe, but when the riots began all the Hindu houses were looted. And the looters were of all ages, from children to grown-ups. Some people had utensils in their hands—pots, pans, ladles—some had knives, some dragged out the furniture. It was tragic. Houses were emptied with the residents still inside them. But then they went on to the women; they assaulted them, raped them, and that … that was by far the worst.'

She paused, shaking her head.

'This particular incident must have occurred in November. My husband had a fever and was home from work, resting. Our neighbour at the time was a Gujarati—not a Sindhi but a Gujarati Hindu. The rioters broke into his house, raped his daughter in front of him. And then they killed him,' she said heavily.

'As soon as my husband heard the ruckus outside, he got out of bed and told me to take the children upstairs. He was working for the police, so he took out his revolver and was ready to shoot anyone who tried to break into our house next. Outside the house sat a *ghoda-gaadi-walla*, appointed to drive around the ladies of the house in his horse-drawn carriage. He was a good man, a Muslim, and when he saw the mob approaching our house, he warned them that a policeman lived there and they would be shot down if they tried to break in. So the mob didn't dare come near our compound. He saved us that day, the *ghoda-gaadi-walla*.

'That was when my father-in-law decided it was time for us to leave. My husband also agreed. So one day, not long after this incident, he went to give in his resignation...' her voice trailed off.

'... but it was not accepted,' Maya finished.

'Why not?'

'Well, the riots had just begun in Sindh. They couldn't let their police officers leave just then. And so when my *dada* went to hand in his resignation, it was simply rejected. Unlike Punjab or Bengal, the Sindh province did not split, nor did its resources or police force. The Sindh police were the only force not allowed to leave their stations. It was their duty to control and curb the riots. After all, refugees had just begun to pour in from across the border.'

'It all happened so fast,' the old lady explained. 'The same day that my husband went to resign, an opportunity arose for me to leave Karachi. My father-in-law's brother, a big businessman, happened to have two tickets, but couldn't leave just yet as he hadn't sold his business. So my father-in-law told me that the rioters were after young women, the city was no longer safe and, still horrified by the incident, he reminded me of our neighbour's daughter. He said I must take the children and leave immediately.'

'Just like that?'

'Just like that,' Maya echoed.

'Were you afraid?' I asked, wondering what it must take to leave your life behind at just a moment's notice.

'I wasn't even thinking about that. My husband wasn't home; he had gone to give his resignation. How could I just leave, how could I just go without saying goodbye, without speaking to him? It was so tragic, I didn't know what to do.'

'Dadima left without him. She was put on a ship to Bombay,' Maya said.

'I know my father-in-law meant well, but he forced me to leave. I was in tears as I packed. I left everything. I told my *aayah* to keep all our belongings, the furniture, clothes, everything. I couldn't take it, I couldn't sell it. She helped me pack just one suitcase. In that we put nappies, the children's clothes, my clothes, and that was about it.'

'And your *hamam-dasta*, the mortar and pestle,' offered her daughter, Shobha.

'Yes, of course, the *hamam-dasta*. The *aayah* put that in too, but I did not know at the time.'

'And then you left?'

'Yes, then I left. When we came to India, we put in a claim for the house because the government said that all refugees should put in a claim for the belongings they had left behind. But what did we get for that claim? A mere Rs 100 a month. It was nothing.'

'When you were leaving Karachi, did you ever think you would return? That perhaps the violence would die down after a while?'

'No, never. I knew even then that it would be permanent.'

I would have imagined her answer to be different, for there to be more disbelief and longing, if not in her voice then at least in her eyes, but they too were impassive.

'She is not really sentimental…' Maya offered.

Her grandmother sighed. 'The house, the things in it, they are just material possessions. *Bura toh laga, beta*, I felt bad—not about leaving the city or the house, but about leaving my husband behind. We had barely been married for, what, six or seven years. We had two young children. How could I leave without him? When would I see him again? How would I know he was safe? How would he know I was safe? I remember sitting in that car on the way to the port and crying the entire ride, holding on to my children and weeping … not out of fright, but out of sheer uncertainty. In hindsight, I know it was the right thing to do. Who knows what would have happened to us if I had stayed back? So though it was difficult, it was the right thing to do…'

The lump in my throat grew and I nodded slowly. Then, attending to a curious detail of her story, I asked, 'You went to the port in a car?'

'Yes. Very few people had cars in those days, but this was my father-in-law's official transport.'

I looked to the other two women for clarification. 'My great-grandfather was with the Port Trust as a customs collector,' Maya explained, 'so all this *gaadi-shaadi*, the cars, came with that. He was part of the educated elite. In fact, most Hindus in pre-Partition Sindh were educated elites, usually with government jobs.'

Suddenly, her grandmother sat up straighter, looked at me and said, 'All Sindhis came to this country as refugees. They came with nothing. Zero. No money, no business. They left everything behind. I came with one suitcase and two children and built a new life here. I am proud of that.'

Sighing deeply, she settled back into the sofa. She had sailed to the Indian shore, but her Sindh, the entirety of the province, had remained in Pakistan. It was ironic that the words 'Hindustan' and 'India' were both derived from 'Sindh'[4] yet now Sindh itself lay on the other side of the border. Not even a small sliver had been allocated to India. But what India did receive was the majority of the Hindu Sindhi population,[5] who had all left behind their homes, land, businesses, culture and sense of identity.

Clearing my throat, I asked her, 'So what had you heard about India before you came here?'

'*Kuch nahi*, nothing. I had barely thought of the words "India" or "Pakistan". Like I said, for the family it was just Sindh. So when I boarded the ship, I didn't think it was "India" that I was going to. I just thought I was going to my sister's house in Bombay.'[6]

'Oh, you had a sister here! And so why did you just bring one suitcase; was it because of the little time you had?' I asked, confused.

'*Nahi nahi*, not that. We were told not to bring anything. So I just took the basics, like clothes and nappies. Even our pockets were checked before we got on to the ship.[7] You had to leave *everything* behind,' she said, repeating it for good measure.

And so, because they couldn't bring anything else with them, they had brought the intangibles. They brought the weather; the humid, salty air of the Karachi port; the culture, language, accent and script. They brought old family recipes of crispy twice-fried potatoes. They brought their names, and with those they brought their histories. Often, the most important things cannot be seen, and so it appeared that, by leaving everything behind, the Hindu Sindhis brought with them the most crucial, yet invisible, parts of their being.

'You left everything behind, but your *hamam-dasta* crossed the Arabian Sea with you,' Maya beamed.

* * *

'Yes,' she smiled back. 'I still don't know how that happened. Maybe the *aayah* put it in and it was just not found during the checks on the ship.'

'Did you cook a lot in Karachi?' I asked.

'No, not really. I would oversee the cooking, and I can cook well, but I don't really enjoy it.'

'It's a curious thing, isn't it?' I said, surveying the pestle and mortar seated on the marble table. 'Imagine the priorities of the help at the time. The woman of the house is leaving, she is going to a new land. There, of course, she will have to feed her children, herself. She will have to make *sabzi* and dal. And for that what will she need? Spices.'

'And to crush the spices, she will need the *hamam-dasta*,' Shobha said with a smile. She carefully reached forward and brushed it with long, graceful fingers.

'Dadima left it here, and it's been in my kitchen ever since! We use it almost every day,' Maya said.

I reached out to pick it up.

'Be careful, it's quite heavy,' the old lady warned.

'Yes, it is made of brass,' Maya added. 'In Hindi, brass is *peetal*. And in Sindhi we say *pittal*,' she enunciated the soft double T. 'The bowl at the bottom is the *hamam* and the stick is the *dasta*.'

It was a beautiful old object. It bore the tarnish of years of use and weather, which gave it its character. The inside of the mortar did not shine but glowed. It bore lines and scratches, a result of the constant contact with the metallic pestle. The bowl itself was an odd angular shape, with a large open mouth and its body cinched in the middle, but every edge was softened, as though it had been handmade. The exterior bore a crosshatch pattern. The pestle was unusually long. It was thin at the top, where it would be held, and thick and strong at its base. When I tapped the bowl with my fingernail, it created the same kind of short yet sharp metallic sounds that temple bells make—a hollow reverberating echo.

'Use Brasso over it and it will shine!' offered its original owner, sitting back and smiling, quite pleased with the suggestion.

'Yes, maybe,' Maya replied, 'but why do you want to make it shine? Its tarnish reminds me of the history that lives within.'

'*Arey*, it will look good. Then you can display it as an antique in your living room!'

'Dadima...' she laughed, 'the real joy is in using it every day in my kitchen, like you did in yours!'

'When did you get this?' I asked, taking the *hamam-dasta* onto my lap and studying its shape.

'I had bought it from some bazaar in Karachi right after my wedding. It probably cost about eight annas.'[8]

Then Savitri Mirchandani took it from my lap and placed it back on the table. Gripping the *dasta* tightly, she told me about its use. 'In those days there were no automatic mixers, and so if you wanted, for instance, black pepper powder, you would use this. All the masalas would be ground fresh at the time of food preparation; we hardly ever crushed spices beforehand and stored them as we do today. Kala namak, garam masala, lal mirch. It would *kooto*, crush, all the spices. Not grind, but crush. For grinding we used the *sil-batta*, a large, flat stone slab called the *sil*...' she drew an imaginary shape in the air, '... and a cylindrical grinding stone rolled on top of it called the *batta*, which we used for grinding all kinds of mixtures, ginger and onion, and other ingredients for different chutneys. The thing to remember is this: if you want your spices to be rough and coarse with larger granules, use the *hamam-dasta*, and if you want them to be fine and powdery, use the *sil-batta*.'

'But you didn't bring that...' I said.

'No, though I wish I did,' she replied, laughing. 'It was used more, but was also heavier.'

'What else do you wish you had brought?'

'I have forgotten everything ... all the things in our house, I cannot remember them. But there was something I had thought about in my first few months after coming here...'

Three pairs of eyes looked at her expectantly.

'A cradle! *Your* cradle,' she said to her daughter. 'My mother-in-law had given us a cradle for you to sleep in as a baby, and you loved it. It was so beautiful, hand-carved out of wood. If I could, I would have brought that. But no matter how much you try to take, it will never be enough, and some things will always get left behind.'

'How long were you by yourself before your husband joined you?' I asked.

'Well, it took me three days to come from Karachi to Bombay by ship. It was the month of November. There were all kinds of people on the ship, but we travelled in a first-class cabin. The crew told me that it was the very same cabin in which Fatima Jinnah, Muhammad Ali Jinnah's sister, had come from Bombay to Sindh, and now we were making the same journey across the other way! When I got off at the port in Bombay, I went straight to my sister's house, and what a chaotic house that was. Overnight it had transformed from a home into a refugee camp. Many people known to her family had migrated to Bombay and were living with them. It was a small flat, one bathroom, one latrine and twenty people!'

'What neighbourhood was this in, Dadima?' Maya asked.

'At that time it was called the Fort area, but now it is Kala Ghoda. My children and I stayed with her for one and a half months, after which I saw an advertisement for a small room in a fairly good locality on Marine Drive and discussed it with my sister. She agreed that it was a good idea to set up my own home, seeing as my husband would hopefully join us soon.'

'Did you get any news of your husband?'

'No, nothing. I didn't even know whether he was alive or dead. There was no word of him for six months, no letters, no news through anyone else who came from Karachi. I couldn't write to him because the postal service had been suspended. In January 1948 we heard of Gandhi-ji's assassination and I thought to myself that if a Muslim had killed him, there would be riots everywhere for sure. And if my husband was alive, he would not be able to come to us. But thankfully he somehow managed to make his way to Bombay soon after. He went straight to my sister, who told him about the new flat, where he then came to meet me and the children. Because he was in the police, on the journey across he wasn't checked as rigorously by the authorities as the common people and was able to carry a few things, like my wedding sari and these gold *jhumkas*.' She gestured to a pair of earrings and a regal-looking purple silk dupatta that had once been a sari, both of which lay on the table next to her. I looked at the dupatta and, following my gaze, she said, 'I wore this sari at my wedding reception. It is made of Benarasi silk. But over the years it became too frail and we had to cut it to the size of a dupatta.'

'And the earrings?'

'Ah, those I bought for myself after my wedding! You see, they have filigree work done by hand.' She held one out and I picked it up, dangling it in the air. They were umbrella-shaped *jhumkas* made of pure yellow gold, the round shape created by delicate filigree work.

I asked her to put them on so I could photograph her, in response to which she laughed and said, 'Oof, you are making an old woman wear such bright, young jewellery!'

Her granddaughter helped her fasten the earrings, then delicately draped the dupatta across her shoulders and stood back, admiring the sight.

'Beautiful,' I smiled. 'Just where they belong.'

As I focused the lens on Savitri Mirchandani's earrings, I thought about her husband. I imagined him shuffling through the house before he left, looking only for those things that were precious to his wife: her sari, her jewellery, things that would make her happy, things that would remind her of their Karachi, perhaps concealed within his luggage so that the authorities would not take them away. I thought of the pride their granddaughter felt every time she wore the dupatta that now belonged to her. I thought of how objects that were once bought for their utility—a sari, for instance—acquired a new and alien preciousness as their context and environment changed. How much care Maya must put into draping it over herself, how delicately she would fold and store it in layers of newspaper, in the hope that this precious inheritance from her grandmother would never fray, never weather. How lovely it was that parts of Sindh still lived with her.

As I photographed her, a question suddenly popped into my mind and I put down my camera. 'What is the Sindhi word for Partition?'

* * *

'*Batwara*,' the old lady offered spontaneously, but then stopped herself, as though giving it another thought. 'No, no, that is in Hindi.'

'I have never heard of a Sindhi word for Partition,' said Shobha, her eyebrows knitted together.

'Me neither,' Maya said. 'I've just always said the Partition; I don't know if there is a Sindhi word. It just struck me now when you asked her. We never use *batwara*; not her, not anyone. Maybe *judaai* ... but that means separation, and that too in a different context.'[9]

Three blank faces stared back at me until Savitri Mirchandani spoke. 'In the Sindhi language there is no word. We only call it Partition. The land was partitioned, *Partition ho gaya*. I remember, after we came to India, my husband and I always used to say, "Sindhi is a dying language."'

'Why would you say that?' I asked.

'Look, the Punjabis use *batwara* because Punjab was split in half. It was divided, and so for them this is a literal term.' And then slowly, as if weighing every word, she added, 'In India, the Punjabis still have some Punjab, the Bengalis still have some Bengal, and so their languages continue to be spoken, continue to flourish. But Hindu Sindhis have no Sindh; no part of it exists on this side of the border. And so perhaps that is why Sindhi is a dying language.'

'Language is bound to soil...' said Shobha, her voice full of a sadness not necessarily felt by her mother, 'and we no longer have any soil of our own.'

'Essentially, stateless,' Maya completed the thought.

'How come you never taught Sindhi to your children or grandchildren after you moved?'

In her pragmatic tone, Savitri Mirchandani said, 'There was no point. Just after the Partition, people of my generation still spoke in Sindhi to each other. But to integrate into society, we had to learn Hindi or Marathi or some other language. The Sindhis are very good at adapting to any circumstance.'

She was right about that, I noted. Straight through the heart of Sindh cuts the river Indus in its grand and unpredictable ways. Over the years, Sindhis had learnt to adapt effortlessly to its dramatic change in course, altering their lives to that of the river. At times it refused to yield any crops and at others it blessed the villages in abundance. Its feisty nature was capable of both providing and destroying life. As a result, the people of Sindh were not just accustomed to change but lived with the acknowledgment and acceptance of unpredictability. As the years passed, they became good at adapting to any circumstance. And so the thousands of stateless Sindhi refugees who had migrated across to Bombay and other parts of the country had adapted to new lives and nationalities in the most fluent of ways, gradually and unknowingly letting go of Sindh.

'Sindhi sounds a lot like Gujarati, actually. In fact, the closest comparison is the Kutchi language,' Maya said. 'But even among Sindhis there are different sub-castes—we are Amils—and each of these sub-castes will have a different dialect depending on the region.'

'Can you speak it?' I asked her.

'No,' she said slowly, 'I am conscious of my pronunciation. It still feels somewhat foreign on the tongue. I can understand when she speaks to me in it, but I always respond in Hindi or English.'

'That is exactly what we did as children,' Shobha laughed. 'Growing up, she did try to speak to us in Sindhi, but we always responded in Hindi or English.'

Her mother nodded. 'See, that is why my husband and I called it a dead language!'

* * *

'So what happened after your husband joined you in Bombay?' I asked.

'He was recruited into the police force, but lost seniority by nearly three years in his first position—though that did not matter to him since any employment was welcome at that point.'

'During the 1942 Quit India Movement,' Maya said, 'my *dada* had been a part of Pandit Nehru's security when he came to give a speech in Karachi. During that speech, people apparently threw stones and there was a riot; Dada saved him from the mob. After the Partition, the family lived in Bombay, then Delhi, and then in Rajkot, where Dada worked for a few years as an IPS [Indian Police Service] officer in the Gujarat cadre, and finally back to

Delhi, where he was recruited by Nehru—who remembered him from 1942—into the Intelligence Bureau.'

'You lived in so many cities in India after being in Karachi for most of your life before that. Did you miss it at all? Did you not wish to go back?' I asked.

'We did go once, with the children in 1959, but by accident,' Savitri Mirchandani replied.

'What do you mean?'

'My father had been posted to Cairo,' said Shobha, 'and the only way the Indian government would send families on transfers to Egypt in the 1950s was by ship. When we arrived at the Karachi port the crew went on strike, and so we were docked there for twelve days! We spent our days at Hotel Metropole and then came back to sleep in the ship at night. That was it.'

'Like I said, by accident…'

'She did show me the nursing home where I was born, though,' Shobha continued. 'That's the only recollection I have of the city.'

'But your passport, it would say "born in Karachi"?'

Shobha nodded and shrugged. 'It does. But I have never felt any connection to it. It's simply a word on a document. Nothing more, nothing less. For me, home has always been Delhi, but I have often wondered about this disconnection from the city of my birth. Even in '59, we were there for nearly two weeks but didn't venture out to discover the city.'

'How come you didn't show them around, Dadima?' Maya asked her grandmother.

For a few minutes she said nothing, and then she spoke. 'I was upset. Very upset.'

'Why?'

'Because I remembered,' she sighed. 'I remembered everything about Karachi—how we lived there, grew up there. And being there again and not being able to call it my own made me feel unhappy.'

'I took Dadima there again in 2006 and then it was quite different,' Maya told me.

'Yes, when we went together, we travelled around Sindh. It was still upsetting, but we tried to find places familiar to me. But I could only recognize the customs office where my father-in-law worked. I couldn't find my home. It had been over half a century and they had broken down the old buildings and built two- or three-storey houses instead.

'So many roads had changed. Karachi had expanded so far beyond the old boundaries. I couldn't recognize anything. Both houses, the one I grew up in and the one I lived in after marriage, no longer existed. All gone. But we did find the area around my father's house—though only because it was in front of a large hill and Jinnah's *kabar*, his grave, is there.'

'But when we went to Hyderabad in Sindh,' Maya recalled excitedly, 'things were different. The city is about two hours away from Karachi. Though the area where Dadima was born had changed, the core of the city had remained relatively untouched. I remember, we had set off in the small streets of Hirabad, the colony where most Hindus lived before the Partition, with only one mission in mind: we were determined to locate my grandmother's family home, where she had spent the summer holidays until she got married.

'Many of the old *havelis* still stand there, complete with the dates when they were built and the names of the families that originally lived in them engraved at the entrance. In a way, you could say they were testaments to the affluence of the people who lived in them. Not a single member of my grandmother's family still lives in Pakistan, so it was difficult to locate the house. But the locals did direct us to the original resident of one of the *havelis*. I will never forget that day, for when my grandmother met this woman, two complete strangers in the twilight of their lives, their connection was almost immediate!'[10]

'Did she take you to the house?' I asked.

'Yes, we saw the house. But first we sat with her for a long time, sipping chai and talking about the history of Hirabad. She was a Hindu. Her name was Leelawati Harchandani, but everyone called her Dadi Leela.' While the word *dadi* means paternal grandmother in Hindi, it means older sister in Sindhi. 'She had been called that for nearly six decades! At eighty-eight years of age then, she was the oldest living Amil Sindhi in Hyderabad. She used to be an educator and worked for the upliftment of women in school systems through music. After the Partition, many of the Amils fled, but she remained because of music. She sought her mentor's advice on whether she should continue living in Hyderabad and he told her nothing would happen to her, not to worry. Back then, when we met her in 2006, there were very few Hindu families still living in the area—no more than could be counted on her fingers. The rest had vacated Hirabad in 1947.

'Naturally, I was curious as to why she chose to live in Pakistan. When I asked her, she recalled an anecdote from her childhood: "When I was a little girl, my headmaster told me I had three mothers. I remember getting very offended, as though he was saying things against my father. Then he explained to me who the three were. He said the first was my mother who gave me birth. The second was my mother tongue. And the third, my motherland." I guess that was why she remained in Sindh, for the motherland. Till today, I remember that conversation vividly.'

'Had she ever been to India?'

'Oh yes. As long as her health allowed, she would travel to an ashram in Pune every two or three years. Her last trip had been in 1998, when apparently many people asked her questions about India–Pakistan relations and such. She said, "I told them not to ask me anything about *siyasat*, politics!" She actually fell ill on that trip and rushed back to Pakistan for fear of dying on foreign soil! She hadn't been back since, but her wish was for her ashes to be immersed on her death not in the Ganga—as is customary for most Hindus—but in the river Indus—Sindh—that flows through the land she considered most sacred.'

A warmth slowly settled into my heart.

'And the house?' I asked.

'I described whatever I remembered from the house to her,' Savitri Mirchandani said, 'told her it belonged to my aunt and uncle, who used to be a public prosecutor in the area. It turned out that she was actually a friend of my aunt's and so she knew the house. Her young nephew took us there and we even met the inhabitants, a police officer's family who had migrated from Aligarh.'

'The thing is,' Maya smiled at me, 'we always try to look for tangibles that connect us: the homes we lived in, the schools we went to, the bazaars we shopped at. Some things we find and some things we don't. Whatever the result, I knew this was a journey I wanted to, and had to, make with my *dadi* while she was still able to travel and make these crucial connections. The trip was important for us: for me to discover, and for her to rediscover.'

I nodded. 'Do you ever find yourself thinking of either Karachi or Hyderabad or Sindh now?' I asked her grandmother.

'After that last trip, after seeing how much things had changed, I don't think of anything at all. *Kuch nahi sochti*,' she repeated. 'It is all in the past.' With that, the three women began talking amongst themselves about this land they belonged to, so far from where they sat now in Delhi. As I listened to grandmother and granddaughter narrate their separate versions of the same experience, I couldn't help but feel a twinge of jealousy. Maya had been able to do what I could only dream of doing, for no visa is granted now for the place my grandmother was from in Pakistan. But Maya had taken her grandmother back to where she was born in Sindh, back to where she had lived in Karachi. And though her grandmother felt little nostalgia for the land of her birth, Maya's own voice was steeped in the pride and delight of having shared the experience of travelling across the border with her. Her sentences were stitched with passion and endearment for a land, a culture, a world that were hers by inheritance.

18

FROM THE FOLDS OF LIFE

THE HOUSEHOLD ITEMS OF SITARA FAIYAZ ALI

'THE GREEN SHUTTERS,' SHE said, tapping her forefinger on the photograph in her hand. 'I still remember these green shutters.' She looked at me, eyes moist with the recollection of a place never to be seen again, and continued, 'My father built this house in Dalhousie with his own two hands. Brick by brick he built it, with great love and passion.'

Then, with a sigh, Sitara Faiyaz Ali put the photograph down on the coffee table and looked past me straight out the window of her Lahore home. Her movements were deliberate and slow, graceful and refined. She wore a grey salwar kameez with a pink floral pattern and matching grey and gold earrings. Her face was still childlike and youthful, quite beautiful in a soft and gentle way; only the thin web of wrinkles around her mouth and eyes betrayed her age. Her silver-white hair was parted down the middle, styled to the back, wavy tendrils surrounding her forehead. A pistachio green sheer dupatta covered her head and fell in waves across her arms. She closed her eyes, fingers to her lips, until her face broke into a smile. As she opened her eyes, that smile seemed deep enough to hold the memories of summers spent in the house with green shutters.

'Sometimes,' she said in a dreamy voice, 'sometimes when I close my eyes, I can still see the house. Even seventy years later, in my memory that house is still a home.'

Then from the table she picked up the same colour photograph, and a decades-old black-and-white one, also of the house. Holding them side by side, she gestured to the older image. 'This is the house as it looked in 1947,' she said, 'and this,' she pointed to the later one, 'is a photograph a family friend, Dr Farrukh Khan, took of it decades later when he travelled across to India to visit his own house. Every wall was raised, every floor put down, every tree planted and every window fitted by my father. I remember it well. We had a drawing room, dining room, three bedrooms on the first floor and one bedroom on the ground floor. The hills at the back were quite high, as if enveloping the house within their altitudes. He had even bought the plot next door to build a house for his four daughters. This one, he would say, is for my son.' She smiled.

'Now, you see how the structure remains unchanged in this new photograph? The wooden window shutters, all the glass windows, the circular sun room, the roof. Everything remains unchanged.' After a pause she added, 'Well, everything except the ownership.'

I placed both prints on the table and studied them. Both showed the same profile of the house and indeed looked identical regardless of the time that had passed. Taken from a corner of the front garden, both showed the main door flanked by a row of long, rectangular windows on its left and another row of windows encircling the sun room on its right. The second storey of the house followed the same pattern of windows and shutters. Sheer white curtains could be seen behind every window in both prints. The house was built in typical Himalayan fashion—vertically oriented, with multiple buildings of peaked roofs, presumably having derived inspiration from the mountain forms themselves.[1]

The black-and-white photo was set in a grey-checquered paper frame with a black border. Due to the nature of its development in the studio, the blacks of the image were rather dense and the whites quite bright. Much of the image's detail was lost to overexposure, though in the mid-tones, the gritty grain of the film still showed the angular shapes of the open windows and the textures of shadows, grass and trees. In contrast, the coloured image was a breath of fresh white and teal green, the house surrounded by tall cedar trees and short, luscious bushes and shrubs. Its multiple windows reflected the clear sky above it. Here, the front three steps of the house, which had been all but lost to illumination in the old print, could be seen made of red brick. The front door, painted the same green as the window shutters, was bolted and secured shut with a brass lock. The house seemed to be in great condition even decades later, save for a single sheet of tin that had come loose just to the right of the main door.

'Were you born here in Dalhousie?' I asked, gesturing to the picture.

'No, this was built by my father in 1943–44 as a summer house, but we were only able to spend two summers there. I was born in 1924 in a city called Lyallpur, which during the British Raj was named after the then Lieutenant Governor of Punjab, Sir James Broadwood Lyall. During the Partition it came to be a part of Pakistan, and in the 1970s it was renamed Faisalabad.'

'After King Faisal of Saudi Arabia,' added her daughter Shahnaz, seated beside her.[2]

'Yes. It used to be very beautiful in the 1920s. Wide open roads, wide open fields of cotton, wheat and sugarcane, and fruit orchards. The Chenab river would irrigate these fields. It was never an old city. In fact, it was one of the first planned cities built in British India. Because of its rich natural resources, it housed the University of Agriculture.

'My father, Mian Afzal Hussain, was the principal of the University and later went on to become the first Muslim vice-chancellor of the Punjab University in Lahore for two terms— one before Independence, from 1938 to '44, and one after, from 1954 to '65. He was a very educated man, having obtained his MSc from England. In 1938, he hired a classmate of his, an Englishwoman named Anna Molka—married to a Muslim gentleman, Sheikh Ahmed—to begin a Department of Fine Arts at the University. She, along with a Bengali woman, Ms Zutshi, began teaching painting and music. Most of their students were Hindu, but after the Partition all those students left and naturally

Muslims took their place. Ms Zutshi would often tell us about the burkha-clad ladies who would come to her class!'

Her daughter leaned in. 'I think the most important thing to learn from my grandfather's life,' Shahnaz said proudly, 'was his determination to educate, regardless of whether the students were boys or girls, Hindus or Muslims. And not just conventional education, like the sciences or law, but also the humanities and the performing arts. He thought them essential to our understanding of culture and tradition.'

Her mother nodded and then slowly rose from the sofa, gesturing for me to join her. The living room we sat in was divided into two areas: a formal sitting space on the left, to which she made her way now, and a more intimate space on the right, where we had sat looking at the photographs. She walked to a side-table shaped like a half moon and picked up a photograph, handing it to me with pride. Sitting within an aged silver frame was the portrait of a distinguished-looking middle-aged man. His warm angular face sported a salt-and-pepper beard that crawled all the way up to his hair. He struck a pose, looking into the distance, clothed in a smart grey Western suit and black striped tie. On his lips was a hint of a smile, the same one he had passed down to his daughter.

'Abba-*jaan* was a very farsighted educationist. He educated us all. It was his most precious gift to us.'

'Ammi and two of her sisters studied up to BA, while the fourth among them has a PhD in geography,' Shahnaz put in.

'I was the third,' the old lady said in response, holding up three slim fingers. 'In total, we were five siblings: one brother and four sisters. We spent our childhood in Lyallpur and Lahore. *Par taksim ke samay*, at the time of the Partition, we found ourselves in Independent India—in Dalhousie.'

'*Taksim ke samay*…' I repeated, beginning to form my question, but she stopped me, placing a soft hand over mine. Her dense brown eyes were amused at my almost hasty advancement to the topic.

'I will tell you everything. Come…'

My cheeks reddened as I reminded myself that remembering the past was a difficult and gradual exercise. Some things sat at the very core of one's existence, and the slightest indelicacy in handling such memories could tarnish or distort them forever. I told myself to be patient.

She made her way back to the sofa in the other part of the room, where a tray with cups of hot tea had now been laid for us. Shahnaz offered me one, and then, bringing my pen to paper, I said, '*Toh bataiye*, tell me from the beginning.'

* * *

'The truth is,' she said softly, neither to me nor to her daughter, but as if to the room at large and to all the photos of her ancestors neatly displayed on the sideboards and walls, 'I haven't thought about it for many years. But even now there are things from that time I cannot completely forget. The house with the green window shutters in Dalhousie, my father's dream house, is one of those things. And 1947 was the last time we ever saw it.'

She pointed to the wall on the right, where a photograph hung of both sides of a big family. 'I was married in 1945. My husband's ancestral home was in Batala, in Gurdaspur district, which is now in India. His grandfather, Chaudhary Faquir Hussain Khan, was a very prominent politician and the landlord of a village called Bharowal, also now in Indian Punjab. They came from a line of warriors, their ancestors having fought for Maharaja Ranjit Singh in his army… In fact, there is a cannon that sits in front of the Lahore Museum, cast in 1762 under the Durrani Empire and used by many throughout history. Its name is Zam-Zammah, and legend has it that its construction was funded by the people of Lahore who donated their kitchen utensils. It was the biggest in the subcontinent at the time.'

'If you've read Rudyard Kipling's *Kim*, you know about the Zam-Zammah, as the story begins with the cannon,' Shahnaz added. 'And so in popular culture, for Kipling was ever the Lahori, it is known as Kim's Gun!'

'Well, my husband's ancestors used that cannon in the battles they fought for Ranjit Singh,' Sitara Faiyaz Ali said. 'Generations of warriors! Though he did not join any army, my husband was a civil supplies officer during World War II and would get transferred to different cities for his work. In 1946, after Shahnaz was born, we got transferred to Gurgaon, a village near Delhi, where we lived until 1947.'

I smiled as I listened to the mother-daughter duo, realizing that the story of a family could never be completely narrated as an undeviating account. It was, in some ways, exactly like one's memory: perforated, additive, subtractive and a cohesive amalgamation of everything that came before and during one's existence. The story of a family was, after all, spun from the memories of many. It explored its tangents, dug its tributaries and flowed into the various veins where its history took it—from the armies of Maharaja Ranjit Singh to the agricultural university of Lyallpur, and from the teal-green shutters of a cottage in Dalhousie to Gurgaon, a small village on the outskirts of Delhi that has now transformed beyond recognition into a bustling metropolis.

'In Gurgaon, the three of us lived in a rented house,' she continued. 'There were two rooms at the front and a courtyard at the back. Everyone would tell us to stay inside because of the *bandars*, the monkeys roaming the streets! "Keep a close watch on Shahnaz," they would say, because the monkeys could just take her away!' she laughed. 'Anyway, it was a small, quiet place with only a few officers stationed in the vicinity, and there was no one else around. We were happy there but in the summer, when it became too hot, we would all flock to the hills. That's why Abba-*jaan* had built the house in Dalhousie in the first place. Oh, the cool, crisp mountain air, the unending winding streets, the trees, the birds … it was lovely!'

'So, in the summer of 1947, when Shahnaz was a year and a half old and her sister was all of four months, I took them both with me to Dalhousie. It was like a reunion; the whole family had come up from Lahore. Notice of the Partition had been made public in June, but the hill stations were quiet. Naturally, the newspapers printed speculative stories about where the border would sit, which cities it was likely to encompass within Pakistan, and the riots in towns which had religiously intermingled populations, Lahore being one of them. But, like I said, Dalhousie was quiet and calm, and not close to the border either.

'We didn't even know how bad it truly was until my husband came to get me in August. I wonder now how he must have made the journey to the hills all alone. Delhi was engulfed in communal riots,' she said, using the old word *fasad*, 'and he arrived so suddenly, without any notice, and said that we were leaving for his ancestral village. He had also received a transfer from Gurgaon to Mianwali, a city in the middle of the country, certain to be a part of Pakistan, and had already shipped our household items and furniture by the goods train. So we left, but my father stayed behind in this house.'

She picked up the black-and-white photo and held it not as one holds a piece of paper, casually between thumb and forefinger, but like she was holding a rare historical artefact or a precious gem. She cradled it in her palm.

'It was to be a while before he left Dalhousie to come back to Lahore, but he did return eventually. He just couldn't believe that the country could ever be partitioned. When my husband told him of the Hindus who had infiltrated Delhi, and the Muslims who had fled the city, he refused to believe that such a significant portion of the population could just be uprooted!'

'How come?'

'Well, our family always supported the Unionist Party. My father's half-brother, Sir Fazl-i-Hussain, was a founding member, along with Sir Sikander Hyat Khan and others who were opposed to the Quaid-e-Azam's vision of Pakistan as an independent nation of Muslims.[3] Not to mention, my husband's grandfather, the landlord in Bharowal, was also a unionist.

'And so that is where we went, to make sure his family was safe and then find a way to get to Mianwali. We left by road from Dalhousie and reached district Amritsar. We drove slowly through it, stopping in Tarn Taran and then finally reaching Bharowal. Because of my husband's family's influence, no one had dared to attack their village. They were friendly with the Sikhs there. In fact, because he knew how dangerous the trains were during that time, for a few weeks after the Partition my father-in-law, with the help of an army convoy, would transport people across the border. *Musalmaans* to Pakistan and Hindus to India. It went on for a few weeks, and only after all the people had been brought safely across did they migrate. My mother-in-law used to tell us that, when they finally left Bharowal, they opened their home and granaries to the public. Their house was in a safe area, so the Hindus who came to district Amritsar could take shelter and use the grains to cook and the fruit orchards to eat.'

'And what was your journey to Mianwali like?'

'*Beta* … you can imagine what it was like. We were lucky to have a vehicle to get across; otherwise, who knew what would become of us? We saw many riots along the way. Villages, homes, roads, all destroyed. And whatever happened on that side happened on this side too. We went from Amritsar across the border to Lahore, and from there finally to Mianwali. When we reached Lahore I cannot say, because the border wasn't as it is now. There were no fortifications. We saw gunmen and army officials, and that was it. That was the border. But as we drove through Lahore, it became impossible to recognize the city I had once lived in for so many years. Mall Road was painted with flames, the buildings were burning, there were blockages all over the city. Sikhs and Hindus had barricaded certain roads with bullock carts, upon which were heaped entire households— furniture, bags of grain and sometimes even their children, *bache-*

vache, sitting atop the mountains of belongings, unaware of and unprepared for the journey that lay ahead.'

She paused and looked down at the photograph still cradled in her right hand.

'We had become enemies all of a sudden. I still don't understand; despite having lived through it, I cannot explain exactly what happened at that time. It was as though we were living through some awful dream…' She let her voice linger in the silence of the room, infusing it with hurt, confusion and grief. 'But it was real. Every single moment of it was real and unforgettable. And we were frightened. My husband drove the car through the violence with two young children and a wife, all the way to the middle of the new country. When we reached Mianwali, our belongings hadn't yet arrived. But still we were happy to have a roof over our heads. "*Shukar hai aa gaye*," I remember saying at that time, "thank God we have got there"— that was what we felt, relief at having arrived safely. And, quite frankly, I had no idea what was safe in those days—after having seen what humanity was capable of. Who was safe, who could be trusted, when all the men and women of Undivided India had been considered the same, brothers and sisters of the same soil, up until then?' she asked rhetorically.

'This is what astonishes me,' Shahnaz said softly. '*Angrez chale gaye*, the British left, we gained our Independence, we gained freedom. But amidst all that, we separated ourselves, divided ourselves from our own…' In the same soft, small voice, she whispered, 'Ammi, tell her about when Daddy left us to go back to India.'

'He went back?' I asked in disbelief.

'Yes, he had to,' Sitara Faiyaz Ali replied. 'He left us for a few weeks at the end of August, right after we had gotten settled in a guesthouse in Mianwali. He went back to India, to a small village called Algon near Amritsar. His mother's relatives were stranded there and he went to bring them across. But when he reached there, he saw that everyone had been murdered, and the women had fled, some hiding in the fields, some in the wells and some dragged away for marriage or other pleasures. But his cousins, uncles and aunts—they were all dead. He went around the village, checking the homes that had been ransacked or burnt, looking for any sign of life. He found a Christian boy who told him that the Sikhs had attacked Algon in search of Muslims. Then he led him to a man who he thought might still be alive. My husband checked his pulse. He was unconscious but alive, and drenched in his own blood. Mahmood. His name was Mahmood. My husband picked him up and brought him across the border and admitted him in a hospital in Lahore. He survived, but my husband's family did not.'

Her voice turned into a grave whisper as she said the next words: 'Many lives and many things were lost in the days of that August. Many things. And those that survived, well … there they are.'

* * *

She gestured towards the window at the far end of the room, where the table had been set in a rather unconventional manner. Several objects were placed neatly on a cream-coloured eyelet tablecloth embroidered with a floral pattern. I stood up and walked towards it, the two women following me. I placed both palms flat on the edge of the table, surveying the items before me, waiting in anticipating for an introduction, longing to touch but not daring to just yet.

'All of these objects came to this side of the border during the Partition,' Shahnaz said, and then after a moment corrected herself. 'Well, some of these things came *back* to this side! They are from the houses in Bharowal and Dalhousie and some from Gurgaon.'

The older woman then picked up each object individually and told me about its original ownership. Often, the way she touched the surfaces or grazed the nooks and crannies was more telling than the particularities, which she hardly lingered on. How she perceived each object; how she carried herself in the presence of these things that had come so far from their origins, and were so seemingly out of place in this modern, fast-paced world; the engravings in what was now a foreign language altogether; the handmade contours, which were marks of patience and delicate craftsmanship—this touch, these gestures were what I was most interested in. How did we handle our own tangible histories? When there are no voices telling us about their importance or associated memories, how do we then explore the physical remains of our past?

I watched as her slim fingers made their way towards the utensils and wrapped themselves around the neck of a brass vessel. She picked it up with great care, as if to display its metallic heaviness. A small circular pattern covered the entire surface, and the edge of each circle bore a dark residue of oxidation. The elegant neck of the spout curved high. She traced her index finger along the round body, all the way up to the slim neck and around the sharp spout.

'This belonged to my husband's mother.'

With that single sentence, she moved on to the next item: a pair of silver bowls. One was larger, lower and flatter, shaped like an ashtray almost. The smaller one, more conventionally bowl-shaped, had a pattern of a wreath of flowers, almost like four-leaf clovers, along the top edge. The once-brilliant silver had dulled to a faint sheen, but still the bowl looked regal and unique in its shape and form. The other bowl was plain, but for a single line drawn around its circumference.

'These are bowls cast in real silver, made in Kashmir,' she said, holding up the smaller one. It rested in the centre of her palm as her fingers fanned out to accommodate its shape. 'They were part of my trousseau that I had taken with me to Gurgaon. They came on the goods train, along with the fruit bowl.' She pointed at the filigree-patterned fruit bowl on the table. Each leaf in the pattern had been individually tended to with a fine needlepoint—to the extent that every vein in every leaf was visible.

'And what is this?' I asked, pointing at a curiously shaped object that resembled a very ornate vintage egg cup. It was a metallic cup in the shape of a lotus, each petal individually engraved with delicate patterns, held up by a stem. It was forged in a dark grey metal, likely coated. Unaware of how to hold or handle it, I simply peeked into its hollow, where I saw that the pattern of petals was replicated.

'Dessert,' said the woman, smiling. 'This was a cup used to serve dessert!'

'For a special occasion?'

She shook her head. I smiled. What a world of difference a few decades made, I thought to myself, as the ornate was now reserved for an existence behind frames of glass in china cupboards and antique cabinets, never to be opened or admired or touched.

'From the time of my wedding,' she said, patting pink silk salwar kameez. I raised an eyebrow and she beckoned me closer. 'Not the cloth, the *zari* brocade. Look at the embroidery thread, this is real silver and gold, and this is what I wore to my *nikaah*.'

As I came closer to the cloth, my face barely two inches away from its onion pink folds and buttons, I gasped. The fine silver embroidery covered the entire outfit.

'Over the years, the clothes have frayed, but the *zari* is pure, so nothing will ever happen to it! If you set this on fire, the cloth will burn completely, but the *zari* will just collect in a pile, ready to be reused again. That's how you know if the *zari* is real as well.'

'Look at this,' said Shahnaz, her fluorescent pink nails running over the second salwar kameez. A green, gold and pink pattern adorned the chest area of an ivory-coloured kurta. 'I wore this on the day of my own *nikaah*, and over the years, as the cloth has frayed, I've removed the *zari* border and sewn it on to other clothes.' Nostalgia coloured her voice and she looked at her mother, proud to be the keeper of this family heirloom.

'And then we have the old photo of the house, of course.'

'Yes…' I said, distracted still with the thoughts of luxurious clothes sewn with threads of real gold and silver to supply several generations of a family with tangible memories. 'Who lives in that house now?'

'Well, the last we heard, two brothers lived there with their families. They likely claimed it after the Partition. People who migrated from the other side either claimed many abandoned properties or the government allotted the homes to them in lieu of what they had left behind. Don't you remember, Shahnaz, when you were younger and we lived in Jhang, we were allotted a house that had once belonged to a Hindu family? It had been abandoned and many things still remained in it when we moved in. It was built in a typical Hindu style—the railings and banisters fitted with beautiful statues of dancing girls, the windows of stained glass… Do you remember?'

Shahnaz nodded, a wide smile on her lips. 'You know, many years ago, my husband and I were at a party in India, and the hosts, a Sikh couple, told us that their family used to be *zamindars* on this side of the border. At the time of the Partition, as they migrated to India, they had to leave everything behind in their large *havelis*, but the men … the men hid in the folds of their turbans whatever little they could—valuables, jewellery, items that could be sold when they got across, money, anything small that would fit. People did everything they could at that time to guarantee they would have something when they got to the other side. Like Ammi said, we were lucky that we had a vehicle and that our possessions had been put on the goods train, but if not for that, we also would have nothing…'

Her gentle-faced mother told me that meeting me had reminded her of the past. '*Hindustan yaad aa gaya*, I remember so many things about it so vividly now.'

'Do you not think about it otherwise,' I asked, curious, 'when you touch these objects?'

'We hardly ever take out these objects,' she said sadly, 'hardly ever. But sometimes, like I said, when I close my eyes, I can see the Dalhousie house. Yes, that is as clear as the sky.'

Shahnaz held her mother's hand tightly, her touch a comfort, complementing and encouraging the occasional novelty of visiting the past. Her deep yellow dupatta reminded me of the wheat fields of Lyallpur her mother had described at the beginning of the conversation.

'It is not always possible to remember everything,' she said. 'Gradually you forget the things you never thought you could. Things that were once so deeply embedded in you—a house, a landscape, a possession.' She looked straight at me, still holding on to her mother's hand. 'Time swallows the past, life folds over it. Eventually. Seamlessly.'

19

THE MUSICAL SOLACE
IN MY MOTHER'S PRAYERS

THE GURU GRANTH SAHIB OF SUMITRA KAPUR

'So, YOU ARE HERE to ask me about the past,' she remarked as I walked in. The room was bathed in a deep yellow light of the mid-afternoon sun, the golden rays illuminating wisps of hair that had escaped from under her dupatta to fall around her face. This gave her frame a brilliant sheen as she sat with her back to the door on a low stool by the window. Positioned before her, its pages protected by green and golden fabric, was the Guru Granth Sahib. As I sat down, she gave me a warm smile, one hand reaching out to stroke my cheek and the other resting firmly on the holy book.

'Yes … well, whatever you remember of it.' I offered.

'Oh, I remember everything about my life, ever since I was five years old!'

'How come?' I asked, taken aback.

'That was around the time I began playing music, and I use music as a peg to recall all my life events. What I learnt in school, where we lived, the things I used to enjoy doing—in my memory, everything has always been in parallel with music,' she said in refined English, with a charming accent that went back to the twilight years of the Raj.

Her dupatta slipped off her head and she quickly readjusted it so it would go back to sit atop her lush brown curls. The wife of a former army officer, Sumitra Kapur carried herself with an air of natural grace. Dressed in classic shades of light blue and cream, she wore a salwar kameez with thick Kashmiri embroidery down the front and a cable-knit cardigan buttoned over it. She had no jewellery on except a pair of diamond stud earrings.

'You see, I was born in Rawalpindi in 1929 into a family of musicians and lived there until I was eighteen years old—until the Partition, that is. My father used to work for the railways. Since I was the second youngest child, I only remember him as being much older, retired. My mother, Biji, was his second wife and about twenty years younger than him.'

'How many siblings did you have, Aunty?' My paternal aunt's mother-in-law, she had always been 'Aunty' to me.

'We were four sisters and three brothers. The eldest brother and sister were from my father's first marriage. When I was born, they were already married! The brother was a professor at Lahore College—a Sanskrit scholar with a doctorate in the ancient language of Pali. The sister, I think, was married at a young age to a man from a town called Haripur near Islamabad. Unfortunately, the marriage did not last long, as her husband passed away just five or six years later.

'I still remember when the telegram arrived, notifying us of his death. I can still see my mother walking to the door and receiving the note. That was the day I realized that for my mother all of us children were equal, step or not. How she cried for my eldest sister—those tears I can never forget.'

She looked up at me and continued, 'You see, she had something in common with my older siblings. They had lost their mother at a young age, and my mother, being an orphan, understood how that felt. Throughout her life, she strove to treat every single one of us the same, to love us all equally and dearly.'

As she said this, she smiled, her hand still resting on the holy book and her fingers dancing across the fraying corners of the green fabric.

'Tell me more about music ... did your parents encourage you? Did you play any instruments?' I asked, curious about the peculiar way she collated the years of her life.

'Music,' she said and paused, smiling to herself. She then sighed in a purposeful way, as if to clear the air around her for nothing but musical notes.

'I would have to say that I've always had a special relationship with music. It has been the only constant in my life, and I gravitated towards it naturally. I don't think it's something I can explain very well, but I feel this connection to its notes. It's visceral, and in that I think music has this ability to physically move me—us.' She paused, tilted her head to one side and smiled.

'Like a dance, I move with the music and it moves in me. It is the only thing that I understand and that understands me completely, and it has always been this way. Even when I was a child, I was able to effortlessly sing any song I heard or play any instrument I spent enough time with. True, I might have not been very good in the beginning, but I was a very fast learner and became quite skilled. And you are right—it *was* our parents who encouraged us! Our house was full of instruments; they were prized possessions. My siblings and I were exposed to everything from the sitar to the violin, the piano, harmonium, tabla and even the banjo!'

She lifted her hands and jovially demonstrated how a banjo was played differently from the guitar, strumming the air with her left hand.

'I began performing at the neighbourhood mandirs, gurudwaras and even the Arya Samaj at a very young age.[1] My stepbrother used to have a very close friend, Mr Ram Avtar, who was a musician and lyricist. He would write and compose the songs and I would sing them at various venues and competitions. Many places like the gurudwara would give small amounts as prize money, but I remember distinctly I was never allowed to bring that money home. My parents had taught me that whatever you receive, you give back to the gurudwara, back to your community.

'At home, my siblings and I would often practise together. I would play the harmonium, my sister the sitar, my other sister the tabla, and the fourth played the flute and harmonica beautifully. It came so naturally to all of us. The ability to express ourselves through music was ingrained in us, and so all of us grasped songs, notes and the very nature of sound with ease.'

Suddenly she began giggling.

'Now this I must tell you! My elder sister and I went to the American Mission School and we would walk back home together every day. As the corner of our street approached, I remember we would race each other home. Do you know why? Because both of us wanted to be the first to play the pedal harmonium! Sometimes the road hadn't even turned yet and she would begin running, zipping past me! We both loved that harmonium and at times we would play it for two hours each. It is a little different from the regular harmonium; it is operated by foot and so much fun to play! Oh, I tell you … music always lingered in the air around us.'

She broke into a cough and I fetched her a glass of hot water. 'I get very excited when I remember my childhood,' she said between sips, 'as you can probably tell. And while my memory is still quite sharp, it is ageing that has become the impediment to narrating the past. See how quickly my throat has become *khusk*, completely dry…'

I smiled and told her to take her time; reminiscence was no race. After she had had some more of the hot water, I asked, 'What else do you remember of your childhood, Aunty?'

'Oh… I remember many, many things!' she said brightly. 'Even when we were not practising music, my siblings and I would spend a lot of time together. As children, all of us sisters were very fond of curly hair. It would look so lovely and bouncy. But there were no curling irons or curlers in those days…

'Now, our mother would go to the gurudwara every Sunday and in her absence we were expected to do our homework. But what we really used to do was sit and curl our hair. We would warm up the *silai*, the long knitting needles, wrap our hair around them, and the heat would style it! We lived in a double-storey house and our youngest brother would stand guard at the window. The moment he saw our mother returning, he would shout out, "Biji is coming! Biji is coming," and we would scramble to remove the hot needles from our hair! On her return, she would always see us sitting with our books. But every time she claimed she smelled burning hair, we would giggle behind our books! Oh, she would always say, "I know what you do when I'm gone! *Shararat karte ho*! Naughty children!" She never scolded us but there was no doubt she knew what we were up to.' She threw her head back and laughed.

I couldn't help but notice her hair then. Delicate, round curls framed her elegant face. Still chuckling, she touched them lightly.

Then Aunty's tone grew serious, less playful. 'The other thing I recall very distinctly is that our mother was extremely particular about our education. The area where we lived saw a lot of girls getting married at a young age. Our neighbours would often ask Biji why she bothered so much with our schooling. "They don't have to work, anyway. You have four girls—just get them married off into good households and they will be set," they would say to her repeatedly.'

'Why do you think she was so particular?'

'Well, for a number of reasons, the foremost among them being my eldest sister, the stepsister. It is funny that our neighbours claimed that girls "only" had to be married off and so needn't study, which was exactly what happened to my sister, who was wed at the age of fourteen. But when her husband died soon after, she was sent back to our home and couldn't do anything due to her lack of education. Biji then enrolled her in a teachers' college so she could study and work, be able to stand on her own two feet. After that, she ensured that every single one of her children received the adequate amount of education, curricular or otherwise. Whether it was song, dance, drama, sports—she wanted her children to participate, never differentiating between daughters and sons.'

Her voice exuded sheer pride in her mother, in how farsighted and liberal a woman she had been.

'A professional qualification was important to Biji—to both my parents, actually. As I mentioned earlier, my father worked in the railways with British officers, and he always admired how educated they were, how elegantly they carried themselves and how well they spoke English. So he decided that all his children would speak English and embrace a more refined lifestyle. As for my mother, I remember her words so clearly. "Unless they can live life independently, I will not marry the girls," she would say often.

'You know, a major factor that led her to put stress on education was the fact that she was an orphan herself and couldn't study after class eight. She was from Haripur, and in her youth there she befriended a woman in the gurudwara who was six years older than her: Behen Ram-ji, she always called her. My mother treated her like an elder sister. Her family was very well educated and polished, and Biji spent a lot of time with them. Seeing her read the newspaper or pick up sweater patterns to knit from magazines, my mother was inspired to learn.

'So she studied and made us study as well. Two of my elder sisters and I trained to become teachers. One went on to work as the headmistress of a school in Quetta and moved there with our father. This was much before the Partition. In those days, families would not allow girls to live alone away from home. With our father now retired, for a while she became the sole breadwinner of the family.'

'You said you lived in Rawalpindi until the Partition. But it is now in Pakistan. So, what happened in 1947? How did your family move from there?'

'Now, before we get to the Partition, I should tell you that this sister of mine who worked in Quetta applied for a job in Shimla as tutor to the daughters of the Maharaja of Faridkot. It was a reputed job, very well paid. She would be tutoring the two young princesses. She would spend the six summer months in Shimla and the remaining six in Faridkot in Punjab. Since my sister was unmarried and able to move around for work, she applied for the job and was hired! We lived like lords whenever we visited her!'

* * *

The mention of the popular hill station brought her to the summer of 1947.

'I was around eighteen. It was May, our exams were over and we were travelling to Shimla for a few months, away from the heat and humidity of Rawalpindi,' she said. 'Keep in mind, Partition had not yet happened and we thought we were just going for our summer holidays, so all we had brought were some nice clothes and light sweaters for the cool mountain air. My mother packed some jewellery to go with her more fancy outfits, but for the most part we had nothing of value.'

I hung on to Aunty's every word as she narrated her specific memory of the events of that year. In the course of writing this book, I had become privy to many people's experiences of the Partition, and each one had captivated me. Each story dug a little deeper towards the epicentre, each memory unearthed a new perspective. I had often imagined the Partition as a ball of yarn, held together tightly by the lives of the various people it affected, unravelling ever so slightly with the narration of each experience. Every act of violence, every village destroyed, every hasty departure and every life saved helped me make sense of the cataclysmic event.

'For the most part, I suppose we were lucky,' she spoke softly. 'We made it out alive even before any of the violence began. But yes, we only had clothes with us. You see, we went there thinking we would spend a few months and return. In the meantime, the country was divided. And we were stranded in India—although at the time we thought it was only temporary. No one really believed that we would never be able to go back to Rawalpindi.'

'What do you mean?'

'We loved our city, our neighbourhood. We were born and brought up on that land—so what if it now had a new name? We just figured we would now live in this country called Pakistan. I remember our father saying over and over at the time, "*Hum wapas jayenge*, we will go back, of course we will. Let this violence die down and then we will return." He said it with such conviction too—not a shred of doubt in his voice, which of course was reason enough for the rest of us not to worry. We did not mind living among Muslims, it made no difference to us. We had lived among Hindus, Muslims and Sikhs our whole lives without ever acknowledging the difference. But going back ... that was the only thing that made sense, for that was our home.'

After a moment, she added, 'You do understand what I'm trying to say, right? Home. *Humari mitti*, our land. That was the only place we knew as *our* own.'

I nodded. I did understand. The borders were meant to be open so that citizens could roam freely between the two countries, at least initially. The general understanding was that, even if people found themselves in a country that did not recognize theirs as the majority religion, they could continue to live there if they so desired. It seemed the most natural thing.[2] No one anticipated the onslaught of violence that followed, forcing people to change their citizenship so abruptly.

'Home for us became Shimla, then. We stayed for a while with our sister and then moved to a rented flat,' she said, stressing the word 'rented'. 'My parents lived in that house until they died. They always said, "*Sab kuch toh chhod aye*, we left everything behind in Rawalpindi. We will not buy any more property. Neither do we feel the need, nor do we have the means."

'The jewellery our mother had brought with her was sold, and with that money we completed our education. Otherwise, there was not really a source of income for us, except my sister who continued to work as a tutor. Although, I don't think that mattered much; money was never too important for us as long as we were able to survive. We were all together, alive and educated.

So, for the most part, the atmosphere in our house at the time was surprisingly positive despite all that was happening in the country.'

'So how was it that you found out that the country had been partitioned?' I asked.

'Yes, yes, I will tell you. You see, we were in Mashobra in a compound privately owned by the Maharaja, so we were safe. We did not experience the violence that the people of Shimla did. If riots broke out there, we were not witness to them, which is why I said we were lucky. We actually found out that the Partition had happened in the most mundane of ways. Every week, vendors would come from Shimla to Mashobra to sell their fresh fruits and vegetables. When they stopped at the estate that week, they informed us that the country had been divided! "*Batwara ho gaya*," they told us casually. Imagine that, we didn't even have a radio!'

I gave her a surprised smile and she giggled in return.

'I know, it sounds strange to think of it this way now—such important news being delivered by the fruit and vegetable-*walla*. But that is how it was during those days. In fact, when Gandhi-ji was assassinated in 1948, we did not come to know of it until our postman told us: "*Aaj ki khabar hai*, it's today's news, Gandhi-ji has been assassinated!" The postmen often spread news like this since they went door to door.'

Her voice dropped to a whisper. 'I remember running to my mother with the news, "Biji, Biji, the postman said Gandhi-ji *ko maar diya*, they have killed him." I had no idea who "they" were. All I knew was that on hearing the news, my mother's eyes immediately welled up. I will never forget how sad she was that day.'

She fell silent, and my attention turned to the holy book sitting before her. With her fingers delicately grazing its frail pages, she spoke.

'A neighbour of ours from Rawalpindi had also moved to India a few weeks before the Partition took place—to *Dilli*, I think. But in August 1947 he travelled to Shimla, looking for us. I can still picture him sitting in the majestic living room of the Maharaja's guest cottage, sipping chai from dainty cups. The kids had sat on the ground and the adults on the sofas, and with a note of steadfast determination he had said to my mother, "*Biji, mein wapas ja raha hoon*, I am going back to Rawalpindi. I must go. I have kept some money safe in the walls of my house before I left—Rs 10,000, hidden even from my servants, and now I need that money to start a new life here. I must go back."

'In those days, Rs 10,000 was a lot of money, you see! The reason why he came to us all the way from *Dilli* was to know whether we wanted him to bring anything from our house in Rawalpindi. The gesture warmed her deeply, and she looked at him and said, "Baba-ji, only Baba-ji." She wanted nothing else.' With one dainty hand, Aunty patted the Guru Granth Sahib before her.

'He was a handsome man—broad-shouldered, tall, fair, really *gora chitta* and looked like a typical Pathan.[3] In those days, everyone wore a turban, so it was hard to tell at times whether a man was Hindu, Muslim or Sikh. So, in September 1947, Roshan Lal Khanna changed his name to Roshan Din and travelled across the border to our birthplace. He went to his home, found his money still hidden in the wall and packed it safely in his luggage. Then he went to our house and found that a Muslim family now lived in it. Explaining the situation to them, he asked if there was any chance the holy book had survived the Partition. The family welcomed him in and led him to the back room that had once served as our prayer room.

'Before we left, we had locked the book—Guru Baba-ji, as my mother called it—in a small trunk, as we always did when we were leaving the house for a long period of time. Roshan Lal opened the door to the prayer room and found the trunk still locked, the room completely untouched by time or the communal violence outside. The family was happy to give him the book; they were very decent people.

Along with that he took an old table clock—the antique kind that rang every half hour. "*Bauji ki nishani*," he said, a memento for my father. It was made in America, and the year engraved on its back was 1874, I still remember. So he packed the small trunk and the clock in his suitcase and brought it back to us!'

'How come that was the only thing she asked for? Was your family Sikh?' I asked.

'No, *beta*, we were Hindu. But before the Partition, Hindu, Sikh, Muslim … how did it matter?' she shrugged. 'Everyone mixed with each other and visited the mandir, gurudwara and masjid without any problems. Those were our values, our *sanskar*. I also think that since my mother was an orphan, whoever took care of her as a child might have taken her to the gurudwara, so she really believed in the teachings of the faith. And her friend Behen Ram-ji was definitely a Sikhni, and my mother was quite influenced by her as well. Biji had always been in the habit of going to the gurudwara as well as reading the Guru Granth Sahib at home; she had been able to read the Gurmukhi language since childhood. So when Roshan Lal asked her what she wanted, this book was all she asked for.

'When he came back to Shimla to return the book, we asked him about the house and the neighbourhood—what had happened, what still survived and all that was lost.'

I looked at her expectantly.

'I think what my father had wanted to hear was that things weren't as bad, that what we had heard over the past few weeks from fruit-*wallas* and postmen wasn't true of Rawalpindi, that life had remained the same. He had longed to hear that somehow his Pindi was frozen in a pre-Partition time.'

'But that wasn't the case, was it?'

'No. In fact, it was a miracle Roshan Lal was able to slip past the authorities and travel back unnoticed. He told us that all the old Hindu and Sikh families in the neighbourhood had disappeared completely. He told us about the new occupants of our home. Then he mentioned something that none of us had known, told to him by a man on the journey back to India. Earlier that year, parts of Rawalpindi, especially the areas around Tehsil Kahuta, had witnessed the worst kind of communal riots between Hindus, Muslims and Sikhs.[4] What he described was horrifying, yet at the same time all of us were thankful to have been completely unaware of and unharmed by atrocities that had occurred so close to our home.'

A long silence enveloped the room, and hesitantly I broke it. 'So did you ever miss your life in Pindi then?'

'Oh yes, very often. What I missed was our standard of living. My father was a retired railway official and so we had quite a comfortable life. We often thought about our house and all the musical instruments there. And although we continued to play music in Shimla, it was not the same. I missed singing in the mandirs and gurudwaras. I missed that pedal harmonium. But still I was glad we continued to play because it was important to us. It not only took our minds off the fact that we could never go home, but also brought us all closer together.' She smiled.

'My mother missed visiting the gurudwara in our neighbourhood in Rawalpindi. She soon got Baba-ji, which made it better, but it was still not the same, you know. Home is home.'

'And how did the book come to you?'

'When my mother died, the book actually went to my eldest sister—she lives in north Delhi—because they have a prayer room in their house. After a while she told me, "I don't read it often but I know you are very fond of it, so you should keep it." It's been many, many years that the book has been with me now. I have been in the habit of reading Baba-ji since childhood. I have been seeing this book in my home since I was four or five years old. We didn't get breakfast without praying to it first. It was routine: wake up, get ready, pay your respects and say your prayer, and only then would you get your breakfast and milk and go to school.'

'Then perhaps it was just always meant to find a place in your home.'

'Yes, I think so too. Old things, the remains of our life in Rawalpindi, they hold our history…' she began, looking at the type, reading out the information about the book's publication. It was all in the Gurmukhi script, the Sikh script in which the Guru Granth Sahib is written, but she read it effortlessly.

Turning the pages, she exclaimed, 'Oho! I thought this was the year of publication! But no, this is just the address of the publisher! It must be somewhere over eighty years old now because the pages—come here, look at them—they are so delicate, they have become thin and frail over the years. When you touch them, you can feel their age.'

I put my camera down and came over from where I had been photographing her reading. Carefully, I placed my hand on the open page. Its texture was soft, like worn-out newsprint that had lost its crispness to the passing years. I could imagine the pages originally being deeply golden, but they had now faded to a dull ochre. A decorative red border adorned each page and encased the text within. The black letters stood out, as if they sat on top of the page instead of seeping into it. I could feel each word as my hand brushed over the page.

I tried to compare the Gurmukhi script with that of Hindi. When spoken, the two languages could sound similar, depending on the phrases or the dialect, but they were different when written. Hindi to me was precise, each word complete and almost cut to perfection in its representation. Gurmukhi, on the other hand, looked more organic, fluid. The letters were rounded and grew out of each other instead of sitting distinctly in their assigned space. And since I couldn't decipher the words, the script seemed ornately artistic and abstract. The book itself was thick and hardbound. Considering the years and the travel it had endured, its condition was exceptional. In a few places there were tears and cuts that had been carefully taped up.

'The pages are old, my dear; they tear quite easily now. But I did the best I could to fix them,' Aunty smiled.

'How did your mother acquire this book?'

'Oh, she brought it from Amritsar before I was born.'

'And you still read it?'

'Yes, yes. My husband passed away just recently, and I read it from beginning to end; I've only just finished it. The *paath*, the reading, doesn't have to be continuous, but should conclude within ten days of the death. People would usually go to the gurudwara and tell the *bhai-jis* there to do it, but I didn't want to. I can do it myself, so I'd rather do it at home. It feels more intimate this way. These prayers were taught to us at home. Our parents wanted us to know all the languages around us—Hindi, Urdu, Gurmukhi—and as children we could recite short prayers in all these languages. They instilled such wonderful values in us, *beta*.'

'Is this how you would usually keep the book?' It sat atop a small wooden cot.

'People generally keep it in a room by itself, but I don't have a spare one, so I keep it here, close to me. After I finish reading for the day, I close it and cover it with this fabric, Baba-ji's *rumaal*.' She gestured to the lush green and golden fabric that was spread out under the book.

I remarked how peaceful our surroundings seemed at that moment, in the presence of the book.

'Indeed, it is very peaceful to read it. *Gyaan*, knowledge, this is what the book is all about. It provides us with the knowledge to remember the name of god.'

Then, she began reading a few verses from the book. Her voice was strong, and she stopped to explain certain words to me from time to time. It sounded like a story, one that was meant to teach. Indeed, it seemed to be all a question of knowledge. She faltered a few times but always picked up and carried on without hesitation. Enunciating each word, her tone became gradually musical, but still it was a more straightforward reading than I had heard at the gurudwara. She didn't sing the words, but rather read them with rhythm. Though I didn't understand much, I listened all the same. In some parts her voice became softer and she suddenly spoke to me in Hindi: 'This part, it means that whoever remembers god will have good fortune...'

As she read, her index finger traced each word. It could only be a habit born of years of practice. The book seemed to be a living and breathing thing, something whose pages held the knowledge she craved, something that her parents deemed important. By touching those words, by touching each syllable she spoke, this knowledge seemed to pass through her.

The air around us was calm, the room still bathed in the golden light. The lace curtains created shadows on the wall opposite the window and on the keyboard that stood against it. I closed my eyes and concentrated only on the rhythm of her voice. She read as though she found solace in the words, as if there was belief in them. Her voice was raspy, husky, but always attentive to its tone. It lilted as she read, sometimes fast and sometimes slower, but for the most part her pace remained consistent and unchanging.

The recitation could almost be a song, I thought. Eventually, things do come full circle. Her life, as she had said at the start of our conversation, had unfolded in step with music. It was only fitting that music would be her companion in her old age too.

20

A CONVERSATION OF ERODED MEMORY

THE IDENTIFICATION CERTIFICATES
OF SUNIL CHANDRA SANYAL

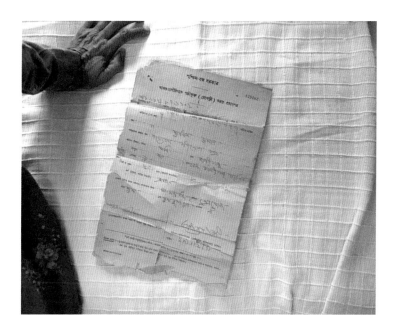

'AN OLD SUITCASE,' SHE said, her arms outstretched, '*itna bada*, this big. It was made of leather that had perhaps once been shiny and firm, but was now worn and shabby. *Bilkul toota-phoota*—completely broken, torn in places with creases across the surface, like small tributaries of a river, or a web of delicate white stretch marks. I found the documents in that suitcase.'

'Where did you find it?' I asked.

'*Suno na*, I will tell you.' Bharati Sanyal leaned forward in her chair, adjusting her thick blue and pink shawl. 'Years after I was married, I was visiting my sister-in-law's house some time in the 1980s and she showed it to me. It was just filthy because, apart from the dust and dirt that had collected over the years, there was also a cockroach nest growing inside and it was covered with little eggs and baby roaches. She asked me to see if there was anything of importance in it and, if not, she was going to throw it. So I took the whole suitcase as it was, full of cockroaches, to my mother's house. There, my husband and I slowly cleaned off all the eggs and insects, removed the cobwebs, wiped off the dirt and then we opened it.'

She clapped her hands animatedly. 'Treasure, there was a treasure inside that suitcase! We took out many old documents, faded and worn pieces of parchment. My father-in-law's matriculation certificate from 1913 as a student in East Bengal, a letter written by my husband when he was only ten years old, and other things. It was the suitcase my in-laws had brought with them when they crossed the border.'

My eyes widened. Her husband, Sunil Chandra Sanyal, smiled and nodded, not saying a word. 'I have brought everything out of the locker to show you,' she said, indicating the precious nature of her findings.

'Your husband was born across the border?' I gestured to the quiet man.

'Yes, in what is now Bangladesh. He does not talk about it much any more, though. It's his recent illness: three cerebral attacks that have eroded his memory, eaten away all the years he once held dear. It is not that he has forgotten ... it's just that he can no longer remember. Even languages have become difficult to grasp. He understands Hindi and English, but mostly only speaks in Bangla now. But I will tell you what you want to know ... *I* remember,' she said confidently.

'How do you remember?'

She laughed. 'He used to tell me things—many, many things—about his life before they migrated to Calcutta. Repeatedly he would narrate the same incidents and I would never tire of listening. Many years ago, I even wrote a poem based on his memories. But what I am trying to tell you is that whatever he remembered then is forgotten now. So I have no choice but to remember for him. How else will memory be passed down, how else will our children know of it? You see, the details of years have blurred into each other, making his mind cloudy.' Slowly she placed her palm over his and smiled. 'But I remember. I remember for him.'

There was always, I thought to myself, a division of family history between its members. Who inherits which details, which anecdotes settle down in whose memory, and who narrates which story was the result of an unspoken, natural allocation of the past.

Here was a man whose past visited him only sporadically, as isolated instances of a life he had once lived. And so it was his wife who filled in the gaps. She was the one who narrated his past, and through this interaction I learnt of the migratory nature of memory. What he had forgotten, she held on to. Not for nostalgia or sentimentality, but for the sheer need to archive. She had become the reservoir and carrier of family history. That afternoon, in the dimly lit living room of their home in Behala, an old and quiet neighbourhood of Kolkata, we began a conversation complex and amalgamated, made up of various languages, voices and gestures. Their daughter Sangita and I mostly listened to the couple, who tried to piece together a faded past.

* * *

'*Inka janam* … his birth?' I asked, and my eyes searched those of the old man.

'On 29 September 1941 in Susang Durgapur village in Mymensingh *zila*,' his wife replied promptly. These were facts she knew by heart. 'He lived there until 1948 and then migrated with his family from East to West Bengal. They were six brothers and one sister, who was already married in Dhaka. My husband is the youngest. The predicament there was such that it was becoming difficult to keep the ladies of the family safe. There were no riots as such, but the air was heavy with anxiety. There were isolated instances of mobs breaking into people's homes and creating a ruckus, but no real fatalities. This is what I have heard from Sasuma, my mother-in-law. My husband's elder brothers were married with wives, and so the family was naturally concerned. The Partition had already happened one year earlier, and they had continued to live in East Pakistan through it. But perhaps something happened, it must have become difficult to remain, and so they took the decision to leave…'

On hearing familiar words, Sunil Chandra Sanyal began speaking in swift Bangla. His wife responded, their daughter intervened, and I found it difficult to comprehend the chaotic conversation. My eyes frantically moved from one voice to another. Sangita asked her father questions and he calmly responded '*haan*' or '*na*', confirming details. If I listened very carefully, I could extract words of English and Hindi from the dialogue. I could understand the names of towns and cities. 'Shillong,' he said at one point, his hands drawing a meandering route in the air, then something about '*ma-baba*', and then the word of all words, '*Bharat*', India.

'Yes, 1948,' his wife finally said to me, 'they left in 1948. He remembers the station being quite a distance from the house, 10 to 15 miles almost, and just beside it was a river. First they stopped in Dhaka and picked up his eldest sister, *didi*, and her family and then arrived in Calcutta. Their mother dropped the children to safety and then went back to East Pakistan to their father. I asked him why they had come and he said that he was too young to consider the reasons. He was only seven years old, after all.'

'Where did he think they were going?'

He looked at me, seeming to have understood my question, and started answering. But his wife stopped him, shook her head gently and began explaining. '*Suno*, listen, when the Partition happened...'

He nodded systematically, waited until she had finished and then said in Bangla, '*Amar kichu mone nei, ami mone korchilam ami berate eshechi.*'

'He doesn't remember anything, he thought he had come on vacation, *ghoomne*,' she translated. 'Their uncle was based in the Bansdroni area of Calcutta and so they stayed with him. But he was certain that soon they would go back to their own village...'

'I didn't know anything...' he said finally in Hindi.

'Can you ask him what they brought with them? If they had planned to leave and it was still safe to leave, what did they bring with them?'

'What did you bring with you when you came to Calcutta?' she asked him in Bangla. His voice was serene and calm as he answered. I looked expectantly at his daughter. Sangita smiled and told me, 'Baba says he came with a lot of happiness in his heart!'

Immediately, my face too broke into a smile and I thought of the sweet, unadulterated innocence of childhood.

'You see,' his wife began, 'he loves Calcutta, feels grateful to be here, to have moved here. But at the time he didn't understand, and so he was happy thinking it was a vacation. It was that simple.' Not wanting to deviate from the question, she tried again. '*Na na*, what things did you bring? Did you only manage to bring clothes? Didn't you manage to bring anything else?'

He looked at her, confused.

'*Jinish?* Things?' she repeated, her voice now anxious. 'What about your luggage? *Saamaan?*'

'Train-*e kore eshechilam…*' he offered.

She sighed and turned to me. 'He does not remember … he just said that they came on a train. What I have heard from my mother-in-law is that the majority of their belongings remained with her husband at home. She had hoped that they would not have to move permanently, that the family could go back to their village when the disturbances subsided. But, just in case, during her short stay in Calcutta, she purchased a plot of land near her brother's home. The children most likely only brought clothes. They couldn't bring anything big or valuable.'

I nodded, thinking about the leather suitcase that Sunil Chandra Sanyal's parents had finally brought the following year. This big, she had shown me, it was only this big. How much stuff could a suitcase of that size hold, and how would they have determined what it would be? There were so many questions I wanted to ask the man whose memory had left him. I watched as he leaned on the wall, silhouetted against the light. He was a small man with dark skin and a round, kind face, with a long neck that bore the folds of many wrinkles, reminding me of the little white tributaries in the old suitcase his wife had described. His demeanour still seemed to be that of a boy, youthful and pure. '*Bachpan*, what was your childhood like?' I asked him in Hindi.

'Back then, I could not … I could not…' his voice trailed off and then he picked up in Bangla.

'Baba could not read or write, he says,' Sangita said, and then asked him the question again.

Bachpan. Childhood. He sat silently, as if thinking about it. Then he spoke for a long time, longer than I would have expected, slowly at first and then more confidently. His words became free and his gestures animated and graceful, as if the many things forgotten at the back of his mind had suddenly dislodged themselves and come to the fore. Had the barrier been broken? I wondered. Had the forgetting been undone? Had he begun to remember?

Sometimes his wife and daughter said phrases or words that I recognized, and in this manner I pretended to follow the conversation, though I had never felt more like an outsider. They listened, transfixed at times and confused at others, and through their expressions I deduced that not everything he was recalling was chronological or even from that time. But such was the power of his soft speech and lyrical tone that, despite not understanding, I too listened. Even their cat, Strawberry, listened, his eyes glistening in the dim light. I made out words like *choli*, a blouse, *zila*, a district, and *maachh*, fish. The whole time, my gaze continued to shift from him to his wife, keenly hoping she would translate everything word for word. She obliged. Each elongated sentence and every poetic phrase in Bangla was explained to me in Hindi or English with equal sensitivity.

'*Achha, bass bass…*' said his wife, softly stopping his flow. 'That's enough.' Then, turning to me, she said sadly, 'I will tell you what he said, but only some of what he remembers is of East Bengal. Most of it is from after they had migrated to Calcutta. Sometimes it pains me to watch my husband's memory get so tangled up that, in a way, it gets unmade. Years of experiences have come undone. Then it just becomes fabrication, like a story he tells himself.'

She paused, and then revealed the greatest truth she had learnt over the years. 'The human mind is a fascinating organ, with the ability to both assist and deceive us.' With a soft laugh, she looked lovingly at her husband. 'Life has its limits, but we never think we are going to reach them. It never feels like the edge of a cliff until you've fallen off it.

'I used to wonder why he would repeatedly tell me his childhood memories, with force and vigour, holding my hand and making me listen even when I had almost memorized them. But now, after nearly twelve years of his forgetting, I realize why he did it. Was it possible that he knew that one day he would lose his ability to remember? And then how would he ever have access to the past, to the gulmohur trees in the garden, to the smell of earthy fish from the pond behind their family home? Is that why he gave them to me, transplanted them? So that they would be safe—safe with someone he trusted? Did he make me responsible for keeping his childhood alive? I really wonder…'

Sangita looked at her mother, her eyes teary, her knees bent up to her chin. With a half-smile, she said, 'He remembers that in his old neighbourhood there was a pomelo tree … quite a common citrus fruit in the area, *khatta-khatta*, very sour, and my father and his siblings would play football under the tree with the pomelo!'

Her mother laughed and continued, 'He remembers a sky-blue blouse. On the day that they were leaving the village for Calcutta, he remembers his neighbour wearing a sky-blue blouse. He also remembers the fish he would catch with his grandparents.'

Then her husband interrupted, prompting her as if he had suddenly recalled another anecdote. She listened, her hands folded behind her head and her small frame leaning back in the chair. '*Bolchhi bolchhi*, wait, wait, I will tell her,' she said.

'One day, his mother and aunt took all the children on a picnic. And as they were passing through a jungle, he remembers wishing he would see a lion!'

As soon as she finished translating, he picked up the conversation from where it was left off, and I found myself wondering about the peculiarity of languages. That was it, I thought. A good five animated minutes of Bangla had been translated into a single sentence in English. There must be so many nuanced, delicate things that were lost in the rendering from one language—long, elastic and expansive—into another language—utilitarian and concise.

My thoughts were interrupted by the mother-daughter duo talking about the family patriarch, and so I asked about that man's occupation and the family's social standing before the Partition.

'My father-in-law was a very educated man, especially for those days,' Bharati said. 'The certificate I found, the one I will show you, belongs to him. I believe he had been somehow cheated out of the family property, and the household was not doing so well. Back then, he was just a teacher in the local school. Around the same time, a man named Naresh Bahadur, who was either the king or the governor of their *zila*, was facing a lot of financial troubles due to the British officers, and he hired my father-in-law as his *muneem*, accountant. In a matter of just a few years, he brought the ruler both wealth and respect, and as a reward was given many acres of land, both to cultivate and to live on. This was how the family became quite wealthy.'

'And the Partition ... was that how they came to know of it—through his position?'

She nodded.

'Were there any riots? Does your husband remember seeing any riots?'

'*Tumi Hindu-Musalman-er* riot *kichu dekhecho?*'

'*Dekha hai.*' His response was affirmative. 'I have seen.' Confused, she asked him again, to which he replied, '*Eituku mone ache, doodh niye ashto je lokta, shey Musalman chhilo. Roj ashto. Kintu sheta je kono* problem *ami jantam na.*'

Smiling, she translated, 'He didn't even know what a riot was. He says he remembers that the milkman who came every day was a Muslim. But the fact that a Muslim was visiting the house and it was never a problem says much about how the family perceived the various religious communities, even after the Partition. He never saw a riot, but yes, when his parents left in 1949, things must have gotten worse.'

He didn't remember seeing any riots, hearing any slogans, or even most of their journey across the newly made border. He remembered only the smaller things, the strange bits of memory that, for reasons unknown, had become lodged between the folds of years. But nothing of the Partition, not a single detail, and I was surprised to learn that something as monumental as the Divide now occupied so little space in his mind.

'So how did his parents finally leave?'

'I have heard about this incident many times from my husband and my *sasu*, my mother-in-law. It was 1949 and the children were all safe in Calcutta. The only members of the family who still remained in Mymensingh *zila* were my in-laws. She told me that one night she lit the kerosene lamp that usually illuminated the rooms and left the coal stove, the *chulha*, burning so that the chimney would keep emitting smoke and make it seem as though someone was still in the house and food was still being cooked. Then, in the middle of the night, the couple fled their hometown by bullock cart for the city of Shillong, from where they got on a train to Assam and finally to Calcutta. Why exactly they left in such haste I cannot say but, like the experiences of many others who became refugees in the wake of Independence, their journey of migration, too, was…'—her voice trailed off for a moment—'… painful and disorganized and, if I can speak of the years that followed, full of lament. It was driven purely by instinct.

'They weren't able to bring much with them. My *sasu* used to tell me about the vast acres of agricultural land left behind. She would describe the beautiful ornaments that she left in the house for fear of being robbed along the journey. Just that one suitcase—that's all they brought. One suitcase full of documents and clothes.'

'*Kuch nahi laye*, they brought nothing,' her husband said, gesturing with his hands.

'My father-in-law drowned in this sadness. He fell ill and eventually died in 1952. Empty-handed, they came empty-handed, and he couldn't bear to live through such a steep fall from grace and the loss of stature. *Humara gaon, humara ghar*, our village and our home, he would weep having left them both behind. There was no other place that belonged to them—or that they belonged to. He died before I married into the family, but I have heard this from my *sasu*.'

'People who have come from East Bengal,' added Sangita, 'feel a nostalgia that is deep and dense. They are uniquely attached to the homeland, to the language, to the food, to the very feeling of being from *that* side of the border.'

'I could never understand why…' her mother spoke to the room. 'I was born here in West Bengal and I don't feel such an attachment to land or culture.'

'*Ab tak khoya nahi hai na*,' said Sangita, patting the floor on which she sat cross-legged. 'You haven't lost your land.'

'Perhaps.' Her mother nodded.

'It is difficult to leave,' I added softly, drawing from the experiences of my grandparents. 'But worse still is to live with the uncertainty of one's return.'

* * *

For a while we sat in the silence of the memories we had unknowingly inherited from our ancestors, the instances of pain and loss that had found their way into our hearts without our ever having witnessed them. Sunil Chandra Sanyal leaned against the window frame, his wife sat picking stray strands off the blue carpet, and I watched the wispy, ghostly smoke rise from the burning mosquito coil next to me.

Clearing her throat, Sangita broke the silence. 'So, would you like to see the documents?'

'Please.'

She disappeared into the next room, returning moments later with a see-through bag in her hands. The plastic had stretched out and was wrinkled in places, and within it were several faded, folded pieces of mustard-coloured paper. She extracted them very carefully, sliding each one out as if in slow motion, and placed them on the bed. Among them were several of her father's school certificates from after he had moved to Calcutta and newspaper clippings about him securing the first division in board exams. From the bottom of the pile she extracted a worn-out, fragile certificate. This belonged to her grandfather, who had died of heartbreak at the loss of East Bengal.

She carefully unfolded it, though any effort on her part to smooth out the paper was in vain. Years had compelled the fold lines to set themselves deep within the fibres of the page. The centre fold from top to bottom had been mended with Sellotape, causing the paper beneath to turn a dark ochre-brown in contrast to the otherwise light mustard. All four edges of the paper were torn, wrinkled and taped up. One corner was discoloured, and in another, words had become nearly illegible. The text was in exquisite longhand, with ink that would once have been midnight black but had faded to a dusty brown.

'Dineschandra Sanyal,' the man slowly enunciated his father's name, eyes shining with joy.

Then, holding it up delicately, Sangita began to read: "'I certify that Dineschandra Sanyal of Jamirta H.E School, aged 14 years on 1 March 1913, has duly passed the Matriculation Exam held in the month of March 1913, and is placed in the First Division. Senate House, 4 June 1913." You see, here is the signature of the registrar,' she said, pointing to an almost faded scrawl in the bottom right corner.

She handed it to me. Taking it in both hands, I held it up to the light. Rays filtered through the mustard page, making its surface appear a glowing golden colour. The tape gave the creases a glossy finish. A few words had faded and many sat between the tears, making their letters difficult to read. The certificate was conferred by the University of Calcutta, which had had many institutions under it at the time. At the bottom centre was a round seal in resplendent red ink, reading 'UNIVERSITY OF CALCUTTA* THE ADVANCEMENT OF LEARNING'.

'This was given to my father-in-law upon completing his matriculation in class ten,' her mother added.

'What did you feel when you first found this document in the suitcase?' I asked her.

'You see, the suitcase would have been thrown away if I hadn't taken it. And this certificate was a matter of pride. To be educated up to the matriculation level 103 years ago was an enormous achievement. I think he must have carried it with him to Calcutta as something he held dear, as well as a document that would serve as proof of identity. I have kept it all these years because it makes me feel close to a person I never knew. Through it, I better understand the drive for education that he inculcated in his family. This is how I became acquainted with him—by keeping something of his close to my heart.'

'And how did you feel when you opened the suitcase for the first time?'

'Immense happiness … how can I describe it to you? I didn't even think twice about the cockroaches or dirt. I just brushed them aside. When I saw what was inside, I burst out laughing with joy—I was that happy. I showed everyone what I had found. "*Dekho dekho*, look what I have found!"' she laughed.

'He passed away in 1952,' said Sangita, 'one year after Baba had written this letter to him when the two were staying with different relatives in different parts of Calcutta.' From the plastic bag she took out a small dark-brown postcard bearing the hesitant handwriting of a child in blue ink. Large-sized words were strung together in small sentences, complete with crossings-out and spelling errors. 'I was first shown this letter when I was about fourteen years old. Baba was so young when he wrote it, I was able to relate to, and could almost feel, his innocence when I held it in my hands. In it, Baba asks his father to send across any educational certificates so he can finally be admitted into a school in Calcutta.'

I smiled and picked up the thick brown postcard, turning it around, unable to recognize anything except the round postmark from Tollygunge, 1951. I put it down on the bed and looked through all the carefully laid-out papers. Picking up one, which was folded twice horizontally, I smoothed it out on the bed and peered at the fading words.

'What is this?' I presented it to the couple.

Bharati knit her eyebrows together, causing her maroon bindi to dance up and down on her forehead. Turning the page around, she looked at me, confused. 'I don't know, *maloom nahi*. I will have to read it…' Her eyes quickly scanned the page and then, taking off her wire-rimmed glasses, she sighed. 'It appears to be a registration document for displaced persons.'

'*Udbastu*…' I said.

Sangita, not understanding, said, '*Ki?*'

'Yes, exactly,' Bharati replied, taken aback by my knowledge of the word. 'Sangita… *Udbastu*, refugee, *ei shabdo ta ato purono je aami nije e bhule gechilam.*' She turned to me and repeated herself: 'It is such an old and obsolete word that I'd also forgotten it!'

She showed the document to her husband, and for a few minutes their conversation was rapid and difficult to follow. He ran his fingers over the paper, allowing his skin to caress each tear and every fold, as if he were being introduced to it for the first time. There was curiosity in his touch—something that came from either discovery or rediscovery after a prolonged period of time. His memory had eroded so irretrievably that he barely recognized the document that legitimized his status in a newly independent India.

'It has his name and his father's name, as each member of the family would have had to have a separate certificate. I will read it out for you,' said his wife, placing her index finger on the frail page. '"Government of West Bengal. [Certificate] Number: 879102. *Praman Patro*," which means proof of identity. "Registry Number: 1647. Name: Sunil Kumar, Family Head's Name: Sanyal, Dineschandra." Then it says that it was issued at a camp on Freeschool Street. Then it lists the present address, village, nearest post office, sex, age. "*Dhormo*, religion: Hindu. *Borno*, caste: Brahmin. Place where one migrated from: Mymensingh *zila*. Police station: Susang Durgapur Village. *Tarikh*, date: 9/12/1948."'

In this manner, Bharati read the full document, carefully holding both ends to prevent any further tearing. Like her husband's touch, her voice revealed an innate curiosity. With every detail she divulged, Sangita's face softened, and at the end she asked her mother, 'Baba went to the camp to get registered?'

'Yes, I suppose everyone had to,' her mother responded, 'but I wonder if he remembers it. Those early years in Calcutta were difficult as it is.'

Sangita then turned to me. 'A couple of days ago, I asked Baba about the family's situation when they came to Calcutta initially. He told me that it was a struggle but he enjoyed it. I don't know whether he said that because he doesn't remember, or whether, now that he looks back at things, even the worst of hardships seem like sweet memories. Like, if I'm going through something difficult now, in twenty years I might think that it shaped me, made me stronger…'

As she spoke, her parents continued to converse behind us, turning over each tattered document and scrutinizing every tear and fold. 'Financially my father went through a lot. He, along with his siblings, used to stay with relatives who misbehaved with them. Every day, after school, he would come home and make *thongas*, those paper bags made of newspaper. The children would sell them to earn a living. And if there was ever an egg cooked for any meal … well, it would be considered a luxury and was equally divided between everyone.'

The end of her sentence was met with silence, as the couple's conversation had also subsided. The old man had begun folding every document carefully back along its creases, laying his palms on the paper to further flatten the folds. His movements were slow and deliberate. With great care he gathered up any torn bits, any taped-up corners, and stacked up the papers in a pile. The registration certificate lay on the opposite corner of the bed and he reached out for it. Resting it gingerly on both my palms, I leaned in and handed over his identity.

His wife, watching these calculated movements, asked, '*Haingo, tomar ki mone aachhe je tomra jakhon ekhane eschhile, ei* certificate *ta banano hoechilo?*'

'She is asking whether he recalls at all the time when the registration certificate was issued,' Sangita whispered in my ear.

The old man's head moved slowly up and down. '*Haan, ektu ektu mone aachhe*. Yes, a little bit.' And then suddenly, with a knowing smile, he moved his head from left to right. 'Or maybe not. But you are here, *tumi to aachho*. You can remember the rest.'

His words, infused with gratitude and love, settled down in the sunlit room. His wife's eyes glistened as she acknowledged the sentiment, and in one swift motion she reached out and held both her husband's hands in hers.

As he went back to folding and packing up the past, she turned to me and said, 'Sometimes I think it's a good thing he longer remembers. You can't hold on to everything, that's just not possible. One has to learn to sift, weigh and then maybe forget. In his case, the forgetting has happened for unavoidable medical reasons, but maybe that's not the worst thing. Forgetting is as important as remembering. We must clear some space, let in some light. Otherwise the world would be too heavy, our hearts would be too heavy. Like his used to be before ... weighed down and overcast with longing.'

As she said these words, I imagined the world to be an over-full plate, dangerously bent in the centre with all the 'stuff' that people were holding on to, all the sifting that hadn't been done, all the dense remembering. In that moment I couldn't help but compare her husband with all the people who had silently been holding on to their pasts. People who, like him, had lived through the Partition but, unlike him, had locked away all the heaviest parts into a silence stored deep within their hearts. I thought about Sunil Chandra Sanyal's incredible lightness, his involuntarily spotless mind, and deduced that perhaps he was lucky to forget—for there existed an entire generation of the subcontinent that did not know how to.

21

PASSAGE TO FREEDOM

THE WORLDLY TRUNK OF UMA SONDHI AHMAD

'*Yahan pe rakh do*, you can put it right here.' Like a musical conductor, she directed with her hands the two people carrying a large brown trunk towards the centre of the room. Having slowly dragged it across the floor, they now lifted it using the metallic handles on both sides and placed it on top of the carpet. '*Sambhal ke*, just be careful, it's very old,' she cautioned, and then, giving the trunk a closer look, asked for a dustcloth. 'She has come just to see this,' she told them, pointing at me.

I immediately leapt from my seat and told her not to have the trunk cleaned. We would look at it as it was—aged, dusty and blanketed in layers of the past.

'Well, all right.' Uma Sondhi Ahmad adjusted her deep-brown shawl so that it covered her shoulders, placed both palms flat on top of the trunk and caressed it. As I followed her lead, the texture reminded me of a painting whose shiny veneer had flaked with the passage of time, leaving its appearance somewhat fragmented. The typically soft leather surface was worn and even discoloured in places, showing patches of the original dark brown, a rusty brick red, and specks of light camel. An ornate metallic latch was used to secure it shut. A geometric pattern sewn in the *kantha* stitch with heavy jute thread embellished the entire exterior. At the edges, the threads stuck out where the stitch had come undone, but on the whole it kept the luggage upright and shapely. I watched her pale fingers point out a beige label on the lid. The paper was badly weathered by usage and time—folded, torn, ragged, scratched—but despite all that, the text was still legible.

'"V.P. Sondhi, Geological Survey of India,"' she read out. 'Ved Pal Sondhi, that was my father. I don't know how long he had this trunk before he gave it to me in Lahore in 1945. But it has been in my memory and in Daddy's possession for as long as I can remember and I've always loved it.' She opened it slowly to reveal an interior lined with patterned fabric in beige and faded teal. 'I used it mostly for books—never clothes, always books. Along with this, he also gave me a small cupboard, which I recently gave to Diya,' she said, smiling at her granddaughter, who was seated next to me.

The trunk commanded the attention of all of us as it sat in its antiquated glory, in the centre of a beautifully furnished living room in Ballygunge, Kolkata. The sunlight created soft shadows around the box's grand shape. The trunk's base was covered in thin sheet metal, likely tin. The sides and straps were also reinforced with metal. Interestingly, despite its age, it was covered with either whole or partly torn original luggage labels. Moisture had seeped into some, laminating them right on to the wrinkles and folds of the leather below. A label on the side, resembling the one on top, read: 'V.P. SONDHI, GEOLOGICAL SURVEY OF INDIA'. But here the 'P' had torn off, as had the entire bottom left hand corner. I ran my fingers over the aged tag, impressed that most of the paper and letterpress ink had survived the years. Not far from it were the remnants of another label with the numbers '63 620' written in thick black pen. And by the handle was a series of labels, pasted one atop another over several trips, with barely readable text.

'Oh, I hadn't ever noticed those!' Uma Ahmad laughed. 'Imagine that!' Then, still smiling to herself, she laid a chain of keys on top of the trunk. Six rust-coloured, elaborately old-fashioned keys in different sizes. They were unlike any I had seen before, hollow bows fitted with lovely, rounded pieces of metal.

'One of the keys fits the lock for the trunk … these all belong to my mother.' She began trying the keys to find the right one, creating soft jangling sounds. 'I think it's the smallest one, but I've lost the lock now! My father gave me another lock once, an unusual beetle-shaped one in brass that had a swinging chain attached to it. But, for the trunk, I always just used one of these.'

I smiled back and beckoned her and Diya to the other side of the trunk. 'Where did this trunk travel before you received it?' I asked, pointing to a label stuck on sideways, half of which had been destroyed. It was more detailed than any of the others on the trunk and I began reading out loud, 'There is a serial number—No. 1817–493000–1245. And then "COM. 241 F" ... "D.R" ... and below that, "*G.I.P.R.*"'

'Great Indian Peninsular Railways, G.I.P.R.,' she offered. This British railway connected Bombay with the interior, designed to increase exports of cotton, silk, opium, sugar and spices.[1] 'Daddy always called this Camel Luggage, to be carried by a camel. He often travelled to sites in Sindh and Mohenjodaro on business.'

'Hmm.' I looked up at her briefly and then continued peering at whatever letters remained: '"TO HOWARH, FROM ... N-A-C" ... or is it G ... and then an R. Nagpur?'

'Yes, it's very possible. The thing is, I don't know how long Daddy had it before he gave it to me. It could very well have come back from Burma, or even travelled to England with him.'

'Did you grow up in these places?'

'I have grown up in many different places, depending on my father's work. Let me give you a little background,' she said, sinking into a white wicker chair on the verandah. I took a seat next to her, and Diya sat on the couch opposite.

* * *

'My father joined the Geological Survey of India (GSI) in 1926 and was its Director General from 1955 to 1958,' Uma Ahmad said, handing me an oval wooden photo frame. A handsome young man in sepia looked back at me. Looking to the left, he had been photographed in profile, wearing a smart jacket and tie. The

411

portrait had a bottle-green cloth frame, around which was a polished wooden one. As I held it out to the light, she handed me its companion. A woman, seated towards the right, also in profile, eyes downcast, wearing a sari, with the *pallu* covering her head and pinned in place at the shoulder.

'My mother, Vidya Vati Sondhi. She was married at the age of fourteen, although, because my father was studying at the time, she didn't come to live with him until four or five years after that. Oh, I remember this sari she's wearing here: soft silk, beige, with lovely lemon flowers. These portraits would have been taken in Jullundur some time in the late 1930s, before we left for England, I think. But I'm getting ahead of myself. Let's start at the beginning.

'My family comes from Jullundur, where I was born in 1931. I have a brother, Mohan, older than me by ten years, and a sister, Ruma, who is ten years younger. My great-uncle had this big house in the cantonment area, a little outside the main city. For the most part, everyone in the family was quite educated, and my grandfather, Bauji, was a landowner—that's where most of the income came from. The house we lived in had an open *aangan* in the centre, a yard around which all the rooms of the house were built. We children played mostly in that *aangan*, and in the summers we slept out there as well, under the starry sky. Bauji used to host many parties outside his study area, the *baithak*, and people from all parts of the Punjab were invited. Over the years, someone from the family had built a big *dharamsala*, a Hindu sanctuary, right next to our home, used mostly by travellers or pilgrims as a rest stop. We had a small fort called Kot Kishan Chand, and we also ran a school for girls, Kanya Mahavidyalaya. In any case, Jullundur became a very integral part of my life as I used to spend every vacation there with my grandparents and extended family.'

And thus, Uma Ahmad began the story of a childhood that crossed the entire subcontinent, as well as the small island of Great Britain which had ruled it for nearly two centuries. One of the first posts her father took with the GSI was in the Southern

Shan States of then British Burma, where he discovered caves full of coffins—an old burial ground—and silver mines along the Sino-Burmese boundary, among other geological investigations.[2] In early 1937, the family came back to Calcutta, where Uma was put in Loreto House and then, just a few months later, Ved Pal Sondhi was granted study leave in England for two years until the end of 1938.

'We arrived in England in 1937, only a few years before World War II broke out, but the terror had already begun to sink in,' she said. 'I was used to moving around in India, but England was in a pre-war state. Everyone at school was petrified and we were told that an evil man called Hitler wanted to conquer us. For the entirety of those two years, we were made to blacken all our windows and participate in air raid drills, hiding in the basements and securing shelter areas. Even now when I hear a siren, my heart jumps! So while Daddy was doing courses and working at various universities,[3] at home, Mummy was sewing nametags on to all of my things, including my clothes, as though I were luggage!

'And you know the most traumatic thing of all? We were all issued gas masks.[4] I believe the masks nowadays are sleeker and more compact, but in those days they were large. I was rather a small child, so everything felt larger. It was a suffocating apparatus, with a long, uncomfortable snout. These masks were issued in individual cardboard boxes, with strict instructions that they be carried at all times, without exception. Fines would even be imposed if anyone was caught without a respirator. Despite all the preparations, I don't think gas was ever eventually used on the British population. But Mummy tells me that I used to have nightmares, waking up screaming that Hitler was climbing through the window to kill me. It was … horrifying, truly, and I didn't think that's what England was going to be like, but there it was.'

'By the autumn of 1938, my father had been transferred to the N.E. Circle of the GSI and so we moved back to Calcutta, where we were given a flat in Park Mansion and I was enrolled back into Loreto House. The nuns were so welcoming, and after all that trauma of war and air raids and gas masks, it truly felt like a homecoming to me.'

She paused for a moment, looking out at the Ballygunge landscape. The *chik* curtains had been partly rolled and raised, and the January sunlight streamed in, illuminating her silver hair like a halo. 'Life was so good in Calcutta,' she said, smiling wistfully. 'It was good. But just a few years later, we had to move all over again, and this time it would truly change my life.'

* * *

'By the spring of 1942, the Japanese had all but occupied Burma, and due to its proximity, Calcutta felt well within their reach.[5] It was then that the office of the GSI temporarily shifted from Calcutta to Lahore, though, as far as I recall, my father still commuted back and forth, quite often by train. Later that year, the Japanese air force did bomb the city, but we had already left by then. We moved to Jullundur for a few months before the school year began. I was eleven and my sister Ruma was now about a year old. When we arrived at the ancestral home, Bauji and everyone insisted that I be put in some sort of classes to pass the time. Nobody spoke English like me—accent and all—not even my cousins, and so I was promptly put in the Kanya Mahavidyalaya, where I first learned some Hindi.

'Oh, oh, I must tell you this…' she began excitedly, laughing. 'My grandmother, Ma-ji, also used this time in Jullundur to "de-Westernize me"! Such a *zabardast* lady she was, very feisty. And so in Jullundur, I would always wear *khadi* salwar kameez. Around her, I learnt to cover my head, to cook, to wash clothes and utensils, all the while sitting on the ground in the outdoor kitchen. After all those years in England and with the nuns, she really made me imbibe the Indian traits that later came to define me.'

'Nani…' Diya said, looking at her grandmother, 'what was Lahore like?'

Uma Ahmad smiled. 'My dear, Lahore was the place that would eventually teach me about freedom, *azadi*,' she said. 'Since we had not yet been assigned a home there, I was enrolled at Sacred Heart Convent School as a boarder. This box I gave to you,' she said, picking up a small wooden jewellery box from beside her chair, 'I painted this box at Sacred Heart.'

'*This* is from *then?*' asked Diya, her eyes wide. 'She gave it to me only two days ago,' she told me. Though it was abraded and cracked in places, assured brush strokes had once painted its scenery of a quaint village road with a few trees and mountains in the distance. Its side was a dark charcoal grey and an ornate and copper-coloured shell-like clasp secured it shut.

'Oh yes,' Uma Ahmad continued. 'At the school, there was a very nice Belgian nun who taught art and I used to love her classes. For a particular assignment, she needed us all to bring a box to paint, and since I was a boarder, I told her that my box would come too late. At the time, my mother was in Jullundur, my father in Calcutta, so who could I ask? I was so desperate to be a part of the assignment that she gave me this plain wooden box… You see, I'm quite certain that the only reason this mundane box has survived for this long is that it was placed inside the trunk when we left Lahore,' she said, pointing to the GSI luggage that would have held her books. 'I would have stored my little trinkets in the box. It's scratched now, but still quite beautiful. I used to love it.'

Diya beamed at her.

'Eventually, we were given residence just opposite Mayo Gardens in Lahore. White House Lane, a beautiful place with lots of trees and plants. There was also, funnily enough, a cotton field somewhere in the area, and some days the entire neighbourhood would be covered in fluffy white, like in a fairytale!'

I furrowed my brow. 'I find it interesting that you arrived in Lahore at the height of the Quit India Movement, and yet you describe the city's gardens and flowers rather than the politically charged atmosphere.'

'People remember what they remember,' she said gently. 'But make no mistake, even we as teenagers were in due course drawn into the freedom movement. At the beginning, I didn't really understand what was happening—neither the struggle nor what it would mean to be free from any foreign rule—until my father's elder brother, Gyan Chand Sondhi, a *khadi-posh* freedom fighter, explained it to me. My world was so small before that,' she said, balling up her fist to show the dimensions, 'so small and so naive. All I knew was that, suddenly, one day all my beautiful silk and muslin frocks were burned in a bonfire and we were made to wear *khadi*. But he explained how the British government was ruining the Indian cloth economy by making us buy cheap cloth manufactured in England. He explained the significance of Swadesi, he told me about the Dhaka weavers, spinning beautiful *mul-mul*, who had had their thumbs cut off by the government.[6] He explained all this and more, and I understood. Teenagers are very passionate, you know, they absorb.

'Now, Gyan Chand Sondhi had a daughter, Usha, who also lived in Lahore. Oh, she was so beautiful, and everyone used to pay attention to her! She was a boarder at the Sir Ganga Ram School and used to spend weekends with us. The school was run by the famous Mrinalini Chattopadhyay, who constantly had visitors like Gandhi-ji and Pandit Nehru and Sarojini Naidu. She even often encouraged her students to participate in the activities of the freedom movement.[7] And because she was a friend of G.C. Sondhi's, naturally, she always invited his daughter, who took me along. But I would mostly just stand around and look reverently at the visitors.

'Anyway, the very first time I went there, my Hindi was still quite terrible. So my cousins and I arrive and—I almost didn't believe my eyes—Gandhi-ji was sitting right there! For some reason, he called out to me. "What's your name?" he asked in English, but I kept quiet; I was shy. And before I could actually say anything, another cousin of mine, Pushpa, declared, "*Ennu kuch ni aanda, Hindi nahi bol sakti!*", telling him that I was unable to converse in Hindi. Now, in an atmosphere where everyone was so zealously Indian, here was this creature that couldn't even speak her own language. I was pretty much ready to sink through the floor. So I just kept quiet and soon people came and began serving food and tea.

'Then suddenly he beckoned me closer, and I looked around hesitantly and literally went crawling because we were all sitting on the ground. He gave me a laddoo sweet and smiled a wide smile. And you know what he said to me? In English, he said, "My Hindi is also very bad!" Because he was a Gujarati and also probably struggling to speak. It was so sweet … I did eventually learn the *chusst*, pure Urdu during my time in Lahore. And even after I got married to a Muslim, you know, his family didn't speak the same kind of Urdu I did … they were from Bihar.'

Slowly, then, she sank back into her chair, allowing her hands to hang over the arms. Running her forefingers over her thumbs, she held them out, pale digits bearing the creases of age. 'In 1945,' she began, 'when the World War ended and the first of the Red Fort trials was under way in Delhi—of Prem Sahgal, Gurubaksh Singh Dhillon and Shah Nawaz Khan[8]—my friends and I got passionately involved, and we all pierced our thumbs with a pair of compasses. You know, like in a child's geometry set? And we put *tilaks* of blood on each other's foreheads. That was how it began, these small acts of defiance, like not standing up for 'God Save the King' after films or singing songs like "*Hindi hai hum chalis karod, mera desh chhod, chhod*"[9] and "*Jhanda ooncha rahe humara*". These were a fourteen-year-old's gestures of patriotism.

'In 1946, my father got transferred to the GSI's Bombay office and was succeeded in Lahore by a colleague whose family we were close to. We had to vacate the house for them, but I still had a year to go in school, and so Daddy suggested that I live with them while Mummy moved home to Jullundur. That's when he gave me the trunk and the cupboard, because all our other furniture was packed away and sent to Jullundur. That is the only reason this trunk has probably remained with me all these years,' she said, patting the trusty luggage.

'By now, my friends and I—a group of about eight or nine girls, mostly Muslim—had begun hearing about stray incidents of communal violence happening around the old walled city. One day, I went to my friend Nuzzat's house. She belonged to an eminent family of Lahore, and they lived in a house with a blue [dome]. When I entered, her old grandmother was presiding from a *takht* seat in the middle of the *aangan*, and she told me that if anything happened in our neighbourhood, any violence at all, we could come and stay with them, that they would protect us, that they had a cellar. "*Apni ammi nu dass de*," let your mother know, she said. I have to admit that when she said this, fear began to creep inside me as well. So many families we knew of had begun offering help like this to one another.

'But oh, before I forget, something strange happened just before my mother moved back to Jullundur. Every day, a Muslim fruit-*walla* would come to our house on a *tonga*, a horse-drawn carriage, to sell his produce. He would often give my sister and me delicious unripe mangoes. Then one day he looked up at our window and said to me in an evil tone, "How many rooms do you have in your house? I will come and live here!" I didn't exactly understand what he had meant by that, but obviously the impending Partition had started playing on people's minds. Even then, it never occurred to me that it was linked to religious communities. And the thought that we would eventually have to migrate from Lahore because of riots and violent activities never even crossed my mind. But, on the other hand,' she paused and brought her fingers to her temples, 'I have seen people with hammers and daggers and sickles and knives, and the hate in their eyes for me, for us. I have seen it. And I will never forget that madness…' She shook her head from side to side.

'What do you mean?' I asked, confused. 'Where did you see this?'

* * *

'In the early months of 1947, rumours began flying thick and fast about Partition, and my school decided that the Hindu girls could give their final matric exams earlier than usual. My mother had come back to Lahore to help me pack whatever I had, and we were to leave for Jullundur the very next day after the exam. The school arranged for a large hall, where about 500 of us girls would be writing our paper. But halfway through, the invigilators suddenly started snatching our answer papers. I was confused till they gestured for us to look out of the window.

'And then we saw them: a mob outside vaulting over the wall, carrying knives and weapons, and this man, running up to the hall, trying to break in, ready to attack us. We began hearing loud voices from outside, yelling and shouting. The girls began screaming and running out, things were happening all at once, no one knew where to go. Even the invigilators were petrified.' She waved her hands frantically in the air. 'They were hysterical, telling us to hurry up. There was uproar in the hall. And then, there was this rather large girl who used to sit behind me in exams. I don't know what school she was from but she began breathing heavily, a laboured breath—I noticed her only because of that. She just continued to stand where she was. I began running halfway down the hall, calling out to her, and she wouldn't say anything. She just stood there, frozen. "*Chalo, chalo,*" I said, grabbing her. "Let's go, we have to go." But she wouldn't move, and she was twice my size! Like a stone statue—petrified.'

Diya and I leaned in closer, holding our breaths, hanging on to every word.

'What happened then?' I asked.

'Well, she just wasn't moving, so I snatched her dupatta and said, "*Chalo,* we have to go now!" as forcefully as I could, and she ran behind me yelling, "*Haye, meri chunni, meri chunni,* my scarf," and finally came out of the hall.' She took a deep breath, her eyes wide. 'I think I saved her life. My god, I'll never forget her face.'

'Outside the hall, there was an area where people were waiting while the exam was going on—parents and all. My car was waiting there and—I am not joking when I say this—that day my car was *full* of girls.' She looked me straight in the eye and repeated, slowly enunciating each word, 'Full—of—girls! We sat atop one another, squished in the back, a few were even hanging on the side steps that old-fashioned cars used to have. I am telling you, it was horrible. Then, one by one, the girls started getting off close to their homes, and by the time I got home I was trembling. My whole body was shaking as the driver told Mummy what had happened. She took one look at me and declared that we were not staying in the city even a day longer, we were to leave that very night. "*Ajj raat di gaddi pakad ni. Ajj raat jana hai etho*," she kept saying, gathering our things. "We have to catch the train tonight, we need to leave this place tonight." We were all ready and packed for the next day, but we took the Geological Survey car that same evening and reached Jullundur.

'You know, after that incident in the exam hall, the newspapers carried a report that said the registrar had been stabbed to death and the building had been burnt down,' she said, looking at us both in angry disbelief. 'Stabbed to death! Can you believe that?'

'Did you ever think back to that day?' I asked, quietly.

'Oh yes, I would have nightmares, wake up screaming and shouting, "Mummy, Mummy, they are catching me!" In my naive head, all I thought was that in England, Hitler had wanted to catch me, and here, this marauder! But wait, there is more … I would wake up screaming about much, much worse in the months to come.'

* * *

'When we arrived in Jullundur, which had always been my safe haven, we discovered that the *dharamsala* right next to our house—we shared a common wall—had been occupied by refugees from Rawalpindi.[10] A building that was meant as a resthouse for pilgrims was given to them as a shelter, and throngs of families had settled both inside and outside the premises. Mind you, Partition had not yet happened, these were only the spring months of 1947, but these people came with the most awful stories of what had happened in their villages. The rage and frustration with which they narrated horrific incidents to us, it was awful. Women who had been raped and tortured, men who had been made to watch, children who were wounded and hurt. They would say things like, "It would have been better had I died", and "So-and-so drowned in the well". All this business that I had heard about in Lahore and had only gotten a slight taste of in the exam hall, all of it was true; these were people who had suffered exactly that. Their homes had been burnt, shops and neighbourhoods destroyed, their families killed… Every single person there had a story to tell about what they had seen and how they had escaped.'

When Uma Ahmad spoke about Jullundur, I noticed that it was mostly in the local dialect; the lilting of her voice, which rarely flickered in her pristine English, radiated in her Punjabi. Like a river, it curved with fervour, contorted into a story, performed the various voices and tones, the sadness and anger. The language of her land allowed for the unhurried expanse of every emotion. I watched her speak with her voice, her eyes and her hands to tell the tale of Jullundur.

'There was this girl…' she said, sighing deeply, her tone transforming into one of absolute heartbreak as she slowly divulged every detail. 'This girl was probably just fifteen or sixteen years old but she was expecting a child and would just continue to sit in a corner all day with a vacant stare, not saying a word. You see, I was not allowed to go to the *dharamsala* by myself. I would usually just watch from a spot on our roof. But whenever Mummy went down with food, medicines and other supplies, I would almost always be with her. Then one night there was a ruckus, we heard the commotion from the house. Sounds of "*Pakdo, pakdo*, catch them", and we thought some thief had entered the compound. Of course, I wasn't allowed to go downstairs but I went up to the rooftop and I saw that this girl was running all over the place.

'She was screaming and running, heavily pregnant, this girl, and everyone was trying to catch her. So the next morning, when Mummy went downstairs, we found out what had happened. The girl, it appeared, would suddenly sometimes become aware of her circumstances. Knowledge would dawn on her that, amidst the riots, *it* had happened to her, that she had been gang-raped, and this child she was carrying was the result. And she would weep and howl and scream and shout and try to kill herself. She was exactly my age. Imagine that, *my age*.' She shuddered at the thought. 'Her mother would tell stories of how it had happened and, oh, after listening to them, I would grow fearful of what the world was capable of and grateful to have been where I was and safe.

'I was present when she actually had the baby, right there in the *dharamsala*, and Mummy went and got baby clothes and all that. I've never seen such a beautiful baby. A boy. You know what a fuss everyone makes if it's a boy...' She turned to Diya, whose eyes were now lined with tears. 'Just think, if it had been born in a house, a normal house, under normal circumstances, how ceremonial the birth would have been. I've often wondered what would have happened to that child.'

'Did you spend a lot of time with them?' I asked through the growing lump in my throat.

'Well, like I said, I would go with Mummy, but we had to be careful. They would often catch hold of her and cry and weep. "*Hath nahi aana*, don't fall into their hands," they would tell me repeatedly. Then one day, a few ladies came from one of the houses and told us that self-defence and *charkha* classes were being offered. *Charkha*, you know? A spinning wheel. They said to my mother, "Your daughter is alone here, would you like to send her over?" So my mother said, "*Haan, ja*, go, it will be something to pass the time." In any case, after seeing the state of the people from Pindi, and not to mention what had happened to that young girl, I was ready. I needed to learn how to defend myself, should anything happen.

'Those classes were an eye-opener for me. To begin with, there was a spinning wheel in the room, but these were not your regular *charkha* or self-defence classes. Rather, they were lessons in how to defend yourself from the enemy—by taking your own life! We were given these ruler-like things with red ink on one end, and whenever the instructors made a noise, we were supposed to cut ourselves, or at least place the ruler with the red ink where we would need to cut ourselves if we were ever harmed. Then these ladies would come around and review the red marks and say, "*Nah puttar, zara oopar kari*, a little higher, a little to the side," telling us where the right artery was that we needed to cut to die immediately. They also taught Gatka, the ancient Sikh martial art practised with wooden sticks. But that was for the more advanced students, so I was stuck with my reddened ruler and it was enough to terrify me.

'After I began taking those classes, I also started sleeping with a knife under my pillow—one of Daddy's fancy Burmese ones. The training put me in such an inexplicably traumatic state that one time, on a particularly hot night when we were sleeping out in the open *aangan*, two cats began howling and fighting, and I got up and brought the knife close to me. I thought that they were rioters, I thought they had come for me—and Mummy shouted from her bed that they were just cats. She got up and calmed me down, but I could have stabbed myself that night. Easily. I had taken out the knife and placed it where they had taught me the artery was...' Her voice was firm.

Silence pervaded the room, and when she spoke again, it was in a voice from the past, suffused with distress and horror. 'They told us again and again in those classes that if something were to happen to us, our families would no longer accept us. "*Tussi wapas nahi ja paoge*," they would say. "You will never be able to go home again." And to add to it, all these refugee women from Pindi continually told me, "*Beta*, don't let them catch you." Anyway, when Mummy found out what the classes actually were, she made me stop them immediately.'

* * *

'Were you in Jullundur still when Partition happened?'

'No, we had been waiting for Daddy's younger brother, Dharam Pal Sondhi, to join us in Jullundur. He was a government official in Canal Engineering and was travelling from somewhere near Sargodha in District Gujrat, crossing the entire expanse of land that was to become Pakistan. As soon as he arrived with his family, we left for Mussoorie; that was some time around the end of June and we were there till Independence was granted. In August, we all sat around the radio and heard Pandit-ji's "Freedom at Midnight" speech and I remember us all being in tears. Pandit-ji had this emotional voice, and at last we were going to be free from the British. I have to tell you that if we blamed anyone for all this, it was the British, in a very educated way. The older uncles, especially the freedom fighter, used to make us realize that the British were squeezing us dry, and so we hated them by then. Of course, now years have passed and I have read so much about the Partition that my views have been shaped differently. But back then ... I don't even know if I realized what freedom from the British meant, or at what cost it came, but we rejoiced at Independence nonetheless. And I was in Calcutta shortly after that, back at Loreto, back under the Mother Superior who called me her "little Punjabi".'

I smiled.

Uma Ahmad leaned forward and patted the Geological Survey trunk, the object that had begun this conversation. A rough sound emanated from under her palms as she grazed its surface slowly. 'I'm actually thinking about this now for the first time,' she said with a sad chuckle, 'how much this trunk has seen, how much it has lived through. First with my father and then with me— Burma, England, Calcutta, Jullundur, Lahore. Every scratch, every label, every mark of wear and travel is...' She searched for the right word.

'A symbol?' I offered.

'Yes, indeed,' she smiled. 'Symbols, if you think about it. They speak to the places this trunk has been, the stations it has travelled through, the times it has seen, the encounters it has had, the history it has partaken in, the inheritance it has become. Oh, it's a strange realm—objects of age—they're impregnated with time, yet discreet in their existence. So many things simply go unnoticed, so many details one just takes for granted.'

She caressed the lid of the trunk and then opened it, examining the piles of saris and other clothes stored inside. For a while, no one said anything. My eyes lingered on her hands, how they touched every loose thread and every label, quiet gestures of love for a time gone by.

A few more minutes passed and then, clearing her throat, she slowly uttered five significant words.

'I never spoke about it.'

* * *

'How come?'

'I don't know, I just never did. Not to my family, not to my close friends. Not even to my husband, Mumtaz, I never told him everything. Perhaps he wouldn't have understood, as he didn't live through it. But, really, it was just too terrifying and vivid for me to talk about. Yes, I was safe and so was my family, but the world around us was changing. It was being dissected, it was bleeding, and the common man was paying the price for freedom in a way that no one imagined they would have to. It was … difficult to discuss it, to even untangle and understand it. It's only now, when I've grown older, that I feel all this might not worry me any more, that it happened too far back in the past, that I might finally shed it.'

Diya wiped her eyes and asked, 'How do you feel about it now, Nani?'

'I feel…' She thought for a moment and then, with incredible sadness, said, 'I feel that Partition divided friends and families and colleagues and people who loved one another, it really did. See, this is why I don't talk about it. It reopens something, something that cannot be changed or undone. Don't get me wrong, I am well out of that time. But I have to say that marrying a Muslim gave me access to the other side. Part of Mumtaz's family lived on that side, so we would visit every now and then, and it's not the same, but it's access, it's something...'

'It's not the same, but it's something,' I repeated, nodding.

'Well, I've gone back a few times now,' she said, brightening up at the thought of Lahore. 'The first time was in the '50s, when my sister-in-law and I had gone for a wedding. I told her that I wanted to go see my old house and school, and she was more enthusiastic than I was. It was so wonderful. We even took the same bus route that I used to take home, and part of it was through Anarkali Bazar. Aapa had forgotten to bring some toiletries and so we stopped at the little *chaurastha* where parents used to wait for their children and there were rickshaw-*wallas* and shops selling trinkets and everything.

'So we stopped at this shop and the shopkeeper took one look at us and said, "You are not from around here," and Aapa replied, "*Nahi*, we are visiting from India." And then she pointed at me and said, "*Yeh Punjabi hain.*"

'He stopped everything he was doing and asked me, "*Tussi Punjabi ho?* You are Punjabi?"

'I nodded, and he immediately told everyone in the store not to accept any money for whatever we were buying. *Meri behna*, he called us, his sisters. Then he leaned in and asked, "Where are you from?"

'"Jullundur," I said.

'And you know, I'm not joking, he became absolutely motionless. His eyes welled up and he looked at me and said, "*Bhenji*, sister, could you not have brought a handful of soil from our homeland? *Tussi mutthi-bhar mitti na ley aande?*" He was longing for the land of his birth, all he wanted was a fistful of soil from it, some *ghar ki mitti*. It was so full of pathos, so full of poignancy.

426

That day I realized that the aftermath of brutally partitioning an entire subcontinent could be reduced to just that one statement. A fistful of soil, *mutthi-bhar mitti*. Till today, how many people, on both sides of the border, have been pining for just that?'

EPILOGUE

WHAT BEGAN AS AN empty corner of a room has transformed into something of an overcrowded study. The white paint on the walls is now peeling in places from having photographs taped on and taken off every few weeks. 'If I see it in front of me, I'll be able to write better,' I say with each new object. Smiling, I recall doing the same thing years ago in the print shop when I would begin work on an engraving or lithograph. That world seems far away now as photographs of antique objects, of the people who own them, of their homes, and documents of research are carefully put up. Then, post-it notes laden with notes on ages, family trees, and dates of birth and death. And lists— many, many lists—with citations and references and question marks. The mood and landscape of the walls keep changing depending on the chapter I am writing.

The wooden vitrine, whose top surface used to be empty, is now piled high with books. Fiction and non-fiction, I find myself reading on everything from the Divide to World War II, from odd tales of the Raj—like how to order a carriage or an elephant for the day—to the letters of Christopher Beaumont, Sir Cyril Radcliffe's assistant; from texts on mnemonics and savants to various Urdu dictionaries; from instructional guides on how to weave traditional Punjabi *phulkari* to a play on the drawing of the Partition line. The tall perch that used to hold a plant now holds eighteen books, dangerously stacked.

My *sheesham* desk is cluttered. I have organized my research into piles. There are cities and there are people, and sometimes the piles transform into who migrated from India and who from Pakistan, who lived at which refugee camp and who went back to visit their home, who brought across the Basra pearls, who slipped the large lock from the *haveli*'s front door into his pocket, who treasured their father's old letters from across the border and who forgot about their mother's shawl at the back of a closet. At other times, these piles are more utilitarian, sorted into which chapters need to be edited and which audio transcriptions need to be sorted. At times, I'm embarrassed by my own ability to effortlessly sort through these various pasts. What used to feel like wading through oil has now become like swimming gracefully with the tide. 'What a strange thing to have in one's areas of expertise,' I muse, 'to be an archivist of memory and associated items.'

* * *

What I had initially given myself a few months to complete has taken the better part of my twenties from me. And, for what it's worth, I'd do it all again, though I can't explain how full my head is at times. Full of stuff that doesn't belong to me: things, names, words, languages, books, emotions, cities, stories, voices, memories. The archiving of so many lives has led me to deduce that ultimately, in these interviews, we always return to the same place; each tale evokes the same sensation of longing, the exact same tone, the words repeated almost verbatim. I feel like a palimpsest, where each new voice is softly pressed on to the last and the many become one. Yet, no matter how many times I hear the same kind of story infused with near-identical emotions, every single experience still feels unique and undeniably exceptional.

Two years into the project, one night I awake in the middle of a dream. It's the most surreal feeling: dreaming with my eyes open. For the first time, I have to locate myself in my own room. The images of the dream are uniquely bizarre and it takes me a moment to recognize them. They are fragments of interviews I've conducted over the past few weeks. Afghans ride through fields by the mountains after ransacking a village; a young woman writes a poem about the nationalist movement in Lahore; a child is saved by her mother from falling off a roof in the middle of the night as they flee; behind a locked door, a Sikh family discreetly hides their jewellery within the flooring; an Englishwoman ambles onto a refugee-packed train in Ludhiana, trying to get to Lahore with her neatly labelled attaché briefcases. And there is rain, so much rain, that I awake almost certain that my room is the epicentre of the *barsaat* season.

To prevent myself from drowning, I begin a blog. I think about all the experiences I have recorded—all the stories of unimaginable sacrifice, convenient forgetting, painful concealment, hesitant remembrance, and prolonged silences—and I know that the only thing I can do is share. I feel uncomfortable holding on to these valuable parts of other people's lives, a sense of biography and responsibility. I cannot let them go, I cannot just *be* with the knowledge of them. Recording, archiving, unravelling, smoothing out and making sense have taken too much time, too many of my months, too much of my heart.

So I write about these objects and their beginnings, about the people, about the landscape, about memory. Soon I begin to get comments from both sides of the border, from readers not much older than myself: 'I wish I had recorded my grandfather before he passed.' 'How can I get my grandmother to tell me about her home?' 'Can you travel to Kanpur to archive the story of my uncle?' 'My *nani* also came from D.I. Khan!' 'My mother-in-law travelled by boat from East Bengal to West, in the darkness of night, clad in a burkha.' 'Today I sat with my *dada* and, inspired by you, asked him about his India.' 'What is Pakistan like? I am yearning to visit my family home near Multan.' 'We used to live on Barakhamba Road in Delhi, what is it like now?' The messages are overwhelming and I can't contain myself as I go through them daily. My heart expands thinking about the cross-border community we are creating together through this work.

To get people involved further, I, along with a friend, set up a digital repository based on contributions—the Museum of Material Memory—to facilitate the collection of objects from various parts of the country that I cannot travel to; to give anyone a platform to exhibit and celebrate their family's material past. It seems I have become the medium, an intermediary, carrying the memories from a generation receding into the past to a generation advancing into the future, both with great speed. I feel a renewed sense of purpose, for my efforts are stirring a conversation. They are forcing artefacts to dust off the years and present themselves as unlikely ambassadors of life across a man-made border, of an unreachable home, of an irreversible divide.

Extract an object from the past and deposit it where it doesn't belong and, decades later, it will tell a story. For better or for worse, I have become that storyteller.

NOTES

FOREWORD TO THE PAPERBACK EDITION

1. See Louise Carpenter, 'Interview: Potter and writer Edmund de Waal on his family's Holocaust nightmare', *The Times*, 17 April 2021, https://www.thetimes.co.uk/article/potter-and-writer-edmund-de-waal-on-his-familys-holocaust-nightmare-fj8xkf6pf.

PREFACE

1. For a more detailed account, see: https://scroll.in/magazine/856901/how-my-book-brought-together-two-families-divided-by-partition-and-united-by-a-house. 'Kehkashan' was what Ali's father, Mian Afzal Hussain, had named the house when he built it, meaning 'galaxy'. He carved constellations of stars and a semi-circular sun into the ceilings of the home, inspired no doubt by Sitara (star) and her sister Suraiya (sun). When the Bedis, who had migrated from Kaller Syedan and bought the house, invited me to come and see it, for four days I explored every corner of a house I thought had been consigned to history. I pored over documents and letters written by Mian Afzal Hussain about its construction from 1932 to 1947, before video calling Sitara Faiyaz Ali to show her the house.

2. Dori Laub, 'The Event Without a Witness: Truth, Testimony and Survival' in *Testimony: Crises of Witnessing in Literature, Psychoanalysis and History* (Routledge, 1991).

3. Ibid.

4. 'Sight and Sound: Challenges and Ethics of Visual Representation of War and Conflict in Asia', Singapore University of Technology and Design, 2018. 'Reporting on the Rohingya: Views from the Field' consisting of Maitrii Aung-Thwin (National University of Singapore),

Lam Shushan (Channel News Asia, Singapore), Sören Kittel (Funke Media Group, Berlin), Taimoor Sobhan (Fortify Rights, Bangkok) and Drew Ambrose (Al Jazeera Media Network).

5. Raghu Karnad, *Farthest Field: An Indian Story of the Second World War* (New Delhi: HarperCollins India, 2015), p. xix.

INTRODUCTION

1. American photographer Margaret Bourke-White, who extensively chronicled the Great Divide for *Life* magazine, was known to have famously written it down as a 'massive exercise in human misery'.

2. 'Chapter 3: The State of the World's Refugees', UNHCR report, 2000, p. 59: 'In the quarter of a century after the end of the Second World War, virtually all the previously colonized countries of Asia obtained independence. In some states this occurred peacefully, but for others … the struggle for independence involved violence. The most dramatic upheaval, however, was on the Indian subcontinent, where communal violence resulted in partition and the creation of two separate states—India and Pakistan—in 1947. An estimated 14 million people were displaced at the time, as Muslims in India fled to Pakistan and Hindus in Pakistan fled to India.'

3. Nicholas Mansergh, *The Prelude to Partition: Concept and Aims in Ireland and India* (Cambridge: Cambridge University Press, 1978), p. 26; A.K. Azad, *India Wins Freedom: An Autobiographical Narrative* (Bombay: Orient Blackswan, 1959), p. 143.

4. From an interview with Pran Nevile at his home in March 2016.

5. Asif Noorani, 'Footprints: Six inches and a world away', *Dawn*, November 2015. Noorani attempts to untangle the immeasurable distance between the six exact inches that separate India and Pakistan at the Wagah–Attari border. Infusing his account with both humour and poetry, he writes: 'Last month … I looked up at the birds flying from one country to another unencumbered by paperwork. It had drizzled an hour or so earlier; the ground on both sides of the Great Divide was damp but the sun was shining brightly now. Nature doesn't recognise any man-made boundaries, otherwise the 100-plus-year-old tree, with its trunk a few inches on the Indian side of the white line, would not have allowed its branches to spread over Pakistani territory, nor would its roots have pierced our soil. Thanks to the Radcliffe Award

many such trees must be enjoying what you may be tempted to call "dual nationality".'

6. Yasmin Khan, *The Great Partition: The Making of India and Pakistan* (New Haven: Yale University Press, 2008), p. 1.

7. Joydeep Gupta, '60 Days to August 15, 1947', IANS, New Delhi, 2007.

8. Jaswant Singh, *Jinnah: India. Partition. Independence* (New Delhi: Rupa & Co., 2009), p. 305.

9. Ikramullah Shaista Suhrawardy, *From Purdah to Parliament* (Karachi: Oxford University Press, 1963), p. 135.

10. Yasmin Khan, *The Great Partition: The Making of India and Pakistan* (New Haven: Yale University Press, 2008), p. 44.

11. From an interview with the family at their home in October 2016.

12. Choudhary Rahmat Ali, 'Now or Never. Are we to live or perish forever?' 28 January 1933. In this pamphlet, Ali published a map of what he believed would be the eventual landscape of Pakistan, opening with the infamous lines: 'At this solemn hour in the history of India, when British and Indian statesmen are laying the foundations of a Federal Constitution for that land, we address this appeal to you, in the name of our common heritage, on behalf of our *thirty million Muslim* brethren who live in **PAKSTAN** [sic]—by which we mean the five northern units of India, viz: Punjab, North-West Frontier Province (**A**fghan Province), **K**ashmir, Sindh and Baluchi**stan**.'

14. See W.H. Auden's 1966 poem, 'Partition'.

15. MSS EUR PHOTO EUR 428 from the British Library.

16. Ibid.

17. *Times of India*, 5 June 1947.

18. Yasmin Khan, *The Great Partition: The Making of India and Pakistan* (New Haven: Yale University Press, 2008), p. 91.

19. MSS EUR A168 from the British Library.

20. Howard Brenton, *Drawing the Line* (Nick Hern Books, 2013), p. 87; IOR/L/PJ/7/12500 from the British Library.

21. Urvashi Butalia, *Partition: The Long Shadow* (New Delhi: Viking, 2015), p. ix.

22. Ibid.

23. Orhan Pamuk, trans. Maureen Freely, *The Museum of Innocence* (London: Faber & Faber, 2010).

24. Dominiek Dendooven, 'The Journey Back: On the nature of donations to the "In Flanders Fields Museum"', in Nicholas J. Saunders and Paul

Cornish (eds), *Contested Objects: Material Memories of the Great War* (Abingdon: Routledge, 2013), p. 63.

25. See Devika Chawla, *Home, Uprooted: Oral Histories of India's Partition* (New York: Fordham University Press, 2014), p. 17: 'Objects also tell us that home can be understood in terms of "belonging" and experienced via "belongings"—items and artifacts of material culture that we choose to carry with us.' Katie Walsh states: 'Thinking about belonging through *belongings* is productive because it is empirically and theoretically attentive to the way in which the home is experienced simultaneously as both material and immaterial, lived and imagined, localized and (trans) national space of belonging.'

26. Andrew Jones, *Memory and Material Culture* (Cambridge: Cambridge University Press, 2007).

27. Elizabeth Loftus, 'How Reliable Is Your Memory?', TED Talks, September 2013, https://www.ted.com/talks/elizabeth_loftus_the_fiction_of_memory?language=en: '… many people believe that memory works like a recording device. You just record the information, then you call it up and play it back when you want to answer questions or identify images. But decades of work in psychology have shown that this just isn't true. Our memories are constructive. They're reconstructive.'

28. Moni Chadha, *By the River of Silver: Diplomatic Chronicles from a Life in Six Continents* (Main Street, 2016), p. 33. In this memoir, Chadha explains how, before the Partition, during wedding celebrations families would borrow items from one another: cutlery, dinnerware, glasses and so on. For easy identification, they would engrave their initials on them. When his family left Rawalpindi for Delhi in 1947, they left behind a majority of their belongings, including a set of silver glasses engraved with his grandfather's name: Arjan Singh Chadha. Five decades later, a friend of the family was visiting Canada and accepted the hospitality of a Pakistani family in Toronto. On the dinner table, a generous spread in typical Punjabi fashion unexpectedly included a set of silver glasses engraved with the name Arjan Singh Chadha.

1. A *GAZ* FOR MY FATHER AND A *GHARA* FOR MY MOTHER: THE HEIRLOOMS OF Y.P. VIJ

1. Since he moved to the city in 2007, Mayank Austen Soofi, the Delhi

Walla, has been the most comprehensive guide to an alternative Delhi. The late Khushwant Singh, author and renowned chronicler of the city, deemed him to be someone who has 'the knack for bringing out the unusual from the usual'.

2. In an article about the house, titled 'Home Sweet Home, Roop Nagar', published on his website (www.thedelhiwalla.com) on 22 October 2013, he writes: 'In their book *Social Aging in a Delhi Neighborhood*, authors John Van Willigen and N.K. Chadha say that Roop Nagar and its nearby "colonies" such as Shakti Nagar, Kamla Nagar and Vijay Nagar "provided housing to the people who were part of a dramatic increase in the population of Delhi following the division of the country into India and Pakistan after independence in 1947".' According to the book, 'there was more than a 103-percent increase in Delhi's population in the 1941–1951 intercensus decade'.

3. See 'Sheen of Antiquity' in Jun'ichirō Tanizaki, *In Praise of Shadows* (Stoy Creek, CT: Leete's Island Books, 1977), p. 11.

4. According to the census of India, Delhi received the largest number of refugees for a single city. Its population grew rapidly in 1947 from under 1 million (917,939) to a little less than 2 million (1,744,072) during the period between 1941 and 1951.

5. The broader basis of vocabulary and syntax, from which both Hindi and Urdu have developed, is called Hindustani. It served as the lingua franca around the city of Delhi to facilitate interaction between the speakers of various dialects like Khariboli and languages like Arabic, Persian and Turkish. According to Abdul Jamil Khan, in his book *Urdu / Hindi, an Artificial Divide: African Heritage, Mesopotamian Roots, Indian Culture & British Colonialism*, the language is 'the linguistic super family uniting all' across north India and in Pakistan.

6. 'Delhi, a City of Refugee Enterprise', *Times of India*, 24 January 2010: 'The massive influx of Hindu refugees after the Partition had changed the very fabric of the city's population, giving it a predominantly Punjabi character. Earlier it had consisted of a mix of Rajputs, Turks and Hindu *baniyas* who had entered the city to serve successive rulers and eventually stayed back'.

7. Gyanendra Pandey, *Remembering Partition: Violence, Nationalism and History in India* (Cambridge University Press, 2001), p. 138. Vazira Fazila-Yacoobali Zamindar, *The Long Partition and the Making of Modern South*

Asia: Refugees, Boundaries, Histories (Columbia University Press, 2010), pp. 21–22.

8. Vazira Fazila-Yacoobali Zamindar, *The Long Partition and the Making of Modern South Asia: Refugees, Boundaries, Histories* (Columbia University Press, 2010), pp. 23–25.

2. BETWEEN THIS SIDE AND THAT: THE SWORD OF AJIT KAUR KAPOOR

1. According to the 1941 Census of India, the population of the old district of Mirpur was 386,655, with approximately 80.5 per cent Muslim, 16.7 per cent Hindu, and 3 per cent Sikh.

2. Luv Puri, *Across the Line of Control: Inside Pakistan-administered Jammu and Kashmir* (London: Hurst & Co., 2012), p. 58.

3. Ibid.

4. Amnah Shaukat, 'A City Under Water', *The Friday Times*, 26 January 2018, http://www.thefridaytimes.com/tft/a-city-under-water/.

5. Sansar Chandra, 'Reliving the Tragedy of Mirpur', *Tribune India*, 25 November 2001; M. Zahir, *1947: A Memoir of Indian Independence* (Trafford Publishing, 2009), p. 160—'Things were now very dangerous in Mukerian [present-day Hoshiarpur, India]. I decided to send Hamida to Mirpur. I thought that Mirpur would be safer.'

6. For a detailed account of the background to the incidents of violence in the state of Jammu and Kashmir, and of Maharaja Hari Singh's accession of the state to India, please refer to Nisid Hajari, *Midnight Furies: The Deadly Legacy of India's Partition* (New Delhi: Penguin Random House, 2015), p. 179–84; and Narendra Singh Sarila, *The Shadow of the Great Game: The Untold Story of India's Partition* (New Delhi: HarperCollins India, 2005), p. 343–56.

7. Dr Karan Singh, *Autobiography* (New Delhi: Oxford University Press, 1989), p. 53: 'The situation was so complex that even a person far more aware of contemporary realities than my father would have found it virtually impossible to come to a neat, peaceful solution … if he had acceded to Pakistan, the Hindu areas of the state would have been virtually liquidated in the wake of communal frenzy sweeping across north India at the time. If, on the other hand, he would have earlier acceded to India, he would have run the risk of alienating a large section of his Muslim subjects who constituted seventy-five percent of the

state… My father's only positive reaction to the rapidly approaching partition was to offer to sign a Standstill Agreement with both the "Dominions" as they were then called.' Also see, Victoria Schofield, *Kashmir in Conflict: India, Pakistan and the Unending War* (I.B. Tauris, 2003), p. 40.

8. Ipsita Chakraborty, 'They Sprang from the Earth: It's been 70 years since tribal forces poured into Kashmir', Scroll.in, 26 October 2017: 'Within the princely state, the Poonch uprising of September had led to violence against Hindus and Sikhs, pushing them out of towns like Mirpur and Muzaffarabad towards Jammu. In October, there would be large-scale massacres of Muslims in Jammu, Udhampur and other districts, sending a tide of refugees towards the west.'

9. *The Times*, London, 10 August 1948: '237,000 Muslims were systematically exterminated—unless they escaped to Pakistan along the border—by the forces of the Dogra State headed by the Maharaja in person and aided by Hindus and Sikhs. This happened in October 1947, five days before the Pathan invasion and nine days before the Maharaja's accession to India.' As a result of the massacre, Muslims, who were in a majority in the Jammu region, became a minority.

10. Syed Manzoor Hussain Gilani, *Constitutional Development in Azad Jammu & Kashmir*, Appendix IV, p. 90: 'Thousands of Hindu and Sikh refugees were pouring over the state borders from India and Pakistan daily, with at least 70,000 Hindu and Sikh refugees in Jammu in early September.' Andrew Whitehead, *A Mission in Kashmir* (New Delhi: Penguin, 2008), p. 33: 'Some Partition refugees, a small proportion but sufficient to infuse Kashmir with some of the tension of the time, used the Kashmir Valley as a corridor to pass through on their way between the two dominions. Thousands of Sikhs from Peshawar and elsewhere in the Frontier travelled through Kashmir… Muslim refugees tended not to travel through the Kashmir Valley, but enormous numbers passed through Jammu district on their way to west Punjab.'

11. See Bal K. Gupta, *Forgotten Atrocities: Memoirs of a Survivor of the 1947 Partition of India* (2012), p. 19: 'November 25, 1947: Throughout the night, I could hear the incessant firing of machine guns and heavy artillery as the Pakistani army and Pathans began their final assault on Mirpur.'

12. Christopher Snedden, *Kashmir: The Unwritten History* (New Delhi: HarperCollins India, 2013), p. 56: Snedden states that a 'great shocked'

Sardar Ibrahim confirmed that some Hindus were 'disposed of' in Mirpur in November 1947, when he interviewed him at Rawalkot in March 1999. There are also references to the incident in *The Kashmir Saga* by Sardar M. Ibrahim Khan.

13. Mr Dharam Vir Gupta narrates a similar account of the fall of Mirpur in November 1947. The interview was conducted by Oral History Scholar, Prince Tomar, on behalf of the 1947 Partition Archive: 'Mr. Gupta recalls picking out innumerable bullets from his three-storey house. The attacks became consistent, bullets and canons were fired. [They] were organized and strategized.'

14. See Christopher Snedden, *Understanding Kashmir and Kashmiris* (London: Hurst & Co., 2015); *Selected Works of Jawaharlal Nehru: August 15-December 31, 1947* (Jawaharlal Nehru Memorial Fund, 1986), p. 345.

15. A similar reunion story was written by Omer Farooq for *Free Press Kashmir* (25 June 2018) titled 'Divided by War, Reunited by Web: The Partition Saga of Two Rajouri Sisters'. In the piece, Farooq talks about two siblings separated during the violent riots in Rajouri, Jammu & Kashmir State, in 1947, and reunited seven decades later, one sister now living in Mirpur in Pakistan-Administered Kashmir and the other in Rajouri, Jammu & Kashmir, India. Their families managed to trace one another online and through mutual friends, and the siblings spoke for the first time since their separation on 27 April 2018: 'It was under such circumstances that Satya Devi, who later became Ghulam Fatima, got separated from her family [in Rajouri]. She was displaced to Mirpur unknowingly. "I do not remember many things," says Fatima. "I remember that a siren was blown and it was a chaotic, war-like situation. I had been married six months ago. It was a horrible situation. I had no *dupatta* on my head. Nothing but clothes which I had on my body." In that war, she even lost the address of her groom.'

16. See Dr Dori Laub, *The Event Without a Witness: Truth, Testimony and Survival*, 'Testimony: Crises of Witnessing in Literature, Psychoanalysis and History' (Routledge, 1991). In this essay, Dr Dori Laub discusses that sometimes a traumatic experience which has long been submerged becomes distorted in that submersion. 'The horror of historical experience is maintained in the testimony only as an elusive memory that feels as if it no longer resembles any reality.'

17. Mrs Promila Gupta narrates a similar account of the conditions of refugees while walking from Mirpur to Jammu in November 1947.

The interview was conducted by Oral History Scholar, Prince Tomar, on behalf of the 1947 Partition Archive: 'She shares that when children became too exhausted to continue walking, family members would place rocks on their chests to weight them down, so they would not be able to follow.'

18. See Bal K. Gupta, *Forgotten Atrocities: Memoirs of a Survivor of the 1947 Partition of India* (2012), p. 23. Bal K. Gupta describes how, during their journey of migration from Mirpur, refugees had to resort to inventive methods to obtain water and food: 'About one to two miles south of the notorious area known as Kas Guua, we all, particularly the children, became extremely thirsty and stopped near a well along the route to drink water. There was no bucket or rope near the well with which to draw water. Finally, in desperation, people started using their turbans and dupattas (head scarves for women) to soak water from the well to quench their thirst and that of the children.'

19. Sunny Dua, 'Reliving August 14, 1947: The Pains of Partition', *Daily Excelsior*, 14 August 2015, http://www.dailyexcelsior.com/reliving-august-14-1947-the-pains-of-partition/.

20. Sansar Chandra, 'Reliving the Tragedy of Mirpur', *The Tribune*, 25 November 2001: According to this first-hand account, the number of survivors from Mirpur who reached Jammu alive was a meagre 3,400. Though we don't know how many set out on that journey, first-hand accounts give the population of Mirpur on the day of the Partition as 25,000, swelling by about 10,000 as refugees from West Punjab poured in.

21. Bal K. Gupta, 'Death of Mahatma Gandhi and Alibeg Prisoners,' *Daily Excelsior*, 30 January 2014: 'The Alibeg Prison was located about two miles from Pakistan's border. It was originally a large Gurudwara that was converted into a prison by the Pakistani army to detain Hindu and Sikh prisoners. It was outrageous that a holy shrine was converted into a slaughter-house.'

22. Sardar Muhammad Ibrahim Khan, *The Kashmir Saga* (Verinag, 1990), p. 55: 'During the month of November, 1947, I went to Mirpur to see things there for myself. I visited, during the night, one Hindu refugee camp at Ali Baig—about 15 miles from Mirpur proper. Among the refugees I found some of my fellow lawyers in a pathetic condition. I

saw them myself, sympathised with them and solemnly promised that they would be rescued and sent to Pakistan, from where they would eventually be sent out to India… After a couple of days, when I visited the camp again to do my bit for them, I was greatly shocked to learn that all those people whom I had seen on the last occasion had been disposed of. I can only say that nothing in my life pained my conscience so much as did this incident… Those who were in charge of those camps were duly dealt with but that certainly is no compensation to those whose near and dear ones were killed.'

23. Bal Raj Madhok, *Kashmir: The Storm Center of the World* (A. Ghosh Publishers, USA, 1992), p. 709: 'The barbarities of the Pakistan troops and civilians on these hapless women who were kept for some time in Alibeg camp before their dispersal to different towns put to shame the worst orgies of rape and violence associated with the hordes of Ghengiz Khan and Nadir Shah.'

24. *International Review of the Red Cross*, June 1998, p. 272: 'On his departure from Geneva in December 1947, Dr Otto Wenger's instructions were to establish contacts with the new governments and Red Cross Societies in India and Pakistan, to ascertain the exact needs of the victims, and to make proposals for further action… By the end of February Dr Wenger's efforts had achieved the following results—the immediate dispatch of aid, by the Pakistan Red Cross, and of medical personnel, by the Christian Relief Association, to the Alibeg camp. The ICRC delegate had visited this camp, situated in "Azad Kashmir" near the border with Pakistan. It housed 1,600 non-Muslims living in appalling conditions.' Mr Dharam Vir Gupta narrates a similar account of the fall of Mirpur in November 1947. The interview was conducted by Oral History Scholar, Prince Tomar, on behalf of the 1947 Partition Archive: '… A couple from the Red Cross came and offered milk powder, washed us and sprayed us with disinfectant. People had become malnourished and their heads, limbs and body parts had swollen up.'

25. Ritu Menon and Kamla Bhasin, 'Homes for the Homeless' in *Borders & Boundaries: Women in India's Partition* (Rutgers University Press, 1998).

3. GIFT FROM A MAHARAJA: THE PEARLS OF AZRA HAQ

1. 'Women's Auxiliary Corps (India) World War II photograph album', Ms. Coll. 1154, Finding aid prepared by Clémence Scouten, University

of Pennsylvania, Kislak Center for Special Collections, Rare Books and Manuscripts, 24 November 2015.

2. Mridula Chari, 'Rare photographs of the women who joined the Indian army in World War II', Scroll.in, 18 June 2015, https://scroll.in/article/722562/rare-photographs-of-the-women-who-joined-the-indian-army-in-world-war-ii.

3. Frank McLynn, *Burma Campaign: Disaster into Triumph 1942–45* (London: Vintage, Random House UK, 2011). According to the *London Gazette*, published on 5 May 1942, Slim was made acting lieutenant-general on 8 May 1942, having in March been given command of Burma Corps, consisting of the 17th Indian Infantry Division and 1st Burma Division.

4. MSS EUR F164/48 from the British Library.

5. Sanam Maher, 'Flashback: Vanity Fair's Lady in Red', *Express Tribune*, Pakistan, 6 August 2014, https://tribune.com.pk/story/756520/flashback-a-peoples-history-of-pakistan/.

4. UTENSILS FOR SURVIVAL: THE KITCHENWARE OF BALRAJ BAHRI

1. Ravinder Kaur, *Since 1947: Partition Narratives among Punjabi Migrants of Delhi* (New Delhi: Oxford University Press, 2007), p. 99. Aparna Alluri and Gurman Bhatia, 'The decade that changed Delhi', *Hindustan Times & Dawn*, August 2016. Ranjana Sengupta, *Refugees: Delhi's Last Conquerers* (New Delhi: Penguin, 2008).

2. Anuj Bahri and Deborah Smith, *Chronicle of a Bookshop* (India Research Press, 2004), p. 44.

3. Aanchal Malhotra, 'How Bahrisons Delhi has been romancing books since 1953: The enchanting history of a bookshop, a family and reading', Scroll.in, 11 April 2015, https://scroll.in/article/719693/how-bahrisons-delhi-has-been-romancing-books-since-1953.

5. STONES FROM MY SOIL: THE *MAANG-TIKKA* OF BHAG MALHOTRA

1. Nisid Hajari, *Midnight's Furies: The Deadly Legacy of India's Partition* (New Delhi: Penguin Random House, 2015), p. 78.

2. See Yasmeen Aftab Ali, 'Understanding Pashtunwali', *Nation*, Pakistan,

6 August 2013; Thomas H. Johnson and M. Chris Mason, 'No Sign until the Burst of Fire: The Pakistan–Afghanistan Frontier', *International Security*, Vol. 32, No. 4, Belfer Center for Science & International Affairs, Harvard University.

3. The man who helped them was called Khanna, related to actor Prithviraj Kapoor's younger brother, Trilok Kapoor. My grandmother, focusing on this claim to fame rather than the details of the Partition riots at this time, was keen to stress how important this man who came to their aid had been. He owned farmlands in Meerut, where he had set up a refugee camp for those who were escaping the violence and riots and coming into Delhi from the Frontier.

6. STITCHES AND SECRETS: THE *BAGH* OF HANSLA CHOWDHARY

1. Shailaja D. Naik, *Traditional Embroideries of India* (New Delhi: Ashish, 2010), p. 103.

2. Claude Cahn, *Roma Rights: Race, Justice, and Strategies for Equality* (International Debate Education Association, 2002), p. 38: 'Hancock completed his analysis by drawing cultural parallels between Gypsies and India. In his earlier survey of Romani linguistics, he had pointed out that 'Indian scholarship in this connection is an intriguing combination of subjectiveness and careful documentation,' and quoted the following claim as an example of the former: 'The very fact that Roma loves buffaloes for their milk proves their origin in the Panjab, where till today, every Panjabi would forgo anything else, but not buffalo milk.'

3. Shailaja D. Naik, *Traditional Embroideries of India* (New Delhi: Ashish, 2010), p. 104.

7. HEREDITARY KEEPERS OF THE RAJ: THE ENDURING MEMORIES OF JOHN GRIGOR TAYLOR

1. Charles Allen, *Plain Tales from the Raj* (London: Little, Brown Book Group, 2000), p. 255.

2. David Davidar, *House of Blue Mangoes* (New Delhi: Penguin, 2002), p. 296.

3. Anne De Courcy, *The Fishing Fleet: Husband-Hunting in the Raj* (London:

Weidenfeld & Nicolson, 2013); Charles Allen, *Plain Tales from the Raj* (London: Little, Brown Book Group, 2000), p. 46.

4. A near-identical image can be found in the archives of the National Army Museum, UK, showing the Qissa Khwani Bazaar massacre. Accession number: NAM. 1977–02–39–1, '*Riots in Peshawar, 1930*', Photograph, India, North West Frontier, 1930.

5. P.N. Chopra, B.N. Chopra, M.N. Das, A.C. Pradhan, *A Comprehensive History of India*, Vol. 3 (New Delhi: Sterling Publishers Private Ltd, 2003), p. 250.

6. MSS EUR F370/1521 from the British Library—Broadcast: 'Some impressions of India', by Sir Cyril Radcliffe (copy of text of broadcast talk): 'I can think of one thing that we could at least say of ourselves: we certainly got about the world. We have been such wanderers that the mud of every country is on our shoes. It is quite an essay in geography to list the places in the five continents in which British soldiers lie buried: and we would need a new list for the British civilian cemeteries overseas. In all recorded history up to the present, no people have ever so mixed its dust with the dust of the wide world. Eccentric, tiresome, interfering, if you like, but surely too, adventurous, ingenious, courageous and enduring. And yes, for better or worse, very remarkable.'

7. 'Take a tablet of Vicks and get rid of the hoarseness of your throat!'

8. The lyrics of the song can be loosely translated to 'Come to me, my love, every Sunday! Run away from here … you! Shall I show you Paris? I'll take you around London? I'll treat you to Brandy, Whiskey and Eggs from hens. Come to me, my love, every Sunday!'

9. Attitudes within British India to the urgency of World War II versus the primacy of Independence were far more complicated than John Grigor Taylor makes it sound here. Gandhi, and those in the Congress who backed him, launched a mass Quit India movement of civil disobedience, demanding immediate independence, while the war was going on. Subhas Chandra Bose, a former Congress leader, famously left India and sided with the Axis, which had expressed support for Independence. It was Jinnah's Muslim League that most strongly backed a wartime alliance with the British as a priority over Independence.

10. MSS EUR F370/1521 from the British Library.

11. Hugh Purcell, *After the Raj: The Last Stayers-on and the Legacy of British India* (The History Press Ltd, 2011): 'The British departure from India

at the time of independence was nowhere near as sudden as the handover of power. Many British citizens chose to stay on—there were 28,000 of them in 1951, and still 6,500 in 1971. They stayed largely because they could imagine no other life but the one in India.'

8. THE LIGHT OF A HOUSE THAT STANDS NO MORE: THE STONE PLAQUE OF MIAN FAIZ RABBANI

1. Raj Chatterjee, *The Boxwallah and the Middleman* (New Delhi: Penguin, 2008), p. 51.
2. Yasmin Khan, *The Great Partition: The Making of India and Pakistan* (New Haven: Yale University Press, 2008), pp. 40–41.
3. Muhammad Ayub Khan, *Tarikh-i-Pakistan aur Jullundur* (Lahore: Asatair, 2002), p. 258.
4. Ishtiaq Ahmed, *The Punjab: Bloodied, Partitioned and Cleansed* (New Delhi: Rupa & Co., 2013), pp. 334–35.
5. Ibid, p. 540.
6. Muhammad Ayub Khan, *Tarikh-i-Pakistan aur Jullundur* (Lahore: Asatair, 2002), p. 164.
7. M. Kaiser Tufail, *Great Air Battles of Pakistan Air Force* (Lahore: Ferozesons, 2006).
8. A full account of the incident can be read on Air Commodore Kaiser Tufail's blog: http://kaiser-footloose.blogspot.in/2008/11/our-trip-to-india.html.
9. Mian Faiz Rabbani, *Ma aur Mamta* (Lahore: Shikrat Printing Press, 2009). An account of this event when Samar and Air Commodore Kaiser Tufail found and carried the stone plaque to Pakistan can be found in this book [written in Urdu], which consists of several short stories pertaining to the Partition. Another story worth mentioning is titled '*Dharm Putr*' (p. 112), an exceptionally visual tale inspired by two real events that occurred in the author's extended family as a result of the Partition riots: in the first, a relative's baby was left behind in India; and in the second, fourteen years after the Divide, a young boy returned to his mother in Pakistan, having been raised as someone else's son in India.
10. The translation of the stone plaque has been done in part by Mian Faiz Rabbani, Kumail Hasan and Sumitra Kapur. But, by far, the most

extensive explanation has been provided generously by Mr Wadood Sajid of the India Islamic Cultural Centre, New Delhi.

9. THE INHERITANCE OF CEREMONIAL SERVINGS: THE *KHAAS-DAAN* OF NARJIS KHATUN

1. Jamil Husain Rizvi, *Pakistan Story* (Zia H. Rizvi, 1973), p. 1.
2. Ibid, p. 24.
3. This is a very particular and evocative way to refer to the Partition, in a classic Urdu.
4. Zafarul-Islam Khan, 'Tomb of Prophet's "descendant" discovered', Milli Gazette Online, 16–30 June 2005.

10. THE HOCKEY FIELD I LEFT BEHIND: THE PHOTOGRAPHS OF NAZEER ADHAMI

1. Nisid Hajari, *Midnight's Furies: The Deadly Legacy of India's Partition* (New Delhi: Penguin Random House, 2015), p. 27; Jaswant Singh, *Jinnah: India. Partition. Independence* (New Delhi: Rupa & Co., 2009), pp. 107, 115.
2. Yasmin Khan, *The Great Partition: The Making of India and Pakistan* (New Haven: Yale University Press, 2008), p. 41: 'Women organized pro-League meetings and encouraged donations of jewellery for the League's cause while their husbands and sons used printed leaflets, persuasions, processions and placards to bring Pakistan into existence.'
3. Beverly Nichols, *Verdict on India* (Read Books, 1944), pp. 184–85.
4. Jaswant Singh, *Jinnah: India. Partition. Independence* (New Delhi: Rupa & Co., 2009), p. 58.
5. Official website, Nazaria-e-Pakistan Foundation, 'Excerpt from the presidential address delivered by Muhammad Ali Jinnah in Lahore on March 22, 1940'. Archived from the original on 28 June 2006. Retrieved on 22 April 2006.
6. Jaswant Singh, *Jinnah: India. Partition. Independence* (New Delhi: Rupa & Co., 2009), p. 319.
7. Sharif Mujahid, *Quaid-i-Azam Jinnah: Studies in Interpretation* (Karachi: Quaid-i-Azam Academy, 1981), p. 205.
8. *Indian Constitutional Documents*, Vol. 1, p. 7; K.M. Munshi, *Pilgrimage to Freedom* (New Delhi: Bhartiya Vidya Bhawan, 2012).

9. Jaswant Singh, *Jinnah: India. Partition. Independence* (New Delhi: Rupa & Co., 2009), p. 182.

10. Ian Wells, *Jinnah:Ambassador of Hindu-Muslim Unity* (Chicago: University of Chicago Press, 2005), p. 229.

11. Jaswant Singh, *Jinnah: India. Partition. Independence* (New Delhi: Rupa & Co., 2009), pp. 204–06; *Fazli Hussain to Jinnah, Papers*, Vol. 16–17: 'The very same Fazli Hussain who in 1930 had written that Jinnah was doing mischief at the R.T.C [22 December 1930, Fazli Hussain Diary, papers Vol. 6] now invited Jinnah, writing to him to say, 'Muslim India cannot afford to lose you. Men of clear vision, independent judgment and strength of character are very few.'

12. Ayesha Jalal, *The Sole Spokesman: Jinnah, the Muslim League and the Demand for Pakistan* (Cambridge University Press, 1994).

13. Yasmin Khan, *The Great Partition:The Making of India and Pakistan* (New Haven:Yale University Press, 2008), p. 40.

11. THIS BIRD OF GOLD, MY LAND: THE HOPEFUL HEART OF NAZMUDDIN KHAN

1. Ancient India had often been referred to as 'The Bird of Gold' or, in the words of Mark Twain, 'A Golden Sparrow'. Of India, he states: 'The land of dreams and romance, of fabulous wealth and fabulous poverty, of genii and giants and Aladdin lamps, of tigers and elephants, the cobra and the jungle, the country of hundred nations and a hundred tongues, of a thousand religions and two million gods, cradle of the human race, birthplace of human speech, mother of history, grandmother of legend, great-grandmother of traditions, whose yesterdays bear date with the moldering antiquities for the rest of nations, the one sole country under the sun that is endowed with an imperishable interest for alien prince and alien peasant, for lettered and ignorant, wise and fool, rich and poor, bond and free, the one land that all men desire to see, and having seen once, by even a glimpse, would not give that glimpse for the shows of all the rest of the world combined.'

2. Hermann Kulke and Dietmar Rothermung, *A History of India* (New Delhi: Routledge, 1986).

3. Though it is not true that Gandhi offered the post of home minister to Jinnah, a similar, more prestigious position was offered. In a private

correspondence (MSS EUR C357 from the British Library) between Lord Listowell and Lord Mountbatten dated 3 October 1978, the former writes, 'You asked me at the end of your letter, "I wonder if you agree the transfer might have been made before the war without dividing India".' Though he does not answer the question in the same correspondence, he does confess a most extraordinary fact:

I never had the chance of convincing Jinnah that he was wrong in insisting complete partition because he was so pathological on the subject that one couldn't move him. On the other hand, I understand that he only gradually became so obstinate and at one time might have been moved if the right arguments would have been put to him in a way that he would have considered them seriously. Personally, I could visualize having the chance of converting him to a unified India if I had been able to get there before his mind had been made up in this obstinate manner. He was the key to partition as Gandhi realized when he made his famous suggestion to me, that I should reform the cabinet, making Jinnah the prime minister.

4. Jaswant Singh, 'Gandhi–Jinnah Talks—Sunset of the Empire', *Jinnah: India. Partition. Independence* (New Delhi: Rupa & Co., 2009), pp. 307–27.

5. Gyanendra Pandey, 'Partition and Independence in Delhi: 1947–48', *Economic and Political Weekly*, Vol. 32, No. 36 (6–12 September 1997), pp. 2261–72.

6. Anand Taneja, 'History and Heritage Woven into the New Urban Fabric', in *Patterns of Middle Class Consumption in India and China*, edited by Christophe Jaffrelot and Peter van der Veer (New Delhi: Sage Publications, 2008), p. 165: 'During the 1947 violence, villagers from Lado Sarai gave shelter to their neighbours, Muslims from the village of Hauz Rani.'

7. Gyanendra Pandey, *Remembering Partition: Violence, Nationalism and History in India* (New Delhi: Cambridge University Press, 2004), p. 140.

12. THE BOOK OF EVERLASTING THINGS: THE COLLECTION OF PROF. PARTHA MITTER

1. See Dutta Krishna, *Calcutta: A Cultural and Literary History* (Interlink Books, 2003).

2. Nisid Hajari, *Midnight's Furies: The Deadly Legacy of India's Partition* (New Delhi: Penguin Random House, 2015), pp. 35–44; Jaswant Singh, *Jinnah: India. Partition. Independence* (New Delhi: Rupa & Co., 2009), p. 301.

3. Somewhere in the middle, I excused myself to take a phone call, but accidentally left my recorder running. Now when I listen to what that bit of recording held, I am overcome with emotion. The couple's conversation was mostly in Bengali—about my name, what it means and how to pronounce it. And then suddenly, out of nothing but pure love, the historian says to his wife, who was unwell, 'My Swasti, are you cold? Shall I shut the window, are you feeling alright today?' She says yes and I can tell that she is smiling when she speaks. Two years later as I write my story on them, sadly, I learn of her demise and think about this love—the couple's small, thoughtful gestures, simple acts of kindness, the feeling of buoyancy, a balmy sensation, cooler than the direct sun, warmer than a winter's day. What I witnessed was true love.

4. See Partha Mitter, *Much Maligned Monsters: A History of European Reactions to Indian Art* (Oxford: Oxford University Press, 2013), p. 89.

5. *Indian Book Reporter*, Vol. 3, pp. 6–7.

6. See Phillips Talbot, *An American Witness to India's Partition* (New Delhi: Sage Publications, 2007), p. 191 onwards. In a letter to Walter Rogers of the Institute of Current World Affairs, Talbot attempted to describe what he was witnessing during the Great Calcutta Killings in August 1946. He recounted that 'watching a city feed on its own flesh is a disturbing experience'. He wrote about the smashed furniture that cluttered the roads, the concrete blocks and anything else that mobs had managed to tear off of buildings to terrorize 'the other'. And then, with a sense of disgust and horror, he narrated the condition of those who perished during the three days of the riots: 'Most overwhelming, however, were the neglected human casualties: fresh bodies, bodies grotesquely bloated in the tropical heat, slashed bodies, bodies bludgeoned to death, bodies piled on push carts, bodies caught in drains, bodies stacked high in vacant lots, bodies, bodies...'

7. Debjani Sengupta, *The Partition of Bengal: Fragile Borders and New Identities* (New Delhi: Cambridge University Press, India, 2016), p. 38.

8. Ibid, p. 39.

9. Tony Rennell, 'Britain 1947: Poverty, Queues, Rationing and Resil-

ience', Mail Online UK, 20 November, 2007.

10. MSS EUR F370/1521 from the British Library.

11. Chandrika Kaul, *Indian Independence, the British Media and Lord Mountbatten*, Vol. 26 of Occasional publication, India International Centre, 2012, p. 2.

12. Jonathan Silberstein-Loeb, *The International Distribution of News: The Associated Press, Press Association, and Reuters, 1848–1947*, Cambridge Studies in the Emergence of Global Enterprise (Cambridge University Press, 2014).

13. LOVE IN THE TIME OF NATIONALISM: THE POEMS OF PRABHJOT KAUR

1. Khademul Islam, 'Our Story of Dhaka Muslin', Aramco World, May/June 2016: 'Muslin, he said, was the name of a legendary cloth made of cotton, fit for emperors, which used to be made way back in the past. Muslin from Dacca had been the finest, he said, from where it used to be shipped to the far corners of the world… The word 'Muslin' is popularly believed to derive from Marco Polo's description of the cotton trade in Mosul, Iraq. (The Bengali term is *mul mul*.) A more modern view is that of fashion historian Susan Greene, who wrote that the name arose in the 18th century from *mousse*, the French word for "foam".'

2. Pran Nevile, *Lahore: A Sentimental Journey* (New Delhi: Penguin, 1993), p. 130.

3. Narender Singh, Surjit Sachar and Prabhjot Kaur, *Kaafle* (Lahore: Punjabi Literary Society, 1947).

14. MEMORY OF A NATIONALIST: THE PASHMINA SHAWL OF PREET SINGH

1. *Last Children of the Raj: British Childhoods in India*, Vol. 1, 1919–1939, compiled by Laurence Fleming, Introduction by Mark Tully (Radcliffe Press, 2004), p. 131.

2. The 1935 Quetta earthquake occurred on 31 May. It had a magnitude of 7.7 MMS, and anywhere between 30,000 and 60,000 people died

from the impact. It was ranked as the deadliest earthquake in South Asia until the Kashmir earthquake of 2005.

3. The Punjabi word 'Khanna' means one quarter. The city was named such because it used to be very small, just a quarter of what a normal city should be.

15. THE LEXICON OF MY LAND IS DEVOID OF EMOTIONS: THE BATTLE-HARDENED MEMORABILIA OF LT GEN. S.N. SHARMA

1. 'General Service Medal (1918 GSM)', Forces War Records, UK.

2. 'War Medal 1939–1945', Forces War Records, UK.

3. Karan Singh, *Autobiography* (New Delhi: Oxford University Press, 2003), p. 2.

4. Ibid, p. 53: 'In retrospect the only rational solution would appear to have been to take the initiative in promoting and presiding over a peace partition of his [Maharaja Hari Singh] State between the two new nations. But that would have needed clear political vision and careful planning over many years. As it turned out, the State was, in fact, partitioned, but in a manner that caused untold suffering and bloodshed, poisoning relations between India and Pakistan right down to the present day.'

5. Ibid, p. 52.

6. Pamphlet insert page 2 of APS FDC: Major Som Nath Sharma, PVC. 1923–1947, the Kumaon Regiment. PVC Series 1, issued by the Army Postal Service, 3 November 1976.

7. Peter Shaunik Sagat, 'IC 1475 W Lieutenant General Surindra Nath Sharma, PVSM; AVSM; 411 Parachute Field Company, the Bombay Sappers, Retired', Indian Armed Forces blog, 29 April 2012.

8. Ian Cardozo, *Param Vir: Our Heroes in Battle* (New Delhi: Roli Books, 2003).

9. Matthew Richardson, 'Medals, Memory and Meaning', *Contested Objects: Material Memories of the Great War*, edited by Nicholas J. Saunders and Paul Cornish (Routledge, 2013), p. 109.

10. Yasmin Khan, *The Great Partition: The Making of India and Pakistan* (New Haven: Yale University Press, 2008), p. 197: 'Another of the quirks of Partition was that many of the first and second generation of the leading officers of the Indian and Pakistani military facing each other across the Kashmiri line of control in wars of the twentieth century had been

close colleagues and worked alongside each other during the days before Independence.'

16. A HEART OF MORTGAGED SILVER: THE ASSORTED CURIOS OF PROF. SAT PAL KOHLI

1. The Cripps Mission was an attempt in late March 1942 by the British government to secure full Indian cooperation and support for their efforts in World War II.
2. Some of the Highlights of 1942, the Quit India Movement, Gowalia Tank Maidan, Bombay, Gandhi Manibhavan, http://www.gandhi-manibhavan. org/activities/quit_india.htm.
3. Pran Nevile, *Lahore: A Sentimental Journey* (New Delhi: Penguin, 1993), p. xii.
4. Ishtiaq Ahmed, 'Forced Migration and Ethnic Cleansing in Lahore in 1947: Some First-Person Accounts,' on the South Asia Citizens Web website, June 2004, in PDF format, p. 4.
5. Renuka Phadnis, 'Meerut scissors make the cut for GI tag', *Hindu*, 10 January 2013, http://www.thehindu.com/todays-paper/tp-national/meerut-scissors-make-the-cut-for-gi-tag/article4292580. ece.
6. 'Delhi has grown as an educational hub', *New Indian Express*, 14 April 2013, http://www.newindianexpress.com/thesundaystandard/2013/apr/14/delhi-has-grown-as-an-education-hub-467923.html.
7. A very famous saying used by anybody who lived or spent time in Lahore during its glory days: 'One who has not seen Lahore has not been born.'

17. STATELESS HEIRLOOMS: THE *HAMAM-DASTA* OF SAVITRI MIRCHANDANI

1. According to the 1931 census, the population of Sindh was about 4.1 million. Approximately 73 per cent were Muslims, 26 per cent Hindus, and 1 per cent belonged to other religions, mainly Christianity and Sikhism. There were about 1,400,000 Hindu Sindhis, concentrated as a majority in the cities of Larkana, Shikarpur, Hyderabad and Sukkur, and as a minority in Karachi. Following Independence, Hindu Sindhis

were expected to stay in Sindh, as there were good relations between the Hindu and Muslim Sindhis.

2. In the days of August 1947, leading up to the actual Partition, Sindh's governor, Francis Mundie, described it as a place that 'characteristically carries on almost as if nothing had happened or was about to happen'. (Haider Nizamani, 'Who orchestrated the exodus of Sindhi Hindus after Partition?' *Express Tribune*, 4 June 2012, https://tribune.com.pk/story/388663who-orchestrated-the-exodus-of-sindhi-hindus-after-partition/).

3. In an IANS account of the sixty days leading up to Independence, it is noted that the phone services had indeed virtually collapsed in Karachi by 1 August 1947 as all the operators were Hindu or Christian women. Thirty Muslim girls were apparently recruited in a hurry.

4. The word 'Sindh' is derived from the Sanskrit word 'Sindhu', which literally means 'river' and is also a reference to the River Indus which cuts through the province. The Greeks, as far back as 325 BC under Alexander the Great, referred to the land as 'Indós', from which comes the modern name for the river Indus. The ancient Persians referred to everything east of this river as 'Hind' or 'Hindū', cognate with the Sanskrit 'Sindh' or 'Sindhu', since in Persian the letter 's' has an 'h' sound. For them, the word 'Hindu' had little to do with religion per se, but referred simply to the culture of the peoples who lived on the other side of the Sindhu River. This combined with the suffix 'stān', cognate with the Sanskrit 'sthan', both meaning 'place', resulted in 'Hindustan', the land on the other side (from Persia's perspective) of the Indus. When the British arrived in the seventeenth century, they adopted the Greek version of the name Sindh, calling the region India. The word 'Hindustan' was in use synonymously with the word 'India' during the British Raj.

5. According to the 1951 census of India, nearly 776,000 Sindhi Hindus migrated to India.

6. From the image of an article by Situ Savur published in the *Times of India* on 5 December 1998, as cited in Saaz Agarwal (her daughter), *Sindh: Stories from a Vanished Homeland* (Black & White Fountain, 2012), p. 118: 'I had barely entered my teens when my family fled Sindh and came to Bombay. My parents had to leave behind everything, except for a few personal belongings, because of their religion. We were Indian

but our parents told me and my siblings that we were running away to India.'

7. Saaz Agarwal, *Sindh: Stories from a Vanished Homeland* (Black & White Fountain, 2012), pp. 132–33: 'Some families were able to carry their belongings—typically their sewing machines and gold jewellery—and property documents. But, at the ports, their luggage was searched and robbed by Muslim National Guards.' Dawn Special Correspondent, '1,900 Hindu–Sikh evacuees sail from Karachi: Smuggling on large scale apprehended', Karachi, 13 September 1947. A paragraph at the start of the story describes the inspection that each passenger and his or her luggage went through before they could board the ship as it was feared that they could carry arms or ammunition: 'About two dozen customs officials, some police sub-inspectors and more of mere policemen were on the job of checking up the contents of the passengers' baggage before certifying it for transit.'

8. The anna was a unit of currency previously used in India and Pakistan. One anna was equal to one-sixteenth of a rupee. It could be subdivided into 4 paise or further into 12 pies. As a result, there were about 64 paise or 192 pies in one rupee. The system was demonetized due to the decimalization of currency in India in 1957 and in Pakistan in 1961.

9. Though the Mirchandani women claim they are unaware of any words used by Sindhis to denote the Partition, there are older words, Rita Kothari argues, like *ladpalayan* (exodus), used by the Hindu Sindhis in this context. Kothari, 'From Conclusions to Beginnings: My Journey with "Partition" , in Urvashi Butalia (ed.), *Partition: The Long Shadow* (New Delhi: Penguin Random House, 2005), p. 45.

10. Maya Mirchandani has described this meeting of her grandmother and Dadi Leela in her piece 'Cross-border memories' for NDTV, published on 18 July 2006.

18. FROM THE FOLDS OF LIFE: THE HOUSEHOLD ITEMS OF SITARA FAIYAZ ALI

1. See Ronald M. Bernier, *Himalayan Architecture* (Fairleigh Dickinson University Press, 1997).

2. See Anatol Lieven, *Pakistan: A Hard Country* (Public Affairs, 2011).

3. See D.N. Panigrahi, *India's Partition: The Story of Imperialism in Retreat* (Routledge, 2004), p. 36.

19. THE MUSICAL SOLACE IN MY MOTHER'S PRAYERS: THE GURU GRANTH SAHIB OF SUMITRA KAPUR

1. A Hindu reform movement based on the teaching and practices noted in the Vedas.

2. In the India Office Archives of the British Library, London, is a letter dated 25 July 1947 sent by Lord Listowel, the last secretary of state for India, to Lord Mountbatten, the viceroy charged with overseeing the transition of British India to the independent dominions of India and Pakistan. Here, the former congratulates the latter on securing an agreement and the support of the Partition Council on important matters regarding a seemingly fair division of the country. He writes, 'It is hoped that it will have a calming effect throughout all the areas affected by the Partition and will help to discourage any large-scale migrations of Muslims to Pakistan and Hindus to the territories of the future dominion of India; it has been disturbing to learn from Indians I have met in this country recently that such migration will be the natural tendency.'

3. *Gora chitta* is a term used mostly by Punjabi women to refer to men with 'typically' Caucasian features: a very fair complexion and smooth skin.

4. Large-scale killings in the northern parts of Punjab in February and March 1947 were termed as the 'Rape of Rawalpindi', where Sikh and Hindu women committed suicide, sacrificed themselves in communal pyres, were forced to kill their children and at times were made to convert in order to protect their honour. Large amounts of money, weapons and other valuables were looted and extracted from the houses.

21. PASSAGE TO FREEDOM: THE WORLDLY TRUNK OF UMA SON-DHI AHMAD

1. Neha Kulkarni, 'Over 100 documents of Great Indian Peninsular Railway to be digitised', *Indian Express*, 12 July 2016, https:// indianexpress. com/article/india/india-news-india/mumbai-over-100-documents-of-great-indian-peninsula-railway-to-be-digitised-2907994/: 'GIPR was incorporated on August 1, 1849, by an Act of the British Parliament. It was planned to connect erstwhile

Bombay with the interior of the Indian peninsula for increasing the export of cotton, silk, opium, sugar and spices. India's first passenger train was run by GIPR on April 16, 1853, from Boree Bunder station in Mumbai to Thane. The GIPR was, subsequently, incorporated into Central Railway in 1951.'

2. 'Pen Portrait: V.P. Sondhi,' Geological Survey of India, p. 6: 'He began his career in the GSI attached to the Burma party and carried out geological investigations in the Lower Chindwin and Shwebo Districts and in the Southerm Shan States… Along with Coggin Brown, Sondhi travelled from Taunggyi to Salween … and Loilem to Mawkmah.' There is a reference to the 'cave of coffins' in Sondhi's handwritten notes. He writes, 'There are descriptions of a burial ceremony in *National Geographic*, Vol. 141, No. 6, page 795–815.' *Records of the Geological Survey of India*, Vol. 48, Part 1: 'The belt of lead-silver-ore of Mawson was founded by Mr. Sondhi.' Mawson was a Shan state in the historical Myelat region in southwest Burma/present-day Myanmar.

3. 'Pen Portrait: V.P. Sondhi,' Geological Survey of India, p. 6: 'V.P. Sondhi was on study leave from the Geological Survey of India from 1937–1938, during which time he worked at the Imperial College of Science and Technology, The British Museum and the Camborne School of Mines.'

4. 'Second World War Posters—Britain at War', *Telegraph* (UK): 'During the Munich Crisis of September 1938, 38 million gas masks were distributed to the civil population [of Britain]. Germany had signed the 1925 Geneva Protocol promising that it would not employ poison gas. But most people expected that Hitler would use it. Special gas helmets for infants were devised and there were brightly coloured "Mickey Mouse" masks for younger children.' Posters were issued by the Ministry of Home Security, with slogans of 'Hitler will send no warning, always carry your gas mask' and 'Take your gas mask everywhere'.

5. '75 years of World War II Japan bombing of Kolkata: How the city of joy fought back', *India Today*, 19 December 2017, https://www.indiatoday. in/education-today/gk-current-affairs/story/japan-bombing-calcutta-world-war-2-1108404-2017-12-19.

6. The Swadesi movement was intended to develop Indian nationalism by following the principles of *Swadesi*—use of domestic products and

production methods, and the boycott of British products, including clothing and other everyday items.

7. Ashraf Patel, Meenu Venkateswaran, Kamini Prakash and Arjun Shekhar, *The Ocean in a Drop: Inside-Out Youth Leadership* (New Delhi: Sage Publications, 2013), p. 74.

8. Nandini Rathi, '1945 INA trials: A rare glimpse from the lens of photojournalist Kulwant Roy', *Indian Express*, 29 August 2017: 'After the Allies won the war, the INA soldiers once again became prisoners—this time of the British. The military logic of the British India government was clear—they considered the INA joinees to be traitors, deserving of severe punishment. The furious, self-righteous government decided to make an example of the INA leaders by performing their court martial and treason trial—the first one was to take place in Delhi's iconic Red Fort, the same place from where Bose promised that INA would declare India's independence.' The three INA generals arraigned for the first trial were a Hindu (Prem Kumar Sehgal), a Muslim (Shah Nawaz Khan) and a Sikh (Gurbaksh Singh Dhillon).

9. Meghnad Desai, 'Hind, Hindi, Hindu, Hindutva', *Indian Express*, July 2012; India's population was 40 crore, or 400 million, at the time.

10. David Page, *The Partition Omnibus* (New Delhi: Oxford University Press, 2002): 'Almost every village in the Rawalpindi District where non-Muslims lived was attacked and plundered in this manner and Hindus and Sikhs were murdered.'

ACKNOWLEDGEMENTS

HISTORY HAS SEVERAL VERSIONS and this book would not have been possible without the various versions of the Great Divide that came before it. Further, it would be unfair to claim this book as just mine, as it is both by those and for those who witnessed the Partition, either directly through first-hand experience or indirectly through inherited memory, and who were kind enough to share their time and recollections with me. They humoured me as I inquired endlessly into their lives, homes, childhoods, families, journeys of migration and rehabilitation, dreams and regrets, tying them all with the secure knot of their belongings and heirlooms.

For that, I thank Achala Moulick, Ajit Kaur Kapoor, Satwant Kaur Rakhra, Gurshane Kapoor, Sukhmeet Kapoor, Gurdeep Singh, Aquila Ahsan, Tayyaba Jawad, Ameta Bal, Amir Ahmed, Laiba Siraj, Azra Haq, Scherry Haq, Balbir Singh Sir, Gurdeep Kaur, Jasminder Gulati, Dharam Bali, Dharambir Chaudhary, Usha Chaudhary, Anshu Bedi, Dr Aajaz Anwar, Fayyaz Muhammad Faza, Gurcharan Das, Hansla Chowdhary, Col Harinder Singh Bedi, Ambassador Gurdip Singh Bedi, Harleen Bedi, Harmeet Singh Baweja, Jiwan Vohra, Shail Bery, John Grigor Taylor, Sophia Lambert, Juliet Cheetham, Kalyani Ray Chowdhury, Amitesh Ray, Karuna Ezara Parikh, Agneesh Ray, Kiran Bala Marwah, Nupur Marwah, Krishan Mohan Sharan, Sumit Sharan, Lt Gen. S.N. Sharma, Kumudini Sharma, Radhika Shaunik, Mian Faiz Rabbani, Moni Chadha, Pran Nevile, Pushpa Doongursee Bhtaia, Malavika Bhatia, Naeem Tahir, Yasmin Tahir, Najma Nazeer, Nazeer

ACKNOWLEDGEMENTS

Adhami, Saleem Adhami, Fateeha Saleem, Narjis Khatun, Shehrbano Raza Rizvi, Lisa Rizvi, Nazmuddin Khan, Prabhjot Kaur, Nirupama Kaur, Preet Singh, Simran Warsi, Prof. D.P. Sengupta, Prof. Partha Mitter, Swasti Mitter, Prof. P.S. Randhawa, Prof. Sat Pal Kohli, Sandeep Kohli, Boogie Judge Kohli, Raj Kapur Suneja, Sunaina Suneja, Dolly Narang, Sangita Sanyal, Bharati Sanyal, Sunil Chandra Sanyal, Savitri Mirchandani, Shobha Mirchandani, Maya Mirchandani, Shraddha Malhotra Bahirwani, Sitara Faiyaz Ali, Shahnaz Akhtar, Abbas Ali Khan, Asif Akhtar, Sumitra Kapur, Kavita Chadha, Sumohini Tek Chand Bhagat, Geeti Bhagat, Surangana Makin, Om Prakash Khanna, Ved Prakash Jawa, Swarna Kapur, Tanvi Baluja Bajaj, Uma Sondhi Ahmad, Diya Katyal, Anjum Katyal, Yash Pal Vij, Kanta Vij, Ram Prakash Vij and Zehra Nasim Haque.

For access to the various documents that complemented my primary research, I would like to thank the following libraries and archives: the Department of Asian and African Studies at the British Library, home to the India Office Records; the National Army Museum, UK; the Nehru Memorial Library, New Delhi; the Centre for South Asian Studies at Cambridge University; the 'India: A People Partitioned' Oral History Archive at London's School of Oriental and African Studies; the Digital Collection and Archives at Tufts University; Concordia University, Montreal; the 1947 Partition Archive; the Citizens Archive of Pakistan; the Citizens Archive of India; and the International Review of the Red Cross.

There are some people without whom neither I nor this book would have evolved the way we did: Mayank Austen Soofi, my dear friend, thank you for reminding me to remain curious in even the most mundane surroundings; my great-uncle, Yash Pal Vij, without whose memories this work would probably never have been conceived; my paternal grandparents, Bhag and Balraj Bahri Malhotra, who stitched my childhood with the threads of their stories; Rajni Malhotra, my mother and foremost reader, who has unwaveringly encouraged every creative pursuit of my life; Anuj Bahri, my father, from whom I inherited the conjoined love of art and literature; my maternal grandfather, Vishwa Nath Vij, who instilled in me a desire to explore the unfamiliar; my aunt Mona Mehra, who, armed with research questions, fearlessly approached many grandmothers and grandfathers; my siblings, Aashna and Aaditya, for enduring many a midnight ramble and countless 'what-ifs'; Sharvani Pandit, for poignantly honest and earnest feedback; Renuka Kelkar, for the invaluable knowledge and sensibilities that filtered into many stories of this anthology; Sudha Sadhanand, for fuelling the work with anecdotes from an honorary Punjabi childhood; my family at Bahrisons Booksellers, in particular Mithilesh Singh and Devendra Bisht, who catered to my every research need, almost certain that I was disappearing behind the high pile of books accumulating on my desk; and, lastly, Shruti Brahmbhatt, Navdha Malhotra, Laura Emoke Gabor and Karan Arora, for gently reminding me not to get lost inside my own head.

I am grateful to the Faculty of Fine Arts at Concordia University, Montreal, from where I obtained my MFA, for providing me with a travel grant and research sabbatical to complete my fieldwork. I would particularly like to mention the members of my thesis jury: Marisa Portolese, for her magnificent photographic eye; Jean-Pierre Larocque, for the finesse and delicacy with which he observed every archived object; Mitch Mitchell, for his guidance on the multidisciplinary nature of modern printmaking; and Cheryl Sim, for situating the artistic production of the work within a larger contextual framework of contemporary fine art. Raymonde April, my advisor from 2013 to 2015 and friend, deserves a far greater acknowledgement for motivating me to plunge into the subcontinent's history. Eric Simon introduced me to the notion of artist as writer and vice versa. Francois Morelli shared his cavernous bond with the chaos and vibrancy of India. Jill Didur continually encouraged my academic pursuits. Maureen Kennedy from the MFA Studio Arts office was a source of administrative support. Rudolf Bikkers from my days at the

Ontario College of Art & Design, Toronto, urged me to excavate the two-dimensional image further. André Seleanu at Vie des Arts shared profound insights on the intersections between fine art and the humanities. And Bonnie Baxter and Michel Beaudry, who were like family in Montreal.

My sincerest gratitude to all those who volunteered to grant interviews, offered new and unexplored insights, and helped facilitate both artistic and literary renditions of the project from its earliest stages: in England, Emma Dawson Varughese, Rajinder Dudrah, Deborah Swallow, Andrew Whitehead, Shrabani Basu, Imogen Taylor and Mike Symons; in Montreal, Jennifer Dorner and Sarah Amarica at the FOFA Gallery, Kakim Goh and Khosro Berahmandi at Festival Accès Asie, and Adele Ruhdorfer and Emily Beauchamp at Soi Publications, all for believing in the work enough to showcase and write about it; in Germany, Julie Alary Lavallée, who explored the work as a visual essay at the Heidelberg Institute under the sub-sphere of *Walking The Line: Art of Border Zones in Times of Crisis*; in India, Eshwara Venkatesam at Ashoka University, Dr Alok Sarin, Krishna Kumar Nair, Naresh Fernandes at Scroll.in, Vikramjit Singh Rooprai at the Youth for Heritage Foundation, Mukta Naik and Pallavi Raghavan at the Centre for Policy Research, Bhaskar Kaushik at the Google Cultural Institute, Prof. Dinesh Singh, Kaustav Bhattacharya, Ananya Sharma, Anuksha Amal and a special word of thanks to Vaibhav Singh, Anand Virmani and the wonderful staff at Perch, Khan Market, New Delhi, who let me sit undisturbed for hours on end in the cafe, reading and re-reading chapters; in Pakistan, Ali Sethi, who encouraged me to write my first piece on this topic for *The Friday Times*, Kanza Javed, who became my guide through Lahore, Asif Noorani at *Dawn*, Dr Asif Farrukhi at Habib University, Karachi, Fakir Syed Aijazuddin *sahab*, Shahnaz Aijazuddin, Anam Zakaria, Tamkinat Karim, Bilal Mustikhan, Noor Qadir, Leena Naqvi, Zain Naqvi, Anam Pugganwala and Khizar-ji.

ACKNOWLEDGEMENTS

Those who have generously and willingly translated letters, poems, books and passages of texts from various languages: Subheg Singh and Sumitra Kapur from Punjabi, Sayantan Ghosh from Bengali, Revati Kulkarni and Simon Desarzens from English to French, and Munir-ji and Kumail Hasan from Urdu. A special note of thanks to Mr Wadood Sajid at the India Islamic Cultural Centre, New Delhi, for the excellent translation of the stone plaque belonging to Mian Faiz Rabbani, engraved with text that was a complex combination of Urdu, Farsi and Arabic. And for both aid and guidance in writing the chapter on Mirpur, my sincere gratitude to Prakhar Joshi, who, during his time at the 1947 Partition Archive, recorded extensive and important oral histories of the region, and Aamir Wani, who has always embodied the very essence of Kashmir. I am also indebted to the significant and detailed first-hand accounts written by survivors of the Mirpur Massacre and the Alibeg Concentration Camp—in particular, Mr Bal K. Gupta's *Forgotten Atrocities: Memoirs of a Survivor of the 1947 Partition of India* (2011).

I would like to thank my publishers, in India and the UK. Ananth Padmanabhan, publisher and friend, for being continually excited by and supportive of my work; my editor at HarperCollins India, Siddhesh Inamdar, for taking utmost care to preserve the essence and vitality of each object explored; Michael Dwyer of Hurst Publishers, for recognizing how deeply the Partition impacted both the people of the subcontinent and the history of the world, and for understanding the need to discuss it beyond India and Pakistan; and my editor at Hurst, Lara Weisweiller-Wu, for so intimately and carefully engaging with the histories of objects, contested geographies and vernacular languages included in the book.

Last but certainly not least, my heartfelt appreciation to each and every person who has followed the progression of *Remnants of Partition* on social media since the project's inception. To all those who have found the courage to broach the sensitive topic of the Partition with their parents and grandparents, who have shared tales of migration and stories of incredible sacrifice, bravery and loss from their families, who have written in with curiosity about the other side of the border, who have found themselves connected to these accounts of the Divide—thank you for your unfailing readership.

My hope is that this work will further promote the recording of oral history on a more personal and daily basis within homes—so that we may rid ourselves of the prolonged silence around the word 'Partition'. So that we may be able to build a database of first-hand recollections that remain the foundation of post-Partition entrepreneurship, resilience, and strength. So that we may discover that memory, not only of the Partition, but of every family and every country, can sometimes resides in the most unlikely sources. So that we may be able to bridge the ever-growing generation gap. So that we may be empowered keepers of our ancestry. So that we may better understand where we come from.